SOCIAL, POLITICAL AND LITERARY WRITINGS

The Collected Writings of John Maynard Keynes

Published for the Royal Economic Society

throughout the world, excluding the U.S.A. and Canada, by

THE MACMILLIAN PRESS LTD

London and Basingstoke
Associated companies in Delhi Dublin Hong Kong Johannesburg Lagos
Melbourne New York Singapore Tokyo

ISBN 0-333-24175-4

and throughout the U.S.A. and Canada by

THE SYNDICS OF THE CAMBRIDGE UNIVERSITY PRESS

32 East 57th Street, New York, NY 10022, U.S.A.

ISBN 0-521-23075-6 (the U.S.A. and Canada only)

Printed in Great Britain at the
University Press, Cambridge

THE COLLECTED WRITINGS OF
JOHN MAYNARD KEYNES

VOLUME XXVIII

SOCIAL, POLITICAL
AND
LITERARY WRITINGS

EDITED BY
DONALD MOGGRIDGE

MACMILLAN
CAMBRIDGE UNIVERSITY PRESS
FOR THE
ROYAL ECONOMIC SOCIETY

George Bernard Shaw and Keynes leaving the Fitzwilliam Museum, Cambridge, on the occasion of the opening of two new galleries on 9 June 1936.
(*Cambridge Daily News*, 10 June 1936)

CONTENTS

General introduction   *page* vii

Editorial note   xiii

1   KEYNES AND KINGSLEY MARTIN   I

2   KEYNES AND ANCIENT CURRENCIES   223

3   KEYNES AND THE ARTS   295

4   HUME   373

5   MISCELLANY   391

Dramatis Personae   422

List of Documents Reproduced   436

Acknowledgements   445

Index   447

GENERAL INTRODUCTION

This new standard edition of *The Collected Writings of John Maynard Keynes* forms the memorial to him of the Royal Economic Society. He devoted a very large share of his busy life to the Society. In 1911, at the age of twenty-eight, he became editor of the *Economic Journal* in succession to Edgeworth: two years later he was made secretary as well. He held these offices without intermittence until almost the end of his life. Edgeworth, it is true, returned to help him with the editorship from 1919 to 1925; Macgregor took Edgeworth's place until 1934, when Austin Robinson succeeded him and continued to assist Keynes down to 1945. But through all these years Keynes himself carried the major responsibility and made the principal decisions about the articles that were to appear in the *Economic Journal*, without any break save for one or two issues when he was seriously ill in 1937. It was only a few months before his death at Easter 1946 that he was elected president and handed over his editorship to Roy Harrod and the secretaryship to Austin Robinson.

In his dual capacity of editor and secretary Keynes played a major part in framing the policies of the Royal Economic Society. It was very largely due to him that some of the major publishing activities of the Society—Sraffa's edition of Ricardo, Stark's edition of the economic writings of Bentham, and Guillebaud's edition of Marshall, as well as a number of earlier publications in the 1930s—were initiated.

When Keynes died in 1946 it was natural that the Royal Economic Society should wish to commemorate him. It was perhaps equally natural that the Society chose to commemorate him by producing an edition of his collected works. Keynes himself had always taken a joy in fine printing, and the Society, with the help of Messrs Macmillan as publishers and the Cambridge University Press as printers, has been anxious to give Keynes's writings a permanent form that is wholly worthy of him.

The present edition will publish as much as is possible of his work in the field of economics. It will not include any private and personal correspondence or publish many letters in the possession of his family. The edition is concerned, that is to say, with Keynes as an economist.

Keynes's writings fall into five broad categories. First there are the books which he wrote and published as books. Second there are collections of articles and pamphlets which he himself made during his lifetime (*Essays in Persuasion* and *Essays in Biography*). Third, there is a very considerable volume of published but uncollected writings—articles written for newspapers, letters to newspapers, articles in journals that have not been included in his two volumes of collections, and various pamphlets. Fourth, there are a few hitherto unpublished writings. Fifth, there is correspondence with economists and concerned with economics or public affairs. It is the intention of this series to publish almost completely the whole of the first four categories listed above. The only exceptions are a few syndicated articles where Keynes wrote almost the same material for publication in different newspapers or in different countries, with minor and unimportant variations. In these cases, this series will publish one only of the variations, choosing the most interesting.

The publication of Keynes's economic correspondence must inevitably be selective. In the day of the typewriter and the filing cabinet and particularly in the case of so active and busy a man, to publish every scrap of paper that he may have dictated about some unimportant or ephemeral matter is impossible. We are aiming to collect and publish as much as possible, however, of the correspondence in which Keynes developed his own ideas in argument with his fellow economists, as well as the more significant correspondence at times when Keynes was in the middle of public affairs.

Apart from his published books, the main sources available to those preparing this series have been two. First, Keynes in his will made Richard Kahn his executor and responsible for his economic papers. They have been placed in the Marshall Library of the University of Cambridge and have been available for this edition. Until 1914 Keynes did not have a secretary and his earliest papers are in the main limited to drafts of important letters that he made in his own handwriting and retained. At that stage most of the correspondence that we possess is represented by what he received rather than by what he wrote. During the war years of 1914–18 and 1940–6 Keynes was serving in the Treasury. With the opening in 1968 of the records under the thirty-year rule, the papers that he wrote then and between the wars have become available. From 1919 onwards, throughout the rest of his life, Keynes had the help of a secretary—for many years Mrs Stephens. Thus for the last twenty-five years of his working life we have in most cases the carbon copies of his own letters as well as the originals of the letters that he received.

There were, of course, occasions during this period on which Keynes wrote himself in his own handwriting. In some of these cases, with the help of his correspondents, we have been able to collect the whole of both sides of some important interchanges and we have been anxious, in justice to both correspondents, to see that both sides of the correspondence are published in full.

The second main source of information has been a group of scrapbooks kept over a very long period of years by Keynes's mother, Florence Keynes, wife of Neville Keynes. From 1919 onwards these scrapbooks contain almost the whole of Maynard Keynes's more ephemeral writing, his letters to newspapers and a great deal of material which enables one to see not only what he wrote but the reaction of others to his writing. Without these very carefully kept scrapbooks the task of any editor or biographer of Keynes would have been immensely more difficult.

The plan of the edition, as at present intended, is this. It will total thirty volumes. Of these the first eight are Keynes's published books from *Indian Currency and Finance*, in 1913, to the *General Theory* in 1936, with the addition of his *Treatise on Probability*. There next follow, as vols. IX and X, *Essays in Persuasion* and *Essays in Biography*, representing Keynes's own collections of articles. *Essays in Persuasion* differs from the original printing in two respects: it contains the full texts of the articles or pamphlets included in it and not (as in the original printing) abbreviated versions of these articles, and it also contains two later pamphlets which are of exactly the same character as those included by Keynes in his original collection. In *Essays in Biography* there have been added a number of biographical studies that Keynes wrote both before and after 1933.

There will follow two volumes, XI–XII, of economic articles and correspondence and a further two volumes, already published, XIII–XIV, covering the development of his thinking as he moved towards the *General Theory*. There are included in these volumes such part of Keynes's economic correspondence as is closely associated with the articles that are printed in them. A supplement to these volumes, XXIX, prints some further material relating to the same issues, which has since been discovered.

The remaining fourteen volumes deal with Keynes's *Activities* during the years from the beginning of his public life in 1905 until his death. In each of the periods into which we divide this material, the volume concerned publishes his more ephemeral writings, all of it hitherto uncollected, his correspondence relating to these activities, and such other material and correspondence as is necessary to the understanding of Keynes's activities. These volumes are edited by Elizabeth Johnson and

Donald Moggridge, and it has been their task to trace and interpret Keynes's activities sufficiently to make the material fully intelligible to a later generation. Elizabeth Johnson has been responsible for vols. XV–XVIII, covering Keynes's earlier years and his activities down to the end of World War I reparations and reconstruction. Donald Moggridge is responsible for all the remaining volumes recording Keynes's other activities from 1924 until his death in 1946.

The record of Keynes's activities during World War II is now complete with the publication of volumes XXV–XXVII. The gap between 1922 and 1939 has now been filled with the publication of volumes XIX–XXI. All that now remains is to publish in the present volume his social, political and literary writings; and, finally, to print certain of his published articles, and the correspondence relating to them, which have not appeared elsewhere in this edition.

Those responsible for his edition have been: Lord Kahn, both as Lord Keynes's executor and as a long and intimate friend of Lord Keynes; able to help in the interpreting of much that would be otherwise misunderstood; the late Sir Roy Harrod as the author of his biography; Austin Robinson as Keynes's co-editor on the *Economic Journal* and successor as Secretary of the Royal Economic Society. Austin Robinson has acted throughout as Managing Editor; Donald Moggridge is now associated with him as Joint Managing Editor.

In the early stages of the work Elizabeth Johnson was assisted by Jane Thistlethwaite, and by Mrs McDonald, who was originally responsible for the systematic ordering of the files of the Keynes papers. Judith Masterman for many years worked with Mrs Johnson on the papers. More recently Susan Wilsher, Margaret Butler and Leonora Woollam have continued the secretarial work. Barbara Lowe has been responsible for the indexing. Since 1977 Judith Allen has been responsible for much of the day-to-day management of the edition as well as seeing the volumes through the press.

EDITORIAL NOTE

This volume is concerned with Keynes's writings in the social, political and literary fields. The sources are Keynes's own surviving papers and the papers of colleagues and friends, in particular the late Kingsley Martin.

In this, as in all the similar volumes, in general all of Keynes's own writings are printed in larger type. Keynes's own footnotes are indicated by asterisks or other symbols to distinguish them from the editorial footnotes. All introductory matter and all writings by others than Keynes are printed in smaller type. The only exception to this general rule is that occasional short quotations from a letter from Keynes to his parents or to a friend, used in introductory passages to clarify a situation, are treated as introductory matter and are printed in the smaller types.

Most of Keynes's letters included in this and other volumes are reprinted from the carbon copies that remain among his papers. In most cases he has added his initials to the carbon in the familiar fashion in which he signed to all his friends. We have no certain means of knowing whether the top copy, sent to the recipient of the letter, carried a more formal signature.

Chapter 1

KEYNES AND KINGSLEY MARTIN

The correspondence between Keynes and Kingsley Martin covers the last twenty-three years of Keynes's life. It began when Martin had been an unsuccessful candidate for an external Fellowship at King's College, Cambridge, with an early version of what became *The Triumph of Lord Palmerston: A Study of Public Opinion in England before the Crimean War* (London, 1924).[1]

To KINGSLEY MARTIN, *10 April 1923*

Dear Martin,

I do not know if anyone has written to you about your dissertation for the King's Fellowship. But I should like you to know that it was the subject of a great many very favourable comments from quarters whose approbation would, I think, have given you much pleasure. You were, in fact, a very serious candidate for election, and many of us were extremely sorry that it did not in the end prove possible to get you elected.

Personally, I thought your dissertation quite remarkably good, interesting and learned and subtle, and in every way excellent. It was a very promising piece of work, as I think everyone who expressed an opinion of it was quite agreed.

I do not know whether you will have heard that Hubert Henderson is to be the new Editor of *The Nation* and that I shall be closely connected with its management. Possibly you might like to do some reviewing, etc. for us from time to time. If so, we should be very glad that you should do so.

Will you let me know when you are back from America, and come round to see me.[2]

Yours sincerely,

J. M. KEYNES

[1] The successful candidate was P. M. S. Blackett. A *dramatis personae* follows p. 422.
[2] Keynes saw Martin on 6 August 1923.

1

There was then a gap in the correspondence. During the interval, Martin spent a year in Cambridge, taught at the London School of Economics and then, in 1927, went to Manchester as a senior leader writer for *The Manchester Guardian*. In 1930, he returned to London as an editor (with W. A. Robson) of *The Political Quarterly*, a journal founded by a group including Keynes, who was also on the editorial board.[3]

To KINGSLEY MARTIN, *2 August 1930*

My dear Martin,

I am sorry to say that it is quite out of the question for me to do anything for the next issue of *The Political Quarterly*. I am still very much behindhand with my existing commitments, and can take on nothing more.

I am rather sorry to hear that you are leaving the *M.G.*, but not entirely surprised. I can well believe that their very non-committal attitude on almost all subjects under the sun does not fit in too well with your temperament.

Yours sincerely,

J. M. KEYNES

I hope you will now do something from time to time for *The Nation*. I have told Harold Wright about your change of plans.

Later in the year, Keynes and Kingsley Martin became more closely involved. Martin was offered the editorship of *The New Statesman* and discussions began for an amalgamation of it and *The Nation and Athenaeum* of which Keynes was chairman. The next letter reflects an early stage in those discussions.[4]

---

[3] See W. A. Robson, 'The Founding of the Political Quarterly', *Political Quarterly*, January–March 1970.

[4] At this time, Martin's position was complicated by the fact that the Faculty of Economics and Politics at Cambridge had approached the University for an additional post, a lectureship in political science. This lectureship was clearly designated for Martin. When he accepted *The New Statesman and Nation* the Faculty Board agreed to cease taking steps to establish the post. (Cambridge University Archives, Minute books of the Board of the Faculty of Economics and Politics, 29th Meeting, 10 November 1930, minute 4 and 30th Meeting, 26 January 1931, minute 10.)

From KINGSLEY MARTIN, *26 November 1930*

Dear Keynes,

I have naturally been thinking over our conversation in King's the other day and agree with you that 'there is a lot to be said for *The New Statesman*'—much more of course if your project about *The Nation* could be brought off. I should have let matters alone and not written on the subject were it not that the *N.S.* Directors seem disposed to move very slowly. I cannot afford to miss the Cambridge job (which is very attractive from many points of view) unless the other thing is in sight and I cannot be sure either when they will appoint or whether in the end they would appoint me.

They are aware that there are reasons for hurry from their own point of view ([Mostyn] Lloyd is terribly over-worked apart from other reasons) but finding new capital is not a quick business and unless they are hurried in some way, I should think they might go on for months without doing anything. It's aggravating; the paper does not seem to be doing badly,—from a financial point of view. My impression is that if they were approached at the moment they might prove very reasonable. I have good reasons for saying so.

[Austin] Robinson of the Economics Board writes to me that the Cambridge lectureship has passed another stage and he adds that he would of course be glad to know as soon as possible when I have made up my mind about applying. I do not know just how soon I must make up my mind, but I obviously cannot leave the question indefinitely and I must plump for Cambridge anyway unless I have any assurance about *The New Statesman*. I cannot even decide whether I should take it if offered unless I know the terms of possible appointment, the position of the paper and other details. Clearly the whole of that might be altered if your *Nation* project came off—one would be editor of a much more stable and influential paper with a good circulation and not bothered all the time by the feeling that one was competing with one's friends as well as battling with one's opponents.

That's the position. I am bothering you about it at this length because I do not feel that there is much more time and your very kind remark that you would like me to be editor of the joint paper, should that prove possible, assures me that you are interested. For many reasons I think Cambridge worthwhile—I believe there is a job for me to do there—but I should have liked to have had the opportunity of knowing what the other amounted to and I can conceive of circumstances which would make it overwhelmingly attractive.

Yours sincerely,
KINGSLEY MARTIN

3

With the turn of the year, matters moved more quickly, as Keynes told a fellow member of *The Nation*'s board.[5]

To J. B. MORRELL, *6 January 1931*

Dear Mr Morrell,

Thank you for your telegram. I will keep 5 to 6 on Friday free. I think the best plan would be if you could come to this house as near 5 as possible. I would then arrange for Mr John Roberts, the Manager of *The New Statesman*, to be round here soon after 5.15. I could then show you the figures and explain the negotiations so far as they have gone, and we could then have our talk with him. Whether I shall be able to arrange for you to see Mr Kingsley Martin at the same time I am not yet certain. But I shall see if I can get him to be here at about a quarter to six. His business would of course be quite different from Mr Roberts's, that is to say he would be concerned with outlining to you his ideas as to the policy of the paper. Mr Roberts's rôle is to discuss with us, in the main, the terms on which the proposed new Company is to buy the copyrights, etc. of the existing papers.

Yours sincerely,
[copy initialled] J.M.K.

To KINGSLEY MARTIN, *8 January 1931*

My dear Kingsley,

I am very sorry to hear of your tiresome attack of influenza. The particular point I wanted to see you about is the following.

Before the Rowntree Trust definitely agree to put up the substantial amount of new capital for which they will be responsible, they want to be satisfied as to the political complexion of the new paper. Lloyd wrote me a letter which I sent on to them. But that did not really get matters much further, since

[5] For a history of the merger negotiations see E. Hyams, *The New Statesman: The History of the First Fifty Years, 1913–1963* (London, 1963), pp. 115–23.

it was primarily a statement as to what the policy of *The New Statesman* had been in the past, a matter on which we are quite capable of judging for ourselves. What is clearly needed by the Rowntrees is a talk with you on lines which satisfy them as to your present intentions and general attitude. The position is much the same also as regards new capital from Mr Charles Wright, Harold's father.

I believe that Arnold Rowntree is to be in London next Thursday, the 15th. Assuming you are back by then, could you meet him at *The Nation* office at some convenient time? I am sorry to say that I may not be present, as I may have to return to Cambridge on the previous day. But in any case, I suggest that you and Harold Wright should meet Arnold Rowntree and have it out with him.

Otherwise everything, so far as I can judge, is going smoothly. But it would be a serious hitch if the Rowntrees were to feel dissatisfied as to the destination of their money. I don't think you will find them, however, at all unreasonable. All through our long connection with them they have been the kindest and least interfering patrons you can imagine.

Yours,
[copy initialled] J.M.K.

From KINGSLEY MARTIN, *16 January 1931*

Dear Maynard,

I saw Arnold Rowntree with Harold Wright on Thursday and we found no difficulty *re* policy. Rowntree expressed himself well satisfied.

I gathered, however, that there is a difficulty *re* the allocation of shares and a real hitch in the negotiations. I went into the matter with John Roberts afterwards and (as far as I can tell without fully understanding the details) I do believe he is trying to make an equitable arrangement, and not, as I fear Rowntree may think, trying to drive a hard bargain. I very much hope the difficulty can be adjusted quickly—delay just now is a great nuisance from every point of view. One point that worries me is that there are contributors, perhaps to both papers, certainly to the *N.S.* (Emil Davies, for instance, who has been with the paper from its first number) who ought to have proper notice if their stuff is not used in the future. I fear we may have to pay them *in lieu* of notice if we push it to the last moment. And of course there are many other reasons against delay. Is there any chance of seeing you before your *Nation* meeting on Wednesday? I shall be at the *N.S.* most of Tuesday and Wednesday I expect.

I find I have just missed Goldie[6] and that he has gone to King's. I'm troubled about him—he sounds so ill and depressed in a letter I've received from him. I feel as if he needs looking after. I suppose he gets looked after all right at King's.

Yours,
KINGSLEY MARTIN

P.S. There was, I hope, no misunderstanding about the question of contributors from both papers. Of course I fully understand that I am to use contributors entirely on merit from both—that is entirely to my interests and to those of the new paper, and what I should want to do, even if it were not stated in the bond. My momentary hesitation when talking with you was due to thinking that you had implied that I was to use an equal *amount* from both papers—a difficult proposition. There should be no difficulty in using the majority of contributors to both papers—it makes an excellent lot to draw from.

Sorry for this screed—I have not got my typewriter here yet.

Keynes arranged to see Martin on 20 January. The amalgamation negotiations proceeded and the first issue of *The New Statesman and Nation* with Keynes as the chairman of the company, appeared on 27 February 1931.

Keynes's next letter concerned his 'Proposals for a Revenue Tariff' (*JMK*, vol. IX, pp. 231–8).

To KINGSLEY MARTIN, *1 March 1931*

Dear Kingsley,

I enclose my article herewith. I am afraid that it is dreadfully long. I have indicated one short passage which might be omitted if you think fit, but even so it will be above 2,000 words, which,

---

[6] G. Lowes Dickinson.

I suppose, means running over the third column, assuming that you don't print it with narrow spacing, which I hope you won't. I should be grateful for any criticisms.

Could I have (sent to 46, Gordon Square) 12 extra pulls of the proof as is my usual custom, partly for the purpose of my foreign rights and in this case chiefly to send it to one or two people such as Ll.G., the P.M. and Snowden, in advance?[7]

I think that the first number looked very well indeed. I liked your first leader and the whole paper had a solid substantial air such as *The Week-end Review* is 100 miles away from. On the other hand the printing, at least in my copy, came out extremely badly. I fancy it may have been the ink, blurred print with many smudges. Whether for this reason or because the type really is small, one got the feeling that the issue was in desperately small print and a bit difficult to read for that reason. As I say, I cannot quite diagnose whether it was bad ink or too little leading or that the type used was very small.

What is this that I read in *The Observer* about G. D. H. Cole trying to raise £25,000 to run a new Socialist weekly?

One other matter. Would you feel averse to taking from me, if I were to write it, an unsigned column about the Camargo Society,[8] what they are doing and intend to do? I think the Society is much worth-while, but it needs more support and it is approaching a critical moment in its history (such a contribution would, of course, be unpaid).

I hope to be able to look in on Wednesday afternoon, late.

Yours ever,
J. M. KEYNES

Two weeks after his revenue tariff article, Keynes returned to the issue, referring to three letters which had appeared in the issue of 21 March.

[7] See *JMK*, vol. xx, pp. 488–9.
[8] See below, pp. 318–24.

To KINGSLEY MARTIN, *21 March 1931*

Dear Kingsley,

I now send you my puff about the Camargo, unsigned of course.[9]

It is as you will see a puff direct, since in the space at my disposal I do not see how I could do otherwise if it is to serve its purpose. I hope you won't object to this. Please feel free to edit it to any extent you feel inclined, for now that I see it, it seems to me rather a dull catalogue. The trouble is that it really is essential to get in all the specific information that I give. Yet it would not be entitled to more space.

Since I saw you on Friday I have been reading the correspondence in this week's paper, which I had not then done. There are obviously a great number of points which ought to be taken up. Yet to deal with them all at once would make a very scrappy affair. So my mind has returned to the idea of starting at once with a series of short single column articles dealing with specific points. I should like to call the series: Economic Notes on Free Trade.[10] My present notion would be to deal in the first one with the exporting industries, that is to say mainly in reply to E. D. Simon's letter. The second one might deal with the standard of living in reply to Ramsay Muir and many others. The third with the reaction of exports and imports on one another, namely, [Evan] Durbin's letter.

This would keep the ball rolling without occupying too much space. If you would like me to do the first of these for this week, will you ring me up as early as possible on Monday morning since it will be on Monday that I must write it?

I liked your own leader this week immensely. It struck just the right note I thought and was strong and interesting.

Yours ever

J. M. KEYNES

[9] See below, pp. 9–10.
[10] See *JMK*, vol. XX, pp. 498–505.

The 'puff' for the Camargo Society, when eventually printed ran as follows:

From The New Statesman and Nation, *11 April 1931*

PLAYS AND PICTURES

The Camargo Society

On the evening of April 26th and the afternoon of the 27th the Camargo Society will present its third production at the Cambridge Theatre. It is to be a gala occasion. The success of this society will be a great factor in the development of ballet in this country; and all who are devotees of dancing should be aware of its activities. The society was founded last year to give opportunities for English dancers, choreographers, musicians and artists to join together in aid of the art of ballet. In its early days it will depend largely on the traditions and the dancers of Russia; but the hope of the society is to discover and foster talent in this country, and to offer a centre where the diverse arts, which the perfect production of ballet requires, can be brought together for our entertainment.

Ballet is an expensive art. It has been ambitious, therefore, of the Camargo Society to offer four productions a year, each of which will be given only twice. For this reason it requires the unstinted support of its well-wishers. Previous productions have shown that there already exists in England much native talent which can find no worthy opportunity or environment elsewhere; for Mme Rambert's admirable Ballet Club can only be for small and intimate productions.

The programme for the third production is of special interest. On this occasion the Old Guard of Russia has been called in to support the budding talent of England. Tamara Karsavina and Lydia Lopokova will both dance. To see them together on one evening will recall the most brilliant days of the Diaghileff Ballet. Anna Ludmilla, the American ballerina, will also join them. For the rest, the dancers, choreographers and artists will be English. The programme will probably include: Constant Lambert's *Pomona* with choreography by Frederick Ashton, and décor by John Banting, followed by Glinka's. *Valse Fantasie*, a famous piece which Karsavina will produce and in which she will appear. The second part of the programme begins with an important new ballet: *La Création du Monde*, composed to the music of Milhaud by Ninette de Valois, with décor by Edward Wolfe; finally, William Walton's well-known *Façade* will be produced for the first time in England as a ballet with choreography by Frederick Ashton and décor by John Armstrong, in which Lydia Lopokova will dance. Here, then, is an ambitious attempt to bring together the best and bravest talent which contemporary London can show. It would be a pity not to support it; and as attendance at the performances is limited to members of the society and their friends, those who wish to help this effort should join. The secretary is Mr Montagu Nathan, 5/42, Campden House Court, W.8; and the subscription for the remainder of the season is a guinea, or a guinea and a half for the better seats. This subscription will cover, besides the third production, the fourth production to be given in June next, when it is hoped that the principal feature will be a performance of Vaughan Williams's new ballet *Job*, to be presented after the designs of William Blake.

The next letter from Keynes concerned a letter from A. L. Rowse, which has not survived, and two pieces in the issue of 18 April: Martin's leader, 'Free Trade Negative and Positive' and J. A. Hobson's 'A World Economy'.

To KINGSLEY MARTIN, *19 April 1931*

Dear Kingsley,

   The enclosed letter from Rowse seems to me most interesting, and of much better calibre than most of the correspondence which has been printed. I hope you will find room for it. It seems to me to need no emendation beyond a small deletion which I have made on page 2, where I happen to know that the suggestion is incorrect.

I almost felt stirred by your 'leader' and Hobson's article to write another letter. But I have decided not to do so. If I had, the point would have been that of course international action such as you propose, or such as he proposes, would be excellent. But who believes that we are going to get any such thing within a reasonable period of time? This applies overwhelmingly to Hobson, with his suggestion of [an] 'international government with powers to over-ride obstructive elements of national sovereignty'. If, however, you do not expect anything to come of these hopes at present, what do you propose to do in the meantime? For your private information, the idea of an international conference has been most seriously attempted by those responsible, but the chances of getting any such thing at present have been absolutely hopeless.

Yours ever,

J. M. KEYNES

P.S. I find that Miss Rees will not, after all, be back in the office this week, but you can certainly expect her on Monday, the 27th.

From KINGSLEY MARTIN, *20 April 1931*

Dear Maynard,

I have now read Rowse's letter and agree with you that it is one of the most interesting we have had. I wish it had come earlier in the controversy. It would have switched some people off into more profitable channels. As regards Hobson's article I was myself displeased with it, but there was a difficulty. I discussed the problem with Hobson and asked him to write an article before the amalgamated paper actually began and if those were his views, it seemed difficult to refuse to publish them in a signed article. You will notice that in the leader, I carefully left a loophole for constructive proposals. I have been very much exercised in mind about this whole controversy, as I think you know. I am not in the least a hard shelled Free

Trader and was quite open to be persuaded about any particular proposal. Frankly, your proposal did not convince me and I felt that the paper ought itself to take some definite line. For the moment I think it has had as much economics as it can bear, but I should like to talk over with you a more immediately constructive proposal for us to advance, when next I see you.

I am glad to hear that Miss Rees will be back on the 27th.

I have written to [George] Rylands asking him to do the Camargo.

About Supplements. I am beginning to think that the Travel Supplement may not be worth doing. What do you think about the Insurance Supplement? That, as you say, should be profitable. [Nicholas] Davenport is anxious to know your view on getting one out in the latter part of May. Would you have time to help at all? I gather from [T.E.] Gregory that the Macmillan Committee has involved a colossal amount of work, but I take it that will be over. I feel, in regard to the Insurance Supplement rather in your and Davenport's hands. It isn't a thing that much interests me but if it is good and can prove profitable, no doubt we ought to have it.

Yours sincerely,
KINGSLEY MARTIN

To KINGSLEY MARTIN, *21 April 1931*

Dear Kingsley,

If you decide not to have a Travel Supplement, that will have my full concurrence. I think it would be wise to have an Insurance Supplement at the end of May, so as not to have to break the continuity. We have had it now for a number of years and got a fair quantity of insurance companies to contract the habit of coming in. But I am afraid that I cannot possibly help. I am trying to rush through the Macmillan Committee work in time to keep my commitment to sail for the United States on May 30. Apart from all my usual work, term has now begun. So I must take on nothing further.

About a definite policy. The trouble, to my mind, is that there are no definite policies except a tariff, devaluation, or an assault on wages. Devaluation has its attractions, but I think any responsible person who has looked into it must reject it firmly, at any rate at the present stage. That is the dilemma which has forced me into the position where I am. For, apart from any other feelings one may have, an adequate reduction of wages is quite off the map and would, according to my theory of the thing, have disappointing results. That may be true of the tariff too. But it is more promising than the others. Don't feel that I in the least dissent from your decision to treat it as you have. I think you have very likely been right from the point of view of the paper.

Yours ever,

J. M. KEYNES

With these letters, Keynes's correspondence ended for the year.

There is, however, one occasion where Keynes is alleged to have made an unsigned contribution to *The New Statesman*, for which we can find no supporting evidence. In his autobiography, *Father Figures*,[11] Kingsley Martin states 'He [JMK] even wrote a fierce footnote—I think the only editorial footnote ever to appear in the *N.S.* not written by the editor himself—to a letter defending the bankers' behaviour.' The only 'fierce footnote' to which this can refer is a long note appended to a letter from R. H. Brand and published in the issue for 12 September 1931. We can find no confirmation that this came from Keynes's pen, for it does not appear in the news cuttings of unsigned notes he kept or in the Keynes Papers themselves. Moreover, the style is hardly Keynes's. Therefore, we do not print it here.

In 1932, no correspondence survives beyond a single letter. During that year Kingsley Martin and David Low visited Russia. On their return, they produced *Low's Russian Sketchbook: 56 Drawings by Low* with a text by Kingsley Martin. Kingsley asked Keynes to review it, with difficult results.

From KINGSLEY MARTIN, *6 December 1932*

Dear Maynard,

It is sometimes best to say what one feels right away and I hope you will forgive this note.

[11] Penguin edition pp. 203–4.

It seems ungracious to complain about your very flattering review—especially when you are terribly busy and did it at my special request. What troubles me is this. If you had attacked the opinions that I think came through pretty clearly, though not dramatically, I should not have minded in the least. Nor should I mind, though I should be sorry, if you said my stuff was bad. But you have given the one impression which I feel to be unfair. The suggestion is that the book is written by a superficial observer who hates everything but is courteous enough to give Russia the benefit of doubts and be nice to it. I think to apologise for Russia is the silliest attitude and I tried to avoid it. You see the stuff in the democracy chapter about the press and the theory of democracy is almost new in this country, I think, and I do not know any satisfactory answer to the argument put forward in it. Similarly the terrible challenge of Russia—as it seems to me—is expressed in a rather new way in the Volga conversations. The points of view are put against each other as strongly as I know how in the space. Is it true or not true that the Russian system provides a complete answer to the problem of unemployment? However the thing I hate about your review and the thing which makes me hate printing it as it stands is that it reads as if you thought my stuff tosh and just wanted to avoid saying so because I am editor of the paper.

These are my reactions and I thought it best to explain them right away. If you had slammed the book I would have been content but I did try to do a serious job and it does offer a challenge, not a bit of polite eyewash.

Yours ever,
KINGSLEY MARTIN

With his letter, Martin enclosed a number of suggestions for changes in the last paragraph of the review. Keynes did not adopt them, but he did alter the review. We print below the version that finally appeared, indicating the one change made by a footnote.

From The New Statesman and Nation, *10 December 1932*

ENJOYING RUSSIA

Low (DAVID). *Low's Russian Sketchbook.* 56 Drawings by Low. Text by Kingsley Martin. (Gollancz), 1932.

We all know that we have amongst us to-day a cartoonist in the grand tradition. But, as the recognition, which contributions to evening newspapers receive by word of mouth round the dinner table, cannot reach the modest cartoonist, one welcomes a book like this as an opportunity to tell Low how much we think of him and how much we love him. He has the rare combination of gifts which is necessary for his craft—a shrewd and penetrating intelligence, wit, taste, unruffled urbanity, an indignant but open and understanding heart, a swift power of minute obser- vation with an equally swift power of essential simplification, and, above all, a sense of talent for beauty, which extracts something delightful even out of ugliness. One may seem to be piling it on, but Low really has these things, and it is a great addition to our lives to meet the tongue and eye of a civilised man and true artist when we open *The Evening Standard*.

Last summer Low and Kingsley Martin made a trip to Bolshieland, and this agreeable book is the outcome. Low's pencil and charcoal sketches are reproduced by some process which, whatever it may really be, looks like lithograph and thereby reinforces the comparison between Low and the litho- graphers of the old *Charivari* of Paris—Gavarni and Daumier and their colleagues. They are *illustrations* in the literal sense of the word—pictures of the inside and of the outside of things at the same time.

Both contributors are at their blandest and most urbane, good guests whose first duty is to be courteous to their hosts. Mr Kingsley Martin does not pretend to pronounce judgements, but he has given us with admirable lightness and discretion the running commentary of a highly intelligent tourist, who contrives[12] to raise in a number of dialogues some of the main issues with which the Russian experiment confronts the observer. A little too full perhaps of good will. When a doubt rises, it is swallowed down if possible. Mr Martin is ready to agree 'on the whole' that it is a grand ideal to turn peasants into machine-

[12] The words 'who contrives...Mr Martin' replaced the words 'full of good will, eager to find sermons in stones and good in everything. When he has a criticism to suggest, it is conveyed in a delicate doubt. He'.

minders. He reflects that 'these people at least have a fuller diet than Chinese coolies, and I don't think they are as poor as peasants in India'. If it is pointed out to him that the only people 'who really suffer from restrictions on free speech are a few educated intellectuals', he wonders doubtfully if he will find a convincing answer in Rousseau or Bentham or John Stuart Mill. When he is told that 'as to fat, they rely on sunflower oil', he remembers that the whole civilisation of Greece was built up on olive oil. This is the right spirit in which to visit Russia, if one wants to enjoy oneself.

J. M. KEYNES

The next exchange followed a telephone conversation relating to the issue of 22 April 1933. Keynes's reaction was in response to two articles—'The Rights of Man' and 'Moscow and the Big Stick'. After the telephone conversation, the following letters were exchanged.

From KINGSLEY MARTIN, [*undated but must be 22 April 1933*]

Sorry not to have had the chance to get this typed. I'd like a long talk sometime if you are ever free to dine with me?

Dear Maynard,

Being a pacifist who wants to change the inequalities of the world as peacefully as possible and with the maximum of consent—which is my position—does not seem to me a justification for not trying to be sincere about the problem involved. (It was your accusation of insincerity which annoyed me on the 'phone. I have a kind of religion of sincerity. It's the one thing I am certain is valuable.)

Take the question of 'class justice' as one example. Surely it is plain that justice is being used as a means of suppressing dangerous opinion in most countries. When an instance which can be discussed occurs in this country we do call attention to it in the *N.S. &N.* and I made a point this week of congratulating the Young Liberals on their protest.[13] But we are, I warmly agree (and said), very mild in this country. In many countries there is now a technique of 'frame up' by the police in the interests of conservative

---

[13] 'The Rights of Man', *New Statesman and Nation*, 22 April 1933.

opinion. Sacco and Vanzetti is only the most notorious of American instances.[14] Meerut is really a terrible case.[15] I do not know if you've followed it. Coatman, who I expect you know—he is Professor of the L.S.E. and conservative in opinion on the whole, was a justice officer in India at the time and described Meerut to me as a 'frame up'. I do, in all sincerity, say that this Russian business is gentlemanly compared to Meerut. The prisoners had committed no illegal acts. They were three (or four was it?) years in an Indian gaol waiting for the inevitable verdict: they have long sentences to serve with no British Government to bring pressure on their behalf. 'Frame ups' with violent extortions of 'confessions' are routine in America, Poland and other countries, as almost any foreign correspondent will tell you. Beating with rubber truncheons and the water torture are commonly used because they leave no marks.

Now I should feel insincere if I did not call attention to these things in other countries, including the British Empire, in discussing Russian methods. Why you should think it insincere to mention them I cannot conceive. It's important for people to know that Russia is not in this matter abnormal and I know that many people value the *N.S. & N.* just because it does not make the usual pretences.

KINGSLEY

To KINGSLEY MARTIN, *23 April 1933*

Dear Kingsley,

Please forgive my outburst on the telephone, and not least because it was on the telephone, where one can never say exactly what one means. Will you read the leader in yesterday's *Spectator* on the same subject, which to my thinking is just right? I do not see how anyone could read yours otherwise than, in effect, as an apology for the Russians. For, after all, to call attention at this juncture to what you allege to be parallel injustices elsewhere simply amounts to saying—'poor dear Russians, why do you English take on so, they are no worse than other people'. At least this is how I find it strikes most readers. And though you meant it the other way round, it works out as a defence of injustice.

[14] Sacco and Vanzetti were two Italian immigrants convicted of murder in 1920 on politically tainted evidence. They were executed in 1927.
[15] A conspiracy case conducted by the Indian Government in 1929.

As for your parallels, for one thing the Russian trial had nothing whatever to do with the question of suppressing dangerous opinion. Besides, even if one were to admit your alleged parallels, I do not remember you writing a leader about the Meerut trial, telling the Indians not to excite themselves too much, because what is going on is no worse than what regularly happens in Russia, and that one must not be too ready to blame England or America or Germany for behaviour which is comparatively mild compared with what people are doing in Russia. I should like to see for once the kind of leader which you would write if the Government in England were to do the kind of things in matters of justice and the suppression of liberty or in the commission of economic errors in the same kind and scale as events in Russia.

I am sure that it is this endless obsession with grievances which completely spoils the effect of what you are trying to say. Although I know it would be injustice, I so often lately after reading the paper want to take up my pen and write to you 'you seem to love a grievance and to love nothing else'. And it makes it worse that running under the grievance there is a sort of subcurrent of defeatism, not the note of a crusade which is going to be victorious, but an undertone of 'and I know nothing can or will be done about it'. And towards any constructive effort on the modest lines which are alone practicable in the present world, your interest very soon gets tepid. You know that the Indian White Paper[16] is broadly speaking the utmost progress which can be made at this stage; yet you are quite ready to inflame, rather than pacify, Indian grievances against it.

Well all this means that you are really by temperament an agitator and revolutionary. No harm in that. And the more frankly you put that point of view the better I like what you write. But when, for my sake or the sake of others, you try to substitute for this, without yourself feeling that you lose your sincerity, a moderate and statesman-like demeanour such as

[16] *The Future Form of Government for India* (Cmd. 4268).

best-minded Liberals would approve, it is then that the flavour which irritates me inevitably creeps in. Alas, it is when you are trying to be 'good' that I feel like this.

This is all exaggerated, I know, and largely unfair, and do not, therefore, pay too much attention to it. But these are the easiest words I can find as a means of conveying from me to you what I feel. We must talk again as soon as we are both free. I am sorry that I cannot come to lunch to-morrow, since I shall not get away from Cambridge until the afternoon.

Yours ever,
J. M. KEYNES

From KINGSLEY MARTIN, *24 April 1933*

Dear Maynard,

I am extremely grateful for your frank, friendly and abusive letter. As to 'defeatism' you are perfectly right. It's corroding, harmful and cumulative. I've tried, recently especially, to keep it out of the paper but it's in the whole atmosphere. I am bitterly disappointed with my failure to give the paper a more constructive or crusading meaning.

Will you spare the time for real talk soon? It might at this juncture be worth while, I think. I would put off other engagements almost any night. Any time this week? Tuesday, Wednesday (best time) Thursday. Friday I'm away. Next Saturday? I have been drafting, while away, a series of articles which might be called 'defeatism'! I *must* get through to something constructive.

KINGSLEY

The next letter concerned Keynes's article 'National Self-Sufficiency' (*JMK*, XXI, pp. 233–46.

To KINGSLEY MARTIN, *9 May 1933*

Dear Kingsley,

I have got to the point of considering whether to publish in England the paper on National Self-Sufficiency, which was the basis of the lecture which I gave in Dublin. It is appearing in

The Yale Review in the United States, and in a quarterly called *Studies* in Dublin. My arrangements with *The Yale Review* prevent it from appearing anywhere before June 18.

Before I take any other steps for disposing of it, I would like you to look through it to see if by any chance you would care to have it, for the *N.S. & N.* It runs to quite 5,000 words, and would therefore have to be split up into either three or four articles;—which is an objection, but perhaps not an insuperable one. Will you let me know how you feel about it?

Yours ever,

J. M. KEYNES

I should suggest a fee of £30 for the English serial rights.

Again there is a gap in the correspondence, this time until the autumn. At the time *The New Statesman* was running a series of Low sketches of important people with brief commentaries.

To KINGSLEY MARTIN, *15 October 1933*

Dear Kingsley,

Here is Einstein—I have had the greatest difficulty in producing it, not able to squeeze out nearly enough words (though I hope the enclosed is the best part of 400), with the result of this rather precious morsel. I only hope it won't be taken or regarded as a precedent for the others!

On Tuesday I only get up [to London] a little before dinner, so I'd rather prefer to have dinner with Lydia. But I am doing nothing that evening, so if you could look in for an hour any time after dinner you'd find me free.

It seems to me that today's news about Germany cannot be taken too seriously.[17] The hideous dilemma is presented— allowing them to call our bluff and re-arm as and when they

[17] On 14 October, Germany withdrew from the Disarmament Conference at Geneva and from the League of Nations.

choose with what results one can imagine, or the horror of a preventive war.

Yours ever

J. M. K.

I should like to see a proof of Einstein on Tuesday (Gordon Square).

Keynes's piece when published ran as follows (see also *JMK*, vol. x, pp. 382–4).

From The New Statesman and Nation, *21 October 1933*

EINSTEIN

Gewiss hast auch du, lieber Leser, als Knabe oder Mädchen mit dem stolzen Gebäude der Geometrie Euklids Bekanntschaft gemacht —thus begins the 'Essay on the Special and General Theory of Relativity'—*Gewiss würdest du kraft dieser Vergangenheit jeden mit Verachtung strafen, der auch nur das abgelegenste Sätzchen dieser Wissenschaft für unwahr erklärte.** It is so indeed. The boys, who cannot grow up to adult human nature, are beating the prophets of the ancient race—Marx, Freud, Einstein —who have been tearing at our social, personal and intellectual roots, tearing them with an objectivity which to the healthy animal seems morbid, depriving everything, as it seems, of the warmth of natural feeling. What traditional retort have the schoolboys but a kick in the pants?—to put a price on the prophet's head in red ink under skull and swastika on the parchment lid of a jam-pot.

Thus to our generation Einstein has been made to become a double symbol—a symbol of the mind travelling in the cold regions of space, and a symbol of the brave and generous outcast, pure in heart and cheerful in spirit. Himself a schoolboy,

* 'Assuredly you too, dear reader, made acquaintance as boy or girl with the proud edifice of Euclid's geometry...Assuredly by force of this bit of your past you would treat with contempt anyone who cast doubts on even the most out of the way fragment of any of its propositions.'

21

too, but the other kind—with ruffled hair, soft hands and a violin. See him as he squats on Cromer beach doing sums, Charlie Chaplin with the brow of Shakespeare, whilst yet another schoolboy, ever chivalrous Locker Lampson, mounts guard against the bullies.

So it is not an accident that the Nazi lads vent a particular fury against him. He does truly stand for what they most dislike, the opposite of the blond beast—intellectualist, individualist, supernationalist, pacifist, inky, plump. It is unthinkable that the nasty lads should not kick Albert. Thus Low portrays him. How should they know the glory of the free-ranging intellect and soft objective sympathy and smiling innocence of heart, to which power and money and violence, drink and blood and pomp, mean absolutely nothing? Yet Albert and the blond beasts make up the world between them. If either cast the other out, life is diminished in its force. When the barbarians destroy the ancient race as witches, when they refuse to scale heaven on broomsticks, they may be dooming themselves to sink back into the clods which bore them.

To KINGSLEY MARTIN, *21 October 1933*

Dear Kingsley,

I thought your review of Ll.G. quite excellent—the best of the many reviews of that book I have read.[18] I also liked CML on the German situation.[19] Sorry for letting you down over Einstein, but it was the best I could do. However you succeeded in spoiling my point in the German bit such as it was by misprinting 'treat' for 'beat' in the translation![20]

Wouldn't it be a good plan to announce *forthcoming* portraits?

Yours

J. M. K.

[18] 'Lloyd George on the War Path', a review of volume II of *The War Memoirs of David Lloyd George*, *New Statesman and Nation*, 21 October 1933.
[19] 'Hitler's Coup', an unsigned article, *loc. cit.*
[20] Above, p. 21n.

1934 was a very difficult year for Kingsley Martin. It began with illness and later included the death of his mother and the final breakdown of his marriage. With Martin's illness, Keynes arranged a rest with Edward Whitley, the senior *New Statesman* representative on *The New Statesman and Nation* Board.

To EDWARD WHITLEY, *15 February 1934*

Dear Whitley,

I am sorry to say that Kingsley Martin is distinctly unwell. He has had a severe attack of rheumatic neuritis together with dyspepsia probably due to the same basic cause. The specialist who is attending him has ordered a cure which will occupy some three or four weeks. The doctor wanted him to go away for this but eventually agreed to let him have it in London provided he did no more than very light work during the period. After that he ought apparently to go away for a holiday of not less than four weeks preferably to a warmer climate.

At present I am afraid that he is not knocking off nearly enough work, but, so far as carrying on the paper is concerned, there is no doubt, I think, that proper arrangements can be made. Lloyd is just back from a holiday and I am hopeful that Leonard Woolf will take a hand at helping. Unfortunately Gerald Barry and Brailsford are both away from England.

The main purpose of this letter, however, is this. Unluckily Martin has lately sunk his surplus income in buying a cottage which, at this time of year, would not be the right place for his holiday, and my impression is that he is feeling a little too hard up for what would really be the ideal sort of holiday for him. As soon as the paper is more prosperous, we probably ought to consider an increase of stipend, which was originally fixed rather at a minimum level. Although I think there is every reason to believe that the present situation, since the incorporation of *The Week-End Review*, is excellent, it would be premature to raise the question of stipend. I do think, however, that it would be a very good thing if we were to give him immediately an extra sum of £100 simply for the purpose of a holiday in his present condition of health. I think this might ensure his doing what is necessary. Otherwise there would, I think, be real risk of a more serious breakdown, since the illness is an obstinate and difficult one very liable to recur. If you were to agree with this and could consult one or two other directors, I feel that we could do it without a formal Board Meeting.

Yours sincerely,
[copy initialled] J. M. K.

Whitley agreed to the proposal.

In July 1934 Keynes became involved in a controversy over academic freedom in the columns of *The New Statesman and Nation*. Earlier in the year, Sir William Beveridge, the Director of the London School of Economics, had written to Harold Laski, Professor of Political Science at the School, drawing his attention to 'the possible harm that his (political) utterances might be doing the school'.[21] There followed in April a painful interview where Beveridge asked Laski whether, given his outside interests and earnings, most notably from a regular column in *The Daily Herald*, he might not be more appropriately paid on the lower professorial salary scale set for such people as lawyers with part-time practices. The School did not consider the issue formally until the summer.

In the interim, Laski went to the Soviet Union on a lecture tour as a guest of the Soviet Government. His visit and his remarks attracted much critical newspaper comment in England. The Principal of the University of London issued a statement dissociating the University from Laski's views and suggesting an inquiry. Sir Ernest Graham-Little, the Member of Parliament for the University, wrote to *The Daily Telegraph* suggesting pressure on the School to encourage it to take action. Using a *New Statesman* London Diary piece on events in Germany as a pretext, Keynes raised the issue on 15 July.

[21] José Harris, *William Beveridge: A Biography* (Oxford, 1977), p. 301.

To the Editor of The New Statesman and Nation, *15 July 1934*

PROFESSOR LASKI AND THE ISSUE OF FREEDOM

Sir,

Do not *Critic*'s complaints about the use made by the German press of your article on Schleicher confuse the main issue? For your article did in fact confirm the view that Schleicher desired a change of regime and was in touch with Paris. Surely the point is not that Schleicher or Rohm or the others were innocent of the charge of being actual or potential political opponents of the regime but that it is disgraceful to assassinate your political opponents. No additional comment is required, except, perhaps, that it adds to the personal disgrace, if they were recently your close friends and colleagues. If, in some cases, the innocent were mistaken for the guilty, that was a very culpable inadvertence, but does not—at least for the outside world—add much to the major indictment.

The same point arises in the case of Professor Laski, if stress is laid on the harmless character and anti-Communistic tendency of what he actually said. Here again what is disgraceful is the attempt on the part of the Vice-Chancellor and the Principal of the University of London to interfere with the liberty of speech of one of their professors. If it is the case that they are mistaken about their facts in addition to being inquisitors, that is a minor indictment; though it is legitimate to remark that those who depart from the regular procedure are very liable to be wrong about their facts.

When, however, you wrote your excellent paragraph last week, the attack on Professor Laski was limited to a few outsiders. It has taken on a much more serious aspect with the intervention of the Vice-Chancellor and the Principal of the University, who have made the strange declaration that 'Professor Laski's action will doubtless form the subject of an inquiry by the appropriate body', and have thought it necessary to disclaim responsibility for his opinions. Is it usual for the University of

London to express opinions on the views of its professors? What is 'the appropriate body' for this purpose? And when did it last function? One had assumed it to be well established in England, as distinguished from Moscow or Berlin, both that a professor is entitled to the unfettered expression of his opinions and that no one but himself has any responsibility in the matter. But it turns out that it was with a wise foresight that the founders of the London School of Economics expressly provided in its charter for the complete freedom of its teachers in the expression of their political opinions.

Much worse, however, was to follow, when Sir E. Graham-Little, M.P. for London University, addressed (on July 13th) a letter to *The Daily Telegraph*, in which, after admitting that 'freedom of opinion and of speech are vested with a peculiar sanctity at the University of London, which was indeed founded expressly to welcome aspirants to knowledge, irrespective of creed, race, or political opinion'—so that direct inquisitorial action is rendered difficult—he went on to suggest financial pressure in the following terms:–

Disciplinary correction of objectionable activities by a member of staff of a college would be best made by the governing body of the college. But the London School of Economics, where Professor Laski functions, has long been regarded as a hotbed of Communist teaching, and such action by the governing body is consequently unlikely. In the absence of a spontaneous condemnation by the School of Economics of this regrettable outburst by one of its teachers, the Court of the University might conceivably take action by reducing the allocation it makes to the London School of Economics, an allocation which in the opinion of many members of the University is excessive.

What are we coming to! It is hard to know how to characterise the monstrous suggestion of the last sentence! Sir E. Graham-Little is obviously unfit to represent a University in Parliament. He also shows—if I, too, may be allowed a minor indictment—a singular ignorance of what is taught at the London School.

These episodes, great and small—and the Government's

Sedition Bill also—emphasise the extraordinary importance of preserving as a matter of principle every jot and tittle of the civil and political liberties which former generations painfully secured in their disgust and horror at similar episodes. Inquisition into opinions, the right of search on vague administrative suspicion, political assassination—all doubtless directed, in the minds of those who practise them, to the safety of the state—belong to the same order of ideas, which, as experience taught us many years ago, destroy civilisation whatever they may preserve.

Too many of the younger members of the Left have toyed with Marxist ideas to have a clear conscience in repelling reactionary assaults on freedom. Thus the importance of impressing on the minds of the Right and of the Left alike that not the smallest breach should be allowed in the fortifications of liberty has become so urgent that for many of us *The New Statesman and Nation* takes on a new importance for the sake of the contribution it is making to this object.

J. M. KEYNES

On publication, Keynes's letter brought him a note from Laski.

From HAROLD LASKI, *22 July 1934*

Private

Dear Keynes,

Your characteristically generous letter in this week's *New Statesman* moved me greatly. Of course I knew you would feel like that. I do not myself understand how anyone who cares for academic freedom as a principle can feel otherwise. I told Beveridge at once that I could not submit to any enquiry by the University or anyone else for the simple reason that to do so would be to admit a right of censorship in the University fatal to the freedom of other teachers. That, of course, is quite apart from the question of the real moderation of my lecture at Moscow which has not, I think, anything to do with the question of principle.

I do not expect to hear anything more about the matter. But what is really disturbing is the way in which all the administrators of the University, from Beveridge downwards, at once took alarm about the possible incidence of my speech on the flow of endowments to the University. It became clear to me that their view was quite definite that the teacher should not say or write anything which 'embarrassed' the University. And 'embarrassment' means money and money only. In those circumstances one is asked, in effect, to subordinate one's insights to the persuasion of rich men that the University in general, and the School in particular, is a 'sound' place for the receipt of funds from men to whom left opinions are anathema. My American experience convinces me that once this temper is abroad the very roots of freedom are torn up. I don't think it matters that people like Graham-Little should spit their little venom. But I do think it serious when people like Beveridge, protesting, of course, that academic freedom is paramount, nevertheless hint plainly that the best way to preserve it is so to act as to prevent the issue from being raised.

But I don't want to inflict a long letter on you. I want merely to say that I am grateful.

Please remember me warmly to your wife.

Yours very sincerely,
HAROLD J. LASKI

Keynes's letter also brought comments both from *The New Statesman* and from its readers, most notably Mr Frank Pitcairn who took exception to the first sentence of Keynes's last paragraph. This led Keynes to another letter three weeks later.

To the Editor of The New Statesman and Nation, *11 August 1934*

Sir,

Marxists are ready to sacrifice the political liberties of individuals in order to change the existing economic order. So are Fascists and Nazis. That is why I said that those who had toyed with Marxist ideas could not have a clear conscience in defending the political liberties of individuals from reactionary attacks.

The question for 'Critic' is whether he is prepared to suspend political liberties as a method whereby to change the existing economic order—with the object, of course, of increasing 'true' liberty later on. If he is, he cannot claim to be a defender of liberty *on principle*. If not, why doesn't he sympathise with what I said about those who have toyed with Marxism? He will find it awfully hard work to be *both* a Marxist *and* a political liberal.

My own aim is economic reform by the methods of political liberalism. If 'Critic' considers this a hopeless enterprise, he must give up defending liberty on principle. But if he and Mr Pitcairn merely mean that the achievement of economic reform would make the defence of political liberty much easier (as, of course, it would), what bearing has this against my observations?

J. M. KEYNES

The next letter from Kingsley Martin touched on this issue and others.

From KINGSLEY MARTIN, *27 August 1934*

Dear Maynard,

The liberty correspondence—excluding the earlier Laski references—has run for five weeks and the letters which are now coming in don't seem to raise new points. I have had ten 'Marxists' to one un-Marxist I should think and that makes things look onesided. The only non-Marxist letter last week was a query from Gerald Shove. As the controversy is bound to arise in some form or other again almost immediately I thought I might well give it a rest, but I am sorry that you are disappointed, and if there is any new point in this week's correspondence I will re-start the controversy.

Would it be all right for Olga[22] and me to come down on Saturday? I think we would probably come by train though if it is a very nice day I might be tempted to motor.

I see I exaggerated the length of time that I was away from the paper in the spring. I was only actually away for four weeks but there were about three others in which I was having treatment and did not work much at the office. I have practically decided, however, not to go to America this autumn after all. Next spring might be better.

There are one or two things I should very much like to talk over at the weekend. Please say if Saturday is not altogether convenient to you and Lydia. I could arrange another day if better for you.

K. M.

[22] Martin's wife.

When Keynes and Martin met at Tilton on the Sunday, one of the matters they discussed was the Professorship of International Relations at Aberystwyth (University College of North Wales). This post had minimal lecturing responsibilities and extensive opportunities for travel. When offered it, Martin found the prospect very attractive.

To KINGSLEY MARTIN, *7 September 1934*

My dear Kingsley,

I shall be up on Wednesday but I have a long list of things and don't know when I shall be free. I'll look in at the office between 5 and 6 if I can manage.

I'd gladly have you move into the A. project if I'd realised you were still considering it seriously. But as I said on Sunday, personally I hope very much you won't take it. Your subject is one which is best done *not* academically and is dingy in strictly academic circles. So the only point is to get *leisure* for writing a large book. But is a large book so much to be preferred to the daily task of persuasion?

Yours ever,

J. M. K.

Russia and Marxism occupied Keynes again in the autumn. On 27 October *The New Statesman* published the text of an interview between Stalin and H. G. Wells. George Bernard Shaw added a comment, to which Keynes replied.

From The New Statesman and Nation, *10 November 1934*

MR KEYNES REPLIES TO SHAW

What is the difference between Shaw and Wells? It is the difference between the clergy and the scientists. Shaw believes that he and we *know* all there is to be known, and it is only our nasty feelings that stand between us and what should be. He takes our knowledge as given and our feelings, our passions, as the variable in the system. But Wells takes our feelings as given and our knowledge as the variable. For him it is a shift in our knowledge which will work the sea-change. Wells is a searcher, an inquirer. But Shaw is such a dogmatist by now that it makes but little difference to his enthusiasm whether it is Stalin or Mussolini. He would have a good word for the Pope (as we see in St Joan), if it were not that His Holiness is so mild and broadminded.

Hence flows Shaw's brilliantly malicious misinterpretation of the atmosphere of the interview with Stalin. My picture of that interview is of a man struggling with a gramophone. The reproduction is excellent, the record is word-perfect. And there is poor Wells feeling that he has his own chance to coax the needle off the record and hear it—vain hope—speak in human tones. Shaw mocks Wells's little pretences which show him pathetically conscious that one must be polite to one's host even when it is a gramophone. He reproves Wells as a bad listener. But, in fact, Wells's weakness is that he can't bear gramophones. He is enjoying the most interesting interview of his life—and he is stupendously bored. Desperately he struggles. Clumsily he coaxes. But it is no good. To the end the reproduction is excellent and the record word-perfect.

Shaw writes that Wells 'has not come to be instructed by Stalin, but to instruct him'. Nothing could be more untrue. On the contrary. it is Wells's trouble that he has never yet found a satisfactory instruction to give. He has nothing to offer Stalin. That is what Stalin might have pointed out, if gramophones could hear.

I ask Shaw and Stalin to allow the possibility that mere intellectual cogitation may have something to contribute to the solution, and also that their traditional interpretation does not fit the present facts. Shaw speaks of the 'standard system' of the economists 'still taught in our universities', and of how 'its completeness and logic reconciled humane thinkers like De Quincey, Austin, Macaulay and the Utilitarians to it in full view of its actual and prospective horrors'. I sympathise with his passage—it is excellently put. But Shaw has forgotten that he and Stalin are just as completely under the intellectual dominance of that standard system as Asquith and Inge. The system bred two families—those who thought it true and inevitable, and those who thought it true and intolerable. There was no third school of thought in the nineteenth century. Nevertheless, there is a third possibility—that it is not true. A most upsetting idea to the dogmatists—no one would be more annoyed than Stalin by that thought—but hugely exhilarating to the scientists.

It is this third alternative which will allow us to escape. The standard system is based on intellectual error. The dispersal of that error and the substitution for it of a sounder economic theory, which is as obviously applicable to our problems as electrical theory is to the practical problems of the electrician, will make a vaster difference to our outlook than Shaw and Stalin yet foresee. Our pressing task is the elaboration of a new standard system which will justify economists in taking their seat beside other scientists. Wells's peculiar gift of imagination lies in his creative grasp of the possibilities and ultimate implications of the data with which contemporary scientists furnish him. At the same time he is a social and political dreamer—or has grown so as he becomes older—much more than a technical or mathematical dreamer; of the school of Plato, not of Pythagoras or Archimedes. Wells's misfortune has been to belong to a generation to whom their economists have offered nothing new. They have given him no platform from which his imagination can leap. But Wells is fully conscious all the same, and justly so, that his own mind dwells with the future and Shaw's and Stalin's with the past.

Not only is the old theory faulty. The facts of the world shift. Shaw and Stalin are still satisfied with Marx's picture of the capitalist world, which had much verisimilitude in his day but is unrecognisable, with the rapid flux of the modern world, three-quarters of a century later. They look backwards to what capitalism was, not forward to what it is becoming. That is the fate of those who dogmatise in the social and economic sphere where evolution is proceeding at a dizzy pace from one form of society to another. In the second half of the nineteenth century it was plausible to say that the capitalists—meaning the leaders of the City and the captains of industry—held the power. It was plausible to say that the economic organisation of society, in spite of its glaring faults, suited them on the whole, and that, so long as they held the power, they would successfully resist major changes coming from other quarters. Nor was it easy to see in 1870 how the power could pass from them by a peaceful process of evolution. Indeed, for another generation after that their effective power increased—mainly at the expense of the aristocratic and land-owning regime which had preceded them. Queen Victoria died as the monarch of the most capitalistic empire upon which the sun has (or has not) set.

If Shaw had kept up with the newspapers since the death of Queen Victoria, he would know that a complex of events had destroyed that form of society. One of the principal causes may have been a sort of natural law which prescribes that the giants of the forest shall have no immediate successors. The leaders of the City and the captains of industry were tremendous boys at the height of their glory; and in due course they became tremendous old boys, with vision dimmed but tenacity and will power untamed. Saplings of the same seed could not survive in their shade. When the giants fell with years, a different sort of tree was found growing in the forest underneath. And much else has happened. The capitalist has lost the source of his inner strength—his self-assurance, his self-confidence, his untamable will, his belief in his own beauty and unquestionable value to society. He is a forlorn object, Heaven knows—at the best, a pathetic, well-meaning Clissold. Lord Revelstoke the first, Lord Rothschild the first, Lord Goschen the first, Sir Lothian Bell, Sir Ernest Cassel, the private bankers, the ship-owning families, the merchant princes, the world-embracing contractors, the self-made barons of Birmingham, Manchester, Liverpool, and Glasgow—where are they now? There are no such objects on the earth. Their office-boys (on salaries) rule in their mausoleums.

Thus, for one reason or another, Time and the Joint Stock Company and the Civil Service have silently brought the salaried class into power. Not yet a Proletariat. But a Salariat, assuredly. And it makes a great difference.

Moreover, the nineteenth century, with all its horrors, suited those in power. They liked it. Well might Marx argue that nothing on earth could bring down those Houyhnhnms, except to organise the myriad Lilliputians and arm them with poisoned arrows. But to-day's muddle suits no one. The problem to-day is first to concert good advice and then to convince the well-intentioned that it is good. When Wells has succeeded in discovering the right stuff, the public will swallow it in gulps—the Salariat quicker than the Proletariat. There is no massive resistance to a new direction. The risk is of a contrary kind—lest society plunge about in its perpexity and dissatisfaction into something worse. Revolution, as Wells says, is out of date. For a revolution is against personal power. In England to-day no one has personal power.

Yet let Stalin be comforted. When I have said all this, I have not touched the real strength of Communism. On the surface Communism enormously overestimates the significance of the economic problem. The economic problem is not too difficult to solve. If you will leave that to me, I will look after it. But when I have solved it, I shall not receive, or deserve, much thanks. For I shall have done no more than disclose that the real problem lying behind is quite different and further from solution than before. Underneath, Communism draws its strength from deeper, more serious sources. Offered to us as a means of improving the economic situation, it is an insult to our intelligence. But offered as a means of making the economic situation *worse*, that is its subtle, its almost irresistible, attraction.

Communism is not a reaction against the failure of the nineteenth century to organise optimal economic output. It is a reaction against its comparative success. It is a protest against the emptiness of economic welfare, an appeal to the ascetic in us all to other values. It is the curate in Wells, far from extinguished by the scientist, which draws him to take a peep at Moscow. It is Shaw, the noblest old curate in the world and the least scientific, who rallies to the good cause of putting the economist in his place somewhere underground. The idealistic youth play with Communism because it is the only spiritual appeal which feels to them contemporary; but its economics bothers and disturbs them. When Cambridge undergraduates take their inevitable trip to Bolshiedom, are they disillusioned when they find it all dreadfully uncomfortable? Of course not. That is what they are looking for.

So I pay my affectionate respects to both our grand old schoolmasters, Shaw and Wells, to whom most of us have gone to school all our lives, our divinity master and our stinks master. I only wish we had had a third, equal to them in his own field, to teach us humane letters and the arts.

Keynes's comments drew a letter from Dora Russell who asked why, if nobody was exerting power to prevent it, Keynes's policies were not adopted in Britain. Keynes replied.

To the Editor of The New Statesman and Nation, *24 November 1934*

Sir,

Dora Russell asks, 'Why cannot we adopt a new economic policy drawn up by Mr Keynes to-morrow, if nobody is exerting power to prevent it?' Because I have not yet succeeded in convincing either the expert or the ordinary man that I am right. If I am wrong, this will prove to have been fortunate. If, however, I am right, it is, I feel certain, only a matter of time before I convince both; and when both are convinced, economic policy will, with the usual time lag, follow suit.

This is the essential point. Are changes for the better prevented by wicked men who know the changes to be advisable, but resist them out of self-interest? Or are they prevented by the difficulty of knowing for certain where wisdom lies? The class-war faction believe that it is well known what ought to be done; that we are divided between the poor and good who would like to do it, and the rich and wicked who, for reasons of self-interest, wish to prevent it; that the wicked have power; and that a revolution is required to depose them from their seats. I view the matter otherwise. I think it extremely difficult to know what ought to be done, and extremely difficult for those who know (or think they know) to persuade others that they are right—though theories, which are difficult and obscure when they are new and undigested, grow easier by the mere passage of time.

I suspect that Bernard Shaw's preference for tyrants is mainly due to his being impressed with the difficulties of persuasion. It is easier to persuade a tyrant to adopt one's policy than to persuade the democracy. I agree with him. But it is not self-interest which makes the democracy difficult to persuade.

In this country henceforward power will normally reside with the Left. The Labour Party will always have a majority, except when something has happened to raise a doubt in the minds of reasonable and disinterested persons whether the Labour Party are in the right. If, and when, and in so far as, they are able to persuade reasonable and disinterested persons that they are right, the power of self-interested capitalists to stand in their way is negligible.

J. M. KEYNES

At the end of November, Kingsley Martin decided to put the Wells–Stalin interview and the ensuing comments and letters together as a pamphlet with appropriate cartoons by David Low.[23] Wells agreed, as did Keynes, but Shaw held back. The result was the following exchange of letters between Keynes and Shaw.

[23] *Shaw–Wells–Keynes on Stalin–Wells Talk* (New Statesman and Nation, 1934).

36

From GEORGE BERNARD SHAW, *30 November 1934*

Dear Maynard Keynes,

I am not at all easy about Kingsley Martin's proposal to reprint all that stuff in *The New Statesman*. I should put my foot down on it at once but for H. G. who has an infatuated belief that he has put Stalin in his place and given me an exemplary drubbing, whereas it is equally clear to me that he has made a blazing idiot of himself.

It is represented to me that you, too, are anxious for the reprint which makes it still more difficult for me to object. However, if you insist, I suggest that you should recast what you said about Marx being a back number, as this will certainly be misunderstood, though of course Marx is an old story to you, as he is to me. But look at the facts. When I read Marx 50 years ago, I could not find an English translation of *Capital* in the British Museum, and had to read him in Daville's French translation. Today the book is the best seller among the serious books in the Everyman Library, and the world is gasping at the Russian revolution, which was put through by men who were inspired by Marx more directly and exclusively than the Reformation by Luther and Calvin or the French Revolution by Rousseau and Voltaire. In such a situation it is impossible for a sociologist of any standing to write about Marx as forgotten and negligible. I have picked Marx's mistakes to pieces as meticulously as anybody; but I am always very careful to reserve the fact that he was an Epoch Maker.

Besides, the Class War is perfectly sound as a proposition in political physics. It is not disposed of by saying that the lines of disruptive strain do not follow the lines between classes; but that the strain is there and can be got rid of only by the abolition of 'real' property is beyond all sane question. At present Marx's demonstration of the blind ruthlessness of capital in the pursuit of 'surplus value' (practically of cheap labour) is producing a dangerous conflict between our obvious balance-of-power interest in an alliance of England and France with Russia and the U.S.A. and the class war pressure to join with Japan in the exploitation of Manchuoko.

Your article reads as if you had never heard of all this; and therefore, if it is to be reprinted, I think you ought to revise it sufficiently to avoid this impression.

I have offered H. G. to write his part in the affair for him and give him a good show; but he says I must 'take my medicine', bless his innocence.

I write with difficulty, very incompetently, as I am still in bed, tired out and run down to nothing, but convalescing all right so far.

Faithfully

G. BERNARD SHAW

P.S. I think the core of the affair—the report of the interview—a complete disappointment considering the eminence of the parties—why give it a pretence of importance by making a book of it?

To GEORGE BERNARD SHAW, *2 December 1934*

Dear Bernard Shaw,

If you feel as you say about publishing the Wells–Stalin business, the advisability of printing it is not so obvious to me that I should feel I ought to press it on you against your own preference. I see, however, from this week's *New Stateman* that it is actually being published *next Friday*—so it seems dreadfully late to interfere.

As for my view of Marx, I said nothing in that article except to accuse you and Stalin of being still satisfied with his view of the capitalist world 'which had much verisimilitude in his day is unrecognisable three quarters of a century later'. Surely it is certain that the picture has changed out of recognition.

My feelings about *Das Kapital* are the same as my feelings about the *Koran*. I know that it is historically important and I know that many people, not all of whom are idiots, find it a sort of Rock of Ages and containing inspiration. Yet when I look into it, it is to me inexplicable that it can have this effect. Its dreary, out-of-date, academic controversialising seems so extraordinarily unsuitable as material for the purpose. But then, as I have said, I feel just the same about the *Koran*. How could either of these books carry fire and sword round half the world? It beats me. Clearly there is some defect in my understanding. Do you believe both *Das Kapital* and the *Koran*? Or only *Das Kapital*? But whatever the sociological value of the latter, I am sure that its contemporary *economic* value (apart from occasional but inconstructive and discontinuous flashes of insight) is *nil*. Will you promise to read it again, if I do?

Wishing for your good health.

Yours ever,

J. M. K.

To KINGSLEY MARTIN, *2 December 1934*

Dear Kingsley,

I have a long letter from G.B.S. from which it appears that he doesn't want to reprint the pamphlet. The relevant sentence in my reply is as follows:–

'If you feel as you say about publishing the Wells–Stalin business, the advisability of printing it is not so obvious to me that I should feel I ought to press it on you against your own preference. I see, however, from this week's *New Statesman* that it is actually being published *next Friday*—so it seems dreadfully late to interfere.'

Presumably you got his permission some time ago. I fancy the old gentleman is weak and ill. He ends—'I write with difficulty, very incompetently, as I am still in bed, tired out and run down to nothing'.

Yours ever,

J. M. KEYNES

From KINGSLEY MARTIN, *3 December 1934*

Dear Maynard,

I have had an extremely amusing time with Wells and G.B.S. I will tell you the whole story some time. I intend to write it down in a few days while it is still fresh. Wells is really a baby. I saw G.B.S. in bed on Saturday afternoon and he is now quite happy about the whole thing. The pamphlet will be out on Friday.

Yours,

KINGSLEY MARTIN

Low has done a superb cover!

From GEORGE BERNARD SHAW, *11 December 1934*

Dear Maynard Keynes,

The pamphlet being now published, my last letter is washed out. Nevertheless let me abuse the one advantage I have over you: the advantage

39

of being frightfully old, and therefore able to remember the nineteenth century, whereas you can only imagine it. And you are hampered in your imagination by the university time lag, which is roughly about half a century. I shall not bother you with arguments, but just put down scrap by scrap the facts that are important to you.

Until about 1860, when Marx and Lassalle and the old International came into the field, the Ricardo–Bentham Manchester school not only faced the horrors of capitalism but actually rubbed them in (Austin's lectures for instance, and Macaulay on the future of America) as a prophylactic against the sentimental reaction. The teaching was candid and clear because the sentimentalists had no alternative system to offer: Tom Hood, Mrs. Browning, and Dickens in *Hard Times* left the Ricardian theorem quite unshaken. The demonstration that it was inevitable, and that all sentimental interferences with it did more harm than good, dominated even its opponents, exactly as you suppose it to have done up to the end of the XIX century, your Cambridge time lag being thus about 40 years.

But this state of things came to an end when 'scientific socialism', 'equipped with all the culture of the age' (Lassalle's boast) knocked Ricardo into a cocked hat by simply saying 'If private property produces all these horrors, let us substitute public property'. When I took the field at the beginning of the eighties I did so as a propagandist of a rival system much more thoroughly thought out than the Ricardian system, which I also had taken the trouble to master so that I could parry all its thrusts and pierce all its advances. This was so generally understood that in 1888, at the meeting of the British Association at Bath, when an innocent old gentleman got up and said that I was entirely ignorant of political economy, the whole audience burst into a roar of laughter, much as if nowadays some old Newtonian were to say that Einstein is evidently entirely ignorant of mathematics. Economics were all the rage; but it was a bad time for poor Marshall in Cambridge. If he had dared to be as straightforward as Austin or De Quincey he would have been fired at the next end of term. If he had gone for Hewins and the Tariff Reform League as Cobden would have gone for them he would have been cold-shouldered by the plutocracy as obsolete and middle class. Vanderbilt, Rockefeller and Morgan were shewing how much better a game it was to abolish competition than to practise it. The Liberal opposition was forced into the Newcastle Program, which was rank Socialism. *Fabian Essays* left Lassalle and Marx behind unmentioned, Webb's list of successful State enterprises being specially staggering to the old school. Marshall and Foxwell dined with the bankers and piffled over little elaborations of theory and graph drawing and affections of being practical men on industrial problems—but they could not get a hearing outside their classrooms with *Industrial Democracy* and the *History of Trade Unionism* setting a standard of proletarian investigation impossible to an academic professor. The new London County Council was captured by the Fabian progressive program; and John Burns, The Man with the Red Flag, was on the way to become the first proletarian Cabinet Minister.

Meanwhile—mark this—Goschen had put a pistol to the heads of the holders of Consols 'Take $2\frac{1}{2}\%$', he said, 'or I pay you off'. And they did. We all discussed what would happen when the fall in rate passed zero and became negative. I said, as I still say, 'Nothing whatever will happen except that dividends will be bigger than ever and we shall have to pay the banks for keeping our uninvested money instead of receiving interest on our deposit accounts'.

The South African war stopped all that by rushing the rate up to 5%, where it stuck until the recent slump.

I could pile up all sorts of facts from the eighties to shew you that your notion of it is postdated by 40 years. The real eighties were far more agitated over economics than the present dole-softened money crisis which isn't a money crisis at all. It had at the back of it hunger riots and the breaking of windows by the unemployed in St James's Street and Piccadilly. When trade revived at the end of the eighties the steam went out of it and the war finished it. And Cambridge forgot all about it, and left you under the impression that I am a curate discouraged by reading Goldsmith's *Deserted Village*! Lord help you, you know nothing about it; and Cambridge has convinced you that you know everything, which is the typical university result. You must shake it off, or Cambridge will nullify you as completely as Parliament has nullified MacDonald.

You are quite right about the *Koran*; but do not therefore go back to the worship of stones or describe Mahomet as 'the accurst Mahound'. Mahomet was an epoch maker; and there is much excellent doctrine in the *Koran*. Marx with his manifesto and his *Capital* also made an epoch; and everything that Stalin reeled off the gramophone for Wells's benefit is still incontrovertible. Mahomet made a mess of the calendar and thought that the mountains were big weights placed on the earth by Allah to prevent the earth being blown away; but he was a very wise man for all that; and Marx, though he thought Ricardo's law of rent was some sort of chemical delusion of Humboldt's, was also among the prophets.

And you Maynard, are not merely Marshall's successor. You are a bright and promising youth, frightfully handicapped by the Cambridge nullification process, with some inextinguishable sparks of culture in you which make you interesting. Hence my writing all this to save you from one or two blunders

41

as to things which happened before your time. In common gratitude for this service give my love to Lydia.

Faithfully,
G. BERNARD SHAW

P.S. Reflect specially on the tragic fact that Jevons, the author of the 1870 *Theory* of P[olitical] E[conomy], and of several divinatory flashes which I seized on and developed, ended a London University Professor demonstrating that a state parcel post is an impossibility. Some nullification *that*: eh?

To GEORGE BERNARD SHAW, *1 January 1935*

Dear Bernard Shaw,

Thank you for your letter. I will try and take your words to heart. There must be *something* in what you say, because there generally is. But I've made another shot at old K.M. last week, reading the Marx–Engels correspondence just published, without making much progress. I prefer Engels of the two. I can see that they invented a certain method of carrying on and a vile manner of writing, both of which their successors have maintained with fidelity. But if you tell me that they discovered a clue to the economic riddle, still I am beaten—I can discover nothing but out-of-date controversialising.

To understand my state of mind, however, you have to know that I believe myself to be writing a book on economic theory, which will largely revolutionise—not, I suppose, at once but in the course of the next ten years—the way the world thinks about economic problems. When my new theory has been duly assimilated and mixed with politics and feelings and passions, I can't predict what the final upshot will be in its effects on action and affairs. But there will be a great change, and, in particular, the Ricardian foundations of Marxism will be knocked away.

I can't expect you, or anyone else, to believe this at the present stage. But for myself I don't merely hope what I say,—in my own mind I'm quite sure.

Lydia sends her love to you and Charlotte.

Yours ever,
J.M.K.

In the New Year, *The New Statesman* published in its issue of 19 January a leading article, 'Complete Impartiality', on a controversy on the choice of school text-books in London. Keynes commented.

To the Editor of The New Statesman and Nation, *21 January 1935*

Sir,

What conclusion do you intend us to draw from your article on 'Complete Impartiality'? Do you want text-books of contemporary political history to be written by persons who have no point of view or *per impossibile* conceal it? The object should be, I suggest, that the young should be made aware of the existence of two points of view and of the warmth and quality of feeling attaching to each; and it is unavoidable that warm-hearted authors should see some facts through coloured spectacles. There was an excellent little book in my youth called *Pros and Cons*, which was the perquisite of the openers in a school debate. It reached, and perhaps excelled, the impartiality of an armament manufacturer. Its point was, of course, that one never sought its aid given so impartially to oneself and one's opponent, until after sides had been chosen. But I should have been sorry if all the intellectual food of my education had been prepared on this model.

I hope, therefore, that Professor Tawney's committee will not expunge from their list the attractively written little books from which you quote—so like what you yourself were brought up on, which made your outlook what it is—but will add others to them of a different colour, even though (which is probable) they are less attractively written.

The liberty not to be impartial is one of the few liberties still left to us, and you must not try to take it away.

J. M. KEYNES

From KINGSLEY MARTIN, *22 January 1935*

Dear Maynard,

I was pleased to get your letter as it makes a good peg for hanging further discussion of this issue on. I could not for the life of me see what your criticism wàs because I carefully avoided last week entering in to any discussion about the line of action. I merely suggested (a) that books were not impartial and (b) that no effort had been made to define impartiality. To discuss the whole issue would have involved another leader.

Yours,

K. M.

In February 1935 the issue of Martin's taking a professorship at Aberystwyth arose again.

From a letter from KINGSLEY MARTIN, *28 February 1935*

The other thing[24] I wanted a futher word about was Aberystwyth. After I turned down the suggestion last autumn they seem to have been dissatisfied with the candidates and made no appointment. It is still open to me for next year (I mean open to me to let my name go forward with a good chance of success) and I have to decide during the next week or ten days. There are some points I'd like to talk over. I've been rather tempted to accept the last few days for one reason or another.

Probably between 28 February and their meeting on 9 March Keynes received another document.

From KINGSLEY MARTIN, *Sunday night* [*3 March 1935*]

Dear Maynard

I've written the enclosed[25] for myself—to stop myself thinking in circles. Its written without art or attempt at finality and I'm sending it you just as it happened on the type-writer. But it occurred to me that you might like to see it. I turned down Aber. in the autumn but when Evans told me they had still no one he was certain he wanted to appoint (which is an absolutely

---

[24] The other matter related to the appointment of Raymond Mortimer as literary editor and complications that arose with David Garnett as a result.

[25] This has not survived.

private remark to me) I could not help thinking about the idea again. Anyway it might interest you to glance at this 'pro and con' and give it back to me.

KINGSLEY MARTIN

After Keynes met Martin in Cambridge, he reported the results to Edward Whitley.

From a letter to EDWARD WHITLEY, *13 March 1935*

I talked matters over throughly with Martin and I have since heard from him that he has decided to refuse the post which was offered him. I agree with you that when the financial results of the year are out, we might well consider whether we could not do something to improve his financial position. But I should be rather inclined to make this a profit-sharing arrangement than a definitive addition to stipend. We shall doubtless suffer wide fluctuations in revenue in the future, as in the past, and when revenue falls off it is an embarrassment to have taken on too many burdens in the good times. A profit-sharing arrangement would progress with our prosperity and fall away when we are less prosperous. In fact, Roberts is already on a profit-sharing basis, since his remuneration fluctuates in accordance with the advertisement revenue. It is difficult to make a concrete suggestion before seeing the figures, but the sort of thing I have in mind is a bonus of 5 per cent of our profits in addition to salary.

Keynes had seen Martin on 9 March. On 15 March Whitley reported that Martin had still not made up his mind about Aberystwyth. Eventually, however, he decided to remain with *The New Statesman*.

There was then over a year's gap in the correspondence. During the interval, of course, both men met regularly at *New Statesman* board meetings and elsewhere.

When the correspondence resumed, it was over a leading article in the issue of 11 July 1936, 'The End of Collective Security'.

45

To KINGSLEY MARTIN, *13 July 1936*

Dear Kingsley,

As you will see from the enclosed, which I send you for publication, I have been unable to make much of your leading article in this week's paper. Possibly, however, my letter might form the basis of discussion. I should like to see the whole matter dealt with pretty fully in, so to speak, a more concrete fashion. I do not think that you ought yet to despair of a British-Franco-Russian understanding.

I liked your article on the Buchmanites[26] immensely. Just right, I thought. But who wrote the second article, saying how much better it would be just now if only there were a few more strikes? It did not sound like Cole.

Yours ever,
[copy initialled] J. M. K.

To the Editor of The New Statesman and Nation, *13 July 1936*

Sir,

I find the conclusion of your leading article on 'The End of Collective Security' difficult to understand. What, to be precise, is the 'frankly revolutionary policy to which Labour is committed'? What is the meaning of the sentence 'Only on a policy of war resistance to this Government can Labour retain unity'?

I infer that you are opposed to any increase in this country's armaments. If so, are you in favour of (a) no armaments at all or (b) inadequate armaments? Yet I do not infer that you favour a policy of isolationism and a complete withdrawal of this country from the affairs of Europe. The conclusion seems to be that you are opposed to this country's possessing armaments so long as the present Government is in power, because you believe that they intend to use them for some sinister purpose of which you disapprove. Could you state what this sinister purpose is?

---

[26] 'God Control', *New Statesman and Nation*, 11 July 1935. The 'Buchmanites' were the followers of Frank Buchman, leader of the Oxford Group and initiator of Moral Rearmament.

I hope you will answer all these questions, even if I give you a chance of avoiding them by adding something positive of my own which, in face of the perplexities of the problem, is probably open to criticism. I desire those countries, whose fundamental policies are peaceful, to be as formidable as possible. I believe that our own country belongs to this group, and can be trusted, whatever Government is in power, not to use its armaments for sinister purposes. The leadership of this group obviously belongs to ourselves, France, Russia and the United States; its membership includes the whole world except Germany, Italy and Japan. We have two tasks before us: first, consciously and avowedly to belong to this group, to give it leadership, body and coherence and to work out means of effective cooperation; and, secondly, to make it collectively so formidable that only a madman will affront it. The first task means that, in common with Mr Duff Cooper, we must seek primarily a close accord with France, especially with its present Government, secondarily an understanding with Russia, and finally, to the limited extent that she will allow it, the habit of intimate conversation and mutual confidence between ourselves and the United States; whilst the recognition of the second task involves us in supporting the programme of rearmament.

Of course I do not deny the existence of a party in this country which totally disagrees with the above policy and favours an understanding with the brigand powers. This party has secured a measure of popular sympathy because some people believe, falsely in my opinion, that this policy is more likely than any other to keep this country out of war. It includes the extreme anti-Bolshevists and the extreme pacifists, so that the line of division cuts across the political boundaries. It is noticeable, however, that those leading conservatives, who avowedly belong to this group, have been strictly excluded by Mr Baldwin from his Cabinet or, as in the case of Lord Londonderry, evicted from it.

I also acknowledge and deplore the disastrous incompetence

and the humiliating failures of our own and the French Foreign Offices. Nevertheless, a state of inadequate armament on our part can only encourage the brigand powers who know no argument but force, and will play, in the long run, into the hands of those who would like us to acquiesce by inaction in these powers doing pretty much what they like in the world, so long as they agree not to lay hands, for the time being, on any of our own imperial interests. Can I not persuade you that the collective possession of preponderant force by the leading pacific powers is, in the conditions of to-day, the best assurance of peace; and that there is no reason to believe that Mr Baldwin or Mr Eden or Mr Duff Cooper is a partisan of the brigands?

Yours etc.

J. M. KEYNES

Keynes's letter provoked a discussion that rumbled on for some months. It also overlapped with the outbreak of the Spanish Civil War on 17 July. Keynes's next letter reflected the course of events and *The New Statesman*'s reactions to them.

To the Editor of The New Statesman and Nation, *8 August 1936*

Sir,

In your leader on the Spanish civil war you write: 'The battalions stand formed—the French and the Russians on one side, the Italians and Germans on the other. But one enigma persists. This country of ours straddles the trenches and fails to recognise the nature of the struggle that has begun.'

In other words, if and when the issue is joined, there will be three possibilities: (1) that we shall assist the brigand powers, (2) that we shall assist those who are suffering aggression, or (3) that we shall stand aloof. When you were arguing two or three weeks ago in favour of keeping this country as weak as possible, I inferred that the explanation must be found in your supposing the first alternative decidedly the most probable. Have I understood you correctly?

If I have, I suggest again that this would be an extreme error of judgement. It may be that we shall stand aloof; but, if by the aggression of the dictatorships the struggle comes, surely it would be insane to believe that Mr Baldwin's Government, or any other Government likely to be in power in this country, will weigh in on the side of the aggressors?

If, however, the doubt in your mind is merely between the second and third alternatives, then I ask again why do you wish this country to be as weak as possible? In common with many others, I do not myself know my own mind between the second and the third alternative. I doubt if it is wise, as yet, to reach a firm conclusion. But I am absolutely clear that the more formidable this country stands, the less likely is the feared contingency to come to pass.

One further point. Your most recent leader suggests that, in your mind, a war between the democracies and the dictatorships is absolutely certain. And you complain against Mr Baldwin's Government for not aligning itself definitely against the dicta- torships. But Mr Baldwin is perhaps wiser than you are. He may be hesitating because he knows that nothing is certain. It may conceivably prove to have been right on our part not to clinch the position; not to crystallise the fatal alignment of forces. The best, the only, hope of peace lies in a policy which does not regard war as certain; which breaks down no bridges and makes no final commitments. Herr Hitler, however disagreeable a creature, is a queer one. National hysterias do not last for ever. Something totally unexpected may suddenly change the whole situation. Your leader on the Spanish civil war enforced on your readers considerations which it is important that they should understand. It was a valuable and interesting statement. But we should combine an awareness of these tendencies and possibilities with a refusal to allow our minds or our decisions to crystallise. It is a nerve-racking thing to pay close and continuous attention to a matter of vast importance, and, at the same time, to refrain from forming any conclusions. No state of mind is more painful than a state of continuing doubt. But the ability to maintain it may be a mark of statesmanship. If I am right in attributing it to Mr Baldwin, he may be serving by his indecisions the best interests of peace.

But one conclusion does seem to be clear. It is better to have strong forces and no clear-cut foreign policy than to advocate no armaments one week and warlike alliances the next.

J. M. KEYNES

The same week as Keynes's second letter appeared, a correspondent calling himself 'A Socialist' asked Keynes four questions

Do you agree with Sir Thomas Inskip's recent dictum that defence has nothing to do with foreign policy?...

Do you agree that the Government were returned to power largely because they promised to uphold the Covenant in the Italo-Abyssinian war, and that they have broken that promise and defaulted on our treaty obligations?...

Do you agree that the Government's abandoment of the collective security system wiped out any distinction between self-defence and the use of war as an instrument of national policy, and makes another great war inevitable sooner or later?

Do you believe in the doctrine 'My country right or wrong'...?

Keynes replied.

To the Editor of The New Statesman and Nation, *15 August 1936*

Sir,

I readily endeavour to answer 'Socialist's' questions.

(1) I do not know in what context or with what qualification Sir Thomas Inskip declared that 'defence has nothing to do with foreign policy'. But, as it stands, I disagree with it. Indeed it is absurd. The Opposition are fully entitled to vote against the Army Estimates if, in their opinion, the effect of increased armaments will be to make our foreign policy more objectionable and injurious to good causes than it will be otherwise. The questions are whether such an opinion would be well-founded, and in what circumstances the Opposition is entitled to threaten

'a nation-wide refusal to fight, or to work, or to pay taxes in case of war, unless and until the Government give adequate guarantees'—to quote the conclusion of 'Socialist's' letter. For I would point out to 'Socialist' that there is a distinction in a constitutional country between voting against the Army Estimates and incitements to sedition.

(2) I agree that the Government's apparently sincere support of the Covenant gained them votes at the General Election. I agree that the League has, collectively, failed in its object and that this country bears a heavy, though not the sole, responsibility for this failure. But, since we have committed no act of aggression and have accepted all the decisions of the League, I doubt if it would be true to say that we have 'defaulted on our treaty obligations'. 'Socialist' almost writes as if he saw little distinction between our behaviour towards the League and Mussolini's.

The discreditable failure of our foreign policy during the Abyssinian War and on many other occasions justifies them, moreover, in re-considering their attitude towards armaments. But the result of such re-consideration is not, in my opinion—far from it—that Great Britain is so actively engaged, or so likely to be in future, in supporting the forces of evil, that all possible steps should be taken to weaken it.

(3) The League has failed to uphold the collective system, and no one now puts much trust in it. But I do not agree that the British Government has abandoned the collective system in favour of something else in such a manner, so far as this country is concerned, as 'automatically to wipe out any distinction between self-defence and the use of war as an instrument of national policy'. The failure of the League, for which we must bear our responsibility, makes war more likely. I do not agree that it makes inevitable a great war in which we shall be engaged.

(4) I do not believe 'that it is everyone's duty to fight in any war in which the British Government alleges self-defence'. But

three points arise. Firstly, I make a distinction between conscientious objection as an individual act and incitement to a collective refusal to obey the law. Secondly, to justify incitement to a collective disobedience of the law, or to sedition, or to rebellion (to take three degrees of action), requires a much graver cause than the grounds which justify parliamentary and constitutional opposition. Thirdly, these acts also require for their justification a reasonable probability of success. Futile behaviour which plays into the hands of the Fascist forces is criminal. In present circumstances it would be crazy and disastrous for the Left to contemplate the use of unconstitutional and illegal weapons of opposition. I should not wish to occupy your space by these obvious and familiar explanations. But 'Socialist's' letter indicates throughout an atrophy of the power to distinguish one thing from another.

Let me return to the real issues. It is impracticable, and indeed unreasonable, to 'demand' a cut-and-dried foreign policy designed to meet future contingencies arising in unforeseeable circumstances as a condition of this country's having a navy; though of course this does not mean that we should not attack a foreign policy we dislike and use all our advocacy to secure specific changes in it. Is it 'Socialist's' idea that the Navy should be alternately scrapped and rebuilt every time that a General Election leads to a change of Government, the scrapping to take place at the behest of the party which has just lost the election? This is a Bedlamite thought. The only practicable course is to form a judgment of probability based on our view of the temper of the country, its motives and ideals, its public opinion in the broadest sense, and the sort of people likely to be in power from time to time in the near future. It is on such a judgement, and on such a judgement alone, that we can arrive at a reasonable conclusion whether we wish this country to be strong or to be weak. Of course, I agree with you that it would be dangerous to put arms at the disposal of Lord Rothermere. But why do you suppose that this is a likely thing to happen?

And if it were, what good would it do to exact pledges from Mr Baldwin?

This leads me to the alternative foreign policy which 'Socialist' puts forward. I make no complaint of his advocating it; I am not yet convinced by it, but I am ready to consider it or some variant of it; I complain only against the extreme conclusions to which he flies in the event of this particular policy being rejected. But let us see what it is. He wishes us to go far beyond the existing Covenant and to demand a new League, the members of which would be definitely committed to give armed assistance to one another in case of aggression. Hitherto an overwhelming majority of the electors of this country have been strongly opposed to our entering into such commitments, and those of us with pacifist leanings, including *The New Statesman and Nation*, have led this opposition. I admit that, in view of the failure of the League as it is at present, we have to reconsider the problem. If we commit ourselves to fight in all wars, will this have the effect of preventing any war? Perhaps. It is arguable. But it would be a terrible decision to take. Do you suppose that those who voted in the Peace Ballot would support it? I believe myself that the average man would passionately oppose it. He wants peace, and he cares about nothing else. But to obtain peace by undertaking to join in every war is a calculation which, even if it be correct, his mind boggles at. On the other hand, the argument that it is dangerous to-day that only the brigand powers should possess armaments carries conviction. And, surely, it should to those who are still capable of distinguishing one thing from another. At any rate, you must make some small progress in converting public opinion before you threaten the Government with unlawful opposition, unless it adopts a policy to which at present the country is likely to be deeply opposed.

Those to-day who cannot endure uncertainty alternate between joining Dick Sheppard's faith of non-resistance and asking us to take up arms of violence on all occasions to defend the world against Fascism. There is something to be said for both. Nevertheless, these are refuges, escapes from the torment of thinking. What relief, what emotional comfort to get amongst like-minded friends with no obligation to talk realities! But this is the cloister, not the world. And in the unresolved perplexities of the world it is the more courageous, and the more useful, course to remain.

J. M. KEYNES

'A Socialist' provided further elaboration of his argument the following week. Keynes replied.

To the Editor of The New Statesman and Nation, *29 August 1936*

Sir,

I am obliged to 'A Socialist' for his further explanations. He holds 'that the situation is already so grave as to require the most drastic action, even including a nation-wide refusal to work, or to fight, or to pay taxes in case of war', unless the Government forthwith adopts a foreign policy which would involve our giving military guarantees throughout Europe, a policy which not even the Opposition have recommended. This is the most practical advice he can give to resolve our problems. Surely it is impossible that there can really be such a person as 'A Socialist'! I disbelieve in his existence.

Nevertheless, this impotent and foolish talk does harm, for it brings the better side into disrepute. And I feel the same, Sir, when in the first Comment of the week you speak of 'the obvious sympathy of the British Government with the Fascist Powers'. You cannot really believe that Mr Baldwin and Mr Eden sympathise with Hitler and Mussolini. You probably mean that they are not opposing the Fascist Powers as firmly as you think they should. If I were on the other side, I should welcome as excellent inverted propaganda your efforts to make out that there is not much to choose between Mr Baldwin and Lord Rothermere, and that the general tendencies of this country are so clearly

54

pro-Fascist that it would be better to have no navy. It is because I accept so many of your criticisms that I deplore this perverse and defeatist view of public opinion.

For, whilst I support the Government's policy (as, I believe, you do) of attempting to secure a general ban on intervention in Spain, I agree with you in wishing that there had been some clearer declaration of where this country's sympathies stand, or ought to stand. I agree with you that our cowardly and misguided policy during the Abyssinian War has done almost irreparable harm. I agree with you that our interest and our safety and our duty alike require that we should consolidate friendly and confidential relations with France and Russia— though, as I have said before, I think that Mr Baldwin is wise to break down no bridges and to avoid clear-cut alignments. I agree with you that we should consult with all other powers how to restore collective security; though I take a more pessimistic view of this than you seem to, believing that brigandage has now gone so far that it is impossible for the time being to depend on rules of law or on promises relating to hypothetical cases. But I am dismayed when I find these views, which command a wide general support, muddled up with cries that the Labour Party should engineer 'drastic action' unless the Government makes military commitments which not even the Labour Party has yet supported; and this country's rearmament should be obstructed because it will probably be used to help Hitler; and that this Government has gone Fascist. Remember that the country loves peace more than it hates Fascism; and in this respect Mr Baldwin represents the great majority. No party will gain power here if it gets to be generally believed that peace comes second in its programme.

The fatal dilemma arises precisely because the Fascist Powers are readier to go to war for their objects than we are for ours. That is the fact not to be shirked, which makes a clear-cut policy impossible and provides those powers with unsurpassable opportunities to bluff. I see no possible reply except to build a navy enormously superior to those of the potential adversaries, without committing ourselves either to use or not to use it—not that I consider this reply satisfactory—and meanwhile to conduct our day-to-day foreign policy free from concealment of our sympathies and with more dignity and candour than of late, but still attempting, however vainly and with however small a hope, to unite Europe and not to divide it.

J. M. KEYNES

A week later, two economists, Abba Lerner and Paul Sweezy, wrote a letter suggesting that Keynes had misunderstood the situation and that

until Mr Keynes recognises that class interests take preference over the supposed interests of the country as a whole in determining the policy of capitalist Governments, he will continue to be surprised at the incredible stupidity that must be attributed to the British Foreign Office by all who boggle at the Marxian approach.

Keynes replied

To the Editor of The New Statesman and Nation, *12 September 1936*

Sir,

Mr Lerner and Mr Sweezy see everything in terms of Capitalism and Communism. This leads them to misinterpret the slant of British public opinion to-day. Capitalists and Communists in this country are, I suppose, about equally numerous, each 1 per cent, perhaps, of the population. The great majority of people are neither the one nor the other, and are just private individuals. But, in that capacity, they have one overwhelming preoccupation—the avoidance of war.

What 'Socialist' and Mr Lerner and Mr Sweezy and perhaps, Sir, you yourself tend to overlook, as an explanation of events, is the overwhelming success of pacifist propaganda in this country. Now that you are minded to criticise the Government for having recently avoided at least three suitable opportunities for risking war, you underestimate the effect on others of the pacifist movement of the past ten years. When the League of Nations was set up in 1919, the country was not pacifist in the sense that it is now. The pacifism of the average League supporter to-day has, unavoidably, weakened the League. Since, at the moment, the capitalist 'anti-reds' do not desire action, this unquestionably plays into their hands. As Sir Norman Angell has pointed out in his brilliant article in the *Political Quarterly*, from which you recently quoted, that is what none of us foresaw.[27] But to see that only is to miss the greater part of the picture. The dominating factor behind this country's policy is not the malice of the 'anti-reds', but the blind determination of the average man to keep out of war, including preventive wars, and out of threats of war, including those which may not, in fact, involve it, and out of hypothetical commitments for war, including those which may help to keep the peace. In this Mr Baldwin represents the country, and that (not Lord Rothermere) is the source of his authority.

You may approve this or disapprove it. There is—there always was—much to be said against a too unqualified pacifism. But those who fail to observe it and interpret everything in terms of Capitalist and Communist theory are blind to their surroundings.

J. M. KEYNES

The next letter concerned a leading article in the issue of 30 January 1937 concerning the trial of Karl Radek and others in Moscow.

To KINGSLEY MARTIN, *29 January 1937*

Dear Kingsley,

I thought your leader this week on 'Will Stalin Explain?' absolutely perfect. The argument convincing, the arrangement beyond criticism, and the style perfectly lucid, severe and to the purpose.

Yours ever,
J. M. K.

[27] N. Angell, 'The New John Bull', *Political Quarterly*, July–September 1936.

I am absolutely baffled for the correct explanation. In a way the speeches of the prisoners make me feel that they somehow *believe* their confessions to be true.

Again, there was a gap in the correspondence until Keynes was recovering from his illness in the summer of 1937. The article that started it off, 'The Need for Action', appeared on 26 June 1937.

To KINGSLEY MARTIN, *1 July 1937*

I interpreted the note 'Need for Action' on p. 1026 to mean that you were (and perhaps always had been—'the position that ought never to have been abandoned') in favour of terminating non-intervention.

Lying in bed, I think a good deal about foreign policy, and sometime this month I'd like to write you an article about it, if you'll have it.

J. M. K.

To-day (though not formerly) crisis has a technical meaning. (The crises were happier and safer, I think, in the days when they were less talked about!)

From KINGSLEY MARTIN, *2 July 1937*

Dear Maynard,

I am delighted to hear that you feel inclined to write an article about foreign affairs. Naturally I should be delighted to have it as soon as possible. I am now desperately troubled about it. I can see no way out at all. Judging by Mussolini's speech yesterday—and now by the Italian note to-day—the Government may have waited too long to take a 'firm attitude'. It has been the same story all the way through—connivance and half-heartedness at a time when firmness would have worked until it is too late for the Dictators to withdraw without hopelessly losing face. The desperate part of the situation is that if this particular crisis passes, there still seems nothing to do, nothing to work for. What constructive policy could be put up to the man who said the things that Mussolini said yesterday? A few days ago he openly boasted that Italian troops had captured Bilbao and that there would be no neutrality about the Italian attitude. Yesterday he pretended there had been no recent Italian intervention. All the diplomacy is just meaningless; we are simply preparing for a war which, I gather, the services now rather expect to be against Italy and fear may be against Italy and Germany at the same time, and with people like Hitler and Mussolini about one sees no place on the slope to dig in and stop.

This week's paper is in my view the dullest and worst we have published for a very long time. I don't think the leader at all satisfactory and most of the articles are dull. This is the result of a number of accidents which I need not go into. If you have any light to throw on foreign affairs I should be delighted, not only journalistically but personally. Of course my trouble is that I could easily write good and interesting articles about them, but I am prevented even from doing that by what appears to be the necessity of having a policy. We have always said, all of us, that if the League idea was smashed up and we went back to anarchy, the situation would be hopeless. We have gone back to anarchy and I think it is hopeless. I could write books about this and head the chapters 'I told you so', but who would read them and what would be the use anyway.

Sorry to sound so gloomy. I don't at the moment see any way out. It is really good news that you are better.

Yours,

K. M.

To KINGSLEY MARTIN, *4 July 1937*

My dear Kingsley,

I agree with you that you ought to be sacked for allowing Brailsford's leader.[28] If you wonder why the left makes so little impression on public opinion, you have here the explanation—producing on the ordinary man an impression of drivelling irresponsibility.

'Critic'[29] left me perplexed as to whether or not he thought Stalin was right to do in Tukhachevsky. Page 2 left me thinking one way, and page 3 the other.

I'll try my hand at an article this week.

Yours,

J. M. K.

[28] 'The Last Chance in Spain', *New Statesman and Nation*, 3 July 1937.
[29] 'A London Diary', *loc. cit.*

To KINGSLEY MARTIN, *5 July 1937*

Dear Kingsley,

Here is the article—rather brash I'm afraid, but I've been trying to be obvious, if that is possible in such an affair.

I very much dislike having anything printed which I have not seen in proof. But if you would instruct the printer to send me a proof by express, it will reach me in time for me to telegraph any corrections.

Yours ever,

J.M.K.

From KINGSLEY MARTIN, *6 July 1937*

Dear Maynard,

I understood the mood of your article so well. I have fought it a score of times; I had after all once written the thesis of *The Triumph of Lord Palmerston*! I have spent unhappy hours trying to work out what policy I should regard as the least bad in Spain and I don't think pretending that we have no interests there or that no 'ideological' differences there matter has been a good idea. It's always been untrue: this country is not a London and will fight for imperial interests. If there was a chance of giving up the Empire I'd have it as an alternative to war, but it's not a chance.

Your article is beautifully done and as an expression of a difference of opinion very inoffensive. But there is no other possible 'Leader' subject and I think I must 'reply' in some way to the article. I've just dictated in about half an hour—the draft of a leader which will give you a notion of what I think must be said. Enclosed also your proof. If corrections are only slight, not altering length, it will be all right to get them on Thursday morning. If you want to alter anything considerable or speak to me I'll be at the office all day tomorrow (Wednesday).

I hope you are better.

KINGSLEY

Will make a very good paper. Many thanks for sending article. I did not like Brailsford leader, as I said but cannot understand why you call it irresponsible drivel! Poor perhaps but why irresponsible?

Kingsley Martin's leader 'A Policy of Delay' appeared with Keynes's article.

From The New Statesman and Nation, *10 July 1937*

BRITISH FOREIGN POLICY

W. H. Auden's poem, Spain, is fit to stand beside great predecessors in its moving, yet serene expression of contemporary
feeling towards the heart-rending events of the political world.
The theme of the poem lies in the comparison between the
secular achievements of the past and the hope which is possible
for the future with the horrors of the present and the sacrifices
which perhaps it demands from those of this generation who
think and feel rightly. Yesterday, all the past. To-morrow,
perhaps the future. 'But to-day the struggle,' his refrain runs.
Auden conceives of 'the struggle' in terms of immediate war
and force, of death and killing:

> To-day the deliberate increase in the chances of death,
> The conscious acceptance of guilt in the necessary murder.

In this he is speaking for many chivalrous hearts. Yet, whilst
he teaches us, as a poet should, how we should feel, the object
of this article is to question whether he rightly directs how, at
this moment at least, we should act.

I view with revulsion the growing tendency to make of the
struggle between the two ideologies (or would it be conceded
that there are three?) another War of Religion, to believe that
the issue can or will be settled by force of arms, and to feel that
it is our duty to hasten to any quarter of the world where those
of our faith are oppressed. It is only too easy for men to feel
like this. The Crusades and the Thirty Years' War actually
occurred. But does it seem, looking back, that it was a duty to
join in them, or that they settled anything? Assume that the war
occurs, and let us suppose, for the sake of argument, that we
win. What then? Shall we ourselves be the better for it and for
what it will have brought with it? What are we going to do with
the defeated? Are we to impose our favourite ideology on them
(whatever, by then, it may be) in an up-to-date peace treaty,

or do we assume that they will adopt it with spontaneous enthusiasm? At best we should be back, it seems to me, exactly where we were. Defeat is complete disaster. Victory, as usual, would be useless, and probably pernicious. It is an illusion to believe that conscious acceptance of guilt in the necessary murder can settle what is mainly a moral issue.

Therefore, and furthermore, I maintain that the claims of peace are paramount; though this seems to be an out-of-date view in what used to be pacifist circles. It is our duty to prolong peace, hour by hour, day by day, for as long as we can. We do not know what the future will bring, except that it will be quite different from anything we could predict. I have said in another context that it is a disadvantage of 'the long run' that in the long run we are all dead. But I could have said equally well that it is a great advantage of 'the short run' that in the short run we are still alive. Life and history are made up of short runs. If we are at peace in the short run, that is something. The best we can do is put off disaster, if only in the hope, which is not necessarily a remote one, that something will turn up. While there is peace, there is peace. It is silly and presumptuous to say that war is inevitable; for no one can possibly know. The only conclusion which is certain is that we cannot avoid war by bringing it on. If, thinking of Spain, someone urges that self-interest does not entitle us to abandon others, I answer that for Spain peace—and to-day, I think, I would add peace on any terms—is her greatest interest. Spain will work out her future in due course. It is not the outcome of the civil war which will settle it. It would be much more plausible to argue that British imperial interests or French security require the defeat of Franco than that the interests of Spaniards require it. Those who believe in the efficacy of war are misunderstanding the kind of power we have to influence the future.

But I do not, therefore, claim that war can always be avoided. I do not need to answer the question whether war is even defensible. The question does not arise, inasmuch as our knowledge of human nature tells us that in practice there are circumstances when war on our part, whether defensible or not, is unavoidable. We are brought, therefore, to the second aspect of foreign policy. The first duty of foreign policy is to avoid war. Its second duty is to ensure that, if it occurs, the circumstances shall be the most favourable possible for our cause. Let us consider the immediate position from this point of view.

By postponement we gain peace to-day. Have we anything to lose by it? Our capacity for cunctation is one of our most powerful and characteristic national weapons. It has been our age-long instrument against dictators. Since Fabius Maximus there has scarcely been a stronger case for cunctation than there is to-day. It is maddening and humiliating to have to take so much lip. We may, conceivably, have to submit to greater humiliations and worse betrayals than any yet. Those who applaud war and believe they have something to gain from it have an inevitable advantage, which cannot possibly be taken from them, in a game of bluff and in the preliminary manoeuvres; though all the time they may be running unperceived risks, which one day will catch them out. But we have to look farther ahead; believing that time and chance are with us, and taking precautions that, if we are forced to act, we can make quite sure. This seems cold and shifty to the poet. Yet I claim the benefit of the first part of one of Auden's stanzas:

> What's your proposal? To build the just city? I will.
> I agree.

leaving to him the second part:

> Or is it the suicide pact, the romantic
> Death? Very well, I accept.

For consider the immediate political factors staring us in the face. At the moment Russia is disorganised and France at a disadvantage. Each is at a low ebb but each needs mainly time. Before long we ourselves will possess the most predominant

63

sea-power in European waters that we have every enjoyed in our history. Meanwhile what is happening to the brigand powers? One of them is busily engaged in outraging every creed in turn. If they could find another institution or another community to insult or injure, they would do so. Both of them are spending a lot of money on an intensive propaganda to persuade the rest of the world that they are the enemies of the human race. It is having the desired result, not least in the United States. No one trusts or respects their word. They have not a single friend or sympathiser in the whole world, for I doubt if even Japan thrills greatly to their croonings. Yet even so, all this needs time to sink in, here at home as well as elsewhere. The full abomination is understood to-day in a degree and over an area much greater than a year ago. These tactics are not characteristic of great statesmen and conquerors. They appear to be morbid, patho-logical, diseased. I gravely doubt their technical efficiency and expect that every sort of idiocy is going on behind the scenes. It is unlikely that those who talk so much nonsense will act quite differently; or that they, who persecute the mind and all its works, will be employing it to the best advantage. It is very probable that, given time, they will over-play their hands, overreach themselves and make a major blunder. It is in the nature of their type of behaviour that this should happen. And if, indeed, the thieves were to have a little more success, nothing is likelier than that they would fall out amongst themselves.

Near the beginning of the Abyssinian affair our Foreign Office was guilty of the gravest and most disastrous error of policy in recent history. It is natural, therefore, to distrust them. But though it has been hateful in its immediate consequences and cruel in some of its details, I am not inclined to criticise the broad outline of Mr Eden's Spanish policy. I should have been afraid if his critics had had a chance to take over from him. The task of a cunctator is always a thankless one. To be for ever allowing the brigands yet a little more rope, to be holding up the cup for them to fill yet fuller is not a distinguished office. It is never possible, unfortunately, to estimate a statesman by his results, since we never have for comparison the consequences of the alternative course. But I do not judge his policy to have been inconsistent as yet with the two prime objects stated above.

I bid Auden, therefore, to pass by on the other side. If he will be patient and unheroic, in due course, perhaps, he will be shown (in his own words):

> History the operator, the
> Organiser, Time the refreshing river.

Keynes's article brought him a challenge from Gladwyn Jebb, then Private Secretary to the Permanent Under-Secretary of State at the Foreign Office.

From GLADWYN JEBB, *9 July 1937*

Dear Keynes,

I have just read your letter to *The New Statesman*. Nobody could more fully agree with what you say than myself. It is, in fact, a point of view which I have for long attempted—quite inadequately—to represent.

For this very reason I should be extremely interested if you could indicate to me—if only in briefest outline—what exactly you refer to when speaking of 'the gravest and most disastrous error in recent history' for which 'our Foreign Office' was responsible 'near the beginning of the Abyssinian affair'?

I hear you have not been too well, and trust that the publication of your letter means that you have completely recovered.

I have just come back from Geneva and Berlin where I assisted Leith-Ross at the Raw Materials Enquiry at the meeting of the International Chamber of Commerce.

Please remember me to Lydia, if she is with you.

> Yours very sincerely,
> GLADWYN JEBB

To GLADWYN JEBB, *12 July 1937*

To dear Jebb,

Rightly or wrongly, I personally am convinced that near the beginning of the Abyssinian affair we could, by firm action, have simply put a stop to the whole thing, and could have done so without material risk. It would have involved framing effective measures and then inviting the League of Nations to ask us to adopt them.

By this means we should have saved the League of Nations, and the whole situation would be completely different. But, as I think, the situation was grievously misjudged.

Yours sincerely,
[copy initialled] J.M.K.

Meanwhile, correspondence with Kingsley Martin continued.

From KINGSLEY MARTIN, *8 July 1937*

Dear Maynard,

I am enclosing a copy of a letter which I have sent to Whitley. On consideration it seemed to me right to report the difficulty, though I don't see any way out of it. I don't see how a paper can have any real independence if it has any advertisements at all!

I am arranging for two copies of the paper to be sent to you direct tonight. I hope that will do instead of the 'pull' for which you ask. That would be difficult to get, as the paper is now being printed, and is not even yet in its final form with your corrections.

Yours,
KINGSLEY

From KINGSLEY MARTIN, *to* EDWARD WHITLEY, *8 July 1937*

Dear Whitley,

As you know, we have for years past published an annual Insurance Supplement. This has been primarily an advertisement supplement, accepting things as they are, but giving *bona fide* information of a useful kind about insurance.

I have not myself been satisfied with publishing so uncritical a supplement on insurance, especially seeing that it was in *The New Statesman* that the Webbs' famous supplement on Industrial Insurance appeared in 1915. People (including, most violently, Sir Arnold Wilson) have suggested that we were not doing our duty in not including the whole question of insurance reform. This year I thought that in addition to a very profitable commercial supplement we could afford a supplement, which would not get much advertising support, on the present position of social insurance. It is particularly topical. Lloyd took it in hand, and the enclosed articles are the result. There are still two to come, one from Miss Rathbone on family endowment, and one from Robson on certain general aspects of the whole problem.

I an writing to you and sending you these proofs, because in view of what Roberts says about the possible effect on the advertiser, it seems right for me to inform the Board. Apparently some of these companies are very touchy and may withdraw their advertisements, purely on political grounds. It is obvious that they have no business cause for doing so, seeing that our ordinary insurance supplement stresses the value of insurance in the present circumstances, and that the commercial value of their advertisements is quite unaffected by editorial criticisms that may appear in the paper. I see no way to meet this danger by any small changes in the articles, even if that were desirable. It also seems to me impossible to change the policy of the paper or not to go ahead with something that may have a real political importance, as well as a good deal of prestige value, because of the susceptibilities of advertisers. If we did that it would mean that the *N.S.* was just like all the rest of the press. I do not see, therefore, what can be done about it, but as there are possibly, if Roberts is right, some hundreds of pounds a year involved, it seemed right to me to mention the matter to you.

The supplement is timed to appear in our issue of July 24th. I may add that neither Willison nor Roberts, who are naturally upset at the possibility of losing the result of so much hard work in the past, opposes the publication of the supplement. They both agree that it is entirely in accordance with the past traditions of the paper and the sort of thing that an independent paper ought to do. But Roberts wishes me to let you know, because he thinks the loss may possibly be really serious.

Yours sincerely,
KINGSLEY MARTIN

P.S. I am also sending a copy of this letter to Keynes.

To KINGSLEY MARTIN, *11 July 1937*

Dear Kingsley,

I enclose in duplicate a letter on the Industrial Insurance articles, in case you may want to send one on to Whitley.

67

As regards Spain I feel glad to have got a pacifist article into the paper—it must be the first one for many months. And now we have each had our say, I have no more to add, unless something arises in subsequent correspondence.*

I still feel much happier with Eden as Foreign Secretary than I should with Brailsford, and so, I expect, do you.

Yours ever,

J. M. KEYNES

To KINGSLEY MARTIN, *11 July 1937*

Dear Kingsley,

Social Insurance Supplement

These articles seem to me quite mild, and I cannot but think that Roberts is over anxious as to the financial consequences. Only two of the articles presumably could be considered peccant, namely, those on Workman's Compensation and Funeral Insurance.

The one of Workman's Compensation is mainly concerned with proposals for clearing up the uncertainties of the existing legislation. The insurance offices would, of course, be entirely in favour of this, since a good deal of the expenses involved arise out of the necessity for litigation. The only reference to nationalisation comes in quite inconsequently at the end, spoken merely as a dogma in the voice of an automaton. Speaking as a director of a company which does quite a lot of this business, I should say that a board would have to be unusually susceptible to be upset by this. It is well recognised by those who are in the business that nationalisation is quite a possibility. And I think the average board would be rather relieved at being let off with the voice of an automaton in place of a reasoned and constructive argument in favour of the change.

As regards the other article on funeral insurance, it has to be

* I have some further thoughts in my mind which I might produce later.

remembered that the great majority of the offices who advertise with us do not do this business at all. I should say that there are only two likely to spend any appreciable money who would be concerned, namely, the Pearl and the Prudential (though I forget for the moment whether perhaps the Britannia and the Refuge have an industrial branch). The Pearl took half a page in our Insurance Supplement, and I think we used to do a little business with the Prudential, but I have not seen much lately. I should be surprised if the total advertising expenditure by industrial offices came to as much as £100 a year.

Moreover, I should doubt whether those concerned would be unduly flustered. This is a well-known, old established controversy in which it is well recognised that everyone is entitled to his opinion. Here again I should say that those concerned would be relieved at being let off with a gas-bag article on the ancient model in place of an up-to-date constructive scheme of what a Labour Party in office could really do. Moreover, in this case, the character of the actual article, wants, I suggest, some consideration. I fancy that the Prudential could produce a devastating reply, if they thought it worth while to do so. It is important to remember and acknowledge that this business has been completely reformed in recent years, and that the Prudential in its handling of it is one of the best conducted enterprises in the country; though it still remains true, I believe, that all the others could be ruined by legislation enforcing on them the same standard as those already observed by the Prudential. The abuses which used to hold have largely been got rid of, and the main question which remains is that of the undue expense of collection. J. L. Cohen, as I could explain better in conversation, is a very unsatisfactory person, and this article should unquestionably be vetted by an expert. I feel a strong suspicion that some of his figures must be wrong, and I fancy that there is a good deal of it which is not up to date. Possibly you might get Swift to look through it with a view to calling attention to any howlers. I have marked one or two passages which look to me suspect. I feel it would be much better to have had either a careful review of Arnold Wilson's book,[30] or a concrete programme as to how Arnold Wilson's programme might be carried out in practice. Cohen makes, of course, a complete mistake in regarding industrial insurance as identical with funeral insurance. The fact of a surrender value is a highly important and often useful adjunct in the mind of the insured.

To sum up, I find the articles, all of them, in fact boring and perfunctory and likely, for that reason, to do injury rather than otherwise to the causes they advocate. But I should have thought that the financial loss which we should incur would be mainly limited to the cost of production of the articles themselves.

The above does not mean that I should not greatly welcome a supplement on social insurance up to the standard of, say, the P[olitical]E[conomic]P[lanning] reports. It is an important subject, and there might be an excellent programme to be evolved in consolidating the various branches of it which have grown up haphazard. I am also entirely with you in holding that we should not be inhibited by advertising considerations; though I think that a genuine enquiry into the subject would prove much more alarming to the advertisers than this one is likely to be.

Yours ever,
[copy not signed or initialled]

From KINGSLEY MARTIN, *12 July 1937*

Dear Maynard,

   Thanks for a useful letter about the Insurance Supplement. I will go into the question of Cohen's figures, etc. before publication. (I have sent article to Swift). It is important to get things right, but I shall be surprised if in this matter Cohen is wrong. Arnold Wilson's book, which Cohen reviewed for us a few weeks ago, was, I think, right up-to-date and Cohen must be familiar in any case with the material. Your comparison with the P.E.P. report raises an interesting question. Is it possible to relate really serious

---

[30] Sir Arnold Wilson and H. Levy, *Industrial Assurance: An Historical and Critical Study* (London, 1937).

research to a weekly paper, as the *Weekend* thought of doing when P.E.P. was started, and as Webb could do with the *N.S.*? Webb, of course, was a complete research organisation all by himself. I think your criticisms of the articles exaggerated; you forget that most people have not your intimacy with the subject. Robson, who also knows it very well, tells me that he thinks the articles pretty good. It is possible that his general, and I gather, constructive article will do something to meet your criticism.

Extravagantly pacifist as I am myself, I find your remarks rather hard to bear! I think if the Government had adopted a tougher line earlier, peace would stand a much better chance than it does. I agree that it is very risky to say boo! to Italy and Germany now, but I think the chance of peace better than it will be if nothing definite at all is said until Germany and Italy are even further dug in. I am delighted to hear that you have another article in prospect. I need not tell you how good it is for the paper.

Hope you are enjoying convalesence!

Yours,

K. M.

P.S. The *only* point between us on foreign policy at the moment is this: If Britain is going to be tough about the contest of Spain or defence of French and British Mediterranean interests, is there any point in pretending that we are not or in putting off making it clear that we are? My enquiries about the F.O. now suggest that they have not the slightest notion where they are going and are completely flummoxed and frightened about what is to happen if non-intervention goes. I don't wonder: it's the result of having no principle at all and sabotaging the only embryonic international system there was. All my *personal* inclination is to join Aldous Huxley and Russell etc. in the pacifist movement! I would personally be happy thus—but it has nothing to say politically. Could the *N.S. &N.* take this view now on the ground that [the] collective system altogether fails so why engage to fight at all? What do you think?

To KINGSLEY MARTIN, *25 July 1937*

My dear Kingsley,

I wonder how the Social Insurance Supplement is getting on. I did not reply to your letter of July 12th because in the meantime I had been without a secretary. But my view about special supplements is really the same as what you suggest. I do not think it is practicable to relate really serious research to a weekly paper, and, in so far as such things can be done by private team work, the P.E.P. method is the right one. Moreover, if a really valuable piece of work is accomplished, it will be of more importance as a work of reference than in one particular week, and it may be rather wasted and inaccessible in the shape of a supplement.

But I draw the conclusion from this that such supplements are really a mistake, and I am dead against them. Apart from the fact that they are generally not very good, they are a frightful bore to the reader, who regards the title of Supplement as a fair warning on the editor's part that he has now reached pages which need not, and should not, and are not really intended to be read. I know in my own case the mere fact that a thing appears in the supplement diminishes at least by a half the chance of my reading it.

I am not sure whether you read *The Telegraph*. In case you do not, I enclose two interesting cuttings of this week.[31] Pertinax is distinctly interesting. But the really flabbergasting thing is the list of leading fallen chiefs. I am at a loss to find any explanation which explains everything except that Stalin is engaged in a systematic destruction of the old Communist Party. It appears that he is succeeding, but how he is managing it remains obscure. Lydia's Russian paper calculates that out of the 2,800,000 members of the Communist Party, something like 25 per cent have been executed, arrested, exiled or dismissed from their offices in the last few months.

For the moment the purge purports to be anti-German. But I confess that it seems to me all very alarming in the long run. Stalin's position will soon be indistinguishable from that of the other dictators, and it would seem to be entirely in character that his foreign policy will be opportunist, and an eventual agreement between him and Germany by no means out of the question, if it should happen to suit him.

In my article the other day, I spoke of the two ideologies,

---

[31] These have not survived.

adding in brackets 'or would it be admitted that there are three', but in truth there are only two: the totalitarian states which are increasingly indistinguishable, and the liberal states. The latter put peace and personal liberty first, the others put them nowhere.

Yours ever,
[copy not signed or initialled]

The next day Keynes drafted a further letter and article for Kingsley Martin. They were never sent, but remain of interest.

To KINGSLEY MARTIN, *26 July 1937*

Dear Kingsley,

Late last night I became suddenly and irresistibly moved to write my second article on foreign policy. It is enclosed, and I should like to see a proof in the same way as last time.

I do not know what feelings it will arouse in you. I must wait and see. But Julian's[32] death last week led me to spend even more time than usual thinking about these things, and trying to disentangle one thing from another.

Yours ever,
J. M. KEYNES

FURTHER THOUGHTS ON BRITISH FOREIGN POLICY

I should like to add to what I wrote in these columns three weeks ago the result of some further meditations, aimed at thinking not coolly, but if possible more clearly, about these matters.

I

'The Prime Minister is more concerned in preventing this country from being involved in a risk of war than in preventing outside assistance to Franco. The Labour Party and the Editor

---

[32] Julian Bell had died on 18 July whilst driving an ambulance in Spain.

of this paper [*The New Statesman and Nation*] are more concerned in preventing outside assistance to Franco.' Would that be accepted as a fair summary? Probably not. For critics of the Government may argue that their policy would diminish the risk of war in the future without running any risk of it at the present time. We cannot tell, however, whether this claim is justified, until they disclose to us in plain language what their alternative policy is. What exactly is the 'much stronger policy' for which they press? For example, would they wish the British Navy to establish an effective blockade of ports in Franco's hands with instructions to sink, if necessary, any vessel which is carrying foreign men or munitions to him? If, on the other hand, they are entirely opposed to anything which even approaches action of this kind, it would clear the air if they were to say so. For with all active threats and ultimatums ruled out, their difference with the Government becomes a comparatively minor one and is a matter of expediency, detail and emphasis. Essentially their policy would be the same, namely to make non-intervention as genuine an affair (which may not be much) as a diplomacy, which is deprived of any threat of force, is able to make it.

This would not exclude a wide field for fruitful criticism of the Government. There is a third policy which has supporters in this country, namely to come to friendly terms with Hitler and Mussolini at the expense of the Spanish democracy. We cannot be certain that the Cabinet is entirely free from such influences. A Government which includes a person whose spiritual home has such an uncertain address as Mr Duff Cooper's requires watching. It may be that Mr Eden sometimes needs more support than criticism. A barrage, such as Mr Noel Baker has kept up on the question of belligerent rights, is obviously useful and important. But there is a clear line of division between keeping the Government up to the mark in the policy of non-intervention and the making of threats the carrying out of which might involve intervention by ourselves.

Our policy, I suggest, should be polite, punctilious, equable but, within its limits, stern and unbending; free both from retorts, reproaches, and minor irritations and from threats and menaces, yet at the same time vaguely disturbing, unsettling and over-hanging; and always offering quietly a complete and generous change of front in response to a change of front on the other side. If this is the policy of the Labour Party, well and good. But I plead for clearness of thought and expression, even if it means admitting that the Government is sometimes right.

II

I turn to another aspect, which involves the relation between our Spanish policy and our re-armament policy but also a wider field. The view is held by some members of the left-wing of the Labour Party and often receives expression in this paper that war may be legitimate and necessary in certain circumstances where no direct British interest is involved—the defence of Czecho-Slovakia would be a good example of this—but would not be legitimate where a British interest, such as unimpeded access by our Navy to the Mediterranean, is at least a part-motive. They would even be reluctant, it seems, to invoke self-interest in aid of a good cause. For 'Critic' writes:– 'It is just because the Conservatives in England and France are beginning to discover that they cannot stomach Italy and Germany in Spain, that it is of vital importance for the Labour Party to be particularly vigilant.' Now it is exceedingly unlikely that this country will go to war without some British interest being in some way involved. It is, therefore, almost certain that, if there is a war, this school of thought will be opposed to it. Thus, whilst they are more or less chronically in favour of risking a war, they are not in favour of any war which is likely to occur. In this way, it is found, they can safely reconcile bellicosity of word with opposing re-armament. Regarded as a personal standpoint, this position can, indeed, have some logic behind it. But as practical politics for national consumption, it appears to the general public as a very foolish sophistication. For it implies simultaneously that its proponents could, yet could not, be in a responsible position. Some of the public can understand opposition to war at all costs; some of them can understand a war to protect vital British interests; and many of them can support re-armament as tending to maintain peace and as an insurance against what may prove an ultimately unavoidable contingency. But when a policy of bellicosity provided no British interest is involved, is combined with a policy of disarmament, on the ground that there will not be a war unless some British interest is involved, the public decide that these people are not to be taken seriously.

You will say that this is an unfair caricature. Whether or not it is so, it is a fair analysis of the impression which is produced on public opinion. It is many years since the Labour Party stood so low in the country as it does to-day. I believe that the explanation is to be found in the impression of an extreme want of wisdom and of common sense which its attitude towards the problems of peace and war has made.

In attempting to do justice to the understandable, and often defensible, impulse of certain individuals to personal protest, the Labour Party has lost its representative character. I say this in spite of holding that in its essential sympathies and objects it is the Labour Party which is most in the right.

III

'Critic' wrote sympathetically last week of this country's running risks of war for Spanish democracy. Does there not underlie this a deep and disastrous confusion between the rights of personal protest and the criteria of national policy?

Many Englishmen are prone to feelings of profound indignation aroused by happenings here and there in the world. It is an old-standing national propensity, of which we often have reason to be proud. Such feelings give rise to a desire for some form of active personal protest, which may range anywhere from writing a letter to *The Times*, getting up a fund, organising a meeting in the Albert Hall to laying down one's life as a true and devoted martyr. To such fanatics of the individual judgment as many of us are born to be, this right of personal protest is an essential and unsurrenderable privilege. No-one should, and as a rule no-one can, interfere with an individual's right to use it up to the limit. Julian Bell was entitled to make his protest with his life. His action was in no way inconsistent with the fact that in other circumstances he would probably have been a conscientious objector. On the contrary, it was deeply consistent, answering in both events to the indefeasible claims of private judgment and duty.

But the position of those who are not acting in an individual capacity, but are advising or representing the nation is entirely different. They have no similar rights of representative protest merely on the ground of their own individual feelings, but only if they are convinced that these feelings are also representative of the great majority.

Now nothing is more certain than that 'Critic's' readiness to run a risk of war for the sake of Spanish democracy is not shared by his countrymen at large. If a referendum were to be taken, his policy would not secure a majority in a single constituency in the country—not even, I should think, in a single hamlet, scarcely in a single house. War resembles matters of faith and belief and differs from most other objects of public policy in that one may reasonably doubt whether even a large majority has a right to enforce it on the minority. But assuredly it is not a matter where the minority has a right to manoeuvre the majority into carrying out its will. Above all, ex-conscientious objectors are not entitled to lead young Englishmen to death for a cause to defend which the average Englishman is in no wise led by his own impulses to honour.

This criticism is based on the assumption that some risk of

war is in question. If there is not, then it falls to the ground and is unreservedly withdrawn. But I ask that we should know where we stand, and that vague rhodomontade should not be used, irresponsibly, as a means of emotional outlet.

J. M. KEYNES

The next, unfortunately incomplete letter enclosed the following extract from *The Manchester Guardian* for 23 July.

Westminster, Thursday

The interest to-day moved from the House of Commons to the House of Peers, when the Lords Spiritual and Temporal met 130 strong to consider the second reading of Mr A. P. Herbert's Marriage Bill. Fifteen members of the Episcopate sat in their picturesque lawn and gay dresses and picture hats.

To KINGSLEY MARTIN, *27 July 1937*

My dear Kingsley,

Why not have a competition on this model? Frightfully silly, but you might get some beauties.

Are you quite sure—thinking twice—that you want Non-intervention to come to an end? Is it your idea that the Span. Gov^t. will be able to buy and import successfully more men and munitions than Hitler and Musso will send Franco free of charge? Or is it your idea that the British and French Navies are incapable (or would you say unwilling) to keep out a single man or a single gun? I should like to hear the argument more fully developed—if it would stand this treatment.

This week's paper prints (for the first time, I think, all these in one issue) bugger, copulation and cissy. Have you discovered what is the optimum percentage of such words from the point of view of circulation? It would be interesting to know—I simply [the next page does not survive].

Dear Maynard,

(1) Enclosed a cheque for seven guineas, but on second thoughts I am not sure whether this is enough. I am sending it any way so that we can both consider the point of principle involved. Obviously the paper can now afford to pay you more and obviously articles of yours are worth more to the paper. What would you think a reasonable figure? Ten Guineas? We ought, I think, to come to some arrangement for the future.

(2) I was disappointed not to get the second article you promised. Did you decide to send it to *The Evening Standard* instead or have you still an article on the stocks for me? There is not in fact any danger of war in the Mediterranean now. Something will be patched up which will let the Spanish people down.

(3) I held up the Insurance Supplement because I wanted to get 100 per cent confidence in the articles before publication. I don't mean that they will please you any way. That would be impossible on such a subject. But I must be sure about Cohen's figures. Swift went into them to some extent for me and reported adversely, but when I cross-questioned him about his reasons, I found him very indefinite. He began by saying that Arnold Wilson was not worth taking seriously and though he had not seen it he assumed that figures in Cohen's article that he did not understand came from Wilson. So I am out for a quite independent examination before the Supplement appears.

Hope you are better and in a really nice place. I have been well but I am afflicted with boils. My sympathy with Job at the moment is very great as my latest boil has sprouted on the side of my right eye and closed it up. Therefore I am in a very bad temper.

Yours,
KINGSLEY

Have just read a brilliant account of Guernica by Steer, the *Times* correspondent who was there, in August issue of *London Mercury*. It is really good.

I knew Steer, a South African, did an article for me about the Ruhr question after I met him reporting in the Saar. Then he went to Abysinnia, married a French journalist in Addis Abbaba, got out safely, but she died of disease almost at once and I hear he went to Spain. Interesting person.

To KINGSLEY MARTIN, *9 August 1937*

My dear Kingsley,

Since I have now given up writing for a living, as I used to formerly, I am content with whatever fee you volunteer. Keep your extra guineas for those who are writing for their living.

I withheld my second article because Lydia, whose opinion I always obey on these matters, did not think it up to standard.

I shall be interested to hear the outcome of your further enquiry about Cohen's article. My dissatisfaction with it, however, is largely based in that I think both he and Wilson are on quite the wrong lines as regards a remedy. The abuse is that industrial insurance is a frightfully extravagant way of saving for the working classes, too many of their hard-earned pennies being wasted. But to suppose that it can be replaced by compulsory funeral insurance for insured persons is, I believe, a complete misunderstanding. The existing policies only serve their purpose in a minority of cases. I doubt indeed if there is any remedy except for the Government to reduce the permitted percentage of expenses down to a figure which probably knocks out this particular business and then offer similar policies themselves through the Post Office. It would have been worth the Provincial's while to pay Wilson and Cohen quite a substantial sum for writing so ineffectively!

My progress is slow but steady, and I now am able to drive out in the car in the afternoon. Much sympathy with your affliction—and your bad temper. It makes you, I notice, just as cross now that you think there is not going to be a war as it did before when you thought there was going to be one. There is no pleasing a really bellicose pacifist! They have got you both ways. And, as for Spain, I am not a bit sure that not making her territory the seat of a general European war is 'letting her down'.

Seriously, it all depends, of course, upon whether the Fascist powers are intending to use the present negotiations as a way of getting out without too much loss of face, or whether the plot is really something quite different, not yet disclosed. Being an optimist, I am still hopeful that it may end in the division of Spain geographically into two states. But, above all, I want the war to come to an end and not to extend.

I enclose another of my *Daily Telegraph* cuttings about Russia. I notice that you have had nothing on the subject for some weeks. Is there any reliable source of information as to what is really happening?

Yours ever,

J. M. KEYNES

Keynes's enclosure ran as follows:

The greatest of historians has told us how where rival ideologies like Communism and Fascism, as it is the present fashion to call them, or the spirit of faction, as he called it, cut across national loyalties they distort the ordinary meaning of words. 'Reckless indifference to the consequences is extolled as the courage of loyalty to those who are of our own political faith; patience that knows when to temporise is decried as cowardice and moderation as a cloak for unmanliness; and ability to see all sides of a question is to be a nervous wreck.'

Did not Thucydides here describe, more than two thousand years ago, the sort of criticism of the Government's policy that was rife on Tuesday* last and was so signally refuted on Wednesday? And is not most of the misery in Spain to-day due to exactly the same causes as the misery then in Corcyra and in so many other Greek States where the democratic faction called in the Athenians and the oligarchic the Spartans to help them in their civil strife? So long as human nature remains the same, says the old historian prophetically, these same causes will produce the same terrible results.

Don't you think this is rather a good historical analogy?

Keynes's next letter to the editor did not appear.

* I don't agree about that.

To the Editor of The New Statesman and Nation, *14 August 1937*

Sir,

In your leading article on *Foreign Office Policy*[33] you attribute a variety of motives. But you do not mention the most plausible explanation of our tortuous diplomacy, namely a dominating desire (rightly or wrongly) to keep this country, if possible and for as long as possible, out of trouble.

Yours etc.

J. M. KEYNES

On 28 September, a *Times* leading article on Japanese aggression in China moved Keynes to comment.

To the Editor of The Times, *28 September 1937*

Sir,

You remind Japan in today's leading article that she is earning the condemnation of the world 'on whom she vitally and inescapably depends'—nevertheless, public opinion greatly underestimates the efficacy of a threat of economic sanctions strictly applied in appropriate circumstances. There is a time for helpless acquiescence and a time for action. But to-day is it not the duty of the United States and of the British Empire and the other 23 nations to warn Japan that they will sever all trade relations with her unless she mends her ways, with an undertaking of mutual assistance against any reprisals on her part? There are at least nine chances in 10 that such a threat would be effective; and its success would have great value for the future as well as for the present. If the United States were to decline our proposal, we could not help it. But we cannot escape blame unless we take some initiative towards positive action.

Yours &c.,

J. M. KEYNES

[33] 14 August 1937.

The next day he wrote to Gladwyn Jebb.

To GLADWYN JEBB, *29 September 1937*

My dear Jebb,

You will probably have seen my letter in to-day's *Times* about economic sanctions against Japan. I do feel that this moment is one of the clear opportunities for decisive action, which would be without risk, certain to be successful and with the most fruitful consequences.

I felt the same at one moment about Abyssinia. I have never felt it in the case of Spain, for there has never been a really clear case. But the present case is surely the clearest of all.

If America will not play, then, of course, we cannot proceed. But it would be a splendid thing at least to put the proposition to her. It is high time that she was forced into the position of having to take clear responsibility one way or the other.

And who knows but she would not welcome the invitation. I shall never forget how, when I visited Washington about three years ago, when Simon was Foreign Secretary, no-one would talk to me (who wanted to discuss nothing but New Deal) except on the question whether I could give an even plausible explanation of why our Foreign Office was refusing to play with them over Japan. I got the same question from the President himself, from Morgenthau and from the State Department. They were begging me even to produce some barely plausible explanation of our attitude. I am sure that the world immensely underestimates the effect of economic sanctions. The case of Italy is, of course, no proof to the contrary. Everyone knows that they were never applied to any adequate extent. If they had been, it would have been another story.

Yours sincerely,
[copy initialled] J.M.K.

Keynes's letter also led him into correspondence with Sir Arthur Salter.

From SIR ARTHUR SALTER, *29 September 1937*

My dear Keynes,

Like all who know you I have been greatly distressed by your illness and hoping for signs that you are recovering from it. I trust that your letter in *The Times* to-day, and its address from London, may be taken as such a sign. I had been wanting to write to you about the Far East, but did not do so because I did not know how complete was the separation from public affairs that was being imposed upon you.

I was therefore extremely pleased to see your letter, both as an indication of your own improved health and also as showing what you are feeling about the Chinese position.

I am encouraged by it to send you the enclosed papers in case you should care to see them.[34] There is some advantage in those who are working on more or less the same lines exchanging notes as to what they are doing.

One of the enclosures summarises some of the obvious facts about Japan's economic position. There's nothing new in this and everything in it is of course known to you, but it may perhaps be convenient to you to have such a summary by you.

My principal object in writing to you is to suggest that one element in the situation is of very special importance. I do not see anything effective being done without America; or the American Government doing anything unless there is a very great change in American public opinion. I think it likely that Roosevelt (whom I do not know personally) and Cordell Hull (whom I do) would both like this to happen, but are impotent without it.

Such a change is I believe possible as a result of the outrages if the religious organisations make the fullest use of the special interest in Chinese affairs that the American missionary work in China, which is on a very large scale, has created throughout America. The periodical reports of different missionaries to their respective churches have created the foundation of a possible movement of opinion which has no counterpart elsewhere. I had a talk with Stimson a week ago and he believed strongly that this might be a factor of quite decisive importance.

There is very great suspicion in the U.S.A.—especially among the 'neutralists'—as to the hidden hand of British policy in America. Lothian and myself have recently been pilloried in a book by Quincy Howe, *England expects every American to do his duty*, which is having an unfortunate success just now; and you of course have in the past been subject to a much more serious attack for your very much more important influence. I have therefore

[34] Not printed.

84

decided not to write anything on political questions in America at present, and I think that anything published by any Englishman there might well do much more harm than good.

This does not, however, preclude private letters if one is sure enough of one's correspondent. And, in spite of the above danger, I have after some hesitation written to Cordell Hull the letter of which I am sending you a copy.[35] Obviously not only the contents, but also the fact that I have written, are extremely secret; it would be disastrous if the fact came out—I would ask you therefore to destroy the letter when you have done with it.

You have, I suppose, a closer personal relation and a greater influence with F.R. [Franklin Roosevelt] than any other Englishman. It occurred to me that, if you can be sure of your letters being read only by him, you might at some stage be thinking of writing to him.

I am also sending you a copy of a note I have prepared for use with several correspondents, with the same point of view in mind, and equally of course confidential.[36]

I do greatly hope that you will soon recover your health completely. Destroy all these papers unread if you think it advisable and don't trouble to reply.

Yours ever,
ARTHUR SALTER

To SIR ARTHUR SALTER, *30 September 1937*

My dear Salter,

I agree with all you say, and am grateful to you for sending me this fuller information. Your letter to Hull could not be bettered. I agree that it is for the American missionaries to work up feeling in U.S.A. But I go even further than you do as to the undesirability of any British propaganda. Long experience has convinced me, as I think it has convinced you, that all the 'sounding' which the Americans encourage before anything is done is really disastrous. It is much better for us to make a public proposal, or for them to make a public proposal, and then deal with it above board.

Moreover, time is short, and any action will have to emerge from immediate feelings. It would, of course, be much better

[35] Not printed.
[36] Not printed.

if the initiative could come from America. But, failing that, it is our duty to make one, though of course contingent on their joining in. I infer from *The Times* having closed their correspondence on the subject to-day and from press rumours about yesterday's Cabinet council that the Cabinet are almost certainly going to do nothing. Not for the first time, they will be incurring deep guilt in the eyes of posterity.

I enclose for your own private information a copy of a letter which I sent to Gladwyn Jebb at the Foreign Office.[37] I feel hesitation for the above reason about writing to the President. But I had half thought of sending him a copy of my *Times* letter with a brief covering note.

My own health is vastly better, but it will be some time yet before I can return to real life. I leave for the country this afternoon. Thinking, reading, and even dictating, does me no harm, but I have to keep down to a minimum of seeing people and particularly meetings.

Yours sincerely,
[copy initialled) J.M.K.

P.S. I return you the copies of your two very private documents.

To KINGSLEY MARTIN, *29 September 1937*

Dear Kingsley,

As you may have seen from my letter in *The Times* to-day, I agreed very strongly with the article you had last week about economic sanctions for Japan. This seems to me one of the clear cases where decisive action is quite without risk, if sufficient join in, and certain to be successful; and there will be united public opinion behind it, (which last it is always necessary to remember is an essential prerequisite of decisive action). So I do hope you will go hammering on along that line. People are quite absurd, in my opinion, in underestimating the effect of economic sanctions. In the case of Italy, as we all know, they have never

[37] Above p. 83.

been honestly and decisively applied. If they had been, it would have been another story.

I have at last escaped from my Welsh prison, very greatly improved in health; though I am not allowed to return to real life for some little time yet. Lydia and I are going to Tilton tomorrow, but for no long time. After that we shall come back to London and probably spend most of the autumn here, since I am not going into residence at Cambridge. We shall hope to see you then.

Yours ever,

J. M. KEYNES

From KINGSLEY MARTIN, *11 October 1937*

Dear Maynard,

I got back from Spain yesterday afternoon. It was interesting but I am very depressed. I have searched for any light about a possible way of even beginning to approach some kind of settlement. This Government is composed of extraordinarily decent people who would talk I think if there was anything to talk about, but there just seem no basis of discussion; and I think we have put off standing up to Italy so long that it is unlikely that she could be induced to withdraw now without a risk that the Government will certainly not run. I was glad that you took the view you did about Japan, though I wish you had taken it about Spain earlier. In my view Spain could have been and still could be saved by a determined effort. I believe Japan, in spite of the apparent unity of some of the important powers, to be an almost hopeless proposition. I don't want to say this in public and Freda Utley is furious with me for holding that view. But I think attention should be concentrated on the Spanish issue where we really could be effective if we wanted to be. However, if people realise that both are really one war, that will be all to the good.

I am delighted to hear that you are better and that there is some hope of seeing you again soon. I should dearly enjoy a talk. I have just been seeing Del Vayo and think I know quite a bit about the Spanish situation. From the point of view of internal politics and military organisation, the government's position is far stronger than I had expected. Its food situation is much worse, but that can be remedied.

I do not know if anybody has told you, but we are producing what I believe will be really an amusing little book composed of 'This England' selections with illustrations by Low, as a Christmas card to be sold on the bookstalls. I believe it will sell really well.

Love to you both,

Yours,
KINGSLEY MARTIN

Did you know that *The Times* suppressed all the 50 letters sent backing you on Japan?—that is how the story reached me—but I'll enquire just when the letters came.

To KINGSLEY MARTIN, *18 October 1937*

My dear Kingsley,

I read with much interest your letter from Valencia,[38] and would like to have a talk. But, although I am getting on extremely well, I cannot be available just yet. The weather is so perfect that we shall stay in the country as long as it lasts.

The difference, to my mind, between the cases of Japan and Spain does not lie in their different degrees of potentiality for evil, but that, in the one case, it appears to me that there is something specific which would be effective if done and might command sufficient general assent to be practical politics, whilst, in the other, I have never been able to see that this was so. I agree completely with Freda Utley.[39] As long as I can remember only a very few have believed in economic sanctions. There seems to be something boring about them and, in addition, there is a prevailing fallacy of the market place that they have frequently been tried and always proved futile. In fact they have only been tried once—in the case of Germany—and were successful. If they had been applied strictly and whole-heartedly, they would undoubtedly have worked in the case of Italy. However, I see it is not good. They are not a form of action, however effective they might prove in practice, about which people's emotions can get roused.

I had not heard about *The Times* suppressing the letters, but I assumed that this was so and that they were doing it by order

---

[38] 'Spanish Diary' by Critic, *New Statesman and Nation*, 9 October 1937.
[39] 'Can Japan be Stopped', a letter published on 9 October.

of the F.O. *The Times* started by being on my side, and I believe still are so, but regard it as their duty to obey authority.

The proposed Christmas book sounds a very good idea.

Yours ever,
[copy not signed or initialled]

From KINGSLEY MARTIN, *26 October 1937*

Dear Maynard,

I happened to see Sidebotham at lunch today and congratulated him on the admirably apt quotation from Thucydides. I found your cutting on my return to the office. It is just a question of which occasion you think calls for which kind of treatment. I am afraid I shan't get much satisfaction in a few years' time when Sidebotham is calling upon me to support the bombing of foreign cities, if I quote back at him his remarks about 'reckless indifference' being extolled as 'the courage of loyalty' and 'patience' being decried as 'cowardice', etc. Nothing was ever clearer to me in my life than the issue in Spain. If we had had a Liberal–Labour government (and there were not even Socialists in the Spanish one) in power in England and there was a rising led by Duff Cooper and Mosley, supported by the City and Hitler, there would be no choice except between complete pacificism and fighting. Remarks about patience, etc. would be irrelevant. That is essentially how I see the Spanish struggle and I believe that if more people had seen it so clearly, we might have helped the Spanish people to win a victory there that would have made a similar situation in France or England, or elsewhere, less probable.

Now that it is clear that not enough people see it like this and that they won't agree with you either about Japan (I don't disagree with you there—it is merely that I felt that we could get no big support), the question of future policy becomes even more difficult. My inclinations get more and more pacifist.

Let me know when there is a chance of having some talk.

Yours,
K. M.

To KINGSLEY MARTIN, *7 November 1937*

Dear Kingsley,

The first leader[40] in this week's paper is apparently intended to incite China to a war to a finish, so long as any Japanese soldier remains on Chinese soil. At the same time, it holds out no hope that any effective assistance from outside is at all probable. Is there not some disastrous confusion of thought and feeling behind this? And next week, for all I know, you will be advising the Chinese to adopt the faith of Dick Sheppard.

I feel increasingly that the paper does infinite harm by its capacity for making the better cause appear the worse, and giving an impression of imbecile confusion of mind and emotion. Garvin at least has the merit that he makes the worse cause appear the worser.

However, I thought Cole's article[41] on the location of industry very good.

Yours,

J. M. KEYNES

From KINGSLEY MARTIN, *9 November 1937*

Dear Maynard,

Thank you for your letter, which is important. I did not know you thought the paper did harm.

I am puzzled in this case because you yourself have been a principal advocate of the boycott policy. As you know, I had doubts about whether it was wise to advocate it again just for the kind of reasons that you now suggest. Mostyn's[42] point was (a) that the governments ought to impose a boycott, and (b) that since it was quite clear that they would not do so, we could at least avoid the taint of treachery involved in actually combining with the Japanese to carve up China. Do you disagree with this, and if so, why? The more I think about it, the more I feel that your letter is a reflection of your own difficulties as well as mine.

On the general question of foreign policy we have not, I think, been editorially inconsistent over Abyssinia, Spain or China. The tone and

[40] 'Is it Peace JEHU', *New Statesman and Nation*, 7 November 1937.
[41] Industry—Where and Why, *loc. cit.*
[42] C. M. Lloyd, the writer of the leader.

attitude of the London Diary has been frequently different from that of the editorials and that by deliberate policy on my part. I regard the Diary as a personal affair and my periodic revelations of the kind of difficulties and doubts that anybody must have today in supporting any foreign policy, have been partly, of course, a relief to me, but also partly the fruit of deliberate policy. I believe that part of the strength of the paper in recent years—I have evidence that it has a good deal of influence—has been that we have been definite and consistent in our editorials, but have also revealed the kind of difficulties and problems that have to be overcome in reaching a policy.

The general line has been to sustain any hope of collective international action as long as that were possible, and to encourage hopes of rebuilding it when it was broken as long as one reasonably could. As it happens, I was talking to Aylmer Vallance at breakfast this morning, before I got your letter, about whether the time had not come definitely and finally to say that any hopes of the kind were now finished, and therefore to advocate the withdrawal of England as far as possible from affairs. This would mean trying to build up a Scandinavian state of mind, and it would mean not trying to save the British Empire. Now that it is clear that nothing effective will be done on the other line, I think that such a change is desirable and I suppose, in view of your letter, that you agree. It will involve a good deal of change of policy all round.

I have only been at all bitter—if I have—in the past because I believed that the chance in the case of Abyssinia was real and that the situation might have been saved by stopping Mussolini in 1935. I know that you hold this view too. Today I am as sorry for Mr Eden and all the rest of them as for myself and the helpless population. I do not think, however, that helplessness in a desperate situation that results from bad actions in the past is a reason for actually changing sides and becoming parties to the evils that one has failed to stop.

As I think you know, I have long been trying to get Mostyn to take a long holiday. He needs a sabbatical year. He has now at last arranged to take a sabbatical term, which begins in January. I imagine the Board will have no objection to this.

Yours,
KINGSLEY

Your letter seems not to have been marked 'personal'; it was open on my desk this morning having been read by Mostyn and probably by both secretaries. I have now discussed it with Aylmer Vallance. We all feel that is a most extraordinary or inexplicable document. I am speculating about why you should decide to be so personally insulting and so completely inconsistent. What is the motive behind your decision to call me an imbecile etc. and to introduce that insult about Sheppard? I am sure that you did not mean to be quite as rude and also (I can't help feeling) as silly as you were in fact. There must be some other reason, perhaps of health, I don't know.

To KINGSLEY MARTIN, *10 November 1937*

Dear Kingsley,

Apologies for not marking my previous letter 'personal'. I meant it as such and forgot that I was addressing an institution, not an individual. When I get a letter marked 'personal' it is generally from a money-lender or a betting tout.

On the main issue I enclose a separate letter which might, if you are inclined, be shown to Lloyd and Vallance.

I am glad to hear that Lloyd is going away for a space. Though I address my complaints to you, and indeed they apply to you, it is very frequently his articles, and not yours, which upset and disturb me most. I thought that to write last week's leader on China, in the face of what one is reading about China's tragedy and heroism, was frivolous and futile and dead to the realities of the world beyond endurance. Just one more opportunity of barking up Eden's tree—that was how the situation seemed to present itself to the paper.

Yours ever,

J. M. K.

Keynes's enclosure ran as follows:

To KINGSLEY MARTIN, *10 November 1937*

Dear Kingsley,

My own view is that we ought to have invited the United States to join us in imposing a boycott. I understand the reasons against this, though I am not convinced by them, namely, (a) that we are not yet strong enough, (b) that the general position is so critical that we must on no account risk any dispersion of forces, and (c) that public opinion is insufficiently homogeneous.

It is also extremely likely that, even if we had taken the action I desired, America would not have responded.

Since, however, there seems no chance of a boycott, and China has saved her honour and her position and character as a nation, it is most advisable in her interests that peace should be concluded as soon as possible, even though it involves what amounts to her ceding a large area of territory. Finally, this being so, we ought to use all our power and influence to get her the best possible terms. It seems to me wicked to encourage her to continue, if any sort of tolerable terms are obtainable, and our duty to get her the best terms we can.

Turning to the wider problem, in my view, our sole and overriding purpose should be made quite sure of countering the Fascist powers at long last. It is precisely because I believe the position to be critical and dangerous that I believe strategic retreats to be necessary and the gradual consolidation of forces absolutely essential. There is no chance except by achieving an almost worldwide consolidation of opinion on very broad issues. Such issues as an enormous majority of the people of this country, for example, and, one hopes in America, are ready to agree about. It is no time for being minority-minded, and those who are impenitently minority-minded are helping the enemy.

You, on the other hand, are perpetually engaged in conducting an indignation meeting, more often than not only secondarily against the enemy, and primarily against friends or, if not friends, at least potential allies, and thereby saving your soul and preserving yourself from all taints. I regard this as unserious and futile and playing into the hands of the enemy. Every sort of motive has to be mobilised on the right side, and the issue must be represented in terms which appeal to the great mass of opinion, as it is well capable of being. It is no good to spit and fume against the powers that be and all the real forces in the world, keeping in reserve, as the final expedient of escapism, throwing in your hand and lying flat on your face before the advancing forces.

I also have another feeling, which may be unreasonable, which ought to be mentioned because it plays a not unimportant part in my own mind. I cannot accept the policy of non-resistance, but I have a very strong objection to sending the average man to fight on an occasion, or at a time, or in circumstances whatever they may be, for reasons which only appeal to a minority. There are no issues on which the rights of the majority are so paramount as in the case of war and peace.

Thus if the issue is to be joined, it must be for reasons which unite the vast majority of right-thinking men. It is this, and not sectional differences and heresies, or too nice an examination of selfish motives which should be one's aim.

Well, that is how I feel and why the paper so often strikes me as injurious to the better cause. I am not sure that I should not like to write publicly on these lines and leave you to expound the opposite in reply. That is, if you really believe the opposite, which I doubt. For I believe that what I am objecting to is due to an uncontrollable minority-mindedness and the old non-conformist urge to save *one's own* soul. But we are at a juncture of the world's affairs when these virtues are vices.

Yours ever,

J. M. KEYNES

From KINGSLEY MARTIN, *12 November 1937*

Many thanks for useful letter.

K. M.

Again, there was a brief gap, until a telephone call sparked off another exchange.

From KINGSLEY MARTIN, *17 January 1938*

Dear Maynard,

I'm sorry I interrupted you at dinner and that you are still so unwell. Lydia must forgive me if she can. I did not think about the time and thought it fairly safe, not realising you would dine before 7.30.

I'm upset about the Webb business.[43] It's so shocking to have G.B.S. writing about her in *The Spectator* when she was the main founder of the *N.S.* and G.B.S. with her. My fault to be caught hopping so badly. I think an article by you would be the one way of retrieving the situation and if you could think of her before her second Soviet youth you might write something short that would be really valuable and please her no end. I think several short things now the only way out. I'm trying to get H.G.W. to say something but he's not sure.[44]

About foreign policy there was so much to say in answer to your last long letter that I put it aside. It meant embarking on a lot of Fundamentals and I was not sure that it would be helpful, though I am very willing and am indeed trying to work out my thoughts in a book just now. If you want to discuss it I'll not funk it.

I'm still hoping you will feel able to do something about the Webb business.

Love to Lydia

KINGSLEY

To KINGSLEY MARTIN, *19 January 1938*

Dear Kingsley,

The only sentence which came spontaneously to my mind was 'Mrs Webb, not being a Soviet politician, has managed to survive to the age of eighty.' But I thought that would not do. The truth is that she is such a complex personality and one's feelings to different aspects of her genius are so mixed that she is most difficult to write about for publication as a living person. That she is the most distinguished woman alive seems to me to go without saying. But this is not the occasion for a perfectly candid examination, and a diplomatic one involved more concentration than I felt capable of yesterday.

Foreign policy and the like must wait until we meet. My own ideas have developed a bit further since I wrote.

Yours ever,

J.M.K.

[43] Beatrice Webb's eightieth birthday had been on 2 January.
[44] Wells did write something on Mrs Webb for the issue of 22 January.

From LYDIA KEYNES, *6 February 1938*

Dear Kingsley

Maynard asks me to answer for your letter about Turner,[45] that apart from being not so carefully written as sometimes in the past, his articles are still clearer, and with a proper angle to mankind. There are very few journalists who are first rate, and Turner even if he does not take trouble still retains the *prima qualita*. Couldn't you talk to him?

Yours sincerely,
LYDIA KEYNES

To KINGSLEY MARTIN, *23 February 1938*

Dear Kingsley,

Yes, I am very glad, looking back, that I thanked heaven a few months ago that we had Eden as Foreign Secretary, and defended him from the charge of being a Fascist.[46]

The gravity and importance of what has happened cannot be exaggerated. But if one is to try and extract any comfort from the disaster, I find a certain amount in the fact that the fissure of opinion has taken place at the most favourable point possible, leaving the maximum of weight and numbers to the Left. As you know I feel nothing more strongly than that in an affair of this kind it is useless to be in a minority. I do not reckon the chances of escaping from that position good, but they are surely better than they could have been with almost any other split, or on almost any other issue. That seems to me the point to emphasise,—the necessity of consolidating as an effective force the *whole* body of opinion to the left of the Government.

But what a miserable figure the Labour Party cut in the debate.[47] Not a single speech of bigness, dignity or importance. Nothing but stale debating points, and personal jibes.

I expect that the future has big surprises for us. I do not rule out the possibility of the Prime Minister having a genuine

[45] T. W. J. Turner, *The New Statesman*'s regular music critic. Martin's letter has not survived.
[46] Anthony Eden resigned as Secretary of State for Foreign Affairs on 20 February over a disagreement on Government policy towards Italy.
[47] On a Labour Party motion of censure on 22 February following Eden's resignation.

success on the immediate issue. If Mussolini was wanting an opportunity to back out of various commitments, this is clearly a heaven sent opportunity for him to do so without loss of prestige. If so, I do not see how one can deny that it will be a benefit on the small stage of the immediate future. If this happens, it will confuse the issue, but, of course, it will not touch the main matters.

I am just back from Ruthin with good reports, and fit to keep one appointment, or see one visitor, a day. We shall be here for two or three weeks, I expect. When can you come round? Would this Friday at tea-time be possible?

Yours ever,

J. M. KEYNES

From KINGSLEY MARTIN, *28 February 1938*

Dear Maynard,

Does something ironical occur to you? A few months ago you wrote an article to the *N.S. & N.* accusing us of war mongering about Spain and Italy and saying that in our hearts we must be glad that Mr Eden was Foreign Minister and so peace-loving an Administration in office. It now appears from Mr Eden's statement in the House—and from a private statement of his views that I heard expressed recently—that at the time you wrote to defend his policy Mr Eden must have been in substantial agreement with our criticism of it; it was in fact forced on him. His criticisms of the PM's policy today have been our criticisms ever since the Non-Intervention Committee showed that it was in fact an Italian device for destroying Spanish democracy and establishing an Italian colony in Spain. If the *N.S. & N.* now backs Mr Eden will you write again and say that we are making war on someone, that Eden is a warmonger and that in our hearts we are glad to have Mr Chamberlain in charge? Has Mr Eden now suddenly become 'not serious' or bellicose?

Controversy—which is rather more than pleasantry since you very deeply hurt me—apart I hope very much that you are better. But I don't know, and as I am fond of you I wish I did know, how you are and also whether one ought to write and worry you about various projects and so on or not.

My love to Lydia

KINGSLEY

On 13 March 1938, Hitler entered Vienna and announced the incorporation of Austria into the Reich. With the encouragement of Kingsley Martin, who used it as a leading article, Keynes contributed another article to *The New Statesman*.

To KINGSLEY MARTIN, *21 March 1938*

Dear Kingsley,

I enclose the article. If you print it as the first leader, I should much prefer, if you agree, that it have no title except the little poem which, appearing with a line under it, should act as a title. I have, however, given a title for use in the Table of Contents and in case you do not approve of the above.

I should be grateful if I might be sent tomorrow a dozen pulls of the proof, if possible in page rather than in galley form, since there are a few people to whom I want to send out advance copies.

I think you are right in making special publicity efforts about the issue.   Yours sincerely,

J. M. K.

From KINGSLEY MARTIN, *22 March 1938*

Dear Maynard,

I am sending with this twelve proofs of your article, 11 without the title and 1 with. It is of course beautifully written, exactly the right contribution at the moment, and very valuable to the paper. I think it will attract a great deal of attention; *The News Chronicle*, for instance, has promised to comment on it on the morning of publication, and I shall also write to Crozier and perhaps to *The Herald* with the same object in view.

I am not quite sure of this question of a heading. You will see how it looks on the page. I think it may look odd in the paper.

Will you please ring me about the article some time during tomorrow.

Yours

KINGSLEY

P.S. I really think you ought somewhere in the article, especially if it is used as a leader, to refer to the *N.S.* which has consistently held the same point of view (though the facts of course are different) through trying times in the past!

From The New Statesman and Nation, *25 March 1938*

A POSITIVE PEACE PROGRAMME

> Sweet Peace, where dost thou dwell? I humbly crave,
>> Let me once know
>> I sought thee in a secret cave,
>> And ask'd if Peace were there
> A hollow winde did seem to answer, No:
>> Go seek elsewhere.[48]

Our troubles are of our own making and our errors were obvious at the time when we made them. The guilt of the Treaty, of French policy for ten years after that and of our own weakness and betrayals since then, we all now acknowledge. But behind this there has been at work another cause of undoing, where we have been, not guilty, but deceived. We have assumed that a negative pacifism, backed by no sanctions and supported by no definite undertakings, would prevail against a positive militarism, whenever and wherever that might arise. If we now look back, is it not evident that positive militarism was sure to arise somewhere at some time? With a slightly different turn of events it would have come, not from Germany, but from Russia. The Japanese agression is largely independent of European totalitarianism. Negative pacifism was most unlikely to stand any severe strain. We have been relying on an illusion.

With the instrument of negative pacifism broken in their hands, the Prime Minister and his group seek for peace, it seems, 'in a secret cave'. Their policy is not lightly to be rejected. To gain time, to avoid at all costs any risk of war, how much there is to be said for it! To keep our own liberties and lives and happiness intact, to attain true isolation in a disastrous world, withdrawing to our secret caves from Cornwall to Orkney as to a cloister, how willingly, and perhaps rightly, would many of us retreat. But if the Prime Minister gathers to his support those whom a withdrawal instinctively attracts, he gains followers who

[48] The poem is 'Peace' by George Herbert.

do not belong to him, and whom he deceives. For this is not what he means. He has not decided, once and for all, to abandon British power in the Mediterranean and to surrender without resistance the more vulnerable portions of the British Empire. Far from it. He is not escaping the risks of war. He is only making sure that, when it comes, we shall have no friends and no common cause. He is forgetting the imponderables of the world, the power of courageous bearing, the majesty of right action, the comfort and stiffening to our friends of faithful words and counsel. He is leaving all the imponderables to the other side, allowing them to exploit the foreseen and the inevitable for purposes of terror and prestige. Yet what a response an act of constructive statesmanship would evoke! Is it impossible to build a bridge between 'I dare not' and 'I would'? What would one do if one had the power?

There is no middle position to-day between non-resistance and a positive pacifism. Within the scope of the existing League of Nations we must, therefore, set out to construct a new European pact open to all the European members of the League, who would give definite undertakings to one another and the power to act by the voice of the majority; since we know by experience that a League with no definite sanctions and a *liberum* veto for each member is useless. The constitution of such a European League could be extremely simple. For example, the three major League powers, Great Britain, France and Russia, would have 10 votes each; Poland and Czecho-Slovakia four votes each; Switzerland, Holland, Belgium, the Scandinavian and the Balkan countries two votes each; the Baltic States and Spanish Provinces one vote each. All the members, subject to the safeguards which follow, would bind themselves to abide by a majority vote as to the fact or imminence of aggression involving two European powers, the appropriate action to avert or meet it, and all other matters, following in general the procedure and principles of the existing League, without, however, any specific guarantee of the *status quo*. It is not essential that all the eligible powers should adhere from the outset. The Pact should begin to function with the three major powers and any others who were ready to join.

If our politicians mean anything by their lip-service to collective security, they have a duty to make some such proposal as this. But there is one urgent matter which they must settle first. The British and French Governments, out of regard both to their own and the general interest, must demand an immediate armistice in Spain and a negotiated peace on the basis of the independence of Catalonia and the Basque Provinces; and, in the event of refusal there should be an end of 'non-intervention' and a free hand to France with our full support. The time has come, on every ground of humanity and policy and the state of public opinion, to end the Spanish war. Does anyone doubt it?

It is also a necessary preliminary to new guarantees that Czecho-Slovakia should at least attempt to negotiate with Germany a reasonable solution of the problem of the Sudeten Germans, even if this means a rectification of the Bohemian frontier. Racial frontiers are safer and better to-day than geo-physical frontiers. But such things will give us no enduring relief except as facilitating a new European Pact, and to the details of this pact let us now return.

The sanctions attaching to the new Pact would be of three orders. The first, financial assistance and the rupture of relations. The second, a blockade. The third, a full military alliance. But the smaller powers with less than four votes should not be committed to join in any sanctions without their own assent in the particular case. The members of the Pact amongst themselves would, of course, accept the results of arbitration, endorsed by a majority vote of the members, in all matters of dispute between them, including frontiers, renouncing altogether the instrument of war. Their general staffs would be in regular collaboration with particular reference to air defence and blockade. But they should be concerned not less with the arts of peace and aim at becoming the nucleus of a new system of freedom in trade and intercourse, so that to be a citizen of the European League would be to enjoy again the old personal liberties. We ourselves should offer on reciprocal terms freedom of trade, freedom of investment, freedom of remittance, and freedom of the movement and employment of individuals, or, failing that, trade and currency agreements going as far as practicable in these directions; subject only to safeguards relating to wholesale or abnormal movements of capital or population. There should be an offer to Germany to make organised arrangements for all German and Austrian Jews who wish to migrate and be naturalised elsewhere.

What would be the relation of the new League to the old League? The new League would be the first-born off-spring of the old, domiciled at Geneva dwelling in amity in its parent's house, sharing all common interests and activities. But the old League should be relieved of its inoperative organs. The articles relating to sanctions should go and all European problems should be handled in the first instance by the new League. When the European League decided to act, the members of the old League, including the British Dominions, would be invited of their own free will to participate in the decision. The hope would be for the blessing of other off-spring, in particular an American League, headed by the United States and limited in membership to the American continents; and perhaps in due course a Pacific League, an African League, a League of Middle and Nearer Asia.

None of these proposals is dangerous. Their whole object is the avoidance of war. But we are suffering to-day from the worst of all diseases, the paralysis of will. Nothing can be more dangerous than that. We have become incapable of constructive policy or decisive action. We are without conviction, without foresight, without a resolute will to protect what we care for. We just rearm a little more, grovel a little more, and wait to see what happens. We mutter the necessity for collective security

A CONTRAST OF DEMEANOURS.

Cartoon by David Low by arrangement with the Trustees and The London Evening Standard.

and do not lift a finger to achieve it. Our strength is great, but our statesmen have lost the capacity to appear formidable. It is in that loss that our greatest danger lies. Our power to win a war may depend on increased armaments. But our power to avoid a war depends much more on our recovering that capacity to appear formidable, which is a quality of will and demeanour.

Mr Churchill understands this vital element of policy, but Mr Chamberlain seems to forget it. The dictators appear much more formidable, the democratic powers much less formidable, than they really are. It is the reversal of that position which will serve most effectively to preserve the peace. If we want to lure the adversary to his destruction, let us sharpen our teeth and silence our snarl. But if we wish to keep him at a distance, the lion's roar is worth more than his power to spring.

We are learning to honour more than formerly the achievements of our predecessors and the Christian civilisation and fundamental laws of conduct which they established in a savage world. We are seeing and enduring events, worse than which have not been seen and endured since man became himself. If we still recognise the difference, not merely between peace and war, but between good and evil and between right and wrong, we need to rouse up and shake ourselves and offer leadership.

Prior to publication, Keynes sent proofs of the article to Philip Noel-Baker, R. A. Butler, Robert Boothby, Lord Robert Cecil, Winston Churchill, Walter Layton, Harold Nicolson and Archibald Sinclair. Some of their comments are of interest.

From ROBERT BOOTHBY, *24 March 1938*

Dear Keynes,
Thank you for sending me your article, which I think quite admirable.
We have had a desperate fight behind the scenes. I only hope this afternoon will not prove it to have been in vain.

Yours,
ROBERT BOOTHBY

From HAROLD NICOLSON, *24 March 1938*

Dear Maynard

A thousand thanks for sending me the proof of your *New Statesman* article which will be of great value to me.

I should quite understand it if the Prime Minister got up and said 'owing to the indolence and optimism of my predecessors we have allowed our defences to decline to a point where we are unable to say boo to the Nazi goose'. What drives me so mad is that the Conservatives should pretend that German dominance in Eastern Europe is not a direct disadvantage to this country.

I absolutely agree with you that there is no middle course between non-resistance and positive pacifism, and that we must recover the capacity to appear formidable. I quite see that it is almost impossible to recover that capacity in the Central European theatre but we ought, by the exercise of sea power, to be able to recover it in Spain. I am beginning to believe that Karl Marx was right and that the judgment of statesmen is finally influenced by their economic interests.

Yours ever,
HAROLD NICOLSON

From WALTER LAYTON, *25 March 1938*

My dear Maynard,

I like your article immensely; but how are we to mobilise enough energy of opinion to turn the tide? Is it too much prosperity or insular muddled thinking that has paralysed the nation's will power?

I hope the health is steadily improving. Regards to Lydia.

Yours ever,
W. T. LAYTON

From ARCHIBALD SINCLAIR, *26 March 1938*

Dear Keynes,

Thank you so much for your letter of the 23rd March and for your telegram. I am so sorry that you cannot lunch on Monday. I hope you are making a good recovery, but I am sure you are right to go slow and not to go about until you feel quite fit.

I read your article with great interest. I agree with it and am doing my best to expound its main proposition—that we must make up our minds whether we are for non-resistance or for constructive peace; and I agree with most of the argument which follows. Nor would I attempt to deny that the League system will never work smoothly and perfectly either on the side of collective resistance to aggression or on the side of peaceful change until there is some such system of federal government as you suggest. Pooled security requires for its full and effective working pooled sovereignty.

Nevertheless I am afraid we have got to work there by slow degrees. The recent utterances of Ministers, supported by the ministerial press, have severely shaken the confidence of the people of this country not only in the League as it exists to-day but in the possibility of making it effective; still more is this the case with other countries on whose support you count but which are nearer than we are to Germany and contrast with dismay the weak and irresolute policy of the democracies with the swift and decisive strokes of the dictatorships. I should therefore regard your proposal rather as a goal than as an immediate objective, but I entirely agree that it is one towards which we ought deliberately to set our course.

I hope you will let me know when you are returning to London. It would give us very great pleasure if you would both come and lunch with us one day.

Yours sincerely,
ARCHIBALD SINCLAIR

To SIR ARCHIBALD SINCLAIR, *4 April 1938*

Dear Sinclair,

Many thanks for your letter of March 26th. I am very sorry that my health still stands in the way of my taking an active part in things.

I agree that my article suggests a goal rather than an immediately practicable policy. But, from the point of view of the Opposition, this is what one wants. It would only be by gradually increasing the confidence of the minor powers that one would be able to make such a scheme as I have in mind a success. But, if anything at all is to be done about salvaging the League of Nations, surely it must be somewhat on these lines. What one wants is that the British Government should adopt this as its general line of policy, gradually preparing the ground for bringing it into effect. What Europe most needs to-day is a change in the state of mind. And the psychological change which must be a prelude to any useful, constructive policy is bound to be a matter of time and education.

Meanwhile there is one detail about which I feel it would be useful to be active, namely, the refugee problem. Roosevelt has given some sort of a lead in that direction, but I do not know how far he is in a strong enough position to implement it. I have not noticed that we have responded. The least we can do is to be generous and constructive in regard to that problem.

More generally, I feel that it is against some situation, unpredictable in its details, which has not yet arisen that you have to be preparing the mind and organisation of your Party. The mind of the progressive section of England to-day is essentially liberal. The Liberal Party is the centre of gravity and ought to be the focus of a new alignment of the progressive forces. In practice, of course, the Labour Party has to be the predominant member. But they, in truth, are progressively more liberal in their general outlook, and in matter of names every sort of concession should be made.

Now, it appears to me that we shall either stagger along with a certain modified success for the Prime Minister's policy, and a general easing of the tension, in which case there is nothing to be done, and indeed not such urgent need for anything to be done. Or, a new situation will arise of a kind which completes the split in opinion and defines the rift along the crack which has taken place in recent weeks. On the one side of this we should find about one quarter of the Cabinet and about one quarter of the Conservative Party, National Labour, the Liberal Party, a vast number of unattached people calling themselves independents, including the League of Nations Union group, and the Labour Party with its various wings and affiliates. I think it is vital that there should be sufficient liaison and mutual confidence between the various elements of this prospective group that, when the time comes, they can join together coherently and form a genuine progressive political force. This would be in fact a resurrection of the Liberal Party, though it would not be called such.

The present situation is not ripe for any such thing. I feel the important task is to prepare for it, to avoid all occasions which might stand in the way of such a reconciliation of forces and to maintain the most intimate contacts that are practicable in the circumstances. It would not be true to say that there is at present a majority in the country of what, under the above definition, could be called liberal opinion. But this is largely prevented because the Prime Minister has been successful in gathering to his support the great number of people who are against war for any cause whatever, and are, wrongly as I think, regarding him as the champion of that view. Some day they will be disillusioned, and when that day comes there will again exist the possibility of an alternative government.

Yours sincerely,
[copy initialled] J. M. K.

To KINGSLEY MARTIN, *25 March 1938*

Dear Kingsley,

It is a very good paper indeed—all except Fischer's article;[49] the object of that seems to be to cause a loss of sympathy for France and Blum, and its tendency on the whole pernicious,—the sort of article which I imagine Goebbels would willing[ly] pay for. But I agreed with *all* the others, and by no means least with Joad.[50] I have very little doubt that he is right that we hate the Fascists so much and are so anxious to have a smack at them that we tend to argue that that policy is much more bound up

[49] 'Paris in the Crisis', *New Statesman and Nation*, 26 March 1938.
[50] G. E. M. Joad, 'On Not Fighting Fascism', *loc. cit.*

with peace than it really is. However, the situation is admirably put by the whole conjunction of articles.

The objection to the Prime Minister's speech is not so much what he said as his tone and the way he said it. Exactly the same things could have been said differently so as to make a very fine speech indeed. As it is, he manages to give the impression that he is not in the least moved by what has happened, that he will not live up to any of his professions, and that his sympathies are in the wrong place. And he is clever enough to spike opposition by putting forward actual proposals about which there is a very large measure of agreement or half-agreement.

When, in *The Economic Consequences of the Peace* [*JMK*, vol. II, pp. 188–9] I quoted a verse of Shelley without acknowledgement, I was generally believed to be the author. I hope that the same thing will happen this time! There is another verse in reserve almost as apposite as the one I quoted.

> Then went I to a garden, and did spy
> A gallant flower,
> The crown Imperiall: Sure, said I,
> Peace at the root must dwell.
> But when I digg'd, I saw a worm devoure
> What show'd so well.

Yours,

J. M. K.

The advertising made a very fine show. I hope the cost has not been ruinous and will bring in at least some return. But past experience suggests scepticism. Such benefit as one gets is probably more in the long period than in the short.

From PHILIP NOEL-BAKER, *29 March 1938*

My dear Maynard,

How very good of you to send me a copy of your article. I need not say that I read it with the utmost interest and was in very much agreement with all the main principles, though naturally not on all the detailed points. I meant to quote it in the House on Thursday night but found that Attlee had taken all the points I had meant to use![51]

I do hope you are really better.

Again many thanks,

Yours ever,
PHILIP NOEL-BAKER

P.S. Our Party always does much better in the House than the newspapers make them appear to do. In fact, the Government have come out awfully badly in all the recent Debates.

Keynes's article was the subject of comment in *The New Statesman* from 'A Socialist' welcoming his conversion to an International Peace Front and asking whether Keynes accepted the Government's view 'that the single-handed defence of the whole Empire against all comers is an "absolute" duty quite apart from circumstances on foreign policy'.

To the Editor of The New Statesman and Nation, *3 April 1938*

Sir,

In response to the letter signed 'A Socialist' I certainly do not accept 'the Government's view that the single-handed defence of the whole Empire against all comers is an absolute duty, quite apart from circumstances or foreign policy'. Let me quote as the text for this letter another verse from the poem which furnished the text for my article;

> Then went I to a garden, and did spy
> A gallant flower,
> The crown Imperiall: Sure, said I,
> Peace at the root must dwell.
> But when I digg'd, I saw a worm devoure
> What show'd so well.

Civilisation and liberty are a fairer cause than the integrity of our possessions. But to-day it is these, and not the Empire,

---

[51] On 24 March the Prime Minister refused to provide guarantees to France if France attacked Germany because Germany had attacked Czechoslovakia. He also appealed to the Czech Government to solve the problem of the Sudeten Germans.

which are in immediate danger. Because the Prime Minister does not register strong emotions about them, he tends unfortunately to gather support from the many people in this country who, rightly perhaps, prefer peace to any cause whatever. That he registers strong emotions about the Empire is overlooked, at present, by these supporters. And when danger in that direction does arise, the issues will probably be so inextricably tangled that those who love civilisation and liberty will not find it easy to stand aside. So we look like enjoying the worst of both worlds. Meanwhile protests are in vain. 'The immediate job', in Mr Kingsley Martin's words, 'is to overcome the party particularism which stands in the way of a union of popular forces.'

J. M. KEYNES

After another burst of severe tension over Czechoslovakia in the period around local elections, Keynes was again commenting on *The New Statesman*'s position.

To KINGSLEY MARTIN, *28 May 1938*

Dear Kingsley,

I am very much better indeed and the efforts I have been making here seem to have been good for me rather than otherwise. We shall be here until Whit Tuesday. It will be very nice if you can motor over during Whitsuntide. But let us know beforehand, since I have to space my engagements. Our telephone is 54184, Cambridge.

I liked your leader.[52] I am sure that that is the line to take. But I do not believe that the time has yet come when one can do any real business with the Totalitarians. However, if one had the nucleus of what you suggest with other powers it is perfectly possible that the day may come when they will think it

[52] 'What We Ought To Do', *New Statesman and Nation*, 26 May 1938.

worthwhile to give in. Until they are really ready to come to terms I am a little scared of doing anything which would mitigate in the slightest degree their financial stringency, which undoubtedly plays a large part in the background—particularly in the case of Italy.

Do you really believe that the Germans have actually been supplying munitions to the Spanish Government? Lydia gave me the same gossip from her Russian paper. But surely the certainty of the Italians finding out about it would inhibit such Machiavellian anti-axism.

Apart from last year's profits I see that the circulation of the paper goes from strength to strenth.

Yours ever,

J. M. K.

In late July, Martin consulted Keynes over an article he had received over Richard Thomas and Company's new facilities at Ebbw Vale. The firm, which was basically the creation of Sir William Firth, had agreed to developing the site in 1935 after Government pressure. In 1938, before all the bills were paid the firm was facing receivership and its bankers, Lloyds, approached the Bank of England. The Bank and other bankers agreed after an investigation to put up £6m, and a Control Committee including some chairman of other steel companies and the Governor of the Bank, took over the company's management. Naturally this caused comment.

From KINGSLEY MARTIN, *22 July 1938*

Dear Maynard,

I received the enclosed article about Ebbw Vale.[53] The writer is very far from satisfied with it, but can do no better himself partly because his knowledge was confidentially obtained and cannot be used. He suggests my sending it to you and one or two other people for criticism or additions. I gather that it is difficult not to be libellous as well as indiscreet.

I greatly enjoyed myself at Tilton on Saturday and will try to come down again some afternoon before the summer is over.

Yours,

KINGSLEY MARTIN

[53] The article 'The Ebbw Vale Affair', appeared on 6 August 1938.

To KINGSLEY MARTIN, *25 July 1938*

Dear Kingsley,

The enclosed is very good, I think, so far as it goes, though it is distinctly on the mild side. If I had been writing it myself, I should have been a bit fiercer. And I think there is more that could be said without any sort of risk of libel. For this is a case where the facts speak for themselves. I enclose some rather interesting cuttings from *The Financial Times*, which, judging from internal evidence, your author has not seen. He could glean a good deal of useful facts from these. They should, however, be taken in conjunction with the recent statement made by the Chairman on behalf of the Company, a copy of which he doubtless has, though I have not one by me to send with this letter.

Points which might be brought to his notice are the following:—

1. I doubt if there is much in the criticism that with 'planning' the project could have been carried through quicker or cheaper. If the Chairman's account is to be accepted, the increase of prices only represents from 10 to 15 per cent, and a considerable part of the increased costs is due to the difficulty of the Ebbw Vale site.

2. So far as the Bank of England is concerned, or rather their subsidiary the B.I.D.,[54] their assistance has been given on extremely generous terms, since they are taking up ordinary shares at more than twice their present value in the market. On the other hand, the major part of the finance which is being provided by the Big Five is on distinctly more serious terms than are suggested in the article. For they not only take security in front of everybody else and arrange for its rapid repayment out of the gross receipts, so that they are lending at $4\frac{1}{2}$ per cent for short term with negligible risk; but they are also taking conversion rights for several years ahead, so that if the project turns out right they can acquire an important interest in the

---

[54] Bankers' Industrial Development Company.

equity after the event. In short, they are coming in at both ends, thus ensuring that they can share the fruits of success with a minimum participation in the risks.

3. I think he underestimates the extreme technical importance of the new works. I understand that they not only produce, by a process not otherwise available in this country, all the steel sheets required for the whole of our tin-plate industry, but are also capable of providing the whole of the sheets required by our motor industry. Altogether their potential output will be about ten per cent of the total output of the country, and since it is in a specialised product, in value a good deal more than this. The motor industry has been complaining bitterly about the high price and poor quality of their existing supplies. The new plant enables us to be the cheapest producers in the world, for home trade and exports, in the tin-plate industry, the motor industry and, I believe, also in products required by some aspects of the building industry and steel furniture. It is said that there is nothing of equal technical efficiency anywhere in the world, since these are the only works freshly laid out from the start with a view to the new technical processes.

4. The nature of the new control seems to me to be open to more criticism than is made. It takes two forms. There is an ultimate committee which will probably be largely controlled by the Bank of England, which is not likely to function unless the concern gets into difficulties. I see no objection to this. It consists of responsible, impartial authorities, representing both the new and the old debentures and the public interest. What is objectionable is that Richard Thomas have been compelled to accept as directors in the concern itself the Chairmen of three other steel concerns. If I remember right (this needs checking) one of these is not a competitor, and can be regarded as impartial, but the other two are competitors. It is practically admitted that the object of this is to prevent Richard Thomas from competing unduly with the less efficient concerns—one of the euphemisms concerned is that it is with the object of

'orderly' marketing. The object is quite definitely to prevent the cheapest producer from collaring the trade and bringing down prices to what they ought to be. The danger to Richard Thomas is that it will lead to their working at less than capacity, and thus failing to reach the low costs that ought to be possible. The duty of these outside directors is, we are told, 'to see that the joint interests as regards quotas of all the producers are duly safeguarded, as well as to see that the industry as a whole develops along orderly lines'.

5. I doubt if there is much in the criticism that, for technological reasons, not much extra employment will be given in South Wales. I am not well informed as to the amount of direct employment, though I should have thought that would be substantial for such [an] enormous works. But there is also the coal produced locally, the transport, the local services, and perhaps (I am not sure of this) local iron.

Yours ever,

[copy initialled] J. M. K.

In late August 1938 the Czechoslovakia question moved to the fore as the German army began ten weeks of manoeuvres in Czech and French frontier areas, called some reservists to the colours and extended the term of service for conscripts, amongst other measures. At the same time, Anglo–Czech negotiations were continuing.

From KINGSLEY MARTIN, *25 August 1938*

Dear Maynard,

I hear from Lydia that you are better. That at least is good news. I am intending to ask Cole about an article on your storage proposals[55] next week; if he is interested he should do it well.

---

[55] *JMK*, vol. XXI, pp. 456–70.

I was annoyed about *Truth's* attack on our advert. [56] They were of course quite right about the nature of it; Roberts, I really believe, was just simple and nice-minded and thought it all right! The two moneylenders we carry have been vetted and, I understand, advertise in *The Times*. But in my view it would be better not to carry any moneylending adverts. What do you think?

The situation is now terrifying. I heard today at only one step removed of the details of a confidential report brought to Vansittart from Germany. Hitler is quite confident that he can attack and that we and the French will do nothing; the Reichswehr are opposing him but are in a weak position having done it twice before and been wrong. The report was an S.O.S. from a highly placed person in Germany asking for a public declaration from Simon to the German people as well as Hitler that war will be world war. Hence Simon's coming statement on Saturday. I am doubtful of its working, and, even if it does, what next? Hitler, the same report says, does not intend the Henlein negotiations to come to anything. Pray God he changes his mind.

I have been talking over what the war will mean with a scientist on a special A[ir]R[aid]P[recautions] committee. I honestly do not believe that our sanity will stand it. I know some tough people's sanity will; it has in Madrid and Barcelona. But all our kind will be dead or in prison (though I doubt if they will get that chance) or mad in the first twelve months. It is all utterly mad for we cannot help the Czechs; we can only bomb Germany and be bombed ourselves. We ought to do everything possible to persuade Hitler not to march, and, if we fail, keep out. But we shan't do that of course. There are doubts in the French Government, I hear, but I will take a bet that the French General Staff will regard it as their last chance. When one thinks it out all through, it is the French who are really to blame for the Czech frontier, the Ruhr and for Hitler. It is a ghastly mockery and tragedy that we should all pay for their sins—apart from our own—once again. The only interest of the war, if it comes, will be watching for the coming of revolutions as in 1918. But I believe that that will take years and I think the expert view is that we may well be beaten. Hitler is short of food and raw materials now; he will have all the S.E. European resources as his own in no time however if war comes. That is the way of giving them to him quickest.

If you have any private or public comments to make on this lunatic situation before I force myself to write again next week I'd like them.

Next. Have you in mind any one who can edit the *N.S.&N.* supposing I go away or give up the job? If there is war it will probably get suppressed

---

[56] *Truth* had attacked one of *The New Statesman*'s personal advertisements as being an attempt to arrange homosexual liaisons. The advertisement, which had appeared a month earlier, was from a young man wanting to get in touch with a holiday companion who stated that he was 'not interested in the fair sex'.

very soon any way; if there is not I need some one badly. Vallance is invaluable, but most of the time with Beaverbrook: Lloyd is the one person now who can run the paper while I am away and he is terribly often unwell. He is now absolutely indispensable because there is no one else to leave in charge. There ought to be. I have made up my mind as a matter of fact that if this crisis passes I shall not go on editing much longer. There are a number of reasons for this that I won't go into now. If you do think of anyone, please let me know.

K. M.

To KINGSLEY MARTIN, *26 August 1938*

My dear Kingsley,

I fancy we have been becoming a recognised clearing house for this type of 'personal' (there have been others in more veiled terms)! I wonder how many replies are received! As regards money-lenders, I should prefer to decline them *all*.

Yes, I suffer from much about Cz-Sl. The only morsels of comfort I can offer you are the following:—

(1) *Russia* is the key to the position. She will have to be the first to lend material assistance. (Will she?)
(2) Germany is *equally* vulnerable to air-raids.
(3) The Cz unaided can give a pretty good account of themselves.
(4) The inevitable never happens. It is the unexpected *always*.
(5) In a world war Hitler will be beaten and knows it. I agree with you that we should bluff to the hilt; and if the bluff is called, back out. I prefer, meanwhile, meiosis and bogus optimism in public.

As regards editors, I refuse to waste my grey matter inventing successors prematurely. But when I do, they'll produce such a shock that you will certainly withdraw your resignation.

Yours affectionate,
J. M. K.

117

To KINGSLEY MARTIN, *27 August 1938*

Having put on my mantic robe and concentrated, my further reflections on Cz-Slo are—Hitler's speech at Nuremberg[57] will be violent and amount to a quasi-ultimatum demanding a revision of frontiers. After many *parlez-vous* this will be granted. He will again win the appearance of a major success. And it will be without war. What we ought to work for is a maintenance of Cz-Slo's integrity apart from frontier revisions. As a preliminary we ought formally to ask Germany her intentions and demand an international conference. If she refuses it, invite collaboration of U.S.A.

J.M.K.

On 7 September, *The Times* in a leading article suggested that the Czech Government should consider revising its frontiers so as to make the country a more homogeneous state in cultural terms. The British Government issued a statement denying that such a view was Government policy.

From KINGSLEY MARTIN, *9 September 1938*

Dear Maynard,

I am glad you agree with the decision not to have any discussion this week of the pros and cons of *The Times'* case. As you say, it could do no good at all at this juncture, whatever its abstract merits. But do not, please, turn on me for mentioning it in the *N.S.* a little while ago! It was you who said to me some time ago that we *must* discuss frontier revision at some point. The truth is that in the middle of negotiations like these there never is a point at which one can be sure of doing good rather than harm though obviously times when one does harm rather than good. If you start thinking of the various repercussions of what you say it becomes very difficult to say anything. *The Times*, of course, has done a terrible amount of harm. We were all sure that when further, and, I believe, disastrous, concessions were forced from the Czechs, the only hope this week was to stand by them. Coming from *The Times* at such a moment a suggestion of further pressure may well have supported Ribbentrop, who is, rumour has it, keeping everything from Hitler except the general notion that England will not come in. I am told

---

[57] At the Annual Congress of the National Socialist Party, scheduled for 5–12 September.

the idea of the leader at that moment came from Dawson, backed by Horace Wilson and Lord Allen. If it is true that Horace Wilson was in it, Chamberlain may have been too, but about that I have no evidence. Cockburn in *The Week* (a special issue came today) says *The Times* consulted the German Foreign Office!

I don't think Hitler will accept the terms. He is more likely just to keep on the pressure or to demand a plebiscite. This last would be his cleverest move, because a large section of opinion here would hesitate about it, and even those who saw its enormity would feel that a permanent blackmailing weapon in Czechoslovakia, which the Czechs could never deal with drastically, would be almost equally disastrous. This is an issue which we may have to deal with next week.

I won't ring you up next week unless I hear from you. Perhaps it is too tiring for you and I have been wrong in doing so. I am afraid Lydia may think that I have only been after gossip. That would be a mistake. At a time like this it is really essential to have consultation with experienced people who are concerned with the influence of the paper and I am particularly anxious to have your objective advice. Everyone here is horribly close to gossip and worked up. If you feel inclined to write or ring up after Hitler's speech next week I should be glad, but tell Lydia I won't take the initiative in bothering you again.

Love to you both.

Yours,
KINGSLEY

It is just suggested to me that Hitler who always consults astrologers may march tomorrow because Saturday is his lucky day! That would be quite in keeping and fulfil your prediction that the unexpected always happens.

To KINGSLEY MARTIN, *11 September 1938*

My dear Kingsley,

Please don't imagine that I have weakened on the wisdom of frontier revision. Indeed the latest concessions are such as to make one feel even more than before that in the long run frontier revision is a cleaner and *safer* remedy. I was simply trying to be emphatic about what you say yourself—that it is plain as a pikestaff that at this juncture one must back up the Czechs, and particularly *not* suggest to Hitler that he can get what to him seems more.

Also (as I was trying to say on the telephone) this shot is very far from *certain*, as the success of other home rule measures has shown. The present proposals insert a wedge between the Sudetens and Hitler. It is not such a jolly thing to be a German to-day and the Sudetens, and not least their leaders, may genuinely *prefer* the present plan. It is not impossible that the peace and amity of Switzerland may eventually come to pass.

I believe in living from hand to mouth in international affairs because the successive links in the causal nexus are so completely unpredictable. One does well to evade *immediate* evils.

I cannot imagine a nastier crew than your alleged conspirators behind *The Times* article—particularly Allen who has raised my nausea for years past. Geoffrey Dawson is a very *queer* personality and with a good side to him, however nefarious his methods.

I don't expect any resolution of these positions tomorrow. There is time yet, and there may easily be wisdom (as King-Hall suggests this week) in reserving fire—though this is very unnerving to those not behind the scenes. If only one had ultimate confidence in Neville and Halifax!—which I at least haven't, though I don't yet reject the idea that they may be doing very well. Every day the force of world opinion is gathering force and the cup filling up.

Lydia was so firm on the telephone because I had finished a long bit of dictating only a minute before you rang up. But telephone talks *are* very tiring.

Yours,

J. M. K.

From KINGSLEY MARTIN, *13 September 1938*

Dear Maynard,

My worst fears about the effect of the effort to solve the Sudeten problem inside Czechoslovakia appear to be confirmed. The news this afternoon is that there are widespread acts of provocation throughout the German-speaking areas and that the Czechs are described in the Berlin press as shooting down the Germans in large numbers. I understand that the French General Staff expects Hitler to march in a few days. The other pieces of news. The British Government's attitude on Saturday was so weak that the French were almost desperate and even the very moderate statement that was obtained from them on Sunday night was extracted by Daladier after six hours pleading on the telephone. The reason for this is not purely ideological. I heard today from an excellent source that the strategic and military position is regarded as almost desperate. Of course there may be propagandist reasons behind this, but I gather that the Government thinks not only that it will take some time for the Americans to come in, but also that the German air fleet can accomplish to a large extent a blockade of England almost at once, and that the French air position is appallingly bad. That Italy would stop up the Mediterranean is taken for granted.

Looking back at it today, I realise that I made a mistake a fortnight ago *in the way* I referred to frontier revision. There is only one way in which the Czechs would probably listen to it, and I gather that in a last emergency they would have been prepared to revise the frontier so that the areas with 90% Germans would be excluded, if they had had an absolute guarantee of the new frontier from England, France and Russia. I put it in the worst way possible and so did *The Times* at a much worse moment and of course with apparent authority. This proposal is now being considered, but probably too late. I think that I shall have a very careful leading article this week, saying that the Germans obviously intend to play Sinn Fein tactics in Czechoslovakia, which cannot be dealt with while Hitler is mobilising on the frontier, and that given such a guarantee as I have spoken of, frontier revision might be the safer course for the Czechs. In my view it was the only possible way of saving a world war and I regret I did not go into this fully three weeks ago. Not that anyone would [have] taken any notice! We said it with great clarity and force in March and I have referred to it several times since, but we have not emphasised sufficiently the necessity of the guarantee.

If you have any thoughts on this when you have read the paper tomorrow morning, I should be glad if you would ring me up.

Yours,

KINGSLEY

Pierre Cot[58] is apparently singled out as the Jaurès[59] of the next war. The German, Italian and now French Fascist papers are discovering him,

[58] Formerly France's Air Minister.
[59] Jean Jaurès was a pre-1914 French Socialist leader who was an important intellectual force behind pre-war French re-armament, even though he was a pacificist. He was assassinated on 31 July 1914.

obviously by pre-arrangement and supported by Hitler who specifically referred to him in his speech as the manufacturer of war and the saboteur of French air strength. He was just stopped from speaking at Sedan where his destruction was demanded on posters, etc. One paper said he 'ought to be shot'. He is now confined to his house under police protection.

Between this letter and the next the Prime Minister made three flights to meet Hitler on 15, 22 and 29 September. As well the Czechs mobilised their armed forces and the French did so partially. In Britain, the Government recalled Parliament, mobilised the fleet, issued gas masks in areas likely to suffer from bombing and began digging trench shelters in London Parks.

On 30 September the Governments of Britain, France, Germany and Italy reached agreement at Munich. Under the agreement Czechoslovakia was to cede certain Sudeten German districts to Germany immediately and to hold plebiscites in other areas before the final frontiers of the country were determined.

To KINGSLEY MARTIN, *1 October 1938*

My dear Kingsley,

These are my basic reflections so far:–

(1) This settlement would not have been too great a price to pay for peace. But with any sort of honest policy peace was never genuinely at risk. The pacific impulses of the nation have been shamelessly exploited and the final piece of stage management was as wicked as it was skilful.

(2) We have suffered one of the worst pieces of trickery in history. Honourable international policy has suffered a terrific reverse by the unscrupulous intrigues, quite unsupported by public opinion, of our own pro-Nazis. But they have played their cards so damned well, that more than usual of the wisdom of the serpent is needed on our part. (The attitude of *The Times* must have been revolting to almost everyone.)

(3) Russia (and of course France too in a different way) has been greatly to blame. Why, on earth, didn't she invite officers

from our W[ar]O[ffice] to inspect with their own eyes the Russian state of preparedness? There has never been any convincing evidence of Russia's reliability, and she has played straight into Chamberlain's hands, making it as easy as possible for his policy of ignoring her.

(4) It is *not certain* that the present settlement may not be a good thing in the long run. Viewed quite drily, there is a great deal to be said for it. Hitler's next move is not very obvious or easy.* This makes our right reaction to it exceptionally difficult. The settlement itself cannot be rightly denounced as indefensible and monstrous. What is certain is something rather different:– namely that the sympathies and methods which have brought it about cannot be safely allowed to continue in charge. This time they may, by historic luck, have carried through a necessary thing which decent men could not have accomplished. This means that a frontal attack on the settlement itself is not the wisest course.

(5) I suppose that popular emotion will shortly be capitalised in the shape of a General Election. The most important immediate political objective should be a union of forces against Chamberlain. This is much wider than a Popular Front and will require a very special kind of electoral strategy. I believe that this should be in the first instance a purely *ad hoc election*, without any union of parties or much attempt at an agreed programme. It should be straight anti-Chamberlain, with liberal give-and-take in the constituencies, the most likely anti-Chamberlain candidates being supported by all of us irrespective of his party:– e.g. Winston, Eden, Duff Cooper, Boothby, Nicolson, etc., should be unopposed by Liberals or Labour. *Every* sitting M.P. who is against Chamberlain should be supported by all opposition parties.

(6) One's own state of mind at the moment is painful in the way in which only a *mixed* state can be. Intense relief and satisfied cowardice joined with rage and indignation, *plus* that

* It must be, I should say, an alliance with Poland for the invasion of Russia.

special emotion appropriate to the state of having been *swindled*; the whole nation *swindled* as never in its history.

We are returning to London next Sunday. Come down here any night this week if you are free and have a mind to.

Yours ever,

J. M. K.

Keynes also submitted an article for *The New Statesman*. When he had received the proofs he wrote again.

To KINGSLEY MARTIN, *4 October 1938*

Dear Kingsley,

Your printers did marvellously :– the corrections I have made are not due to them, but to a desire to clarify and, in one passage, expand the argument.

I thought that yesterday's debate did not go too well for Chamberlain, and today's may go worse. A General Election looks rather less likely. I don't yet agree with you that Fascism is strengthened in this country. The damned thing about the settlement is that from our selfish and short-sighted point of view there is so much to be said for it. Good *may* result from what no wise or good man could have brought himself to accomplish. Vile and dirty work can be beneficial to those who do it—Or do you believe in the eternal justice of the world? I don't.

Come down on Thursday afternoon, if when the time comes you are in the mood.

Yrs,

J. M. K.

Local opinion here, e.g. the local builder and his friends, are anti-Chamberlain. An election might not prove a good calculation.

The article appeared in the issue of 8 October.

From The New Statesman and Nation, *8 October 1938*

MR CHAMBERLAIN'S FOREIGN POLICY

The public has handled itself in a manner beyond criticism. But it may misapprehend the motives and purposes lying behind the drama of the last weeks. It imagines that peace has been snatched from the cauldron of war by the skill, courage and tenacity of a single man. It may well be that peace was in danger at the last moment through the Prime Minister's reckless pursuit of his own aims, and his delay in taking the steps necessary to make clear the ultimate position of this country. But even this is unlikely; and the pacific impulses of the nation have been exploited to serve undisclosed aims, which, if they had been disclosed, would have been approved by some but repudiated by many. It can scarcely be questioned that at several stages in the negotiations an honourable settlement could have been secured without any risk to peace, if an unambiguous stand had been taken by this country, France *and Russia* speaking with one voice. Such a stand has been consistently refused. The Prime Minister was never preparing for the actuality of war. The total omission of any reference even to the possibility of military action by this country in the correspondence published in the White Paper, the avoidance of conversations with Russia, the reluctance and extraordinary delay in ordering the mobilisation of the Fleet are not consistent with any other explanation. Neither the Prime Minister nor Herr Hitler ever intended for one moment that the play-acting should devolve into reality. For it would be a mistake to attribute extreme carelessness to the one or insanity to the other of these two astute politicians. The actual course of events has been dictated by the fact that the objectives of Herr Hitler and Mr Chamberlain were not different, but the same; whilst Russian policy has played into

Mr Chamberlain's hands by making it easy for him to ignore her.

The course of events can be made intelligible by the following considerations. Herr Hitler has explained that his ultimate objective is the Ukraine. The Balkans, Western Europe, the Colonies *might* have been the desired sphere of his expansion. But he has openly decided otherwise; and in these matters he is a man of his word. Yet the position of Czechoslovakia, with a well-armed force of a million men, strongly entrenched, and in alliance with Russia, presented a danger to his flank which could not be overlooked and must be dealt with first. The inner diplomatic game has developed, therefore, as follows. We have been bought off by Germany's agreeing to forgo a fleet and soft-pedalling on the Colonies; France by her renunciation of Western aims (perhaps including Spain, so far as Germany is concerned); Italy by her side-stepping the Balkans; Poland by a sacrifice of the Silesian Germans (for the time being) and the hope of a share of the Russian spoils. Only Czechoslovakia had to be sacrificed. The next move, presumably, is a German alliance with Poland with a view to the seizure of the Ukraine, simultaneously with a Siberian venture by Japan (this move being, however, seriously endangered by Japan's blunder in Central China). Mussolini, as he well knows, is left nowhere; but for the rest of the world that is only a detail.

The attraction of this *politik* to ourselves is obvious. Our sea-power and our overseas Empire remain for the present unchallenged; our own peace may be secured for a considerable period; we are given time to complete our air defences; Mussolini's Mediterranean aims are left in the lurch; even the Spanish Government may benefit; and who knows but that in the end Herr Hitler will be the second dictator to retreat from Moscow. If, on the other hand, it should happen that the capitalist branch of the totalitarian faith defeats its socialist sister, how many Englishmen care? It is Russia and Italy which have suffered diplomatic defeat. We and France have only sacrificed our honour and our engagements to a civilised and faithful nation, and fraternised with what is vile. This, at any rate, is the short-run calculation. The Prime Minister thinks it a small price to pay and can swallow with a good conscience a week's play-acting, beginning with gas masks and ending with bouquets, even if it involved a brief moment of harsh plucking at mothers' heart-strings.

The next letter from Kingsley Martin has not survived, but it probably contained in part an idea for a series of published conversations between Martin and various public figures. Keynes's contribution followed earlier ones from Winston Churchill, Herbert Morrison and David Lloyd George, and appeared under the title 'Democracy and Efficiency' on 28 January 1939.[60]

To KINGSLEY MARTIN, *23 November 1938*

My dear Kingsley,

Apologies for not having replied to your letter sooner. It duly reached me. But I have been away from my secretary, and had as much or more work than I am allowed to do in present circumstances.

I agree that your idea is worth following up, and so far as I am concerned I would be ready to give an interview. I am not sure what would be the best way to approach Winston. I doubt if I am the right man, but could do so if other means fail. I think the fee would be important since he has to earn his living by journalism. I should be inclined to get some of the other names first and then, if it looked a good list, write to him direct. He would be more likely to agree after he had had a chance of seeing who the other people were.

I saw you in the distance at the play and wished I could have

[60] *JMK*, vol. XXI, pp. 491–500.

seen something of you, but my duties that day had used me up to the last drop, and I was under orders to get back to bed.

All this does not mean I am worse. Quite the contrary. I am still steadily improving.

Yours ever,

J. M. K.

The next letter went to the Literary Editor of *The New Statesman*. The enclosure appeared, slightly re-written, in 'A London Diary' in the *New Statesman*'s issue of 4 March.

To RAYMOND MORTIMER, *20 February 1939*

Dear Raymond,

I think you were quite right not to give a further notice of 'On the Frontier'.[61] After all, there had been a lengthy one already. I think there were details in the play and in the production of merit, particularly the music. But, unquestionably, it was a failure. And the authors decidedly deserve to be rapped on the knuckles. They are getting too old for so much infantilism and amateurism.

I had a word with Kingsley on the telephone this morning, and was glad to discover from the strength of his voice that he was much better. I mentioned to him that I had written something about the Jooss Ballet, which I was thinking of sending you for Polycritic. He encouraged me to do so. I have written it in a style so as to be suitable for that column. It might be better there, because it is not intended to take the place of an eventual theatrical criticism in the right part of the paper. But, of course, it could be re-written so as to fit the other context. We had the Jooss Ballet here all last week, and Lydia and I went every night, which is rare behaviour on our part. Lydia regards the new ballet, *Chronica*, as 'a thunderbolt', a

---

[61] This play by Auden and Isherwood opened at the Arts Theatre, Cambridge. Keynes then attempted to take the production to the West End.

thing of extraordinary importance and merit. We have been
friendly but critical to this Ballet hitherto. But really now it is
something totally different in degree of merit—and astonishing
surprise.

Yours ever,
[copy initialled] J. M. K.

I saw the Kurt Jooss Ballet last week at the Arts Theatre at
Cambridge where they gave the first performance of the
important new production 'Chronica'. There is a great treat
waiting for London when they open at the Old Vic in May with
this and their other new production 'Spring Tale'. When Jooss
first left Germany and found a *pied à terre* at Dartington Hall,
he seemed to have lost himself. But now, after a considerable
interval, he has fulfilled more than all his promise and surpassed
by a long way anything he has done before. It is arguable that
these two new ballets must be reckoned amongst the most
finished and complete works of art which have been given us
since the war. Both are full length productions. 'Chronica',
which plays for seventy-five minutes without a break, is a
profound and expressive mime, yet extraordinarily rich in
choreography and formal dancing, in a renaissance setting, of
the rise and fall of a Dictator. One would have thought it
impossible with such a theme for art to transmute the political
idea, but the sublimation is accomplished, and, as a work of the
imagination, it is ten times better than their celebrated 'Green
Table'. It is a satisfactory thing that the only example we yet
have, where the emotion of an artist has successfully handled
the contemporary scene with bitterness and political purpose
washed away and beauty and dignity in their place, should be
presented to us by a company of Germans. The style of this
ballet provokes comparison with the later work of Massine. A
good judge who was with me considered that it was superior,
especially in the perfection of its detail and the unbroken purity
of feeling. Jooss, as an independent creator, may have had an

important advantage over Massine in that he has chosen that the accompanying music should be of no importance. 'Spring Tale', by contrast a fairy tale of the lightest, most airy kind, is a perfect vehicle for the incomparable artistry of Hans Zullig, who here shows himself one of the finest dancers of the day. This ballet is successful in giving a contemporary touch and much originality of movement to a traditional theme. And it is no disadvantage to 'Chronica' and 'Spring Tale' that they are magnificently dressed by Madame Karinska. The company as a whole has made marked progress in its technique and is fully equal to the choreographer's demands. If there is such a thing as progress in art, this new phase of the Jooss Ballet is the biggest advance made since the death of Diaghileff.

The next letter, in June 1939, concerned the format of *The New Statesman*.

To KINGSLEY MARTIN, *23 June 1939*

Dear Kingsley,

Since our meeting the other day, and after thinking things over, I have hardened very definitely against pictures. I wish you would enquire what various sample people might think about it. The results of all my enquiries are violently adverse, and I am now inclined to agree.

It is felt that it would completely destroy the character of the paper with very little compensating advantage. Moreover everyone now is trying to introduce pictures, and many people are bankrupting themselves trying to imitate the success of *Picture Post*. It is not as if we were doing badly as we are. We are doing extremely well. It would be a foolish thing to waste our resources on a fiasco, or do anything which would appear to destroy our own rather special character. Do please consider the matter.

If we are prepared to gamble on spending £50 to £100 a week

on increasing circulation, I am sure there are much more characteristic ways of doing it. I admit that you are right in thinking that an isolated article by a distinguished contributor generally does very little for the circulation of that particular week, but I do not think that the same thing applies at all to a regular continuing policy of having, say, one article a week by an outside, distinguished contributor.

At any rate, I thought I had better let you know at once how very violently I am now coming down on the present side of the fence.

Yours ever,
[copy not signed or initialled]

There was another gap in the correspondence until mid-August, just before Keynes went off for a cure at Royat.

To KINGSLEY MARTIN, *14 August 1939*

My dear Kingsley,

I did not feel inspired to write anything in response to your incitement.[62] Nor, so far as I can make out, were those of your correspondents who did respond. There is really nothing to say at this juncture. If there were any legitimate grievances to deal with it would be another matter. As there are none, it seems to me we have to rely on improvising something when chance and fate sends the unpredictable opportunity.

It is difficult to see how some sort of appearance of a crisis in the next month can be avoided, but I shall be extremely surprised at a warlike conclusion. Hitler's argument that he must get Danzig, because it does not really matter either to him or to anyone else, seems to me unanswerable. In due course, Danzig will be incorporated in the Reich, which will leave the *de facto* situation substantially what it is.

[62] 'Peace Terms', *New Statesman and Nation*, 5 August 1939.

I am extremely well, doing quite a lot of work, and taking much exercise. Yesterday, for the first time for three years, I took quite a long walk on the top of the Downs. Tomorrow, however, we are leaving for France for a three weeks cure at Royat, a bath place, much recommended for my complaint. We must see you after we are back.

Yours ever,

J. M. KEYNES

Keynes was, of course, spectacularly wrong as regards the probabilities of war, for on 23 August came the Soviet–German non-aggression pact, on 1 September Germany invaded Poland, and on 3 September Britain and France declared war on Germany.

During the early part of the war—until mid-1940—Kingsley Martin, according to his biographer went through a period of 'wretched indecision'.[63] Keynes was made aware of this both by conversations with him and letters from friends such as Peter Lucas. His views were reflected in a letter to Edward Whitley.

To EDWARD WHITLEY, *3 October 1939*

Dear Whitley,

I have only seen Kingsley Martin once since the war, but, judging from that occasion, and from reports which have reached me, his mind is, I think, in a state of a good deal of oscillation and subject from time to time to moods of extreme defeatism. I cannot feel perfectly sure that he might not suddenly come out in the paper with a leader demanding immediate peace on almost any terms.

I feel rather strongly that there should be no such change in the policy of the paper until it has been fully discussed by the Board and with the rest of the staff; and that a surprise move on these lines would be very disastrous.

[63] C. H. Rolph, *Kingsley: The Life, Letters and Diaries of Kingsley Martin* (London, 1973), p. 237.

I should like to hear from you whether you agree with me about this. I shall try to see Kingsley to-day, and otherwise will write to him. But it would be preferable to let him know how I feel in conversation if possible.

Yours sincerely,
[copy initialled] J. M. K.

Then on 4 October, Martin asked for Keynes's comments on a piece by George Bernard Shaw, entitled 'Uncommon Sense About the War'.

To KINGSLEY MARTIN, *4 October 1939*

Dear Kingsley,

My opinion is

(1) that the article is mischievous and that your editorial judgement should be against accepting it; I think it would do harm both ways—both to the chances of success in peace and to the prospects of success in war.

and (2) that in any case you ought to take the advice of the Censor before publishing it (this applies not to the whole of the article but to one or two extensive passages in it).

If after re-reading it you want to proceed with publication, I agree with you that others should be consulted,*—the available members of the Board immediately and the other two as soon as possible. I should also attach importance to the opinions of Lloyd and Raymond [Mortimer]. If I am in a minority, I still reserve my liberty of action but should if I used it resign from the Board.

From your own standpoint I believe the article would do great harm.

Yrs,
J. M. KEYNES

I wrote you a much shorter but similar letter last night and posted it before I realised that the evening posts don't function— hence this repetition.

* They should have this letter of mine as well as the article.

133

I shall be out from 10.45 to 12.30 and 3 to 5.15 approx; otherwise available on the telephone.

A letter to Whitley carried the story further to the appearance of the Shaw piece on 7 October.

From a letter to EDWARD WHITLEY, *10 October 1939*

It is very helpful to have your letter of October 8th and know your opinion. I had a long talk with Kingsley Martin when I went up last week. He arrived, as I had feared, in an extremely defeatist mood, but I talked him round a bit and, at any rate, he agreed that he must be careful in what he says in the paper. Immediately after this, however, another issue arose, on which I had rather a row. G.B.S. sent in an article which included passages which seemed to me mischievous and untrue and capable of doing a good deal of harm, if they were printed. After much trouble, I was successful in insisting that these passages should be deleted. G.B.S. himself raised no great trouble about this, but it was held by Kingsley Martin, and also by others who were consulted, that the principles of free speech required that we should print what he said, in spite of the objections which I urged. As I have said, we compromised in the end, but I cannot feel in present circumstance, that it is one's duty in all cases to print anything, even if it is mischievous and untrue. There is at present no censorship of opinion as distinct from facts. But we shall certainly jeopardise the continuance of this happy state of affairs, unless we censor ourselves.

You will have seen the form in which the article eventually appeared, which seemed to me harmless, and I took no objection at all to the paper as a whole.

The trouble is that Kingsley Martin fluctuates so violently in his opinions from one day to another, so that one never quite knows what to expect. I know this nervousness is shared by other members of the staff, particularly by Lloyd, I think, before he left the paper, the other day. However, knowing your opinion and being able to rely on your support, I will keep an eye on the situation, though it is not very easy to do so unless one sees Kingsley Martin pretty often.

Keynes then submitted a letter for publication in reply to Shaw.[64] The argument with Martin continued by letter.

From KINGSLEY MARTIN, *10 October 1939*

Dear Maynard,

Thanks for point *re* young men and volunteers—which I'll go into.

Re your letter which I'm glad to have. I have not in fact asked for any precise war aims for some time because I agree with you that they are not definable now. I think there are important things that we ought to do and proclaim, but 'war aims' cannot be published in any detail by the Government, I think. India may well be the most important—almost on the map soon—I find Hoare agrees about its importance but I see little hope of any satisfactory compromise. It's not broken down yet, but it's not going well and if there is civil disturbance, concentration camps again and so on the results in U.S.A. will be very serious. Also it will help U.S.S.R.

Result of recent talk with Cabinet Ministers is my belief that if one section of the Cabinet gets its way we shall soon cease fighting Hitler and join with Germany against Stalin—if the Reichswehr can be persuaded to do so! But I think the odds are against this party winning. It's very complex!

[copy not signed or initialled]

A week later, Keynes was commenting on an article of Martin's entitled 'Peace Terms'.[65]

From KINGSLEY MARTIN, *19 October 1939*

Dear Maynard,

Can't answer your question accurately especially as I do not remember just how I put it in my letter. But I don't know more than one or two for certain.

[64] *JMK*, vol. xxii, pp. 36–7.
[65] *JMK*, vol. xxii, p. 37.

It's a terribly complex business. Bully their government about collective security and you get not what you want but a guarantee of Poland! If no one had bullied them they might have kept out of war for a bit longer any way. Bully them now and the result will be enough to stop them getting peace—which some of their staff want desperately mainly because they still hope Hitler will turn against Stalin—and not enough to make them wage war purposely or for possible and proper objectives. I wrote I believed in the ideal peace!

G.B.S. this week is quite harmless. I have had a correspondence with the F.O., with whom we are on excellent terms strongly approving our publication of G.B.S. and recommending me to cut out an anti-Musso. piece from Wells. This I was going to do any way but I thought it good policy to make a virtue of it. I have seen Hoare and Halifax the last few days. The second is charming, isn't he? The first—well, he is a very able—careerist.

KINGSLEY

There matters stood until Martin asked Keynes for advice.

From KINGSLEY MARTIN, *27 January 1940*

Forgive this messy scribble—secretary's gone.
Dear Maynard,

I'd like your advice. Oswald Mosley has written a very persuasive sort of pamphlet called 'The British Peace and How to Get It'. The usual stuff about Jewish finance and the folly of international talk instead of national construction. I think this line attractive to many people now because few people see how the war can be *won* and how the peace would bring anything much better than the last. At least that is the common view of correspondents and it looks as if we shall in fact get big blocks and not small nations or Federal Union...Any way the question is this—the B[ritish]U[nion] [of Fascists] wants to advertise their pamphlet in the *N.S.&N.* Should one advertise those who want to cut one's throat—or give public proof that the press boycotts Mosley? The advert problem is difficult and I'd like your view.

KINGSLEY

To KINGSLEY MARTIN, *29 January 1940*

Dear Kingsley,

That is a very perplexing problem. In my opinion, one has the right to withhold from the enemies of liberty that which they seek to deprive us of. But on general grounds one would wish to postpone exercising this right, so long as possible.

In the present case I suggest a compromise, namely, to agree to advertise a straight publisher's announcement of their pamphlet, with title, price etc., but not to include any blurb or similar additional matter.

I had meetings last week about my Deferred Pay proposals,[66] both with the Labour Front Bench and with the T.U.C. The Front Bench was not impressive, and it was difficult to see what useful purpose their continued existence serves. But my discussion with the T.U.C. was particularly interesting, responsible and serious, and in an excellent atmosphere. Clearly they were not unsympathetic, but whether they would be prepared to take any initiative in the matter is another question. After all, that is not their affair. Clearly the right course is for the Chancellor of the Exchequer to take the initiative and for the T.U.C. to bargain about it on details. Put across with proper leadership, I do not believe the T.U.C. would object to the plan out of hand. Yet the prospect of the Chancellor doing anything whatever on any conceivable subject appears to be remote.

I should add that I have considerably improved the scheme from the Labour point of view, mainly by 3 additions, namely, full children's allowances, paid to the mother in cash out of national taxation; the deferred pay to be entrusted, if the man wishes it, not to the Post Office Savings Bank, but to his trade union or friendly society or similar body, who would have the control over releasing it to him for special purposes; and the repayment of the deferred pay after the war by a capital levy.

[66] See *JMK*, vol. XXII, pp. 91–9.

With these additions, it seems to me that it would be extraordinarily misguided of Labour to refuse the arrangement, which is not merely a piece of technique for solving the war problem, but is taking advantage of war conditions to introduce important new social reforms and to make a much greater move towards equality than has been made for a long time past.

Please, however, keep this confidential for the time being. I do not want anything to appear in print until the T.U.C. have reached their considered opinion, and when that happens, I shall bring out my own pamphlet as soon as may be. Meanwhile, I am keeping Cole and Laski fully informed.

Yours,

[copy initialled] J.M.K.

Martin's indecision about the war continued well into 1940 as indicated by a letter from Dublin, where he had gone to interview De Valera about Irish views on the war.

From KINGSLEY MARTIN, *25 May 1940*

My dear Maynard,

I am staying here till Friday morning because I cannot get my essential interview until Thursday night. I'll tell you what I can of the situation when I get back.

I have been thinking a lot and with much regret on other things while I walk these familiar Dublin streets. There are several things I'd like to say to you. Broadly I think you were justified in attacking my gloom last Thursday—but you were not right in saying that I was indulging in gloomy never never hypotheses. You may recall that you were annoyed with me early in the war because I said that the small neutrals would fall into Germany and that we should find ourselves in a desperate position. If my pessimism, of which I am much ashamed, were not so often right, I might have cured myself of it. But it's been, blast it, incredibly right, and therefore has got reinforced every week since 1931. Occasionally, as over Norway, I have conquered it and written optimistically—and been writing with a more depressing effect on morale than when I am gloomy. On Thursday my mind was filled with the knowledge of what was actually happening in France which was not in the papers at all. It's inconceivable except to a person of riotous imagination. The result of this was to make me want the views of you and Rowntree on the question of ultimate policy. I know it's been faced by the Authorities and we may all be faced with it shortly. Personally I would rather fight to any bitter end because I and my kind are on a proscribed list for execution, but that is a bad reason for condemning hundreds of thousands of people to death who have not so much to lose. That of course is not a matter for public discussion, but our meeting was not public.

I doubt if gaol is the right remedy for people like me. I think uniform is a better [one] and I intend to seek service of some sort directly I get back to London. Reviewing the past nine months I think the paper has been generally encouraging to the right things. Dick has been great and so has Noel. I have only occasionally been very dour—and I think it's a suicidal impulse that comes over me and which is of course just what the Nazis want to produce. That is why I am so furious with myself this weekend. The paper in general was courageous and good, I think, but the first two Diary par[a]s, *which I thought a brave call to resist against odds* seem now to me to have been mischievous and precisely wrong. For the point about the Nazis is that they are not Martians, but only try to behave like them. Inside those monstrous flame throwers there are little men with souls somewhere, and in the bombing aeroplanes are frightened men who can be defeated. Yes, that was a bad piece of work—emotional and depressing.

It bothers me all the time at such a time as this because people read my words like a bible! I've met casually in official jobs and others half a dozen almost devoted admirers and readers in the most unexpected places between London and Dublin in the last few days!

Yes, it will be good to find a uniform.

KINGSLEY

From KINGSLEY MARTIN, *26 May 1940*

Dear Maynard,

Had a night's sleep and balance restored. Ought not to have worked off a brood on you.

See D.V. tomorrow and back Friday. Difficult to tell here how the news is. R.A.F. seems miraculous.

Here the war is a hurling match. The money all staked on the allies and some annoyance that they do not seem to play up to form. Some realisation of the true situation now penetrating to some minds.

K.M.

To KINGSLEY MARTIN, *27 May 1940*

Dear Kingsley,

Your letter raises more matters and more intense ones than one can well deal with in a letter. I am coming back to town tomorrow and expect to stay until Friday, with plenty of free time. Meanwhile—

(1) I am sure that you are doing your most useful work where you are at present. I have felt that the paper has been useful, and it may very well get more and more useful as time goes on and the opportunities for independence diminish. It is good for you to work off more gloomy and desperate feelings on your friends, and they must not complain if you do so! I am *quite clear* that it is your duty to continue where you are.

I thought there was much in this week's issue to like. Crossman's leader[67] excellent, and Y.Y. very sweet.[68] I rather agree with your own criticisms of the first part of Critic, but, all the same, I do not think it was much calculated to make a wrong impression on anyone.

(2) My objection to discussing remote (or I would rather say unclothed, since I do not mean very improbable) hypotheses is that it is absolutely useless and simply paralyses one for more urgent and necessary activities. It is absolutely useless because one has to know all kinds of unknown details in order to arrive at any decision of the slightest interest. You must not suppose, because other people do not spend their time discussing the worst, that such thoughts do not pass through their minds. Of course they do—but not, in my case at any rate, with that clarity in detail that makes them a proper subject for reasonable judgement.

(3) You are really deceiving yourself in supposing that you have prophetic insight into all that is going to happen. If in private talk one has predicted every conceivable disaster the imagination can conceive, when things go wrong something or

[67] 'Legend and Reality', *New Statesman and Nation*, 25 May 1940.
[68] 'Wishful', *loc. cit.*

other which happens can hardly help bearing some resemblance to one of the predictions. The particular one of which you remind me, where I said I thought your fears were absurd, has in fact turned out, not correct, as you now seem to think, but exactly the opposite of the truth. You told me, if you will throw your mind back, that the Governments of all the neutrals were, to put it shortly, pro-German and that, at the first serious threat, or even without it, they would allow themselves to be dictated to by the Germans. Indeed, you went so far as to say that even their sympathies were often pro-German. In fact the exact opposite has happened. Norway, Holland and Belgium* have come in on our side. Surely you will remember that my reaction was that these neutrals might be terrified, might be blackmailed, might be defeated, but to say that they were not sympathisers with the Allied cause was the absurdity.

(4) Of course, gaol is not the right remedy for people like you. That is to say, so long as it is only to me that they talk. If you put it all in the paper, it might be another matter! The right chastisement for people like you is to write every week with candour and encouragement, leaving your public feeling instructed, with fewer illusions and yet with more resolution.

There is one point I wish you would think over before we meet—the question of an additional Director. What would you say to Leonard [Woolf]?

Yours ever,

J. M. KEYNES

Keynes also wrote an encouraging note to Richard Crossman, who had worked on the paper since 1938.

* Which remains true even though they surrender.

To R. H. S. CROSSMAN, *27 May 1940*

My dear Crossman,

Just a line to say how much I like your leader in this week's paper. You are, of course, only too right that the lamp-posts are still untenanted by those who ought to be there. In the Treasury, in particular, there is not a sign of a new broom.

If this goes on indefinitely, the strongest agitation may become necessary. But, as I read the situation, all that has to wait for the end of the battle. It is not of absolutely immediate importance and must wait until other matters have been stabilised. To the best of my belief, the entourage in No. 10 are under no illusions.

My mother has been looking up some old correspondence which I wrote to her when I was in the Treasury during the last war. I find that, as late as the end of 1917, I was still in a state of violent rage against the incompetence, madness and wickedness of those in authority.[69] I was then pretty near the centre of things, in daily contact with the War Cabinet. Yet I evidently thought things then pretty nearly as bad as some of us think them now. Yet we did win. I suppose that the others, though in different ways, were worse!

At any rate, as you say in your leader, we have this time crossed the watershed much earlier.

Yours sincerely,
[copy initialled] J. M. K.

From KINGSLEY MARTIN, *2 June 1940*

Dear Maynard,

Life becomes much more tolerable as real danger appears. Reality is never too difficult, because action removes fear and conflict. The almost intolerable thing is the doubt, conflict, sense of guilt and responsibility—above all the muddle—of a period during which some leadership is required and there seems no escape from a direction which leads to a terrible, if not necessarily

[69] See *JMK*, vol. XVI, pp. 265–6.

a completely disastrous conclusion! At the moment things seem fairly clear. The next drive will almost certainly be towards Paris, with Musso making things difficult in some way in the French rear. The R.A.F. should help the French and let us be bombed. Everything really depends on whether the French can hold against the same tactics that smashed thro' before. They won't permanently hold the Somme, I guess, but may do so long enough to enable them to hold the second line protecting Havre and Paris. If so and the German petrol and pilots begin to run short, there is a chance. All propaganda apart the B[ritish]E[xpeditionary]F[orce]'s performance is really extraordinary and there was obviously nothing wrong with the morale of the French in Belgium. Indeed I gather they have sacrificed themselves to enable the British to get away and to give Weygand some time to dig in.

The chance of victory is better as a result of the attack. Stalemate was as good as could be expected from the sitzkrieg. I listed all the asset factors at the beginning of last week and told Brailsford (rather to his surprise in view of my usual pessimism!) to make the first *N.S.* note this week a description of these hopeful factors. I am not too hopeful in my heart, but I agree with you about the useless and paralysing result of dwelling on the dangers. My general view of this war ever since we guaranteed Poland without Russia has been the same as L-G's and I still think, tho' not with assurance, that I was right in backing his attitude last October.[70]

As regards the paper. There is no doubt at all about its influence. Just because it has endlessly discussed the problems and conflicts, been partly pacifist and 'left' etc. it has been responsible for converting more people of the pacifist and left way of thinking than anything else—except Hitler. This has long been part of my depression. We are the most valuable of government propaganda organs because we are more candid than most other papers. Moreover there is a feeling that we have been substantially right along with Churchill and the Labour people—or some of them.

Comic at Liverpool airport the other day. I arrived to find that the C.I.D. man in charge and the immigration officer had just had an argument about who should read the *N.S.* first. The immigration officer kept back my passport till last until I was wondering why. The reason was that he wanted the chance to speak to the editor of a paper he called his bible!

As to this question of gloom and prophecy—it is now of no importance and egotistic to discuss it. Possibly I'll amuse myself by writing about it at some length in a memo sometime. You have not, I think, quite understood about it. It is not that I have claimed any special foresight or that I have foretold all disasters in order to be right as you suggest. The point is that

[70] In the autumn of 1939 Lloyd George had favoured a patched-up peace with Germany. See K. Martin, *Editor* (London, 1968), ch. 14, entitled 'Lloyd George and the Policy of Despair'.

it has long seemed to me certain, not hypothetical—that Germany would overrun Europe if permitted but that the result of pressing for resistance would be a war too late—that is when it would be desperately dangerous and appallingly destructive of civilisation. Chamberlain would obviously *never* do the things we asked—collective security, Russia and the democratic appeal to the anti-Nazis everywhere—and the result of our making these demands would be to force him into a war with the minimum of allies and on the worst possible terrain. This is what has haunted my mind—that we who opposed him would not get the action we wanted in time and should be indirectly at least responsible for the war. It was this I got desperate about because so few of my friends seemed to feel this and I could see it as almost a certainty. They were right not to worry about it, I suppose, because there was no alternative line of action. I was always searching for a way out. War did come just like that (see a series of articles I wrote about the invasion of Austria and after) and I felt and feel a ridiculous amount of guilt about it. Similarly about the neutrals. You, as always, were extremely optimistic. You said things were going well and that all the neutrals would rally to us. As usual then reacting to optimism I no doubt exaggerated my case. But I knew

(a) that in each neutral government there were pro-Germans—so much so as I now know that British staff secrets were always passed on to Germany if confided;

(b) [that] people who, while not pro-Nazis exactly, were afraid to accept support when Britain had so much failed before; and

(c) that in the war of today the mass of the population of any civilised country will prefer up to the very last minute to avoid war if conceivably possible and (however much they dislike the Germans) will even, like the Danes, prefer German occupation to a hopeless war.

I follow neutral opinion a good deal. Britain has had very little support anywhere since Munich and even violent hostility in most neutral countries since we failed to help Poland. You seemed to me quite deluded about the power, prestige and popularity of Britain. Actually the story of Sweden and Norway during the Finnish war, the behaviour of the Quislings and indeed, I think, of most Norwegians and of Sweden since the acceptance of the Danes, the division of the Dutch and the Belgians bear me out.

I could elaborate this but won't. The point is that the division between pro-German and pro-ally or anti-German is no longer the real one—the choice is between giving in (possibly even being a traitor on the one hand) and helplessly seeing your cities and your people destroyed on the other. I could not see that we had any right to call on the small peoples to resist in such circumstances and I did not think many of them would do so effectively, if at all. Nor did I think we should be popular if we tried to get them to do so. And we certainly are not except with a few brave enthusiasts.

That is more than enough. I had not suggested that I should leave my job just now. I meant that I must look for a uniform to put on over the weekend if I could find it. So that I could not think and visualise and so could finally kill in myself much that was most deep-rooted. Great excitement and much sensible organisation going on *re* parachutists as well as some less sensible. One is asked now for identity cards etc. on every main and many side roads. All the able-bodied in this village are in arms. I think Hitler will go for France first, don't you? and then when he comes here, if he does, he will have some device and method we have not considered! I wish our secret service in Germany had not been wiped out at the beginning of the war (as it was—the French too).

Yours ever,
K. M.

I sent a separate note[71] about Leonard. He is the best choice. I'm delighted at the suggestion.

To KINGSLEY MARTIN, *20 June 1940*

Dear Kingsley,

I wrote to Whitley suggesting Leonard for the Board. In response he suggested E. D. Simon instead. I replied that I felt no objection to E.D.S. at all; indeed I had myself proposed him about a year ago. On the other hand, he did not quite fill the bill of supplying us with another director who would be easily available in London, since I know by experience that Simon is particularly difficult to get hold of at short notice. In return, therefore, I suggested that perhaps we might add both to the Board, perhaps dropping Barry, who almost never comes, at the same time.

I now have another letter from Whitley saying that he will mention the names of Simon and Woolf to the Board of the Statesman Company which meets after the meeting of the operating companies next Friday. He adds that another suggestion which has been made to him is that of J. B. Priestley,

[71] This has not survived.

and asks how the Nation Company would feel about that. I shall not have a chance of consulting them just yet, but should like to know what you feel. J.B.P. has his points, of course, and is a sensible fellow who might be quite a rock on certain occasions. On the other hand, it would have the effect of getting the complexion of the Board more mixed than ever, I feel, and there is a subtle distinction of ethos between him and the paper which stands in the way of genuine cordiality. Let me have your own reaction.

Yours ever,
J. M. K.

The next letter from Keynes was in reaction to *The New Statesman*'s losses of staff to the war effort, in particular the departure of R. H. S. Crossman.

To KINGSLEY MARTIN, *10 August 1940*

Dear Kingsley,

That is indeed a blow. I suggest

(1) Vernon Bartlett who must have time to write more than *The News Chronicle* now have space to print.

(2) Tom Harrison

(3) As a general utility man, Connolly whom I have already mentioned.

(4) If Cole is more or less permanently gone, on that side of things one of *The Financial News* young men. I can never remember clearly which is which, but Dacey who edits *The Banker* might not be bad; or there is W. T. C. King. Or Mrs Austin Robinson when she is nearer at hand than Cornwall.

Daily journalists, now deprived of their usual space, are perhaps a promising field.

Yrs,
J. M. K.

From KINGSLEY MARTIN, *13 August 1940*

Dear Maynard,

I enclose a letter for publication[72] that I received to-day from Brailsford. He is at Dartington for a few days and he has 'talked the matter over with Liddell Hart, Julian Huxley and Elmhirst. If you think the formula sound, can you pass it on to the mighty?' I think the best plan will be to publish the letter and discuss the whole issue in our front notes, especially the part raised by Julian Huxley's letter.

I did not want to discuss on the 'phone this morning the various questions you raised. The problem of editorship has now become very great because people who used to be in agreement and used to hold certain principles are now perforce in agreement on only one thing—the general necessity of resisting the Nazis. All the ground is slippery and everyone slips at a different place and tries to dig his heels in at some point of decency or humanity with the result that no two people I know say the same things that they were saying a little while ago or really feel happy about what they say. Nor is it possible to rewrite everyone's contributions. That is a long story but on the whole I am quite proud of the job that we have done.

Yours,

KINGSLEY

P.S. Dick [Crossman] holds that (1) It is important from the propaganda point of view in Europe and the USA to make an offer. (2) This offer should if possible be one that Hitler will reject and that the USA should regard it as unreasonable for him to reject.

To KINGSLEY MARTIN, *14 August 1940*

Dear Kingsley,

I am afraid that the enclosed [letter] seems to me to be great rubbish from the practical point of view. Even in peace time it would be nearly impossible to check the position, and the notion of having a neutral commission in the occupied areas, which would check up the amount of foodstuffs supplied to the army of occupation could only come from a brain which is either lunatic or indecently self-deceived.

We could not possibly propose such a formula, not be[cause] it would not be satisfactory if it were literally carried out, but

[72] 'Mr Hoover and the Food Blockade', *New Statesman and Nation*, 17 August 1940.

147

because, whatever Germany might say, we could have no possible assurance that it would be.

If I were you, I should try to persuade Brailsford to withdraw the letter. In any case to omit the last paragraph, which follows the formula, which seems to me to be exceedingly mischievous.

One has to face the fact that there is no middle course. The blockade is not a humanitarian instrument. We must either give it up or use it to the limit. Supplying ammunition to people in America whose real object is to force us to give it up at the risk of forfeiting their sympathy if we don't seems to me to be something from which it is one's duty to abstain.

Indeed, it would be difficult to think of anything more mischievous. I think it would be much better, even if he presses for its publication, to decline to print it and deal with the matter at the appropriate moment editorially. Julian Huxley's own plan is totally different from this of Brailsford's and quite free from the same objections, in my opinion. Indeed it is excellently double—or treble-edged. If we encourage and assist the accumulation of essential foodstuffs earmarked for the occupied and enemy areas in reasonably accessible positions and then make it clear that these will be immediately released in favour of any area from which Germany effectively withdraws its occupation, one has at the same time an encouragement to the populations of those areas and the very practical advantage that, once the moment for relief comes, it can be brought into operation without any serious delays of organisation. During the first six months after the last war, when I was particularly concerned with this matter, it was a nightmare that, when one had ultimately overcome all the obstructions, there was a prospect of a time lag of anything up to three months before any effective quantities could possibly be bought, paid for and arrive; yet the facts of the situation made it frightfully important that arrival should follow pell-mell upon the decision to allow them.

Yours ever,

[copy initialled] J. M. K.

From KINGSLEY MARTIN, *16 August 1940*

Dear Maynard,

I had the brainwave this morning that Francis Williams was free and I have just seen him. I have asked him to come and help on next week's paper, and I think he is a very possible person for Assistant Editor. He has the great merit of having been an editor and therefore been accustomed to things like libel and so forth. He has much improved, I think, since he left *The Herald*, and incidentally would probably do the City page better from our point of view than Davenport is now doing it. He also has very good contacts with the Ministries of Labour, Supply, etc. I have thought of no one nearly so good. The disadvantage is that he is a dull writer, but I need his writing less than his editorial help. It is urgent that something should be fixed fairly soon, because it looks as if I shall have to have my tonsils taken completely out, which means three weeks away. They seem to be dangerously bad. I have known this for a long time, but have hoped to avoid it. If I am going to have giddy fits purely as a result of tonsil poisoning, I shall have to tackle the matter fairly soon.

We are pretty short-handed because Cole is not able to do much work and Dick leaves this week.

Yours,
KINGSLEY MARTIN

To KINGSLEY MARTIN, *25 August 1940*

Dear Kingsley,

I do not know Francis Williams personally and, though I have no doubt read a good many articles by him, I do not remember any signed ones. However, the suggestion of using him sounds plausible. His minor contributions to this week's paper are all right, though there is scarcely the scope for saying more. I expect you are right to have your tonsils out. I have the same trouble and, in my case, they decided against removal. But you are younger. I am afraid our parents neglected us in that respect. Perhaps you will have disappeared into retirement before this letter arrives.

There was a lot in this week's paper I liked. I am gradually acquiring a real passion for Y.Y.! But I think Brian Howard on

Posters super-assinine.[73] I wonder if you read his stuff. He proposed that 'every London street should be plastered with pungent, comprehensible posters and leaflets proving that Germany has been enslaved by a faction consisting of insanely ambitious, boundlessly corrupt, bottomlessly inhuman nihilists who are superbly organised only because the laws and natural rights which might interfere with that organisation are hateful to them'. This not only sounds silly, but is exactly the opposite of what the Mass Observation people are recommending on the basis of their experience.

Also Crossman on the Bridgehead of Freedom seems to me to be getting dangerously near hot air. Isn't it time he produced the rabbit out of the hat? He goes on writing articles suggesting that he has some concrete statement of our aims in Europe which will work miracles for the announcement of which by Attlee and Churchill the time is now appropriate. But he never tells us what they are,—except that 'any future peace will demand as intimate links between Britain and Europe as those now being forged between Canada and the U.S.A.'. What this means in concrete terms I cannot visualise.

Yours ever,

J. M. KEYNES

To KINGSLEY MARTIN, *10 December 1940*

My dear Kingsley,

The somewhat defeatist initial note[74] in this week's paper is followed up by a total omission to make any reference to what is happening in Greece or to the Anglo-Greek successes in any part of the paper. Won't this produce on the reader an impression of serious lack of balance? There seems to be some Freudian censor who forbids any good news to reach the level of consciousness.

Yours,

J. M. K.

[73] 'A Last Minute Lesson from the Spanish Posters', *New Statesman and Nation*, 24 August 1940.
[74] 'Tell America', *New Statesman and Nation*, 7 December 1940.

From KINGSLEY MARTIN, *10 December 1940*

Dear Maynard,

The Italian news occupied several columns the week before last—Leader on it—because there was much to say. There is definite news this week, excellent news and the paper begins with it. Last week a note was planned but scrapped because there was little definite news and no comment to make that was not in the dailies and which was worth scrapping other notes for. It would, I agree, have been better to incorporate a few sentences in the first note saying that the Greek advance was proceeding.

Is there something Freudian about the fact that when the paper seems interesting to many people your comments are confined to occasions when you find something that annoys you? Our victories pass you by.

Yours,
KINGSLEY

Glad to see you've got back to Gordon Square.

To KINGSLEY MARTIN, *17 December 1940*

Dear Kingsley,

Your letter of December 10 has only reached me to-day. You will have discovered that in the meantime I had found something I liked!

Your main duty is to criticise, and that makes questions of tone and balance so extraordinarily important. I so often find myself almost driven to dislike criticism, which in fact I think absolutely justifiable and most necessary to make, by its environment, and especially by attempts to exploit the war in favour of something you want anyhow on the bogus ground that it will promote the winning of the war, when quite likely it won't. I think that the critic, if he is to be valuable in war time and pull his full weight, has to maintain an extraordinary, and possibly impossible, urbanity of soul.

Yours ever,
[copy initialled] J.M.K.

151

The next letters concerned a complaint about the Air Ministry's use of individuals, who were not professional journalists yet were preparing material for the press. The article 'Amateur Communiqué' appeared in the issue for 11 January 1941.

From KINGSLEY MARTIN, *17 January 1941*

Dear Maynard,

Thanks for sending Cadbury direct to me. Why (a) the Air Ministry did not communicate with me, but chose this roundabout method, and (b) L.J.C. did not come to me direct, are questions that need not now be asked. David Garnett's letter, which you will see in this weeks's paper,[75] will probably satisfy the Air Ministry, and my correspondent who was very fully vetted, will probably reply and make any outstanding points clear. Of course this is all part of a row between some people in A.I. 6, who want compulsory censorship, and the newspaper people there, who know that would be fatal and who had built up an organisation to work with the press. They were thrown out. The facts which the Air people had given to Cadbury were not, as far as I can make out, at all accurate, and the attack that this controversy sprang from started in *The Times*, which wrote very strongly indeed about the matter.

Thanks for your letter about the function of criticism. As you say, it is difficult, and it is not easy to say anything more useful about it in a letter.

Hope you flourish,

Yours,
[copy not signed or initialled]

From KINGSLEY MARTIN, *2 February 1941*

Dear Maynard,

Many thanks for your letter.[76] Members of the Air Ministry approached me directly about a statement in the article which had upset them, and I hope to put the matter right. Had a very interesting lunch with them about the whole affair—an old controversy with a hornets' nest in it of which I was ignorant and into which I trod. I am glad that you objected, as I did, to the round-about way of approach.

The City is rather a puzzle, because if we have no City article Roberts thinks we should lose much or all of our City advertising. He may be right, although Davenport's weekend before last's contribution about nationalising

---

[75] 'Amateur Communiqué', *New Statesman and Nation*, 18 January 1941.
[76] This has not survived.

the banks (with which I agreed) can scarcely have encouraged them to advertise. It may be that Francis Williams would be the best, if I can still get him. Indeed, I may make another shot at getting his editorial help. I am bothered about this subject. George Schwartz is very helpful in many ways, but I doubt if his capacities are editorial. Brailsford is now by no means always well, and if I should have to be away through illness or otherwise for a week or two, it is not easy to see who could be left in charge. Leonard is difficult to bring from the country nowadays, and Mostyn is in Cambridge and out of touch with events.

I have been having troublesome twinges of neuritis, which are apt to keep me awake at nights now and are merely warning symptoms that it is a hell of a long time now since I had a week or two without immediate responsibilities. I am proud of having kept my tonsils in check, but these things do bother me when there is no obvious person to take over, even for a short time. People whom I had thought of, e.g. Douglas Jay, are all now getting absorbed into the war machine, or getting called up. John Strachey might have served, but he is now getting a R.A.F. commission.

This week was rather aggravating. On Tuesday I received an official notice from the M[inistry] of I[nformation], suggesting that no reference should be made in the paper to Weygand and as little as possible said about Petain. As a result, it was very difficult to deal with the foreign situation, and we discussed general stuff on the front page when we ought to have been talking about the invasion business in France, news about which was released to the papers on Thursday after we had gone to press. However, such troubles are inevitable. Roberts tells me that our circulation figures have now reached the respectable height of 32,000 fully paid over six months, but that our actual circulation is 34,000, apart from a couple of thousand or so 5s. subscribers.

I hope you find the Treasury interesting and worth while. Please remember me to Lydia.   Yours,

                                                        KINGSLEY

This invasion business. If Hitler does invade it will be with four times the force our generals and commanders expect. If their preparations are good, he won't invade. They think 30,000 by troop carrier at night the absolute limit; if he does invade it will mean he has about 10,000 troop carrying planes ready, we a few hundreds. Could they come behind Dover (not worrying about casualties) seize the shore guns from behind and hold the Channel for the day? Of course, with other dispersed landings in Ireland, Scotland and East Coast? Don't know.

From KINGSLEY MARTIN, *6 February 1941*

Dear Maynard,

E. D. Simon's famous calendar has a quotation from J. M. Keynes today, which I am sticking up on the wall of my room here:

> Words ought to be a little wild, for they are the
> assaults of thought upon the unthinking. (J. M. Keynes)[77]

I have this as a permanent weapon!

Seriously, on the matter I wrote to you about the other day. Whitley writes to Roberts that he is not well, but wonders whether a Board meeting ought not to be called without him. I do not know whether this is necessary—there are very few to attend it—but I think something will have to be done to find an assistant for me who could, at a pinch, carry on if I was away. As things are at present I do most of the donkey work, and as long as Brailsford can write that is not too bad. But he is not always well and is probably going to America for a time before long, and George Schwartz, although useful, will not, I think, make an editorial understudy. We may have a situation in which it is very necessary to have somebody to keep closely in contact with things, as well as someone to sit in an office. I think we are in a position to offer a good salary. The paper is doing very well in circulation and is probably making a good deal of money. We have, of course, saved largely on salaries, e.g. Willison has gone to the Ministry of Supply, and the staff is altogether smaller.

My own inclination is to make an offer to Ritchie Calder, who has a constructive mind and absolutely first-class information and experience on the home side. He is constantly called in to the Ministries of Health and Home Security on shelter and health problems, and has a very wide acquaintance official and unofficial. He is young and keen, and if a bomb dropped on me he could probably make an excellent paper of his own sort. I sounded him on the subject the other day and found that he might be disposed to leave *The Herald*, even at a considerable drop in salary, provided it left him time to write elsewhere. We should have to offer him, I think, £800 a year,* which in the present circumstances we could easily afford. We should have to alter our arrangement with George Schwartz, which is entirely temporary, and to whom we now pay £30 a month. He would have to have something smaller or be paid at space rates. The difficulties that I see are that Ritchie ought nominally to give *The Herald* six months' notice

---

[77] *JMK*, vol. XXI, p. 244.
* He now gets £1,200 plus.

(but there might be ways out of this), that we should have to give him some reasonable security for the future if he left *The Herald*, and that coming here might raise difficulties about his reservation from military service. On this last point I must talk to an expert.

As you know, I have been for a long time looking for somebody who could give me rather more freedom from the office and, more important, take my place if I were ill or away, and since Dick Crossman went I have not been able to find anyone. I have now made up my mind that Ritchie is about the best bet. Do you know him and would you like to meet? Are you ever free for lunch or dinner? If so, I would ask you to come and Ritichie to meet you.

I am afraid the French news looks very serious.

Yours,
KINGSLEY

What do you think about City?

Drop it and hang the adverts? A lot of money.

To KINGSLEY MARTIN, *7 February 1941*

My dear Kingsley,

That is a lovely quotation in Simon's calendar. I had forgotton it, yet am not ashamed of it. I should like to meet Ritchie Calder. Will you and he lunch with me at the United University Club in Suffolk Street one day next week at 1.30—Wednesday or Thursday?

But about employing him I have two reserves. In the first place I do not very well see how we can give him security having regard to Crossman. I should have thought Crossman was immensely better for our purposes, and I should be very reluctant to block his return in due course. Surely he is our man in the long run.

The other reserve related to Calder himself. I think he is a very good journalist. Some of his work I like. But he does seem to me much more fitted to be a daily journalist than a weekly, lacking the reflective spirit appropriate to the latter. I should say that he is a natural-born liar, ready to take up good causes, but rather inclined to turn other people against them. If it is simply a case of getting him for the time being, I should not press these points. But to put a future obstacle in the way of Crossman would really be a disaster.

On the other hand, I do not agree with you any less than usual that it is very important to get a regular and reliable standby. And I have no constructive suggestion to make. So the real difficulty remains your sentence about 'some reasonable security for the future' for Calder. That is just, it seems to me, what we cannot give him.

We might have a word about the City page when we meet. It used to be alleged that we had to have a City page in order to get prospectuses. We never did get them and, anyhow, there are now none to be got. I doubt whether it greatly affects the rather small number of company reports we receive. It would scarcely be sensible for the Midland Bank to print Reggie's speech merely with a view to hostile comment on our City page. I should say that the reports were now got mostly because the companies have formed the habit and we have got on their list, and they think we are as good as anyone else for general publicity.

I do see, however, that it is a little dangerous to drop the feature altogether. What about a fairly substantial page once a month, called 'A Financial and Economic Review', or something of that sort, for which someone on *The Economist* might be available, such as Tyerman?

Yours ever,
J. M. KEYNES

From KINGSLEY MARTIN, *10 February 1941*

Dear Maynard,

I have asked Miss Robertson to try to get Ritchie for Thursday. It's a good day for me. But I had meant you to lunch with me for once!

Crossman of course is the ablest person we could ever hope to get but I had not thought that it was likely he would return. Perhaps I am wrong—but his ambitions go so far and he has moved into such completely different circles. I'll sound him one day about it: interesting to know whether, assuming the war ends within a year or two, the idea is still in his mind.

Ritchie has done mainly daily journalism and he does not write particularly well. Not sure that I know what you mean about a 'liar'. His mind is primarily scientific and constructive and I think he very much wants to get away from daily journalism. He really knows a great deal about social problems from a non-academic angle. He would not be good by himself perhaps: he knows nothing of foreign affairs, for instance. But I think the daily paper side of him is artificial and that he is capable of constructive thinking on a pretty big scale. I don't know whether it is a recommendation or not but H. G. Wells who is a close friend of Ritchie seems to regard him as a sort of successor on whose shoulders his mantle may fall! This is illuminating as well as absurd. Ritchie has none of H.G.'s gifts though he is growing and has imagination. What he has is a mind for detail and actuality which H.G. lacks more than anyone I ever knew. I should say he was capable of contemplative journalism.

Thanks for remarks *re* City. We will meet on Thursday anyway.

KINGSLEY

I thought Ironside's letter about the last war best so far but I should like to see Sheppard's face or hear Stalin's comment! Have you read the book by Koestler[78] I wrote about last week. Glad you commented on the 'humbug of finance'.

To KINGSLEY MARTIN, *12 February 1941*

Dear Kingsley,

As we may not get any conversation alone on Thursday, just a line in reply to your letter. I, of course, have no idea about Crossman's plans. But, if, as I had rather hoped and expected, he takes up politics, it seemed to me that a part time journalistic job in London of the weekly rather than daily description might exactly suit his plans, and give him a means of livelihood consistent with his ambitions.

Yours,

J. M. K.

[78] *Darkness at Noon* (1940).

An item in the 'London Diary' on 22 February and a letter from Martin opened a new discussion.

From KINGSLEY MARTIN, *20 February 1941*

Dear Maynard,

I have often been puzzled over a remark you made to me a few months ago. You said that if no shipping at all came to our ports we have a year's supply of food in the country. The experts I have talked to lately do not in any way support this statement, and I am very puzzled about the basis of your calculation. The food and shipping situation looks to me extremely serious. If I am wrong it would help me to know why!

Yours,

KINGSLEY

To KINGSLEY MARTIN, *26 February 1941*

Dear Kingsley,

Sorry to learn that you have scurvy in the office. It is all due to taking your news from Haw-Haw.

At this time of year the actual stock of food is not, of course, so good as it is soon after the harvest, unless one makes an allowance for the growing crops. But I am not aware that there has been any serious deterioration in our stocks position so far as the large tonnage commodities are concerned, of which we usually keep heavy stocks, such as wheat, sugar, oil-seeds, whale oil, etc. The shortages are mainly confined to articles of which we have never had appreciable stocks in hand, such as meat, bacon, butter, and cheese. Apart from meat, these are not really large tonnage articles, and the shortage is partly due to our having had to economise dollars, a necessity which will shortly be much mitigated. Moreover the genuine shortages are exaggerated by the way in which the demand for one thing slops over into another. For instance, the consumption of cheese is in excess of what it used to be and yet does not satisfy the demand, which is diverted from eggs, meat, etc.

Moreover even the shortage of meat is rather deceptive and is largely the consequence of a miscalculation on the part of the

the Ministry of Food, by which they arranged to have an enormous amount of cattle in the country at this time of the year, none of which would be fit to be slaughtered. We have nearly twice as many cattle on the hoof in the country to-day as we had a year ago. But until the spring grass comes along we are short of feedstuffs to fatten them off.

In my personal opinion there is no reason for serious concern about food for a long time to come unless losses become worse than they are; though you can find statisticians inside, as well as outside, Government offices who can discover a serious situation a year hence in projecting the bad news forward without allowing for the possible offsets. A good working test for the outside observer is the number of pages in *The Times* and other papers. As long as *The Times* prints 8 to 10 pages a day, practically the whole of which is imported, the position can't be too bad. For, in spite of the newspaper lords in the Cabinet and its near neighbourhood, we shall presumably cut the daily papers before we starve. There could be enough economies in imported newsprint to double our consumption of cheese, and still leave us with substantial newspapers, if this was coupled with some reasonable reduction of stocks of paper.

As usual, our troubles are much aggravated by muddle which time may partly remedy. We can't, of course, import all we should like, but there are still no shortages which we cannot make good by reasonable, and in many cases desirable, economies.

The above is, of course, not for quotation, but merely in the vain effort to reassure you.

Yours,
J. M. KEYNES

There the correspondence ended until after Keynes's return from America in August, when the matter of Robert Lynd, a regular columnist, came up.

From KINGSLEY MARTIN, *9 October 1941*

Dear Maynard,

A point on which I would like your advice. Y.Y. has now been writing a weekly article for the *N.S.&N.* for 20 years or so. He is, I believe, a fixed habit with a large number of readers of the less political type; I remember when I had a chance of testing some readers' opinions in a circular letter years ago that I found that a great many people who liked David Garnett's 'Books in General' also liked Y.Y. I think there are a particularly large number of women who like him, and he undoubtedly appeals to a section of our public who cannot stand too much acrid realism. On the other hand, the number of such people is unknown and those who complain that in the present paper shortage Y.Y. every week is a waster of space, is undoubtedly growing. This opinion has come to me from many quarters and not wholly from the Left, or even from the intelligentsia.

Policies are (1) try to get Y.Y. to contribute fortnightly or less often. I suspect that this would fail. Writing for the *N.S.* is a habit with him and he would more probably answer that if the series was once broken he would prefer to leave off. This is only a guess and anyway I can try. (2) Leave him off altogether. Apart from personal considerations, which are comparatively unimportant, this would have the disadvantage that I should always be looking every week for some article to relieve the political side, and that the number of writers who can do things that are amusing and well written is very limited. Against this it is true that we have some scientific and literary articles which are held over months because the natural space for them is occupied by Y.Y. But they would not strictly be substitutes. They would provide no assurance of pleasure to those who like a piece of mellow philosophising each week. Thirdly, we could keep Y.Y. on as he is now, and, fourthly, I can ask him to shorten his weekly piece. I doubt if this last policy would be worth much. He needs some space to develop his quality.

I would be grateful for your observations on this. I hope you are more optimistic about Russia at the moment than I am.

Yours,
[copy not signed or initialled]

To KINGSLEY MARTIN, *14 October 1941*

Dear Kingsley, ·

My feeling is exactly the same as it was last time we discussed the vexed question of Y.Y. I do not read him always, but the taste for him has grown on me, and I should greatly miss him if he departed and so, I believe, would a large number of readers. I should say that people are not wildly enthusiastic, but it is a habit they have formed, the breakdown of which they would feel keenly. Also it would be a frightful nuisance to you to find something corresponding if he were to disappear altogether. That does not mean that the ideal plan would not be, particularly with the reduced size of the paper, for him to appear fortnightly rather than weekly. I should favour that if you can persuade him. But you will remember that last time it was discussed with him he was quite clear that it must be once a week or not at all. I suppose it is just possible that, being a little older, he may now be a little lazier. And also that he will recognise the force of the argument arising from the drastic curtailments in the size of the paper. So it might be possible to try it on. If so, I suggest that the most delicate way would be to make it clear that, if it is disagreeable to him to make any change, we continue on the weekly basis. If you could get him fortnightly, that would be the best of both worlds.

Yours,

J. M. K.

From KINGSLEY MARTIN, *7 November 1941*

Dear Maynard,

1. There is a further cut of paper from $22\frac{1}{2}$ to 20 basic and also a serious threatened cut on the supplementary. This may make it extremely difficult to maintain the character of the paper. It looks as if we may be cut to 12 pp. Now is the time to make any kind of fight we can. The M[inistry] of I[nformation] is very sympathetic but not, I think, powerful. I think the Beaver,[79] who obviously has no time for such matters of detail, nevertheless really decides them. *The Spectator, Time and Tide* and ourselves are sending a memorandum on the subject, of which I will send you a copy, to the suitable man at the Ministry of Supply, to the M. of I. and to anybody else who may be useful. The thing is quite absurd because the amount of paper required is negligible and, to take only two examples, there were 24 different women's papers dealing with knitting on a single bookstall this week, and a number of

[79] Lord Beaverbrook.

trade and technical papers carry weekly scores of pages of advertisements of
articles which cannot be bought and which are only advertised because
of E[xcess]P[rofits]T[ax]. However, you know the arguments and I won't
repeat them. If you think of anyone useful to talk to yourself, or of
anyone else you think we ought to approach on this subject, I shall be
glad.

2. I think we ought to have a Board meeting to discuss policy in view
of the paper cuts and other matters. I sounded Priestley, as if from myself,
as a possible director, and he, I think, was pleased. That was some time ago
and the matter ought to be decided.

3. Priestley's 1941 Committee is not a very important body politically,
but has built up a considerable contact with Americans. I addressed it not
long ago at a discussion week-end on the implications of 'freedom from fear
and want', with particular reference to projects of Anglo-American co-
operation for the reconstruction of Europe after the war. It is now suggested
that there should be a private meeting of people who are working on different
lines of American-British co-operation and who need some guidance on the
question of the use of the food surplus that is being stored, and on many
other problems of Anglo-American co-operation. I was asked whether I
would approach you to come for an hour to Hulton's house in Hill Street
to give some advice on these matters. A suggested date is December 11th,
but most nights in that week or the week before it would do. If you should
feel inclined and could spare the time it might be worthwhile. It would not
mean preparation and it might usefully direct a number of people who are
working in odd and perhaps mistaken ways on these matters.

I enclose a small pamphlet that was written originally months ago and was
rather unsatisfactorily revised to bring in the Russian war and the Atlantic
Charter.

Yours,
KINGSLEY

To KINGSLEY MARTIN, *12 November 1941*

Dear Kingsley,

The copy of the letter to the Minister of Supply has now
reached me. It seems to me excellent and persuasive. I hope it
will be successful.

But, if it is not successful, I am sure the right solution is to
reduce the circulation, not to reduce the size. Possibly a cut to

14 pages would be practicable and not below that, but I should prefer it to remain at 16.

On the telephone I forgot to answer your passage about Priestley. We must talk about it at the next Board.

But the nearer the idea approaches, the less keen do I feel. I found that Raymond, who was dining with me last night, was horrified at the idea, since he considers that Priestley is the enemy of all we stand for!—the leading anti-highbrow in the country.

Yours ever,
J. M. K.

To KINGSLEY MARTIN, *13 November 1941*

Dear Kingsley,

I have looked through your *Propaganda's Harvest*[80] with much interest. It is a very good little paper. One minor correction. It was not Sir Auckland Geddes who talked about the pips squeaking, but Eric Geddes. He invented this perfect expression in an election speech at the Guildhall in Cambridge, during the Coupon Election, which was only reported in the local paper. It would have been entirely lost to fame if my mother had not cut it out and sent it to me, and it was impressed on my memory when I came to write *The Economic Consequences*.

The phrase about the hard-faced men, which you quote, I stole from Stanley Baldwin, who invented it. I was sitting in Chalmers' room in the Treasury having tea on the first day of the new Parliament after the Coupon Election. Baldwin, who was then Financial Secretary and had the adjoining room, poked his nose through the door, as I can see him now, to us at tea. I asked him—'What do they look like?' And he replied by the famous phrase—'A lot of hard-faced men who look as if they had done well out of the war.'

Yours ever,
J. M. KEYNES

[80] (London, 1942.)

I will be glad to come to a private discussion with the 1941 Committee, but December 9 or 10 would suit me better than Dec. 11.

From KINGSLEY MARTIN, *14 November 1941*

Dear Maynard,

Many thanks for your letter with interesting stories. I am preparing an edition of this little book for America and may want to ask you one or two further points of fact. For instance, I have had a letter from Hamilton Fyfe, criticising certain details and saying that Northcliffe never did any propaganda in the United States but went over purely on financial questions. I am not sure how to look this point up though I have no doubt I could ferret it out. I have strong recollections of Norman Angell telling me stories of Northcliffe's propaganda in the U.S.A. and wonder whether you remember anything about it.

I have given the 1941 Committe your message. They have promised that the meeting shall be strictly private and I think the date chosen is December 10th. Would you book that? They are all very grateful to you.

I think you might be able to help us further about paper by a judicious intervention with Bracken and perhaps Layton. They may be very unwilling to embark on a new principle of differentiation but it may be possible that without admitting this principle they may grant us without fuss a small additional supplementary, since a supplementary is already granted on the understanding that there are some papers that cannot live on the basic ration. I think that is what we should try for; not try to alter the basic ration, which is to be reduced to 20 per cent at the beginning of December, but to ask for an additional supplementary. I am hoping to see Harold Macmillan privately on the matter. He is another person who, I think, might be sympathetic, and I expect you know him well.

You are mistaken in referring to 14 pages. Technically speaking, we can only move by 4's. I am quite clear myself that we should go to 12 rather than sacrifice circulation. Omitting all advertisements we could make a respectable paper at 12. The problem arises at a lower point than that. Whitley has just written saying that any sacrifice is preferable to reducing circulation. Roberts is keen in the same sense and I only begin to hesitate at a point which is so small that we might seem too small to do our job or to be worth the 6d. If we were too small we should automatically reduce the circulation and so solve the problem that way! But there are strong arguments in favour of reduction of size, even if necessary to 8. If we got down there attention would be called to our problem and we should be more likely to get a change. Moreover, it is extremely difficult to cut circulation because we have no casual readers now and the problem of rationing subscribers on any basis of equality seems insoluble. If we believe that what we have to say is important, if may be better to say it to our whole public rather than to stick to the idea that we are a cultural paper wanted by a comparatively small audience. In the kind of situation which we are confronting an 8-page paper read by a very large number would really be much more important than a high-brow affair of twice the length.

Awkward about Priestley. I did not know Raymond felt so strongly. I am still rather in two minds myself but am inclined to stick to a view favourable to him.

Yours ever,
KINGSLEY

From KINGSLEY MARTIN, *12 December 1941*

Dear Maynard,

I was glad you could come on Wednesday. I think it interested and helped you.

I have a lot to say on the subject of the second front which you raised at dinnertime, but on one point I should like to make sure that you have the facts correct. In our issue of October 25th we published a leader called *Amateur Strategists*, which definitely stated that any possibility of another front in Europe was off, though we defended our view that it would have been good policy. We have not advocated a second front in Europe since then though we have on one or two occasions referred to the controversy and suggested, as I strongly hold, that a mistake was made in choosing Libya. I think you must have been confused by the fact that we quoted Stalin on November 29th, pointing out that he had been misreported. I believe that you are entirely incorrect in thinking that this argument is only put out of insincere and propagandist reasons from Russia, and remembering our earlier conversation on the subject I do not believe you have ever examined the case. I am myself convinced that technical arguments were overwhelmingly in favour of a Continental offensive. That this was not attempted was due, I believe, to a decision at the beginning that it was not worthwhile since Russia would immediately collapse. I rather resent your view that this has been an irresponsible campaign inspired by Russia. I have friends in the War Office who told me from the beginning that all the argument was in favour of a Western offensive, but that the prejudiced view of Moscow's strength was so immovable that all our forces would be dissipated and nothing done to draw Hitler's troops to the West. This judgment of the W[ar] O[ffice] proved to be correct. Of course if Russia could win the war without us being on the Continent it will not much matter, but even so it seems to me a serious gamble to have taken.

Yours,
[copy not signed or initialled]

To KINGSLEY MARTIN, *5 January 1942*

Dear Kingsley,

I thought your article about relations with America in the paper of December 26th [*sic*] most excellent.[81] It seemed to me quite an inspired analysis of the situation.

I see that the meeting on Friday has been put at 2.15. I shall, at any rate, be there long enough to make it clear what my opinion is.

Yours,
J. M. K.

The summer of 1942 saw a long argument between Keynes and Martin over a Second Front in western Europe to reduce German pressure on Russia. It began with a *New Statesman* article on 15 August entitled 'The World Front'. Keynes initially replied with a letter to the editor.

To the Editor of The New Statesman and Nation, *22 August 1942*

THE SECOND FRONT

Sir,

In this week's leader you write: 'The Second Front can never be a purely military operation; it is—whether we like it or not—part of a European revolution against Fascism. That may be one of the real reasons why it is postponed so long.'

Do you seriously believe this?

KEYNES

[81] 'Muddle in the Pacific', *New Statesman and Nation*, 27 December 1941.

From KINGSLEY MARTIN, *19 August 1942*

Dear Maynard,

I have sent your little letter to the printer with a monosyllabic affirmative by way of editorial reply.

I should not have thought any close student of recent events could have felt any doubt about the answer to the question. Indeed, ever since Crossman and I started to talk about revolutionary war on the Continent in 1941 we have constantly tried to analyse the motives for an Imperialist rather than a European strategy. That the fear of having to support the revolutionary forces has been *one of* the motives is really, I should have thought, beyond question. De Gaulle went so far as to protest against any suggestion of using the fighting French forces in the war in France until it was won, when, he explained, they would be needed to keep order and to put down the Reds. This is a particularly striking and definite example, but it can be supported by many other instances.

I am reminded of this by the conversation we had when you dined one night last winter at Hulton's.[82] I had in fact left off urging an attack on the Continent because I knew that it was not regarded as a possibility for the near future, but I assumed that it must be this summer after Beaverbrook's promise to send material to Russia. You suggested that I was irresponsible in urging a Second Front at all. I did not feel at liberty to say what I knew then and know now in much greater detail. One member of the Cabinet had taken precisely my view, with full expert knowledge, and had urged invasion of the Continent the very week that Germany had attacked Russia. If his proposals had been carried out I think the war would now be over. He was supported by two other members of the Cabinet with different proposals a little later. I have not recalled this incident until provoked by this week's letter. I have been reminded of it by other people who were at the table on that occasion, and asked why I had not rubbed it in.

A charming example, which unfortunately I cannot print as a footnote, was the case of one of the chief members of the Staff who in an argument on the Second Front was asked what he thought the British Army was for if not to be used to collaborate with revolutionary forces on the Continent. He replied that the British Army was to occupy the Continent after the war. In a word, he accepted the pattern formulated last year by Lord Halifax and pictured again now by Harris of Bomber Command. According to this picture we have only to bomb Germans enough and they will crack up, and Britain and America between them will occupy Europe. This is, I think, the

[82] Above, p. 162.

SOCIAL, POLITICAL AND LITERARY WRITINGS

way to defeat or stalemate in the war, and I am surprised that you should wish by your letter to range yourself on that side of the most crucial controversy of our time.

Yours,
[copy not initialled or signed]

From KINGSLEY MARTIN, *24 August 1942*

Dear Maynard,

I was a bit puzzled by your letter because the statement you queried was so very much an understatement! It is not the sort of thing that one can prove in detail in public, e.g. one cannot quote De Gaulle's statement that his army was for use in keeping order in France after the war and not for invasion, nor can one quote the arrangements now being made for building a kind of French Gestapo to follow up the invasion if and when it happens. I know people engaged in this matter in Political Warfare, in the War Office, in the Foreign Office and elsewhere, who would all agree that one of the great obstacles to getting on with preparing a Second Front last year was the fact that all our Secret Service, all the mind of the Foreign Office (not to mention a number of Ministers who were still in office) was directed to the continuous fight against Communism. The concept of an invasion which would mean, as Tom Wintringham put it, each soldier carrying three guns, one for himself and two for factory workers who might turn out to be Communists—this has indeed been a very difficult concept, which even now has not been fully accepted. I think perhaps you have not followed this controversy behind the scenes. It can be amusingly illustrated by any comparatively Left-wing broadcaster on the European Service who finds the guts taken out of what he says, because to appeal to the Left on the Continent would amount to offending some or other exiled government here or some or other important person in the Foreign Office or elsewhere. Have you, for instance, seen Hoare's protests when anyone makes an anti-Franco remark?

I am reminded of the conversation at Hulton's we had last winter when you imagined that I had no expert authority for suggesting that the Second Front was on the map. At that time three Cabinet Ministers, presumably with full knowledge of possibilities, were in favour of it, one at least strenuously. If the *N.S.* had said that there were no technical difficulties in a Second Front and not many arguments against it, or, if we had said that the difficulty felt in collaborating with a revolutionary movement on the Continent was the most important reason against, I should have seen reason for criticism. But I do not believe that anyone who has heard the arguments discussed could doubt that this has been, as we said, one of the factors. You

168

will remember my point last year always was that it would get more and more difficult to make use of the '1,000,000,000 Allies'.[83] (By the way did you ever read that book by Dick Crossman and me?* I think the reasons why it has been difficult to collaborate with these allies was pretty clearly foreseen there in 1940.) Raymond, who knows the French situation very well has now come round very much to my view of this because he emphasises that the more hungry people get the less chance there is of finding them fighting allies. How deeply reluctant the Foreign Office still is to accept the necessity of working with revolutionaries on the Continent has just been revealed to me once again. When there really is a job on foot they try altogether to exclude the Political Warfare people and to use their own contacts, who are apt unfortunately to be trained entirely in the pro-Pétain–pro-Franco school and to be 100 per cent opposed to the French and Spanish working class who are our only serious potential allies in those countries!

Sorry to have written at such length about all this, but I take it that you would like a fuller answer than could be given in a footnote.

I have been asked recently if I would go over to see groups of people in the United States who want to see me. If I went I should not make public speeches and should not want to be over for more than three or four weeks at the most. I find that those in charge of this at the M.O.I. are in favour of this and think they could arrange a place on the plane for me if I go and come back before mid-November. I believe this would be very good for me and the paper. It depends, I think, on whether Leonard Woolf will be prepared to look after the paper for a few weeks.

Yours
KINGSLEY

To KINGSLEY MARTIN, *28 August 1942*

Dear Kingsley,

I am glad you have written. For when I saw your reply in the paper I regarded it as an excusable fib, since obviously you could not say the opposite—a conclusion which I should expect most of your readers also drew. I now see that the explanation is that you really mean something quite different.

The real point seems to me to be this. You believe that it would greatly facilitate the success of the Second Front, when

---

[83] Scipio, *A Thousand Million Allies If You Choose* (London, 1940).

* Crossman, who is very anti-Communist (indeed, always has been) would agree with me on all this. It was he who started the 'revolutionary war' line in the *N.S.* 1940.

the time for that arrives, if meanwhile we were organising a Communist revolution in France, Spain and elsewhere. Now, if you were to start by saying that, in fact, we are not organising a Communist revolution in European countries, you could point to formidable evidence in favour of the truth of what you say. I do not believe that Sam Hoare is organising or even encouraging a Communist revolution against Franco. We are, superficially at least, working in with De Gaulle, whom I have never heard accused of Communist sympathies. We are in very close touch with the Government of Queen Wilhelmina and Prince Bernhardt, and I never saw people who looked less like Communists; and so on.

There is also another thing, which I think may be true. It is rather difficult to draw the line between encouraging or countenancing Communist revolution and making a mess of things generally for the enemy. There are very likely people who make decisions at a fairly low level who draw the line in a different place from where you would, and probably in a different place from where I should. But obviously it is not very easy, taking everything into account, to know just where it ought to be drawn.

Now, if you will put it that way, namely, that we ought to be organising a Communist revolution in Europe in the interests of the Second Front and are in fact not doing so, one might not agree, but could not possibly object to this as a reasonable statement of opinion. But this is not in fact what you did say, and that still seems to me, on the basis of everything I know, quite balmy. I agree that my knowledge is far from comprehensive and probably covers a field which does not overlap very much with your sources. But in one or two subjects where I can check you (I am afraid I cannot particularise further), I can from certain knowledge say that you are mistaken.

I shall be interested to see whether in the near future the word does not go round quietly to drop for the time being the public agitation for a premature Second Front. But, of course, a premature Second Front has no connection with a Second Front at the earliest practicable opportunity.

On another matter: Bernard Swithinbank,[84] an old friend of mine, who has been for sometime the District Commissioner in Pegu, has now been appointed Adviser on Burma to the Secretary of State. He has his own ideas about the future situation of Burma, which you would probably find sympathetic, and is not very happy about the trend of official opinion. He would welcome the opportunity of a talk. Could you see him sometime or get him to come round? A telephone call to the Burma Office or a letter would find him. He is not at present, I think, on full-time duty in the office.

Yours,

J. M. K.

Written before seeing this week's paper. I see that this time you have answered No—which is much more plausible. Also the explanation of what you really mean confirms my surmise above.

From KINGSLEY MARTIN, *28 August 1942*

Dear Maynard,

I expect you have seen the Henry Luce Fortune supplement about Anglo-American relations in reconstruction after the war etc. I thought it interesting and asked John Strachey to do an analysis for me. The enclosed two articles are the result. They contain an odd new *cujus regio* doctrine for this century. I'd very much like your opinion. I think they will interest you and if you've time to look through them I'd be grateful.

On the subject of your letters and my footnote. I did not at the time think I was being rude—the footnote seemed about in the spirit of the letter. But I see it has been regarded as an interchange of 'amenities' and if it was rude I apologise. There is never any point in rudeness. I expect the footnote should have been the one I put in this week's issue.

Yours,

KINGSLEY

[84] A school friend of Keynes's from Eton.

From KINGSLEY MARTIN, *4 September 1942*

Dear Maynard,

Thanks for putting me on to Swithinbank whose fame I know. My Burmese friends talk of him with something like reverence. He is lunching with me on Tuesday.

No—there was no 'fib'. Your original question was read in two ways, the answer to the first being 'yes' and to the second being 'no'. People who have spoken to me on the subject have been divided about equally into those who thought me obviously right that the Second Front had been postponed because our people could not think in terms of aiding revolution and those who thought you right in suggesting that politics no longer postponed the Second Front *now*. I wrote the second letter signed W to clear this up.

I am writing now to ask you to give me advice on a rather urgent point. I may go to U.S.A. for a few weeks. Leonard and I agreed that it would be good to have an entirely different Diarist outside the usual circle, while I was away and hearing that Bob Boothby was leaving the Air Force and coming back into politics (having made matters up with Winston) I asked him to write the Diary if I went away. He wired that he would like to do so and I expect to see him probably Monday lunch or dinner. Since then it has been suggested to me that his reputation is so muddled by his financial past that he is the wrong sort of person to have writing in the paper and will give it a bad reputation etc. This is important. I don't feel it myself, but if others do I could tell him at once and explain to him or get him to write under a pseudonym. My own view is that he must reinstate himself and that he is a very good journalist and that his name will interest people and do us no harm and himself good. Would you tell me on the 'phone on Monday whether you agree? If you felt strongly against him I should regard that as very important.

K. M.

From KINGSLEY MARTIN, *9 September 1942*

Dear Maynard,

I suppose we were cut off by the Exchange. Perhaps the girl thought the argument wouldn't be conclusive. Actually, I am rather puzzled by what you now say. We have said this business about aiding revolution in Europe in the paper quite consistently since Dick's article on the fall of France, 1940. At one time I was called on by a gentleman from the War Office to know whether I would help in organising the anti-Fascist revolution in Spain, and they got so far as having me vetted by M.I.5 as official organiser of suitable possible leaders.* Then that phase passed. Then there was another move in the same direction for the V Campaign. When you analyse the opposition movements in different countries in Europe, sometimes you find that they are almost wholly nationalist as in Norway, and sometimes that they would be predominantly Communist, as probably in France. All this I think we have said a good many times and have made it clear that the type of invasion we have envisaged involved suitable political propaganda and the provision of arms for those who were willing to fight. There have been many tentative things done in this direction, but political objection is certainly one factor in making this half-hearted.

I am not quite sure from your letter and remarks on the 'phone whether you think this view silly or sensible, but I don't think there is anything that needs clearing up about it. As regards 'political prejudice' that, as you know, is a complicated story. I think it is one of the reasons that dictated the strategy of dispersal instead of a European front which became practical politics as soon as it was clear that Russian resistance would be strong. Beaverbrook and I (a combination that I find embarrassing) advocated the immediate planning of the European Second Front the day that Germany attacked Russia, and I think political prejudice is, as we said, one of the reasons that such an attack has been postponed. But I don't really know whether you differ from me in any of this, or whether, for some reason, you want an argument. Actually, I was urging even before the war the largest possible combination of genuinely anti-Fascist forces from the Nationalist to the Communist, and you will find in *1,000,000,000 Allies* a pretty fair summary of the reasons which I believe have prevented this being done. The book would need some changes now to bring it up-to-date, but the main argument remains, I think, intact, while the importance of the thesis has been immensely increased by the German–Russian war.

Many thanks for your wise counsel about Boothby. I am not sure whether or not I am going to the U.S.A. I am glad you are having a few days' holiday and apologise for inflicting Strachey articles on you. He seems to me to have moved a very long way to the Right. When you come back to London I want to persuade you to have lunch with me and Priestley one day.

Yours,
KINGSLEY

Last year the cleavage of cooperate or not with Russia was quite definite. Halifax made a speech outlining a bombing victory with no collaboration with Russia à la Moore-Brabazon.

* Obviously secret.

To KINGSLEY MARTIN, *10 September 1942*

Dear Kingsley,

I feel that these articles of Strachey's are rather a muddle, and that he has not perhaps put his finger on the fundamental initial point.

On the first page of his first article he explains how under the *Fortune* scheme there is to be free transferability of everything, and the convertibility of dollars and sterling into gold is to be maintained at a fixed rate. But there is not a word of explanation how this is to be done. If it were successfully achieved by some means to be disclosed hereafter, I doubt if the particular difficulties raised by Strachey would arise. Or, put it more moderately, they would only arise if the means to be disclosed hereafter included a domestic policy which would be inconsistent with some of the objects of our future domestic arrangements as he conceives them. It does not follow that they need be. For example, suppose each country was to agree to lend the other for an indefinite period without interest whatever sum might be required to maintain the convertibility between the two currencies at a fixed rate, we should be perfectly free in our domestic policy. If, on the other hand, the proposed arrangements involved various interferences, they are just as likely, I should have thought, to interfere with the functioning of capitalism as of socialism. At any rate, it is quite impossible to comment on the scheme from the particular angle which Strachey has chosen until the authors of it have disclosed what kind of technique they have in view. It may be that Mr Buell's 'closely argued report' discloses all this. I have not read it. If it does, then that ought to be an important part of the summary of the scheme.

Apart from this, I doubt if the *Fortune* proposal deserves to be taken quite so seriously. I have not heard that they have produced any particular reaction in U.S.A. And, from what I know of the trend of opinion there in official circles, I can confidently say that it is not at all in the direction suggested.

After all, the officials we are mainly dealing with in discussing post-war arrangements are out-and-out New Dealers.

I am back in town and would be delighted to have lunch with you and Priestley. We could then discuss the spread of delusion and insanity on the point of facts amongst your contributors and what can be done about it.

K

From KINGSLEY MARTIN, *12 September 1942*

Dear Maynard,

Thank you for taking so much trouble about the Strachey articles. I find it hard to tell how far the Luce 'America's Century' opposition is important.

I'll try to fix something with Priestley. I'm not very hopeful about the 'delusion and insanity'. If I'd got someone to make the remark that politics had nothing to do with strategy or some equal delusion of that kind I might have you now privately arguing on my side. As it is I'm quite fogged about your argument. Your earlier letter made it clear that you did not differ much on the facts: the cause of your complaint is the more obscure seeing that the *N.S. & N.* has certainly argued the case with much moderation & as much fact as we were allowed to mention, & you have not until now decided that in some odd way you disagree. What about I don't know.

I'm off to U.S.A. end of month for 3–4 weeks.

Yours,
KINGSLEY

From KINGSLEY MARTIN, *21 September 1942*

Dear Maynard,

Thinking over your correspondence I thought it might be a good plan to write a short memo summarising my view. I have not spent any length of time over it. It is not meant to be complete but it gives a general view.

I have written in the margin (p. 6) [p. 179] a new point which reaches me which may be thought to support the other side of the argument. I hear via the Turks and others that the state of brutalisation of the Germans who have fought on the Eastern Front is so appalling that it provides a new argument against pitting our soldiers against them. Apparently many thousands of them have become sub-human killing machines. Some of the Turks who have seen the Crimea say that literally nothing remains, that it is quite beyond human imagination to have conceived of such destruction or of such brutality. I can see that this may be used as an argument for us

175

to fight a purely defensive war and to try to win by bombing. I also hear from the best French source that the chance of obtaining active resistance in France, which has been excellent until the summer of 1942, is now probably passing. The de Gaullist from whom I hear this is one of the best: he holds that the country is now disintegrating under Nazi oppression so much that by next spring it will definitely be too late for any Second Front. If that is so all my argument for the last year will have been correct, but it will also become true that the only hope of invasion in 1943 lies through North Africa and Italy.

If you happen to have time to look through this document I shall be very much obliged if you will give me a ring. I shall be fire-watching here all tonight and, of course, obtainable tomorrow. I only want you to tell me one thing when you do. You urged me to justify my view in the paper. I can do so on the broad lines of this memorandum. Do you think it would be good to publish a summary of its points? They have, of course, all been made in the paper from time to time.

Formalities are not yet completed, but I expect to go to the United States for three or four weeks starting probably next week. I am looking forward to seeing you at 1.15 at the Ivy on Wednesday.

Yours,
KINGSLEY

WHY THERE IS NO SECOND FRONT

To answer this question precisely would be to assess the relative weight of technical and psychological factors. I do not pretend that I can do anything of the sort—which is the reason why our demand for a Second Front has been so cautious and understated. But that it is to a large extent what the Germans would call a *willensfrage* and not merely a technical matter I am prepared to assert with all confidence and indeed with knowledge.

Note that questions of this sort always are *willensfrage*. Many things have been done in this war, which, according to the rules, were technically impossible. The Germans do them all the time. It is because technical difficulties only yield to the determined will that Napoleon and other generals have always emphasised that there was in war no such word as impossible. The story of war teems with examples of victories due to the determined use of the resources available at the time when they could be effective and the defeat of those who waited until the proper amount of shipping, of guns, men, etc. were ready and who therefore lost by sticking to the text-book rules. Lloyd-George, who understands these matters, said from the day when Germany first attacked Russia, that now and now only was the opportunity of a victory which had seemed outside our capacities, but that we should never seize it unless orders were given to the General Staff to make a Second Front with what we had and at all costs. If we did that all production would leap up—as was proved oddly enough by the spectacular effect on production of the Dieppe raid which was thought to be the beginning of the Second Front—the shipping space which was now spent in bringing food, etc., would in fact be diverted and we should achieve, with general approval, that war austerity which everyone agreed to be necessary but which we should never achieve until we were far more deeply and urgently 'in the war' than we had so far been. As long as the technique was to ask the Admiralty and the Ministry of Shipping and the Army and each of the experts whether this or that was now possible, we should be told it was impossible. Only when the political decision was made to act would the technical problems be overcome.

That non-technical factors have over-ridden technical we know from a variety of sources. Sir Roger Keyes has described with great precision how important operations which were in his view perfectly possible and certainly desirable were turned down because of timidity on the part of some of the Staff. He did not allege political factors, but just incapacity to seize opportunities and make decisions. These non-technical factors have been present throughout and they are in part at least due to political, ideological, class—whatever you like to call such influences.

Let me only give illustrations of which I am sure. When Germany attacked Russia the chance of a western front was not only the idea of some Left ideologists; it was at once seized upon by more than one Cabinet Minister and inside experts with full knowledge of the facts. I cannot particularise, but, to take only one example, there is no doubt that the Brest Peninsula could have been taken, that at some cost, submarine bases like Lorient, etc., could have been wiped out from land and sea. Instead an immense number of aircraft were lost, with little effect, on bombing Lorient and on trying to sink the Gneisenau and Scharnhorst. But this relative efficiency was not the main reason for pressing this expedition. The main reason was to start a bridgehead which would keep German troops and aircraft on the west and be the beginning of a Second Front. This and many other possible European fronts were much discussed and favoured by experts and Ministers.

When assessing why they were all turned down it is impossible to omit the following considerations:–

(1) Generals and Ministers have both to my knowledge expressed views that betray a bias quite fatal to any such enterprises. One sentence repeated recently by a high-up sticks in my mind: 'It's not our business to pull Stalin's chestnuts out of the fire.' This is a significant repetition of what Stalin said

about us in 1940 and what the Americans said about us up to Pearl Harbour. It is always a fatal view which betrays the difficulty of any genuine working alliance among sovereign states. In the case of Russia it betrays in expert quarters the deep prejudices which have always made co-operation impossible. They appeared in the famous remarks of Moore-Brabazon who wanted Russia and Germany to destroy each other and who told a friend of mine when he was attacked that he had merely said in public what all the Cabinet said in private. But I do not wish to put too much stress on the utterance of a particular Minister. I merely point out that this hope of the two Totalitarian Powers killing each other like Kilkenny cats has been one of the chief factors in our politics for years; it became apparent to the world (including J. M. Keynes) at Munich; it is still in my opinion one of the dominant factors in our military as well as our political decisions. No reason to speak as if it were very strange or wicked; it takes a determined effort for any resident of this small island not sometimes to fall for this tempting line of wishful thinking.

(2) Those who actively took this anti-Stalin line and opposed a Second Front consciously on this ground are not now conspicuously in the key positions of politics, but I believe them still to be powerful, especially in the Foreign Office. That they were powerful last year at the critical moment of decision we know from articles by Margesson and Halifax who outlined an alternative idea of winning the war by bombing, in terms which made it apparent that he was speaking after consultation with colleagues who had decided not to attempt to win the war in company with Russia, glad though they were that Russians were killing Germans.

(3) Further, it was freely said that Russia could not hold out six weeks and that she would give in, make peace and leave us to another Dunkirk. Mr Churchill still, I have been told, believed this last until his recent visit to Moscow and I therefore believe that this factor played an important part in 1942 just as I know it did in 1941.

(4) When I made inquiries in 1941 in quarters where the technical factors were known I learnt that there were grave difficulties that could only be overcome by courageous men who knew their mind and who were not confused by any of these anti-Russian feelings. But my informants assumed that they would certainly be overcome in 1942, if the U.S.S.R. continued to hold on through the winter. If Russia did hold on, a Second Front this spring was certain. Why was there not one? Greater shipping difficulties, Libyan disaster and so forth? Clearly no, since bad as these were, our resources in 1942 with almost all Germany's forces held in the east were unique and however bad the shipping position we were certainly better off than we had been in 1941. If preparation had seriously begun in the winter

of 1941 it was impossible that we could do nothing in the Continent in 1942. The size would be dictated by technicalities; the capacity for some Second Front was indisputable.

(5) I understand the reasons to be the following. Admittedly the strain of Japan, reverse in Libya, etc., were important, the decisive factors were again non-technical.

(a) Cherwell and Trenchard—I do not know who else is influential with Churchill in this matter—were particularly successful in persuading Churchill that Germany could be defeated by a vast bombing programme. Air development was separate from sea and land and the immense departmental war which we all know about on the question of the disposition of bombers, their use as part of combined operations or for separate bombing, has been one important factor. No dive bombers, no torpedo bombers, no transports for invasion—continuous manufacture of civilian bombers. Technically I believe this to have been a disastrous mistake, but I am obviously not qualified to give more than an opinion based on listening to the arguments. I quote this because the emphasis on bombing by itself was at once a reason and a proof of the failure to go all out last winter in the preparation of a Second Front.*

(b) The natural tendency of our Chiefs of Staff is all against a Continental expedition. We have never reckoned to fight on the continent without great armies trained on the continental model. Our manpower goes into manufacture, naval and now air. Military comes second. This tradition is naturally greatly reinforced by the fall of France, Dunkirk and the continuous inferiority induced by German victories. One who has watched our generals at close quarters said that 'we have performed a remarkable feat in producing a staff of pacifist generals', while another with similar opportunities said to me that the chief reason why we had no Second Front was that our generals 'are afraid of the Germans'. They have good reason. I am listing reasons, not assessing blame.

(c) For generals trained in this tradition the natural instinct is to throw everything into Imperial defence and rely on blockade, and on other Powers to defeat Germany. Thus we find the armies of Britain being wiped out, or surrendering or driven out in all distant parts of the world, and a front, in Libya, which cannot prove of more than secondary importance and which diverts an immense amount of shipping and material at a terrific cost in sea, tonnage and sailing hours, while the opportunity of winning the war in Europe is neglected. The one front, France, where the air umbrella would

---

* The argument for attempting to win by bombing is reinforced by reports of the sub-human stage of brutalisation said to have been reached by Germany's Eastern armies. This is the strangest argument for a defensive strategy!

179

be decisive, if not for victory, at least for withdrawing Germany's air force and other power from Russia, is neglected, while our power is dispersed in a score of places all of which could be readily retaken, if an attack was made at the heart while the Russian armies remained powerful and in the field. This I believe will be regarded as almost incredible strategic folly by historians. That we, any of us, for a moment accept it as anything else merely shows how difficult it is for a country to face new circumstances and break with traditional ways of looking at national problems.

(d) There remains one factor, in my view the most important of all. Just as the habit of guarding and conquering in backward countries disperses our forces and the mystique of bombing which has proved a failure when tried by Göring, still prevails for traditional reasons here and fits in with the prejudice against Russia as a secure or potent ally, so the kind of warfare and the habits of mind required for the war of liberation on the Continent require changes in mentality which have proved too much for our staff. On this I could recite a lot. From the time that France fell it became difficult to envisage any method of unity except in conjunction with anti-Fascist elements on the Continent. That meant in some places purely national elements, but in others socialist, communist, perhaps even, anarchist elements. It meant a repudiation of several respectable and sometimes Catholic 'governments', after Russia was brought into the war it meant a much more definite alliance with the 'left' at home and abroad. Some day the story of the internal conflict caused by this dilemma, so difficult for a Catholic and conservative Foreign Office, will be told. Sometimes the party of activity seemed inclined to win. Plans were made for fomenting and helping revolution in Spain and in Italy for instance. They were abandoned, not I think for any technical reason, but because they were highly distasteful to a whole set of interests, which thought more of the social results of the war than of beating the Germans. Directly that liberation view was entertained, the technical difficulties became different and less. A large number of air and sea and combined operations carrying arms to people in revolt and sustaining bridgeheads wherever possible so that the Germans would have to send back air and land forces to deal with them and with the sympathetic revolts that would arise all over Europe— this could certainly have been done with a good hope of creating a Second Front where the revolt was strongest and our landing most successful. St Nazaire was encouraging about the chances of landing and the degree of support. But, most important of all, note that complete success was not necessary. Such a front or series of fronts would certainly have served the united cause by giving Hitler two fronts if they had been begun early this summer. I have never found anyone to deny this. The truth is quite simply that guerilla warfare such as has played so important a part in China, Russia and Yugoslavia does not appear in the manuals of British military science and is extremely repugnant to our conservative instincts. Read the story of the British attitude to the 'native' (mainly Chinese who have been fighting for five years) in Malaya where guerilla warfare was suggested, or, for that matter, in India. In Europe the same prejudice exists against the unofficial soldier especially if he is likely to be some sort of revolutionary.

(6) My conclusion is that as things are now going *there will be no Second Front in Europe in 1945* even if the Russians hold on and keep the mass of Germany's troops engaged there. The same factors that prevented the Second Front in 1942 will continue to operate in the next years however much production there is. Indeed there will be terrible new arguments next year against doing what is perfectly feasible in 1942; the Germans will be stronger in the west, the capacity of the submerged allies to resist will be terribly diminished by executions, by discouragement and by starvation. On this experts on Europe, including it seems Sir Samuel Hoare, agree. Sir Samuel, I understand, argues that we shall soon be too late in Europe which will give in of necessity if no aid comes from us. Add to this strong reports from France that resistance, which was ready in spring 1942, is now dropping as well the guise as [of] a military factor [in] spring 1943. In that case the tragedy will indeed be complete. There will be no way of defeating Germany unless indeed the weight of bombing may in the course of years smash up so much that this crack on which it seems popular to gamble in high quarters should appear in Germany before it appears here—which I should not have thought probable in a Germany with the vast area of conquered Russia to develop and with no scruples about the number of our potential allies [to] die of starvation.

(7) The logic of the policy of Britain and America in not running risks to fight now on the Continent while it is possible, is a peace which accepts a German Europe. My friends who follow German thought carefully tell me that there is complete confidence in Germany that such a peace must follow our failure to attack in 1942. That is the logic. I do not think it will happen because logic is not our strong point. Actually we are more likely to go on for years in a giant and destructive and utterly inconclusive bombing and blockading match. Hoare's warning about winning in time for the victory to have any meaning or to save anything we want to save is precisely to the point.

When Martin returned from the United States, he had a proposal for an American edition of *The New Statesman*. On 8 January, the Board discussed the matter.

From KINGSLEY MARTIN, *8 January 1943*

Dear Maynard,

Many thanks for your help today. But my fears about the Board were confirmed. The argument is not at all over and the Board has gone away without really thrashing the points out, leaving to Roberts to find all the technical difficulties. He got Whitley and Low to stay behind and talk after the Board was over and Whitley is obviously not very happy. After all he doesn't know who the Walshes are and it is natural that he should be anxious before passing over our subscription list to them and that there should be a very definite legal arrangement about the return to us. I don't know whether you know the Walshes. They work in close contact with *The New Republic* and many other people we know. I don't know whether you can reassure the Board about Walsh's complete reliability? They are now close friends of mine, but of course I cannot produce proof that Richard Walsh is an honest man. I don't mean that Whitley was going back on his vote, but he was wanting to be very definite indeed about a legal contract. This is all right, but not the real point. If our arrangement only relied on legal phraseology enforceable as between us and a firm in the United States whom we did not know, I should hesitate myself.

There will be a lot of minor details to work out and if Roberts is still quite unpersuaded—it was the great reason for wanting a complete Board with a couple of hours to talk—it will be difficult indeed to carry the scheme through. However, I will talk the matter out with him when I can and we will draft a letter and send it to the Board.

I fully understood how terribly busy you were and it was good of you not to mind my pressing you so hard about having a longer time for the meeting. But there are some things that can't be settled by force of intellect in a few minutes, because if the settlement is real it has to be an agreement as well as a victory.

Yours,
KINGSLEY

To KINGSLEY MARTIN, *12 January 1943*

Personal and Private

Dear Kingsley,

When you have worked out the details of the proposed contract for the American edition, perhaps it might be useful to let me give it a look through before it goes round to the Board.

I was greatly perplexed by Roberts the other day and did not feel satisfied that I had reached an explanation why he felt so hot and bothered about it all. The reasons he gave were hopeless, and most of them seemed to be pure fabrications. As to what really moves him one can make the most uncertain conjectures. Yet it is very important to get him reconciled to so significant a new development. I do not know the Walshes except by name. But I did not gather that his opposition was based on any particular distaste for them.

Yours,

J. M. K.

To KINGSLEY MARTIN, *24 January 1943*

Private and Personal

Dear Kingsley,

I have had a private and personal letter from Whitley, from which it appears that he is weakening seriously on the American project, though no new arguments are produced. I suppose Roberts has been working on his feelings meanwhile. He proposes that there should be another Board to discuss the matter. No harm in that, if we can have a cut-and-dried contract in front of us to discuss. How, by the way, are you getting on with that?

Yours,

K

Brailsford ought to be pensioned off as soon as possible.

From KINGSLEY MARTIN, *26 January 1943*

Dear Maynard,

I had a similar private and personal letter from Whitley and agree with you that a Board is desirable if we can have a much more definite scheme to discuss. Some days after the Board, Roberts wrote a short business note to Walsh, asking how long a photostat process would take, and whether he fully understood that any agreement would mean all subscriptions, etc. coming back to us after the war and our probably cancelling the arrangement after the war. I think he feels sure that the Walshes cannot really agree to this.

I wrote a longish letter to Walsh going into matters a good deal further. But you realise, of course, that the business arrangements must be in Roberts' hands, and I told Walsh that he must write on these business points to Roberts. The big question involved is the time factor. Roberts will argue that at best we can only rely on getting the paper to the New York reader in $2\frac{1}{2}$ to 3 weeks, and that this is not a sufficient improvement to make the change worthwhile. Two weeks would certainly make it worthwhile. There is some point, obviously not easy to define, at which it becomes doubtful. I am now making further enquiries about how quickly we can do it. I saw the American Office of War Information people the other day and they told me that if I could get a regular arrangement with the British authorities, they believed that it might be easy for our American agent to get the loan of a very early priority copy for photostat purposes from Washington on occasion, if something went wrong with the regular service. In other words, one or two copies already go over in the first priority bag. It is a question of how high we can push the priority up. I am going to see Cruikshank again about this.

As to the contract of which you speak, we now wait for a letter from Walsh, which may, I suppose, be a couple of months! I do not quite see how to expedite things at this stage, because it really is not possible for me to take the business arrangements out of Roberts' hands. Have you any suggestion? Do you think we ought to cable?

I wonder what prompted your P.S. about Brailsford. I am a good deal intrigued. What was it you disliked? His views on Germany, or what? I do not always agree with him, but he is still in my view much the best journalist writing in England. His famine article[85] surely you agree with that. He did not write the first article last week.[86] I'm curious.

[85] 'Famine in India', *New Statesman and Nation*, 23 January 1943.
[86] 'World Plans, Current Facts', 16 January 1943.

Roberts had the very wise idea the other day that we ought to raise Raymond Mortimer's salary. R.M. is paid much less than Literary Editors have been in the past and he is far the best we ever had. Whitley has agreed to giving Raymond £200 extra a year, which still leaves him today very much less than *The Sunday Times* or *Observer* would give him for a weekly article, but I know you will agree about this. He will still receive less than £1,000 with all his writing, bonus, etc. (I am inclined to think that the Board ought to reconsider some other salaries. My own monthly cheque is now £10!)

Yours,
KINGSLEY

To KINGSLEY MARTIN, *28 January 1943*

Private and Personal

Dear Kingsley,

As I said at the last Board meeting, I agree that everything turns upon how much time can be saved. And we must get as clear about that beforehand as possible. But it seemed to me that Roberts thought this a good wicket to bat on against the scheme rather than the root of his objection.

I entirely agree about Raymond's salary. But should not this have come before the Board? Certain other salaries were, I thought, going up automatically because of the profit-sharing arrangements. But I should like to know for certain that this is working out as it should.

My P.S. about Brailsford is an old but ever-increasing grievance. He seems to me to have every defect—almost incredibly misinformed and ill-informed, carrying credulity to the point when it is almost certifiable, extraordinarily tendentious in a frightfully boring sort of way, with bees in bonnets that entirely distort the right balance of attention given in the paper to different subjects without any balanced judgement or wisdom.

It is astonishing how often things which get the paper into general low repute and mockery (which are usually attributed to you, and for which, perhaps deservedly, you get most of the blame) turn out to be from his pen when I look at my marked copy.

You mention his famine article. Of course, that was about as silly and ill-informed as it could be, but I was not emphasising that particularly. Or take the first paragraph in an article which was a week or two earlier, I think, about the wonderful blue print for the new world which Mr Wallace is producing, whilst everyone else is doing nothing, or obstructing him. If one knows so little about what is going on in the world, is it not wiser to hold one's tongue?

Well, apologies for being so emphatic. But there is, I think, something definitely pathological about Brailsford which smears the paper, and I am increasingly of opinion, when people are trying to diagnose what particularly repels them, that that is the major source.

Yours,

KEYNES

P.S. Reading this letter through, I fancy the following is probably the diagnosis of why I feel so emotionally about this. At bottom Brailsford is generally on the right side and espousing generous causes. Yet the effect of what he writes is nearly always to arouse my worst feelings and detach my sympathies from what he advocates. There is no-one such an expert as he at making the better cause appear to be the worse. One dislikes intensely seeing some of the best causes in the world so lowered in their place and their degree.

From KINGSLEY MARTIN, *5 February 1943*

Dear Maynard,

Roberts and I did not want to wait for a Board Meeting to raise the question about Raymond's salary, because it seemed very likely to us that after *Channel Packet*[87] he would have an offer from one of the Sunday papers. It seemed much better that his salary should be raised first by us at once

[87] (London, 1942.)

and not as a result of any kind of competitive pressure. I feel sure that this was a wise move. *The Observer* is nibbling at Raymond, though so far its main effort is to try to persuade him to go to North Africa as a special reporter. It is possible that he may go there for both papers.

I could say a great deal about your very interesting remarks about Brailsford. I think I understand. You are temperamentally opposites; he is a good deal of a sentimentalist and very much a romanticist. Very many readers would react, I think, in precisely the opposite way from you. He writes always as a puritan and a prophet, and that always puts you off. I am puzzled about the particular example of the famine article. I have tested that out and find it pretty accurate, though the finance remarks were admittedly a partial statement of the case. I think that you react from his moral passion about India so violently that when you find something that seems to you an over-statement you decide that the whole thing is rubbish. Actually he follows India as carefully as anyone can outside the India Office, and he often has facts which they do not see fit to publish. I suppose it would not have been any good trying to get you and Noel better acquainted; he is very shy and does not readily display the riches of his mind, which have only been equalled by one or two others in my experience. I often remove from his writings passages of the sort that annoy you and which I cannot stomach. He belongs to a generation which had faith in the future, and he holds on to it in spite of intellectual disillusion. I am continually checking up on the general reception of the paper, and my information does not square with yours. If you take Brailsford on Germany, which he has known very well, I find, for instance, that Crossman who is, as you know, today as well informed as anyone in England on this subject, greatly approves of what Noel writes on that subject. As for the Wallace point, I thought I had changed that. It was a natural mistake for anyone who was in America two years ago and who was an intimate friend of Wallace and the younger New Dealers.

Finally, I do not find in general that the paper is 'in low repute'; on the contrary I think that we have never exercised half the influence we do to-day and I have evidence of this not only from a surprisingly wide section of the public, but also from civil servants. The two places where I know the paper is 'mocked at' are on the Executive of the Labour Party and in the Treasury!

Yours,
KINGSLEY

To KINGSLEY MARTIN, *9 February 1943*
Private and Personal

My dear Kingsley,

Well, I see we shall never agree about Brailsford. A poet is entitled to his emotions with the least possible regard to facts, but is a journalist? I think he has now reached a point when he seizes upon any supposed information which suits his preconceptions and rejects all else with such avidity that it really is a degrading sight. And the better the emotions, all the more upsetting.

I have just looked up again the article on 'Famine in India'. Heaven knows that few can have a lower opinion of the Government of India today than I have, nor is there anyone more conscious of how it has muddled this and most other matters. But the article contained some fantastic misrepresentations of fact, largely inconsistent with its own, perfectly correct, diagnosis of hoarding, and then when it came to its proposed remedy for hoarding overlooked the fact that the greater number of the Viceroy's Council are Indians. The conclusion Brailsford ought to have drawn is that, since the Indianisation of the Viceroy's Council, the once prized efficiency of the I[ndian] C[ivil] S[ervice] and the Government, at any rate on the administrative side, has largely disappeared, which is a sad forecast of what will happen when we have entirely withdrawn our hands. Personally, I am so fed up with India, that I should like to clear out on any terms and at the earliest possible moment. But probably, if I was nearer the facts, I should not have the heart to follow my inclinations literally; and then, I suppose, I should become a victim of Brailsford's ravings on the matter.

At any rate, I can only repeat that I have found it lowering to my morale, and I am not the only one. It has the sort of indecency of the public exhibition of someone in hysteria.

Yours ever,

J. M. K.

From KINGSLEY MARTIN, *11 February 1943*

Dear Maynard,

The fact that you feel like that is important and I take due notice of it. I agree that H.N.B. is highly emotional about the Indian situation, and I see that you too feel strongly about it. He and I took the view from the first week of the war that it was one of the key questions, and deeply deplored what I believed to have been the terrible initial error of declaring war for India without consultation with Indians, and rejecting with contempt the first admirable appeal by Nehru, etc. which offered full collaboration in the war only a few weeks after it started. Behind all the discussion is the knowledge that Winston does not intend to make any move on India if he can possibly help it anyway. The situation is now worsened by Gandhi's fast. I do not quite understand all you say about the famine article, but it is important that the emotions which I thought were kept in check in that article have come through with so much effect upon you. I do not think Noel's judgement is always good nowadays. I know very few people whose judgement has quite survived the strain of the last five years. From the Editor's point of view it would be easier if there were more available leader writers. It is something like a full-time job to keep the coherence of outlook within a small group who must write on a number of subjects.

Hints in the press and elsewhere reveal to me something of the struggle you must be having behind the scenes in Washington. If there is anything useful to be done about post-war agreements with America at the moment I should be glad to be better informed. I know you don't think that these issues should be so strictly private. If you think it might be useful to have an off-the-record conversation with a few of us, I would like to arrange a small lunch. Yours,

K. M.

Two remarks about India:

1. Raymond, who as an individualist intensely dislikes USSR says he thinks Russia the only future ruler for India, etc.

2. I asked (privately) Panikkar, Prime Minister of Bikaner, what he thought about Russia. He is a strict Hindu! He agreed with the suggestion that the USSR might be the only solution since only Bolsheviks would be ruthless enough to destroy Hindu Temples and Moslem Mosques impartially. It's hell to write about.

In March, another leading article, this time 'Hitler's Political Offensive' from the issue of 13 March, caught Keynes's eye.

To KINGSLEY MARTIN, *15 March 1943*

Personal

Dear Kingsley,

The first leader in this week's paper is a good example of the dishonouring stuff which you should not print—the *suggestio falsi*, the inexcusable ignorance, not merely of the hidden realities, but even of the possibility that it might be so. If a chap really knows or suspects no more than that of the inwardness of things, he should keep silent. No harm in the last paragraph, though it is superficial.

. Yours ever,

J.M.K.

From KINGSLEY MARTIN, *17 March 1943*

Dear Maynard,

I am baffled by your letter. Do you mean the front page or the article 'Hitler's Political Offensive'? I cannot imagine why either should be called 'dishonouring' or indeed what you are getting at all. The 'Hitler's Political Offensive' article was written with perhaps too much inside knowledge: the front page seems to me plain sailing. But I know you must mean something or you would not have written.

KINGSLEY

From KINGSLEY MARTIN, *18 March 1943*

Dear Maynard,

I am afraid I can make nothing much of this complaint, and I don't see how any further information would have modified what we said. I see from active propaganda that the long-expected Tunis offensive is just beginning and I have known for a long time that large reinforcements were going out to Montgomery, but the African Front has never meant anything in terms of withdrawing German manpower from the Russian Front, and the best experts I have been able to talk over the matter with have always maintained that a Northern European attack was necessary for that. If that is maturing

I certainly know nothing about it, and that would of course modify what we wrote. In general I think the picture of our relations with the U.S.S.R. is pretty accurate and balanced. The passage about the Big Army school in Washington I wrote in myself as a result of conversations I had in Washington. I remember discussing this point with you on my return and finding that you were in full agreement. At that time Roosevelt had squashed the most extreme members of this party; as far as I can now make out he has had to give way. But there may be politics in this I haven't followed. Relations with the U.S.S.R. do seem to me, and others with much better information who talk to me, pretty bad, and I do not know how I should improve on our leader as a way of giving our public a picture of the situation. A large number of them, you must remember, begin with the assumption that the fault is entirely on our side. I don't see it that way myself, but they have plenty to go on.

I think Eden's visit[88] may really make a great deal of difference, especially as I hear this week that his conversations in the State Department are progressing favourably. Do you think that if we clear up Tunis quickly and invade Sicily and Italy, it will seriously change things on the Russian Front? My military contacts think that Hitler would leave Italy to the Italians and would not divert a single man.

Yours,
[copy not signed or initialled]

From KINGSLEY MARTIN, *21 March 1943*

Dear Maynard,

Desmond McCarthy called in on Friday for no particular reason that I could see except to ask me a question.

D.M. When is the 'Second Front' going to begin?

K.M. The attack in Tunis is beginning this weekend I believe. Montgomery has been very heavily reinforced I'm told. If the Germans are turned out of Tunis I should expect an attack on Sicily and Italy.

D.M. But that's not what I mean at all. When is the invasion going to begin in the West? We must draw off Hitler's troops from Russia before it's too late and we must do it even if it means failure for our army. Not at all for the sake of Russia but to win the war.

Now Desmond is a conservative, anti-Red and very 'non-political'. But I think he is there saying what the majority of *N.S.* readers are saying. The fall of Kharkov, the Russian statement that I am told is quite correct, that Hitler (or rather the General Staff) have been able to withdraw many

---

[88] Mr Eden was in America from 12 to 29 March.

divisions of fresh troops from France for the eastern theatre of war, and now Churchill's bland assumption that the war can only be won at our leisure next year or in some future year certainly seems to justify the school of thought to which I, Lloyd George, Stalin and many others have belonged since the summer of 1941! I always believed that the resistance movements on the Continent plus Russia were, with aid, the instuments for victory and that it would be fatal to wait for the U.S.A. to be ready. I do not repent at any point of belonging to this school. My view that the opposite school is much influenced by an often unconscious fear of Russian victory on the Continent has been borne out in many ways; in the U.S.A. it is no more unconscious or even silent than it was in 1941 here, when Moore-Brabazon innocently blurted out his hope that Russia would be destroyed as well as Germany and said afterwards that he was only saying in public what all the Cabinet had said privately. The remark (in the article you commented upon with such unnecessary rudeness) about the Big Army school in Washington was put in by me; it was the result of conversations in Washington, and when I came back I asked you about this and found that you completely agreed with me.

I think a general strategy of bombing and blockade and waiting was decided upon before the attack on Russia when in fact it was the only plan available to us, and that the full possibilities of victory, years before it seemed possible in 1941, were never realised because of distrust of Russia, and that the plans have never been thoroughly revised to meet the hope of European victory in alliance with Russia. A fortnight ago I asked Herbert Agar (whom you probably know is now Winant's personal assistant and who went to U.S.A. with Winant a couple of months ago) about the Big Army school. He had just got back. He replied that they seemed to have won, and when I asked what this army was for he said that the Army could only think in terms of an AMERICAN victory and still absolutely assumed the defeat of Russia, after which they would need these millions of men to fight an American war all over the world. Herbert is Catholic in his outlook and in philosophy violently anti-Soviet. My view does not come to any important extent from attachment to the U.S.S.R. but to the horror of allowing the Continent to be starved into submission and all the things we are supposed to be fighting for and all the best people in Europe to be massacred or otherwise disposed of while they wait with terrible anxiety for help we have promised and that I believe we could have given them effectively in 1943. Russia gave us the chance of rescue; we have preferred to go to North Africa. Perhaps the Italian offensive will do the trick; I hope so. Much here seems to turn on whether an attack on Sicily and Italy will materially 'take the weight off Russia'. Two experts I asked today differed on this. But certainly not quickly. The Air Force people I've seen have been just bewildered by not making use of their free supplements in France. But views seem to all affected by politics. Perhaps you have information of another front—mine is that it is planned, but not in time to coincide with Russian efforts this year. I hope I'm wrong. What I do notice is that evidence that anti-Soviet prejudice of one sort or another has much influence still accumulates and that when Winston makes a big speech he does not even mention and certainly does not appreciate the resistance movement on the Continent which is, far more than anything else, the aspect of the war that makes sense to me.

You may have something else in mind altogether. If not, you have no justification for calling a very reasonable expression of this view (which incidentally included a carefully balanced argument that Russia always overdid her suspicions) 'shaming' or using other heat-making and abusive comments.

Roberts and I have heard from Walsh today about the American edition. Every condition is answered according to Roberts' satisfaction. Unfortunately I am unable to get any assurance about being able to get the paper over to the U.S.A. in any regular quick way. The summer would be all right, but Cruikshank at the M.O.I. who is exceedingly helpful, tells me that he has still no assurance that even for the best priority next winter's mails will be better than last's. In which case the thing is no go.

KINGSLEY

Excuse messy script—all my own typing.

To KINGSLEY MARTIN, *1 April 1943*

My dear Kingsley,

You have no idea what the plans are; you have no idea what factors affect the timing; if anything is going to happen in time or place different from what you wish, you have no idea what the compelling reasons are;—so your propaganda-conditioned mind falls back on the one thing which is quite certainly false so far as this country is concerned,—namely, that military events are much influenced by an often unconscious fear of a Russian victory on the Continent.

It is, of course, true that there are many people in this country who think it would be much better if Russia does not have it all her own way in Europe and that we play a part which entitles us to have a say in what comes after. But how is it you cannot see that this works in exactly the opposite direction? The people who are over-afraid of Russian dominance are, of course, those who are most urgently concerned that we ourselves should be putting up a good show. The lunatic state of mind which you attribute to un-named persons is absolutely non-existent.

I am not up-to-date about U.S.A. But I agree, as you know, that the American 'big army' scheme does run the danger of being an obstacle to proper concentration on 1943.

However, I think that it is not so much your delusions I object to, but the kind of way in which they peep above the surface of the paper. Suppose you were to have an article saying straight out the sort of thing you say to me in your letter, I should of course disagree, but I might feel, as such things are being said below the surface, something to be said for bringing them up above it. If you were to say in so many words that people in this country in a position to influence military affairs were governed by the motive that they wanted Germany to beat Russia, not the other way round, everyone would know what sort of stuff they were reading.

But, of course, you are in fact much too sensible to write any such thing. You want to have it both ways,—to appear in public as a more or less sane member of society, and to indulge morbidities a little out of sight, letting them however peep out in a disguised or ambiguous form. And that is what always upsets me so. I notice from your letter a further development of the malady. It now appears that an invasion of Europe only counts as a Second Front if it starts on certain parts of the coast of the Continent, and does not count if it starts on other parts.

Yours,

J. M. K.

The next exchange concerned an obituary of Beatrice Webb.

From KINGSLEY MARTIN, *5 May 1943*

Dear Maynard,

I always make a rule of not printing people's private conversation without giving them a chance to see it, even when I am sure there can be no objection. I enclose a proof of an article I have written about Beatrice Webb.[89] It is in a half-corrected form, but will you look it through? If I don't hear from you by 'phone on Thursday morning I shall assume that you have no comments to make.

Yours,
KINGSLEY

To KINGSLEY MARTIN, *6 May 1943*

Private

My dear Kingsley,

I am delighted with your account of Beatrice. It is excellent that you should be filling the paper with her this week and giving some proper appreciation of what she was. I have been dismayed by the futile and inadequate notices elsewhere, only mitigated by Maisky's very charming note. But that, of course, was too *parti pris*. I agree with your judgement that she was the most remarkable woman of our time. I wish I could do something myself for *The Economic Journal*.[90] But it is hopeless to try to find time to do it properly just now. Perhaps I shall return to it one day after the war.

[89] Martin's obituary of Beatrice Webb, which appeared in *The New Statesman and Nation* for 8 May 1943, contained the following story concerning a lady who had sold her name for advertising purposes: 'I cannot forbear to repeat the conversation that followed; it is so characteristic of all those present. She was riding so high on her moral horse that Maynard Keynes said, gently leg-pulling, "But surely you are too severe. We should all give our names for money if only we were offered enough. You would do it yourself for a million pounds." Before Mrs Webb could utter an indignant denial, Sidney Webb, always on the earth and quick to see the common-sense reply, said, "Oh, yes, of course we should if we were offered a million pounds, my dear. But we should do the advertisement in our own way so that we should not be ashamed of it." "You mean", said Keynes, "that you would say 'this is the best cigarette you can hope to get until the industry is nationalised'."'

[90] The notices in *The Economic Journal* were by Leonard Woolf (June–September 1943) and G. D. H. Cole (December 1943).

I thought your handling of the Polish-Russian business last week just right.[91] Naturally the Russians are indignant at having German murders passed off on them, when the knowledge that they have shot the gentlemen in question at quite another address has absolutely confirmed the falsity of the Smolensk story. And equally the Poles are indignant at having had, not 8,000 officers shot, but 16,000, 8 by one enemy-friend, and 8 by the other. But the weakness of the Polish case is that they have in fact known all about the Russian side of the business for months and even years.

Yours,

J. M. K.

In May 1943 the problem of staffing the paper became acute.

From KINGSLEY MARTIN, *25 May 1943*

Dear Maynard,

I enclose a letter from Francis Williams, which is self-explanatory and which states the situation, I believe, very precisely. The only important fact as far as I know that he leaves out is that the relations between Bracken and Grigg are such that that line of approach is much worse than useless.

If you feel that you can write to Grigg, perhaps it would be useful if I make one or two points about the position of the *N.S. &N*. At the beginning of the war Crossman was Assistant Editor, Calder and Aylmer Vallance were both regularly working on the paper, as well as Brailsford and Cole. Aylmer went into the War Office, where it was then believed that the Political Warfare side would be important. In 1940 Crossman and then Calder were both taken from the paper and given, as you know, important Government jobs. I have since managed because Cole has maintained a steady output, while Brailsford has done *very* much more work, and that I have had one or two temporary assistants in the office. These have never been more than stopgaps, and Freda White, who has been helping me for the last two years, is now leaving. This would in itself make a great difficulty, but the situation is really serious, because at the same time Cole's health has broken down badly and he is having to go away altogether for two or three months. Also

---

[91] 'A Case for Plain Speaking', *New Statesman and Nation*, 1 May 1943. The matter in question was the Katyn massacre.

Brailsford has very much aged and is, for health reasons, quite unreliable. His heart has become seriously affected and he cannot be hurried or bothered to do office work; he can only write articles from home. This means that I am now left without any regular assistance in the office and *very* few regular contributors. Others who used to write regularly are also worked up or otherwise unavailable. The situation is quite impossible. If I were ill myself, for instance, next week, I do not know how the paper could be produced except by 'phoning Woolf to come up from the country which would not work if I were ill on a Wednesday! The result of trying to cope with so many subjects (during the greatly shortened hours when the printer can work nowadays) on the crucial two days of the week is that I am liable to make mistakes, which would never occur in normal times, and it makes serious political thinking and planning of the paper almost impossible.

I have searched diligently for any experienced help and come to the conclusion that I must ask formally for someone to be released. Aylmer would be for many reasons the best. In the first place he is 51 and therefore beyond the age when the transfer of his work will make a difference from the point of view of the Ministry of Labour or, as far as the fighting side of the Services go, of the Army. He is himself ready to come, feeling that his present work is of less importance than he had expected. Perhaps there is an additional point in the fact that the Committe on War Expenditure have urged some cutting down in staff and that the War Office may regard him as a person who can be sacrificed without seriously disorganising other work.

I do not imagine that Grigg has warm feelings towards *The New Statesman*. We have been rather rude once or twice lately though we were very welcoming when he took office. I have only met him once myself, but I know a lot of him and believe that personally we should get on very well. However, the immediate point is that whether he likes the paper or not he may agree that it is ludicrous to expect a newspaper of this size and influence to run without the Editor having any editorial assistance on the political and economic side.

If there are any other points about the staff position that you want to know, please give me a ring. I have only noted down those that occur to me as absolutely essential.

Yours,

KINGSLEY MARTIN

P.S. I was very much worried as well as interested in what you said to me about your conception of the future in Europe. I have thought a lot about it and grow increasingly troubled. Perhaps some day soon you could spare the time either to talk to me a little about it, or to meet four or five people to discuss it. I am now engaged in preparing a series of articles on the future of Europe, especially of Germany, and I should like to know more of the school of thought you mention. On the face of it the proposal bewilders me. I happened to see R. A. Butler last night. He still concerns himself, as you know, with reconstruction problems and I found his mind moving in a very different direction indeed. I would certainly like to get clearer about what you regard as the real possibilities before I take a decided line in the paper. I have deliberately avoided doing so until now, but can put it off no longer.

P.P.S. While Miss Robertson was typing this letter Brendan Bracken rang up. He asked me if I would please go to Australia for six weeks, starting in six weeks' time! He seemed keen on my being a member of a journalist party going. Woolf, I think, would edit for six weeks. If Aylmer were free it would be possible and Bracken rightly said it would be good for me and the paper also.

I leave it to you whether this invitation is an additional argument which might help with Grigg or not.

K. M.

The enclosure ran as follows.

From FRANCIS WILLIAMS, *21 May 1943*

Personal

My dear Kingsley Martin,

I have discussed the question of the possible release of Aylmer Vallance to assist you on *The New Statesman* with the people at the War Office in charge of the Section in which he works. It would, I am afraid, be raising your hopes too high to say that they will agree to release him, but I think I can say that they appreciate your difficulties and are prepared to consider the matter sympathetically. Much would, of course, depend upon whether it is possible to replace Vallance in the work he is doing, which work, I understand, may in some ways tend to become more important than less so.

The best course would be for Lord Keynes, if he would agree, to write to the Secretary of State for War asking whether he would be prepared to consider the release of Aylmer Vallance and setting out *The New Statesman*'s need of him and its inability to find anyone else with the necessary qualifications. They promised me that if the Secretary of State for War receives such a letter and asks for advice on the matter from his higher officers directly concerned they will give the matter very careful consideration and will certainly not turn it down out of hand, though, as I say, they cannot of course guarantee that they will be able to advise the Secretary of State for War to release him, since this depends upon a number of questions which are under consideration.

At any rate, my impression is that it would certainly be worth while your trying. I am sorry I cannot be more definite than this.

All best wishes.

Yours sincerely,
FRANCIS WILLIAMS

To SIR JAMES GRIGG, *26 May 1943*

Dear Grigg,

I write this letter in my private capacity as a Director of the New Statesman and Nation Co. We are in the greatest possible difficulty about the higher staff, and the question has arisen whether Aylmer Vallance can be released from the War Office.

The Ministry of Information support this; and I gather that he is not doing such vital work where he is that his immediate superiors are likely to be desolated at the idea of losing him. But it is thought that your authority will be required before anything can be done.

If Vallance could go back to the paper, I should be much happier in every way about the way in which the work would be carried on, and I believe that the public interest would be served, if you could agree to his release.

I do not know how far you will want to be bothered about the details, but broadly the case is as follows: at the beginning of the war Kingsley Martin was Editor; Crossman Assistant Editor; Calder, Aylmer Vallance, Brailsford and Cole all working regularly for it. Vallance went into the War Office when it was believed that the Political Warfare side would be more important than I believe has turned out to be the case. In 1940 Crossman and then Calder were taken by the Political Warfare people. Cole has been working until now, but has just suffered a breakdown of health from overwork and is having to go away. Brailsford is very old, far from well and, in my judgement, so queer in his views that it is exceedingly inadvisable for the paper to depend on his services too much. The breakdown of Cole and the difficulty of making much use of Brailsford has now put the Editor into an impossible position. He has no responsible person to help him. If he falls ill, the position would be exceedingly awkward; and he cannot get away on any special jobs such as are proposed to him from time to time by the Ministry of Information. Vallance is 51 years of age, a very experienced journalist capable of covering the whole field. *The New Statesman* now has a prodigious circulation and exercises, one way and another, a great influence on opinion here and abroad. It is rather essential, I think, to see that its work can be properly done.

So, unless Vallance really is doing work with you which is important and indispensable, I do very much hope you can agree to let him go.

Yours sincerely,
[copy initialled] K.

From KINGSLEY MARTIN, *27 May 1943*

Dear Maynard,

I forgot one thing I meant to say on the 'phone. It is possible in view of future developments that they think important that the War Office will not be keen on releasing Aylmer altogether, but may be willing to give him a period, say six months, of absence with the understanding that they can have him back later if they want him. I say this on good advice having heard recently of cases which would act as precedent for this.

Yours,
KINGSLEY

To KINGSLEY MARTIN, *3 June 1943*

Dear Kingsley,

I happened to see Grigg personally yesterday. He told me that they have a new job in view for Vallance which only he could do satisfactorily. If that comes off, they would have to keep him. But if it does not come off—and I gather this is not by any means certain—then Grigg agrees to release him.

Yours,
J. M. K.

From KINGSLEY MARTIN, *3 June 1943*

Dear Maynard,

Thank you for sending me this letter from Grigg. I agree that it is only 'moderately discouraging'. I understand privately that while it is admitted that Aylmer has too little important to do now, there is a scheme on foot to give him a job with correspondents on the Continent after invasion. But other people are in the running for this job and I am not unhopeful.

Yesterday Bracken asked me to go and see him. He tells me that the idea is to send four people connected with the press, headed by Walter Layton, to Australia. He and Gervais Huxley, head of the 'Empire' at M.O.I., were very pressing indeed. I told them it was absolutely impossible unless I got Aylmer, and that if Aylmer was able to come I should then have to consult the Board and go into the whole matter. Bracken said he would take the matter of Aylmer up further through Francis Williams on the ground that they needed me to go to Australia, and that I could not even consider it unless Aylmer were released. I was careful not to commit myself, and that is how the matter now stands.

Yours,
KINGSLEY

I have young man of 21 coming in the summer as a 'trainee' on the chance of his turning into something but that will be as much liability as asset for some time.

The next issue that arose came from a leader on 27 July, entitled 'Arms in Sicily'.

To KINGSLEY MARTIN, *27 July 1943*

Personal

Dear Kingsley,

As an old friend of Francis Rodd, I must protest rather strongly against the ignorant and libellous reference to him in Brailsford's first leader this week. So far from being an Oxford Grouper, he has been deeply distressed by the fact that his wife was. No doubt, he knew Volpi, who was formerly, I think, Italian Minister of Finance, just as he knew every prominent person in Italy. But he was extremely *persona non grata* to Mussolini and very decidedly not in with the regime. I can even add that his tendency to heterodoxy is such that he is also decidedly *persona non grata* to our own Governor of the Bank. The whole thing is ridiculous.

Apart from this, the article is another example of fudge and humbug and morbid psychology. We are not to speak to anyone who has been a Fascist; we are not to speak to anyone who is a Catholic. But we are to support a Government which has the support of the majority of the population. I suppose the explanation is the obsessional delusion that some minute underground group is in fact a majority of the population. It all seems pretty unrealistic. However, that is not the point of my letter, since the paper is quite entitled to be un-realistic.

So, you will see I still wish that you would bring yourself to stop his contributions. You will not have much thunder left, I think, when there really is something against which to protest, and that, sooner or later, is extremely likely to happen.

Yours,

J.M.K.

From KINGSLEY MARTIN, *29 July 1943*

Dear Maynard,

Your letter is quite ill-conceived; the particular phrase which you object to most in the article was written not by Brailsford but by me, after the most careful enquiry and at Raymond's suggestion. Raymond has actually twice rung up Rodd's sister-in-law to check this point and finds that she has been present at Oxford Group weekends at their house when Francis Rodd has spoken on 'Ethics and Industry', etc. When Lady Rodd became too conspicuously associated I have no doubt that Frances Rodd withdrew. I inserted the passage myself at Raymond Mortimer's suggestion (the printer actually made a slip by putting 'backers' instead of 'backer' after 'Volpi'). There is a great deal else that I could say on the subject of Rodd on the testimony of close acquaintances, but perhaps that is hardly necessary. For the real point is a different one. What appears on the front page unsigned is editorial and the result of really careful consideration. In this case it would have mattered very little if it had been written by me, Brailsford, or another. Half-a-dozen of us, including a prominent M.P. and a Treasury official discussed the matter at great length before the article was written.

The very strong language which you have taken to using to work off feelings which I suppose are difficult to express in the Civil Service, is provocative and unjustifiable. I should not find it difficult to reply with similar phrases, but what would be the object? You have not even carefully considered the points you make. Nowhere was it suggested that we ought never to 'talk to any Fascists'; on the contrary, what is suggested and what is held very strongly in the House of Commons and elsewhere, is that there is a danger of far too little change being made in Italy and of the general result of our intervention being inadequate to release the forces of democracy, especially in Italy. This is not a bizarre view and certainly not especially Brailsford's.

Yours,

KINGSLEY

On top of Martin's letter, Keynes wrote:

Replied: Sorry, but it is not true that F.R. is or ever has been, a Grouper and a Fascist.   K

The next exchange came after Keynes's return from America after the Anglo-American negotiations on post-war planning (*JMK*, vol. XXIII, pp. 276–301; *JMK*, vol. XXV, pp. 339–92). It concerned an article 'Gifts of God' which had appeared on 16 October 1943.

From KINGSLEY MARTIN, *5 November 1943*

Dear Maynard,

I hear you are back full of classic remarks and stories about the U.S.A. I hope you both enjoyed yourselves more than you did last time.

I am sorry, but not surprised, that you are too busy to come to a Board. It has had to be abandoned as so few could come. You have probably heard that we have got into what is probably the worst libel action in history. I feel that the Board should be fully appraised of the facts and so I have drawn up the enclosed very confidential memorandum.[92] It is of the utmost importance that these facts should not be known to the other side. You will see that the article was published only after the most careful vetting by a

---

[92] Not printed.

lawyer, who saw the author and his evidence. It may be better if this memorandum is destroyed after being read.

I am more sorry about this business than I can say. It looks, however, as if it may coincide with the defeat of Germany and therefore attract little attention.

Yours,

KINGSLEY

To KINGSLEY MARTIN, *9 November 1943*

Private and Confidential

My dear Kingsley,

When I got back, I found your letter. What a dreadful story! I agree that it ought, if possible, to be considered by a Board Meeting.

I have no doubt that it should be settled out of court, if possible. But, of course, if the other solicitors see that, they may demand higher damages for a settlement out of court than they would be likely to get from the court. If it goes into court, then alternative (3) on your page 11, seems to me to be much the best, that is to say, to be completely abject and make no defence whatever. In this case, it would be essential, I should say, to go the whole hog and not to go into the box at all. For, if you do, you are bound to be asked what steps you took to corroborate the story, and then, sooner or later, you are in for the whole narrative, which, as you say, will reflect no credit.

I should say that points (4) and (6)[93] on your page 11 are not worth pursuing, but I am afraid that there may be a risk of what you fear under (5).[94] (8) has its dangers, in view of what you relate about D.C.'s politics and personality, although, if it were to come up, the advantages are obvious.[95]

How soon do you expect the case to come on?

Yours,

J. M. K.

[93] Alternative (4) involved action against a detective agency concerned with the matter and (6) a possible line of defence.

[94] That the party's lawyers might discover the anonymous writer of the piece or that a detective agency was involved.

[95] Going to all possible lengths to keep the matter out of court.

From KINGSLEY MARTIN, *11 November 1943*

Dear Maynard,

Many thanks for your letter. I agree with each of your points.

I enclose a copy of a letter I have just sent to Whitley in reply to some points he raised.[96]

Yours,

K. M.

The case did not go to court, but *The New Statesman* agreed to apologise publicly and pay the two ladies involved a total of £850.

There then was a lull until Martin received an article on the Bretton Woods agreement.

From KINGSLEY MARTIN, *14 September 1944*

Dear Maynard,

I believe you know Hammersley. I enclose an article he has sent, for the *N.S.* to publish. It seems to me that we must do so, and I feel that an answer is really required. I do not feel that anybody except yourself can do it properly.

The Daily Herald correspondent in Washington, Arthur Webb, had lunch with me today. He was awestruck with the brilliance of your performance at Bretton Woods, and said that you succeeded in explaining these matters to journalists in the simplest language, etc. No one has done this in England, and until there is some authoritative statement from yourself, I think that the usual writers on this subject, who do not want to crab something important, but are full of doubts, will hesitate to do so. If you are simply too busy to do it, it can't be helped, but unless you do, Hammersley's piece will be followed by a lot of other articles and letters supporting his view, or defending Bretton Woods, perhaps on grounds which are just those you would not wish. Please let me know if you feel you can't do anything about it. I expect to publish Hammersley next week. *The Daily Express* is starting an attack!

A lot of important things have happened since I saw you. One of them

[96] Not printed.

205

is that Crossman is definitely coming back to the paper a few months after the defeat of Germany, which I know will please you.

Yours,
KINGSLEY

I greatly enjoyed seeing you both the other night.

To KINGSLEY MARTIN, *15 September 1944*

Dear Kingsley,

In my opinion this article should be rejected. It is altogether below par, mainly based upon a pure misunderstanding of the document, and quite grossly misinformed. There are only two ways of replying to it. One would be a couple of sentences, saying that it is wide of the mark and based on a misunderstanding of the document. The alternative would be to expound in detail what the document really is. That could not be done under a good many columns.

Yes, I know Hammersley. Before I went to Bretton Woods I had brought him round to the Joint Statement. The only differences between this and the Bretton Woods Plan are from his point of view, in the right direction. I can very possibly bring him round again if I spend two hours with him. But it simply is not practicable for me to undertake individual missionary work like that. Nor, unfortunately, am I free to write articles.

If you want to get to the bottom of this question of whether a return to the gold standard is involved, read the last issue of *The Banker* where Einzig puts the case that it is a return to gold, and is answered by Dacey. I believe that in the next number of *The Banker* there will be a rejoinder from Einzig and a further comment by Dacey. If you look at these articles, you will see that it is not the sort of subject on which you would be inclined to give a lot of space week after week, and it cannot be dealt with very briefly.

My suggestion, therefore, is this. The Chancellor has agreed to my having a talk with a select group at Chatham House, provided no sort of publicity is concerned. McAdam is therefore collecting a party of about thirty at 5 o'clock on October 4th. I am suggesting to him that he should invite both you and Hammersley. This will enable you to suggest to Hammersley that he should put off publishing something which is largely based on misapprehension until he has had the opportunity of the above discussion.

I am very glad to hear that there is a prospect of Crossman coming back.

Yours,
MAYNARD KEYNES

P.S. I might add as possibly some further indication that Hammersley and Boothby and many others are completely off the rails; that out of a large concourse of competent economists at Bretton Woods which included in our own party those of such different schools as Robbins, Robertson and myself, as well as many others from a great number of countries, not a single one thought that there was anything whatever in the gold standard allegation. It is not the position which any competent person can sustain when he is fully acquainted with what is proposed.

Again, there was a lull of several months until an article 'Sanity in Poland' in the issue of 14 May 1945 brought Keynes a series of complaints.

From L. J. CADBURY, *14 May 1945*

Dear Maynard,

I should normally have written this letter direct to Kingsley Martin. As, however, he is away I do not know who is editing the *N.S. and N.* I fear Brailsford is having a good deal to say in matters.

This week's issue, particularly the opening Notes, is really monstrous. I should very much like to know if you feel as critical of it as I do myself. If so, even though we are minority shareholders, ought we not to do something about it?

In reading the Notes, I had in mind particularly the section dealing with Anglo-American–Russian relations, as last Friday afternoon I had a long talk with Paul Winterton who, apart from occasional leave, has been *The News Chronicle* representative since 1941. He returned home last week as he just could not stick it any longer.

What possible justification is there for the following sentences:–

But Mr Eden, egging on Mr Stettinius in a campaign to vilify Russia and (incidentally) to split the British Left on the eve of a General Election, doth protest too much. What is important is that the Russians would in all probability not have troubled to arrest these men if Moscow's suspicions of the West had not recently deepened.

One reason for this deepening of suspicion is apparently because we declined to promise the Soviet Union vast post-war credits. A diplomatic way, of course, for stating goods for which we never expected to be paid. It is a little difficult to see why we should be taken to task for refusing to send goods to the U.S.S.R. on these conditions. Anything we can spare from home consumption we require in our endeavour to re-establish our position in export markets where we expect to be able to continue normal peace-time trade on business conditions.

Though it is only a very minor consideration, one cannot altogether forget that we have never had any credit as far as the Russian public is concerned for all the military supplies we have sent or even for the raw materials delivered under the Agreement I negotiated.

The U.S.S.R. is obviously more powerful, at any rate on the Continent of Europe, than this country and can without great difficulty make itself almost completely self-sufficient. Nevertheless, we can be extremely useful to her if she is prepared to play ball with us. If we are going to encourage her to play the last thing we want to adopt is the policy of unvarying boot-licking which the *N.S.&N.* appears to advocate.

Is there anything we can do about it, particularly at this very critical moment in our relations with the U.S.S.R.?

Yours sincerely,

L. J. C.

To L. J. CADBURY, *15 May 1945*

Dear Laurence,

I could not agree more than I do with what you say about that shameful article in last Saturday's *N.S.&N.* about Poland. After reading it I had it in mind to write to Leonard Woolf, who is Acting Editor, to ask how he could have taken responsibility for so monstrous a comment. I failed to do so at the moment, however, being over-occupied in other directions. It was all the more unnecessary because Kingsley Martin's article from San Francisco on the same subject[97] was perfectly reasonable and proper and, indeed, exceedingly interesting.

The note in question was not in fact by Brailsford, but by Aylmer Vallance.

I am sending on your letter to Leonard Woolf. There have been several things in the paper lately which, in my judgment, passed all limits of decency, but this particular one was about the worst. Compare it, not only with Kingsley Martin's excellent contribution from San Francisco, but with the most interesting and judicious comment in *The Economist* last Saturday.

Yours sincerely,
[copy not signed or initialled]

From VIOLET BONHAM-CARTER, *15 May 1945*

My dear Maynard,

I must write you a line to say how horrified I was by the first article (front page) in *The New Statesman* of this week—accusing Eden of 'egging on Stettinius to vilify Russia'.

If they are so ill-informed they should go out of journalism. Alternatively: if they possess the information which is at the disposal of everyone of us, and yet write such stuff their intellectual dishonesty deserves a far worse fate.

I believe you have some power and authority in their counsels. How can you allow them to 'rip' on like this? I am really sickened by them. They make me feel ashamed *for* them.

Ever yours,
VIOLET

My love to you and Lydia—the war in Europe over and Mark still alive—is a great relief to me. He has been fighting hard every *inch* of the way since Good Friday—and 2 brother officers were killed in his company—one close!—only a week ago.

[97] 'Shadows at San Francisco', *New Statesman and Nation*, 12 May 1945.

To VIOLET BONHAM-CARTER, *16 May 1945*

My dear Violet,

I could not agree more than I do with what you say about that shameful article in last Saturday's *N.S.&N.* about Poland. It was all the more unnecessary and inexcusable because Kingsley Martin's own article from San Francisco on the same subject was perfectly reasonable and proper and, indeed, exceedingly interesting.

It makes me deeply ashamed to be connected with the paper. But the position of the directors has become very difficult. The successors of the old *Nation* group represent a minority and can do nothing by themselves. The Board seldom meets. We have established a tradition, which, of course, is in many ways wholesome, that the Board will not interfere with editorial discretion. But I agree with you that this vile thing does overstep the limits of decency. Nor is it the first example of what seems to me to be shameful intellectual dishonesty.

I am now writing to Leonard Woolf, who is Acting Editor in Kingsley's absence in San Francisco. I cannot think how he allowed it, since I know from conversation that he has agreed with me in feeling ashamed about some earlier passages which have occurred.

I hope you are feeling fairly cheerful about electoral prospects. All my good wishes are with you and the [Liberal] Party. I should view with great alarm a substantial victory by either of the major Parties.

I hear, by the way, that you are now one of the Governors of Sadlers Wells. In that connection you will have come across one aspect of CEMA[98] activities through the Covent Garden project. As Chairman of the Covent Garden Committee, I am closely concerned with this. After a talk with Dyson this morning, I am encouraged to think that we shall eventually reach a really satisfactory plan, acceptable to both sides. But the main

[98] The Council for the Encouragement of Music and the Arts, of which Keynes was chairman.

point is that we really must recover Covent Garden for Ballet and Opera of a national character. It is a great step to that that we have succeeded in persuading the Treasury to put some money into it through CEMA. But I should like to engage your sympathies.

My love to you and Bongie, and affectionate congratulations on Mark having got through it all. I should think one can assume that they will let him off for the rest.

Yours ever,

[copy initialled] M. K.

From a letter from JOHN ROBERTS, *15 May 1945*

For some time I have 'sensed' your unhappiness about the paper. Frequently of late I have found myself, in varying degrees of heat, in disagreement with some of its views, and although I have nothing like your knowledge and information to support my views, I have nevertheless felt strongly that there has been too frequently an insufficient weighing of the facts or a deliberate blind eye to facts which, with more detachment, would have been considered. Sharp once wrote in a leaflet about the *N.S.* 'if the facts don't square with the theory the theory must go'. Some of our contributors, in my opinion, are too inclined to reverse this. As you say, such contributions are by no means from one pen. I have hated, for example, Joad's recent effusions in the paper.

From a letter to JOHN ROBERTS, *16 May 1945*

Thanks for your letter of May 15th. I am afraid that Vallance's note about Poland last Saturday has really pushed matters beyond bearing. I am receiving letters of protest and am deeply ashamed to be mixed up with the paper. I am writing to Leonard Woolf about it. A point is arriving, I think, when the directors simply cannot disclaim responsibility.

It is all the more unnecessary and inexcusable because Kingsley's own article from San Francisco on the same subject was perfectly reasonable and proper and, indeed, very interesting.

From RAYMOND MORTIMER, [*May 1945*]

Dear Maynard,

I'd like to come to see you some time next week if I could. My situation on this paper is becoming very awkward. Last week the front page comments on the Polish row went beyond what I could stomach. I shall of course talk to Kingsley as soon as he returns, and I would rather you said nothing to him about this until I have seen him. But if this paper is going in for a policy of supporting Russia against both the liberal democracies and against England, I do not see how I can go on.

Yours ever,

RAYMOND

To RAYMOND MORTIMER, *18 May 1945*

My dear Raymond,

I am not at all surprised at your letter. I was deeply disturbed and horrified by that article, and am personally ashamed to have any connection with the paper. It happens that before I got your letter I had already received strong protests from others concerned. I have passed these on to Leonard. When Kingsley Martin returns we must, I think, grasp the nettle and open up the sore, etc., etc. This has to be treated, I think, not quite in isolation, but as the culminating outrage of a series.

I cannot think how Leonard passed it. Possibly it may have been written at the last moment after he had left the office. It was all the more unnecessary and scandalous in as much as Kingsley's article on the same subject in the same issue was perfectly reasonable and proper and also very interesting.

My present feeling is that Vallance should no longer be entitled to contribute to the paper, and I am afraid Brailsford is not much better. Kingsley himself is, of course, deeply responsible. On the other hand, my marked copies are always telling me that the passages which I find outrageous are seldom from his pen. I frequently disagree with Kingsley, but that is another matter. I do not so often find him outraging the decencies as the scum which he attracts round him.

212

Let us have a talk next week. Would you like to come to lunch one day or take supper with us in the kitchen one evening? (Are you raising the matter with Leonard meanwhile?)

Yours ever,
[copy initialled] M.K.

To LEONARD WOOLF, *15 May 1945*

Dear Leonard,

I enclose some correspondence with Laurence Cadbury, which speaks for itself. What, if any, action do you think it is one's duty to take about it, if one feels as you see I do? I should like to have the correspondence back.

Yours ever,
[copy not signed or initialled]

P.S. Since writing the above, I have had the enclosed letter from Violet Bonham-Carter. It was indeed a very vile passage, which leaves one thoroughly ashamed of having anything to do with the paper.

P.P.S. Since writing the above I have had another dismayed protest from one closely connected with the paper. I do not think you can expect people to go on much longer without having the sore opened up.

From LEONARD WOOLF, *19 May 1945*

Dear Maynard,

I entirely agree about the article, although the responsibility is of course mine. It is appalling. I was in a difficult situation last week and I dare say looking back I made a wrong decision. The two days holiday in the middle of the week meant that all the proofs had to be passed on Thursday. I arranged that Vallance should write the front page and leave it with the printer early on Thursday morning so that I could not see it before it was in proof. We all spent the whole of Thursday at the printers and everything

213

had to go straight on to the page and it was understood that the printers could only print on Friday if there were no serious alterations to be made. The pages with material which I had not read were promised for 2.30. The front page however was only ready for me to read at 5. When I read it, I felt as you do about it and told Vallance so. It was considerably worse than it is now. The difficulty was that the article ought to have been rewritten entirely, but that in the state the printers were in that meant beginning all over again on Friday for them and quite probably not getting the paper out until Monday. I also had an engagement which made it necessary for me to catch the 6.45 latest to Lewes. In the end I told Vallance that he must put in certain alterations and additions which I thought would make the article tolerable. But I agree that they did not and that it would probably have been better to have rewritten thearticle and have held up the printing.

As regards what action it is your duty to take, I think it would be wrong to confuse this case with anything against Kingsley. It should be raised at the Board meeting, but the responsibility is mine and it shouldn't be counted against Kingsley.

On the general question, after my experience of the last four weeks I think it is a mistake to have MacKenzie on the paper. I like him and he is extremely intelligent, but it is hopeless to have communists in 'key positions'. However I understand that he is not going on. I don't understand Vallance. Up to this incident I had always thought him to be a first-rate journalist and second rate in everything else, but also some one whom one could trust to be reasonable up to a point.

Yours,
LEONARD WOOLF

To KINGSLEY MARTIN, *29 June 1945*

Dear Kingsley,

I have been meaning ever since you returned from America to get you to come round for supper one evening. But I have always seemed up to the limit of my physical capacity in engagements, so it has got put off. Could you come to supper at Gordon Square on next Wednesday, July 4th, at 7.30?

I thought your own contributions from U.S.A. very good indeed,—your very best level. But, as you may have heard, I have been more than dismayed at some things which have appeared in the paper in recent times.

Yours,

J. M. K.

From KINGSLEY MARTIN, *21 July 1945*

Dear Maynard,

You made some criticism the other night of Cole and now that I have the opportunity of improving things with Dick back and more staff, I'd like you to be more specific. He knows much more than he writes because he sees a lot of 'secret' stuff still, but these are no doubt things he is not so much in touch with and a suggestion from you about what they are and of anyone who might help would be valuable.

You could be of immense value to the paper now if you would make suggestions. I am very receptive to sense and know there are gaps and faults galore. Cole has written for this week what seems to be a good article on Article VII and Bretton Woods etc. But we could do with an extra contact on domestic matters. Who? What parts seemed to you specially weak? New people will soon be available.

I wish that on one of the rare occasions we had for talk about the paper time had not been wasted in an abusive wrangle. I don't follow your technique here. In any case H.N.B.[99] is retiring and on the particular points you raised we seemed, when I examined them not far from agreeing. Also on all the main subjects—Russia, U.S.A. etc. But the important thing is the paper and any concrete suggestions would be welcome.

Yours,

KINGSLEY

To KINGSLEY MARTIN, *25 July 1945*

Dear Kingsley,

The particular points where I thought Cole not sufficiently well informed have now dropped out of my memory. They were not, I think, very important, but suggested that he was not in as close touch as he used to be. The best way, I think, would be that I should watch the paper from that point of view for the next few weeks, and if anything does crop up I will call your attention to it.

[99] Brailsford.

Is there any more news about Whitley's shareholdings?

Yours,
J. M. K.

The second last exchange followed the American Loan Agreement.

From KINGSLEY MARTIN, *1 January 1946*

Dear Maynard,

It's been a bit difficult to know how far to give in the paper any of the inside story which I have heard from Washington. I am anxious to consult you about anything that might be thought to come from you. I feel that the enclosed at least is safe to say, and that it is only fair to you to say it. I should like to add a great deal more. I have had fairly long reports both from Washington and from people over here. If I don't hear from you I propose to publish this piece as a Diary paragraph.

I am afraid this must have been rather a vexatious homecoming for you.

Yours,
KINGSLEY

The enclosure ran as follows:

Argument about the American Loan, as far as this country is concerned, is now over, at least for the time. But in the United States, bitter feelings about Britain continue to be expressed. Official circles of Washington of course understand the British case. It was American politics and lack of political leadership that prevented a happier outcome. I am told that the three days' exposition of Britain's post-war position given by Lord Keynes to a group of American experts was the most masterly and persuasive thing of its kind ever done. No-one can so combine technical mastery with an appeal to moral and common sense. At the end of it Mr Clayton made a statement which showed that he knew that it was in the interests of America as well as Britain to make the loan 5 billion dollars and only to charge nominal interest. Economically, I repeat, as well as psychologically in America's interest. Then up rose Senator George threatening to lead a Southern revolt against this British attempt to outsmart America. Back came the American negotiators; the loan had to be much smaller, and at 2 per cent. If there had been a strong political leader in the United States, Senator George would not have mattered. Once again one recognises the tragedy of Mr Roosevelt's death. We in this country have to remember that the American public still cannot face the fact that Britain stood alone for a year in the war and lost absolutely more men than the United States with three times the population; that most Americans are not economically educated and think in simple terms of money, not of realities, and believe they were generous to wipe out lease lend and that it must always be generous to lend money to anyone at 2 per cent.

To KINGSLEY MARTIN, *3 January 1946*

Personal and Private

Dear Kingsley,

I find it rather difficult to answer your letter or comment on the enclosure. As an impressionistic picture, I suppose it is not more remote from the facts than what usually appears in newspapers. In the very broadest outlines it was all something like that. On the other hand, a good many of the details are quite inaccurate, particularly the following:—

(1) Clayton made no such statement as is attributed to him. There were other people who in private conversation got a bit nearer to that, but nothing of the kind was ever said at the conferences by any American representative.

(2) It is true that the influence of Senator George led to trouble. But this was on the question of the size of the loan, not the rate of interest. The Americans were standing out for the rate of interest before the Senator made his views heard.

(3) The importance of Senator George is not that he could lead a Southern revolt, but that he is Chairman of the Senate Committee which will have to pass the loan.

(4) What is said about the absence of strong political leadership is, of course, quite true. But whether we should really have gained by the survival of Roosevelt is a matter on which I have never been able to make up my mind. If he had been in full health and at the height of his political power, the answer would probably be Yes. But, if he had just not died and the position

217

in other respects was the same as it now is, we might have come off worse. Suppose Winston had survived too, undoubtedly there would have been brisk messages from one to the other, and very probably indeed Roosevelt would have used his authority to get us better terms. But the result of this might very well have been a repetition of Wilson and the League of Nations after the last war. If, in current circumstances, Roosevelt had offered us considerably better terms than those to which American opinion would readily respond, I fancy that Congress would almost infallibly have thrown them out. And then where should we have been? The advantage of the present set-up is that the Administration have, to the best of my belief, squared the people in Congress who really matter, so that, although there will be a great deal of noise when the loan comes up, it will in the end go through.

(5) The last sentence of your note is entirely true in my judgment. It is also true that the Americans we were dealing with would, I think, have liked to have given us considerably better terms, if they had judged that public opinion would stand for it. But, as I have said above, the position in this respect was nothing like as clear-cut as is suggested in the note.

Whilst there are certain aspects, vital from our point of view, which the Americans obstinately overlook, there are also, I think, some aspects which people here obstinately overlook, for instance the following:–

(i) This is not the funding of a war debt. The Americans agreed totally to wipe off the war debt. This is new money for us to build up our political and competitive position. That makes a vast difference. There is no sort of analogy with last time's war debts.

(ii) The waiver clause, which is rather better than appears obviously on the surface, is so worded that we are not in fact required to pay any interest whatever until we have recovered to a position when we can well afford to do so. My estimate is that until the volume of our exports is at least 60 per cent above pre-war we pay no interest at all.

(iii) The Americans were extremely scrupulous, although most people here believe otherwise, in not putting financial pressure on us to exact political concessions. On the matter of Preferences we have agreed to nothing whatever beyond what we agreed to when we signed Article 7 of the Mutual Aid Agreement some years ago. Indeed, if anything, our commitments are less under the new proposals than they were then. There was great pressure on the Americans to associate the loan with civil aviation, bases, shipping and any other matter in which any pressure group in America happened to be interested. Clayton scrupulously resisted all such pressure.

(iv) We are not the only people in the picture. The Americans are much more conscious of that than we are. They want to give us very decidedly better terms than anyone else, but they do not want to have too obvious a discrepancy between the terms they give us and the terms they give others. In practice they are charging the French per annum during the early years about twice as much as they are charging us, without any waiver clause (I pointed that out in my speech, I think).

What is prominent in my mind, but not easily emphasised in public, is that they treated us like gentlemen, that there was as intense a desire on their part as on ours that there should be no break in Anglo-American intimacy, and that they were doing their damnedest all through to give us as good a deal as their own perfectly frightful local politics would permit.

Yours,

MAYNARD KEYNES

P.S.

(v) On my return I discovered that, in some circles at any rate, people's minds were much more disturbed about the abbreviation of the Bretton Woods transitional period for the sterling area than the financial terms of the loan. This, I believe, was largely due to misunderstanding of the arrangements. Unlike the loans that they are making to other countries, the

American loan to us is free money, not tied to purchases in U.S. and available for expenditure by us in any part of the world. The amount of it has been so fixed that we shall only need about half of it for our own expenditure in the United States, and the other half will be available precisely for the purpose of releasing the earnings of the sterling area in other parts of the world, so that they can get paid by us in dollars for what they supply and can consequently purchase themselves in the United States. Now, it should be obvious that when something like half the loan is provided for the express purpose of liberating the sterling area and would not otherwise be required at all, one's case against anticipating the Bretton Woods arrangements for the two or three years in question is pretty weak and, indeed, cannot possibly be sustained. Most people seem to believe that the whole of the loan is required for our own expenditure in U.S. But that most certainly is not the case.

*　　*　　*

One final reflection. If the negotiations had broken down and we had not got the loan, I do not believe the Labour Government could have lasted a year. One sometimes wondered whether this might not be in the minds of some of those who seemed so complacent at the idea of things breaking down. I personally felt this as an additional reason for insisting on an agreement. It seems to me it would have been a real disaster if, for the second time, a Labour Government should be destroyed by an external financial situation, for which they could scarcely be regarded as primarily responsible. I should not care to contemplate the consequences of that when what had really happened had become perfectly clear. I doubt if the poor, silly Cabinet caught a glimpse of that possibility, or probability as I should view it, even out of the corner of their eyes. For I think most of them were almost completely oblivious of the prospective factual background.

From KINGSLEY MARTIN, *7 January 1946*

Dear Maynard,

Sorry about the muddle. I thought I'd taken the right precautions. Your letter is very interesting. It's not easy to make a correction because the general effect, as you say, is not untrue and the facts given are wrong in emphasis rather than in substance. It was good of you to write so long and informative an account.

I've tried seriously in this paper to present the prime alternative to the loan and, accepting it, to say what was involved for the Government. I think it was fairly clearly said and understood that the alternative was another 'blood, toil and sweat' period and that the Government would need great courage to put that over. It may have been impossible. The Cabinet had this in mind, as far as I could judge from circumstances.

Best wishes to you both for 1946.

                                                                KINGSLEY

To KINGSLEY MARTIN, *9 January 1946*

Dear Kingsley,

I agree that no correction is necessary. No harm done. When I penned so many words I thought that I was going to be in time to give you the material.

In my view a great deal more was at stake than another spell of blood, toil and sweat. If that had been going to lead to something eventually beneficial, very likely we ought to have been prepared to put up with it. My conviction is that the *consequences* would have been even worse than the *process*. A permanent splitting up of the world into separate economic blocs, of which ours would be far the weakest, founded on sand and almost certain to collapse within a brief period, would have been a major disaster, at any rate for us.

I don't think people have realised that it was not merely a question of the alternative being difficult to attain, but that, in any desirable or acceptable form from our own point of view, it simply did not exist. There has been a great obfuscation of people's minds, mixed up with the general state of coma which

221

now prevails and thriving only in the false paradise in which we live, about what our present position in the world really is.

Yours,

MAYNARD KEYNES

The final exchange concerned Keynes's appointment to the first meeting of the Bretton Woods Institution at Savannah.

From a letter from KINGSLEY MARTIN, *21 February 1946*

I hope your appointment is what you desired. I have an uneasy feeling that you were right in saying in a recent letter that Britain is living in a fool's paradise. If anyone can pull us through on the financial side you will.

You may have seen an asinine paragraph in today's *Daily Express*. I don't know that anything useful can be done to stop or reply to this kind of silliness.

From a letter to KINGSLEY MARTIN, *22 February 1946*

My appointment as a Governor of the Bretton Woods affairs is ornamental rather than otherwise. The chap who really does the work is the Executive Director and he is not yet nominated. It is really my own fault that I am going on my journeys again. But it is a case of a rather formal conference, with not much work, down in the South in the warm weather, and my doctor thought it would be a good idea to go. In addition to this, I had a sentimental feeling at wanting to be in at the birth of these institutions after having spent so much time and strength on them. I should not be away more than four or five weeks.

I heard there was something in *The Daily Express* to the effect that I was responsible for you—which Heaven forbid! But I have not actually seen the text. Certainly it should be ignored.

Chapter 2

KEYNES AND ANCIENT CURRENCIES

On several occasions between 1920 and 1926, Keynes worked at a history of ancient currencies. In his correspondence with Lydia in 1924 and 1925–6, he reported that bursts of work on the subject kept him from working on his *Treatise on Money*.[1]

Although subsequent research has meant that many of the details of Keynes's story require revision,[2] the fragments which emerged from his research are of sufficient interest in themselves to merit publication, for they show Keynes turning his mind in an unexpected direction.

From Keynes's efforts over the period, the first surviving fragment dates from 1920.

NOTE ON THE MONETARY REFORM OF SOLON

According to Professor Gardner's interpretation of the authorities, Androtion makes out Solon's reform to consist in a change from the Aeginetan drachma (proportion 73 to 100), whereas according to Aristotle, Solon's change was from the Aeginetan drachma to the Euboic drachma (proportion 70 to 100). Professor Gardner thinks that the account of Aristotle is the correct one. He believes, therefore, that Solon changed the standard from the Aeginetan to the Euboic and that the change from the Euboic to the Attic was effected by Peisistratus fifty years later. I have not seen any direct evidence of the supposed further change of standard under Peisistratus.

I suggest that Professor Gardner has misunderstood Aristotle's statement and that there is in substance no contradiction between the statement of Androtion and that of Aristotle.

---

[1] See, for example, *JMK*, vol. XXIX, pp. 1–2.
[2] For example, the whole account of the monetary reforms of Pheidon and Solon, *in so far as* it is attached to them personally, must now be rejected. For a recent statement on the consensus view and essential references see M. M. Austin and P. Vidal-Naquet, *Economic and Social History of Ancient Greece: an Introduction* (London, 1977), pp. 56–8 and 214–17.

The confusion arises out of the assumption that the mina was the unit which was kept constant, whereas better sense could be obtained by supposing that Solon introduced both a new mina and a new drachma, keeping the talent constant.

According to Aristotle Solon introduced two changes. He made a new mina $\frac{63}{60}$ of the old mina. Further he divided this new mina into 100 new drachmae, whereas the old mina had been divided into 70 old drachmae. Consequently the new drachma equalled

$$\frac{70}{100} \cdot \frac{63}{60} \quad \text{of the old drachma.}$$

$$= \frac{73 \cdot 5}{100} \quad \text{of the old drachma}$$

which nearly agrees with Androtion, who is making a portmanteau statement of the net effect of Solon's two changes on the relation of the new drachma to the old drachma.

According to this interpretation the alleged discrepancy of the two authorities is explained away by supposing that Aristotle was comparing the number of new drachmae in the new mina as compared with the number of old drachmae in the old mina, whereas Androtion was comparing the value of the new drachmae to that of the old drachmae.

The above calculation fits in sufficiently accurately with the weights of the coins. The Aeginetan drachma was 94 grains according to Gardner, and 93 grains according to Ridgeway.

$$\frac{93 \times 73 \cdot 5}{100} \quad \text{yields 68·35 grains as the weight of the drachma}$$

resulting from the Solonic reform, which is sufficiently near to the Attic drachma.

The matter may be put also in this way. The Aeginetan table was:—

$$70 \text{ drachmae} = 1 \text{ mina}$$
$$63 \text{ minae} \quad = 1 \text{ talent}$$

In place of this Solon substituted:—

$$100 \text{ drachmae} = 1 \text{ mina}$$
$$60 \text{ minae} \quad = 1 \text{ talent}$$

the weight of the talent remaining unchanged. This seems plausible as it agrees exactly with the table which was current in Athens in later times. This makes much better sense than Gardner's view that Solon made 63 minae to the talent instead of 60 as formerly. If this were really the case it would be necessary to invent also a reform of the table of weights by Peisistratus as well as of the change of the drachma standard. I notice that Ridgeway translates Aristotle in the opposite manner to Gardner, and in accordance with the above theory. Gardner does not seem to attempt to harmonise with the rest of his account his view of what Aristotle said about the mina.

That the Aeginetan table had 70 drachmae to the mina is borne out by the archaic Aeginetan Mina weighing 6585 grains, mentioned on page 149 of Gardner. If this was the weight of the Aeginetan mina and if 94 grains was the weight of the Aeginetan drachma, it follows that there were 70 drachmae to the mina. The table for the three standards works out then as follows:—

	Aeginetan	Euboic	Attic
Drachmae to the mina	70*	100	100
Minae to the talent	63	63	60
Proportionate weights of drachmae assuming the talent the same in all these standards	100	70	73·5

The statement of Androtion that 'when men repaid coins equal in number but less in weight they were actually advantaged, while those who received were not injured' derives its force, I think, from the fact that the creditors were receiving back as many legal tender drachmae as they had lent and would therefore not suffer at all until prices had risen in proportion

---

* In the Assyrian cuneiform inscriptions there are 60 dr[achmae] to the mina.

225

to the debasement of the currency, which might take a long time and even when it occurred might not be connected with the debasement. So long as prices are not affected a man who receives back as many Drachmae as he lent, is not injured even though the Drachmae are lighter coins.

Of the remaining early fragments that survive, one further one which, to judge by the paper on which Keynes was writing, antedates 1923, is of interest.

The fall in the value of money throughout almost all periods of recorded history deserves a brief discussion. It has been effected in two ways, if not by the one then by the other—by an increased abundance of the metal of which the money is made, or failing this by a diminution of the metal content of the monetary unit. It is convenient to call the former *Depreciation* and the latter *Debasement*. If the course of history and nature does not occasion the former, man generally falls back upon the latter.

When first the use of money supplants barter, a coin is no more than a quantity of bullion, of which the stamp may certify the quality and indicate the quantity, but which will not circulate except for its bullion value. In this elementary stage the expedient of debasement is not available. It cannot appear, until with the development of contract the conception of a money of account has emerged, and the coins issued by a state have acquired the character of *legal tender* and enjoy a *cours forcé* as the legal discharge of obligations calulated in this money of account. It is at this stage that money, in the sense in which we understand it, makes its entry into human institutions.

For this reason the History of Money begins with Solon, the first statesman whom history records as employing the force of law to fit a new standard coin to an existing money of account.*

* That is to say, according to one interpretation of those celebrated measures for the relief of debtors, over the details of which the mists of history and confusion had descended even in antiquity. The original authorities consist (i) of brief direct accounts of the reform of Solon not less than 250 years after the events which they described by Aristotle (in *The Constitution*

The scarcity in Greece of the precious metals must have caused in his age an appreciation of the standard, that is to say a tendency of prices to fall, which was intolerably oppressive to that indispensable class in ancient, as in modern, society, which carries on the business of agriculture with borrowed money.*

As in all later ages, the appreciation of the standard called for the remedy of debasement. Solon, perceiving in his wisdom, that in such circumstances the interests of society required that the weight of capitalism and the dead hand upon the active workers should be lightened, so became the first of the long line of statesmen, of whom the latest is Lenin, who, throughout the ages of private capitalism, have employed debasement wisely to diminish its weight or rashly to sap its foundations. The sage who first debased the currency for the social good of the citizens was suitably selected by legend to admonish Croesus of the vanity of hoarded riches. Solon represents the genius of Europe, as permanently as Midas depicts the bullionist propensities of Asia.

After the primitive debasement of Solon ([c.] 590 B.C.) the campaigns of Xerxes in the fifth century by releasing the treasures of Persia† allowed prices to rise by the de-

of Athens) and by Androtion (quoted by Plutarch in his Life of Solon), and (ii) of the contemporary Solonic Poems from which, however, the nature of reforms can be gathered by inference only. Solon certainly carried through two distinct measures, a Seisachtheia for debtors and a change of monetary standard. It is disputed whether the Seisachtheia, or in the language of the ancient authorities 'the cutting down' (ἀποκοπή) of the debts consisted, besides the release of those imprisoned for debt, in the total cancellation of mortgages on land, in a partial abatement of them, or merely in a diminution of the interest charges. The change of standard consisted in the adoption as the legal tender of Attica of a drachma 27 or 30 per cent lighter than the Aeginetan drachma previously current. The effect of this was to reduce the metal content of the money with which debtors were entitled to discharge book debts expressed in drachmae. It is uncertain whether Solon himself introduced the Attic drachma of classical times or whether his measure consisted in establishing the already existent Euboic coin as legal tender in place of the Aeginetan. The Attic drachma of classical times is to the Euboic drachma as 73:70. I prefer the argument for the former hypothesis. In the latter case the Attic drachma was introduced by Peisistratus (550–527 B.C.).

* The withdrawal of money from circulation into the treasure of Athens on the Acropolis may have been at the bottom of the troubles Solon was dealing with.

† From the sixth century B.C. to the discovery of America the currency history of Europe has been dominated by the ebb and flow of the metal tides of the East. In epochs of peaceful trade, balance of commerce has always been (as it still is) in Asia's favour, the needs which they could satisfy in us being most numerous and urgent, at any rate before the day of

preciation in the value of silver, and so preserved the parity of the Attic standard; the Peloponnesian wars, by restoring to the active circulation the temple hoards of Greece performed the same service for the next generation; and when again towards the end of the fourth century B.C. the force of this was spent, the conquests of Alexander inflated the Mediterranean with the spoils of Asia.*

Manchester and of cotton, than what we could furnish to them, and the valuable produce of the East far more portable for the trade of caravans than anything, except bullion, which the West could send in return. Pliny states the annual drain of the precious metals from the Roman Empire at what was in relation to the production at that time, the prodigious figure of £400,000 to India and £800,000 to the East generally. The mines of Thrace, Spain and Germany could do little to make this good, and from the time of Caracalla onwards the decline in the supply of gold and silver, by reason of the drain to the East, especially for the purchase of slaves, has been remarked by every historian of the later Roman Empire. Before the discovery of America, there was no period at which gold was sufficiently abundant in Europe to furnish the regular standard of value—excepting, as barely European, the *aureus* of the Eastern Empire. Was not the English sovereign, as established by the Act of 1816, the first monometallic gold standard in European history? If, on the other hand, the Eastern drain was the occasion of an unbroken history of debasements from Augustus to Henry VIII, this same demand has in more recent times carried off the redundant supplies first of the Spanish Main, then of Cripple Creek, Ballarat and the Rand, and thus saved Europe from a greater depreciation than that continent could have experienced with advantage. Only since the German War has the United States disputed with Asia the right to wear the ass's ears of Midas.

* The quantity of the precious metals current in antiquity, according to tradition and conjecture, varied from extreme scarcity to what even now we should consider comparative abundance. Pliny declares that Rome could not find above 1,000 lbs (Roman) weight of gold (about £30,000) in payment as ransom to the Gauls (390 B.C.) (for figures as to the amount of gold at Rome at other dates also see Pliny's *Naturalis Historia* Lib. XXXIII). Herodotus affords several instances of the great rarity of gold in Greece before the fifth century B.C. Yet, according to the same authority the gold reserve of Xexes was £4,000,000 (reckoning, very roughly, that a gold daric was about a pound sterling); and the annual revenues of the Persian King in gold and silver together about £3,500,000 (taking silver here and elsewhere in this note at the old British parity). The reserve of coined silver in the Athenian Acropolis amounted, according to Boeckh, to £2,350,000, apart from gold and silver vessels, before Pericles spent it on the embellishment of the city, or, more strictly, before the Athenians borrowed the money from the gods at the nominal rate of interest of $1\frac{1}{5}$ per cent. (The above is a higher figure than the £1,500,000 at which Thucydides placed the coined treasure of the Acropolis in 431 B.C.) The gifts of gold from Croesus to the Delphic oracle were worth above £500,000. Sparta's subsidies from Persia were of the magnitude of £1,000,000 (British subsidies to Europe between 1793 and 1816 were £57,000,000 and between 1914 and 1918 £1,700,000,000). The treasures of Delphi yielded nearly £2,500,000 to the sacrilegious Phocians. These traditional figures (as to which see, especially, Boekh's *Public Economy of Athens*) seem reasonably compatible one with another, and indicate the general scale of the period. With Alexander the Great we reach, if the historians are to be trusted, a different scale altogether. The treasures collected by the conqueror at Susa, Persis, Pasargadae and Persepolis were £44,000,000 (out of which £200,000 was allotted to the scientific researches of Aristotle). The reserve of Ptolemy Philadephus (284–247 B.C.) was estimated by Appian at £45,000,000. Boekh justly remarks that, if these great sums had not been hoarded or

The influence of these events, duly reflected in the rising course of prices, obviated the necessity for several centuries of any further debasement. The Attic drachma, constant in weight and fineness from Solon to the fall of Athens,* shares a rare distinction, in length of virtuous life, with the *aureus* of Constantine, the English shilling of 1601, and the Spanish pieces of eight (reckoning with the last named their nearly identical successors the dollars of Mexico and Maria Theresa).

As the Attic drachma was a silver coin nearly equivalent to the franc,† it is possible to follow, very roughly, the general movement of prices in terms intelligible to ourselves. The broad conclusion of classical writers is that, if we start with the age of Solon (590 B.C.), prices had doubled by the age of Pericles (450 B.C.), had increased threefold by the end of Demosthenes (340 B.C.).‡ Real wages over the same period were fairly constant. It appears that at all dates a week's unskilled labour purchased

wrought into vessels, the effect upon prices must have been far more vehement than was in fact the case. In the course of succeeding centuries, Asia recovered her ravished riches, and conjecture has placed Europe's total stock of gold by the end of the Middle Ages not above £12,000,000 to £16,000,000. Between 1492 and 1731 Spain imported into Europe from America $6,000 millions in gold and silver, apart from undeclared imports.

* Ignoring the very slight change from the Euboic to the Attic drachma, if it was the former and not the latter which Solon established, and confidently repudiating the view (*vide* Gardner, *History of Ancient Coinage*, p. 148) that Solon's coin was double the later drachma and was reduced to half its size by Hippias (510 B.C.).

† I take the drachma, therefore, at 25 to the £, without entering into the exactly correct parity between gold and silver involved in this transition.

‡ This is illustrated by the following figures. In the time of Solon a Medimnus of wheat (1½ bushels) cost 1 drachma according to Plutarch's *Life of Solon*; in 392 B.C. 3 drachmae according to Aristophanes' *Ecclesiazusae*; in 330 B.C. 5 drachmae according to Demosthenes (*contr. Phorm.*); and an inscription shows that in 329/8 B.C. wheat was sold by the state at 6 drachmae the medimnus. A sheep is alleged to have sold for 1 drachma in the time of Solon and for 10 to 20 drachmae at the end of the Peloponnesian Wars. The rate of payment at Athens for attending the Ecclesia, which was originally 1 obol (= ⅙ dr.) had been increased to 3 obols (= ½ dr.) by 390 B.C. and 1 dr. after the time of Demosthenes. A day's wages for unskilled labour was reckoned at 1 obol under Solon, 2 obols under Pericles and 4 obols fifty years later (Aristophanes puts a porter's wages and also the wages of a common labourer who carried manure at this figure). These figures for wheat and unskilled labour are reasonably concordant with one another. In the best age of Athens, according to Boeckh, an economical member of the middle class could support a small family on £25 a year, or about double the wages of an unskilled labourer. When Demosthenes was a youth, his mother, his young sister and himself spent £28 a year apart from his education. Prices and earnings in England may have been about comparable with this in the reign of Queen Elizabeth.

round about a bushel and a half of wheat.* I do not know if historians have remarked how constant this figure has been over long epochs of history. It is as valid for England from the Plantaganets to the Stuarts, as it is for Athens from Solon to Alexander.†

The currency history of Athens during the 250 years so far recorded seems to me to have been a singularly happy one. The value of money was steadily falling (at an average rate over the whole period of one third of one per cent of its original value), that is to say prices were rising, at a rate which was not injurious to real wages or productive of any other awkward economic consequences, and yet as it was just sufficient to relieve debtors (without injustice to creditors)‡ and afforded the necessary stimulus to enterprise, the Athenians were never faced again with the problems of Solon. In these circumstances the city was able to avoid debasements, and there can seldom have been a

* The ratio of the prices of barley and wheat was fairly constant, the former being from a half to two thirds of the latter. The ancient world lived so largely upon cereals that this index is reasonably accurate. An adult Athenian slave received a choenix of grain a day ($= \frac{1}{48}$ medimnus), and according to Polybius a Roman soldier was accorded the same measure. This works out at about 11 bushels a year, as compared with the 9 bushels of the modern Frenchman and the 5 or 6 bushels of the Englishman or American. On this basis of consumption an Athenian labourer with three dependents would spend at least half his income on grain.

† The following conjectures have been made as to the normal rates in England round about certain dates (Walford, *Jl. Roy. Stat. Soc.* 1879 and Thorold Rogers).

	Price of 1½ bushels of wheat	Weekly wages
1400	1/6d	1/6d
1450	1/–	1/–
1500	1/4½d	1/6d
1550	2/9d	2/6d
1600	5/9½d	5/2d
1650	9/3d	7/6d
1691–1702	8/8d	8/8d

The stability is surprising, specially as the statistics which I have thrown into this form were not compiled with this argument in view.

‡ In ancient Athens 12 per cent per annum was considered a very moderate rate of interest. It was no hardship to the lender, therefore, if a fraction of 1 per cent of this had to be regarded as a sinking fund against the depreciation of the money of account. When money is falling in value, the money rate of interest must be considered to include an element of sinking fund; and that debts, on which the interest is regularly paid, should tend to wipe themselves out over a long period is no bad thing.

period in which the vagaries of the currency caused so little trouble.

The influence of the precious metals from Persia brought into the circulation by Alexander involved much wider movements, but not nearly so violent or rapid as they would have been if the treasures of the Persian King had been rapidly dispersed in their entirety, instead of being largely transferred into the reserves of Alexander and his successors.* From this time onwards accurate figures are very scanty. But it seems clear that after 330 B.C. prices rose rapidly.

There follow two typed chapters, parts of which were later re-worked (see below, pp. 244 ff).

I THE BABYLONIAN MINA, THE EGYPTIAN KAT, THE LYDIAN MINA AND THE ROMAN POUND

In the latter part of the second millennium B.C. it was traditional in Nineveh that the weight standard which they then employed had been instituted by Dungi, a King of the third dynasty of Ur *circa* 2456 B.C. Some of the weights which Layard discovered in the Palace of Nineveh bear his name, and Prof. Sayce recorded a Babylonian weight thus inscribed:– One maneh standard weight, the property of Mersdach-sar-itani, a duplicate of the weight which Nebuchadnezzar, King of Babylon, the son of Nabopolassar, King of Babylon, made in exact accordance with the weight prescribed by the deified Dungi, a former King.

This tradition has now been verified by the results of more recent excavations into Sumerian remains in the neighbourhood of Ur. Two objects, in particular, have been found, one from the reign of Dungi himself and one from the reign of his grandson Gimil-Sin (2387 B.C.), which are inscribed with the name of the ancient weight which they are supposed to represent. These weights agree reasonably well with the Nineveh weights of more than 1,000 years later.

* See footnote to p. 228 *supra* as to the reserves of Ptolemy Philadelphus.

The mna, or mina, which Dungi prescribed for Ur in the middle of the third millenium B.C. is, within the limits of our positive knowledge, the earliest standard of weight. Recent discoveries have, however, thrown back the genesis of organised economic life to a date so much earlier than was previously supposed, that weights must have existed centuries and, perhaps, even millennia before Dungi, in whose reign money, interest, contracts, receipts, and even bills of exchange are fully established, the Archaic civilisation of the Sumerians being much more fully developed in these respects than those which succeeded it.

We know not only the approximate weight of Dungi's mna, but also the table of weights then current, which was as follows:-

1 talent	= 60 mna
1 mna	= 60 gin or shekels*
1 shekel	= 60 gin-tur or little shekels
1 little shekel	= 3 she or grains

The most ancient evidence for the weight of the mna is as follows:-

(1) The diorite weight from the reign of Dungi, which is inscribed ½ mna, weighs 248 grammes, giving 1 mna = 496 grammes.

(2) The diorite weight from the reign of Gimil-Sin, which is inscribed 5 mnas, weighs 2510·975 grammes, giving 1 mna = 502·2 grammes.

(3) The Babylonian weights, which were discovered by Layard in 1853 are of the greatest importance, because (bronze and stone together) they are numerous (about 30), many of them have their weights inscribed, they are concordant, and the place of their discovery was such as to suggest that they were authoritative.

(4) The bronze lion, representing a royal talent (120 mna) discovered at Khorsabad and now in the Louvre, which gives a mna of 502·5 grammes and the bronze lion of Susa

* Shekel is the Semitic translation of the Sumerian word.

(resomna) [*sic*] which yields a mna of 506·4 grammes. The last named, being the largest weight, has probably suffered the least proportionate wastage and is therefore the most reliable guide.

(5) This figure is further confirmed by the agreed weight of the stater, which was $\frac{1}{60}$th of the mina, and is given by all authorities at 8·42 grammes (130 grains) which yields a mina of 505·2 grammes.

No primitive weight standard, indeed, is so well authenticated or so undisputed as is the Babylonian mna at 505–506 grammes, and all authorities agree in fixing the standard at approximately this figure.

In spite of a variety of conjectures,* I see little reason to doubt as to what the basis of this weight standard was. The mna was what it said it was, namely the weight of $60 \times 60 \times 3$ she or grains of wheat, just as the qa, the measure of capacity, is the volume occupied by the number of she included in the qa. Thus the unit of weight is given by counting grains of wheat. It follows that the weight of the she must have been

$$= \frac{1}{10800} \ (502–506) \text{ grammes}$$

$$= 0·046–0·047 \text{ gramme}$$

This is, as we shall see below, exactly the same figure (or within 1 per cent) as that of the traditional weight of the grain of wheat as given by the Roman lb., the weight of which we know to a high degree of accuracy. It is also the exact figure for the wheat grain evaluated by Professor Ridgeway.†

These figures seem to me to establish almost beyond controversy that the Babylonian weights were based on a sexagesimal system with the wheat-grain of about 0·047 grm as its monad.‡

---

* E.g. that it represents the weight of a certain cubic volume of water or of stones or has some astronomical significance.

† *Origins of Currency*, p. 182.

‡ Thureau-Dangin approaches this solution (*Journal Asiatique*, vol. XIII (1909), p. 79) and then sheers off in favour of the mna being the weight of a certain cubic capacity of water (a far

Two other measures of weight are to be found in the primitive world—(1) the Kat of Egypt, and (2) the Lydian or Euboic mina.

(1) *The Kat*. The literary evidence (so far as I am aware) is very slight, and the evidence from extant weights very discrepant. Prof. Flinders Petrie suggests that there were two *kats*, one of 142 grains and one of 152 grains. Many of these weights, however, are very small, and on the principle of taking the largest weight as the most accurate, the unit of 152 grains (9·85 grms), given by the 100 outen (i.e. 1000 kats) weight of Bowley is preferable. This makes the *kat* equivalent to about 214 she. If we assume an error of 1 per cent by wastage and substitute 216 she, we have 1 Kat = $6 \times 6 \times 6$ she, and 100 kats = 1 double Babylonian mna. In this case Bowley's weight of 100 outen = $60 \times 60 \times 60$ she. This is plausible because it brings the *kat* on a sexagesimal system.

(2) *The Lydian or Euboic Mina*. The best authenticated starting point for the weight of the Lydian or Phoenician, or, as it was called in Greece, the Euboic mina is, the bronze lion of Abydos, which closely resembles in pose and appearance the lions of Nineveh. He represents a talent and weighs 25657 grms, which yields a mina of 427·6 grms, allowing nothing for wastage. This figure has close literary corroboration in a statement of Herodotus, according to whom (III, 89) the Babylonian talent amounted to 70 Euboic minas. As the Babylonian talent was equal to 60 Babylonian minas, this statement would make the Euboic mina $\frac{6}{7}$ths of the Babylonian mina, that is to say 433 grms. Most modern critics, however, including Lehmann-Haupt,* hold the view that the figure of 70 given by Herodotus is a textual error for 78. I will return to this point later.

more advanced idea than one based on counting grains) partly because he takes the mna, rather than the she, as the ultimate unit and partly because he gets the relative weight of wheat and barley the wrong way round. See also *Revue d'Assyriologie*, vol. XVIII (1921), p. 123. Lehmann-Haupt seems to ignore almost entirely the monads of the ancient systems.

* Since the above was written, I find that Lehmann-Haupt has revised his opinion and now offers an explanation substantially similar to that given below (Pauly's *Real. Encycl.*, art. *Satrap*).

I do not know any theories as to the origin of the Lydian or Phoenician mina. But I offer the following conjecture (on the assumption of the correctness of Herodotus's 6:7 ratio between the Lydian and Babylonian standards).

According to Thureau-Dangin* the qa, or 60 shekels of capacity, consisted of $60 \times 60 \times 2$ she or grains, instead of $60 \times 60 \times 3$ as in the case of the historic mina. He also asserts that the measures of capacity actually discovered are of a size to contain approximately $60 \times 60 \times 2$ grains of barley. He argues from this that 2 grains of barley is the monad of the qa of capacity, and conjectures further that there may have been a primitive mna of weight corresponding to this.† In this case the innovation introduced by Dungi consisted in substituting 3 grains of wheat instead of 2 grains of barley as the monad of his system. If I am right in basing the Egyptian kat (see above) on 3 grains of wheat, then, since the kat certainly existed before the time of Dungi, Dungi's reform also amounted to bringing the Babylonian standard into line with the Egyptian.

Further excavations may settle one way or the other the existence of a primitive pre-Dungi mna of this magnitude. If we can presume the existence of such a standard, it is worth considering whether the Lydian-Phoenician mna current in Asia Minor may not be its descendant, Dungi's innovation having failed to displace its predecessor in the remoter regions outside Babylonia.

If the Lydian mna based on 2 barley grains was six-sevenths (as Herodotus says it was) of the Babylonian mna based on 3 wheat grains, this would make 1 wheat grain $= \frac{7}{9}$ or 0·777 of a barley grain, i.e. 13 wheat grains equal in weight to 10 barley grains. This is very close to (within 2 per cent of) the traditional

---

* *Journal Asiatique*, 1909, p. 93.

† In Assyrian documents of the 7th century B.C. Dr Johns finds that weights of copper or bronze in less quantity than a mina are never referred to in terms of the shekel as weights of silver are, but in the ka (or qa) which was a measure of capacity descended from the Babylonian qa. Possibly, therefore, the barley standard continued in force for weighing copper, the new wheat standard being used for silver. Dr Johns thinks that the ka of copper was just the same weight as 1 shekel of silver. But in this case the term seems redundant.

figure of 3 to 4, i.e. 0·75 as the proportion of the weight of the wheat grain to that of the barley grain. Different strains of wheat and barley vary somewhat in weight, and the above figures are fully as close as one would expect.

In this case the relation between the Lydian and Babylonian standards was similar to that between troy weight and the old avoirdupois, the grain Troy being a barleycorn and the grain of old avoirdupois a wheatcorn,—with the added complication that in the former case the monads were *two* barleycorns and *three* wheatcorns respectively.*

I conjecture, therefore, that in the most ancient times the monad of the Babylonian talent was 2 barley grains. Meanwhile the Egyptian system was based on 3 wheat grains. Dungi's reform consisted, therefore, in introducing the Egyptian system, making 3 wheat grains the monad of the talent. The Lydian or Euboic system, on the other hand, continued on the basis of 2 barley grains.

The Roman Pound

It will be convenient to introduce at this point the most famous weight of all, also with very ancient origins, the Roman lb. The Roman lb. was divided into 1728 siliquae and each siliqua was equal to four grana or wheat grains. Thus the Roman lb. was by definition $1728 \times 4 = 6912$ wheat grains. The weight of the Roman wheat grain $= 0·047$ gramme more rather than less, which, as we have already seen, is practically the same figure as that of the monad of the Babylonian mina.

Thus the Babylonian mina was *said* to consist of 10800 wheat grains, and the Roman lb. was *said* to consist of 6912 wheat grains, and the actual ratio between the two, given by the universally agreed weights of these standards, is in fact 10800 to 6912. This seems to me to be a strong argument in favour

---

* The legal definition of the grain avoirdupois in the reign of Henry III (1267) is given by 'An English peny, called a sterling, round and without clipping, shall weigh 32 wheat corns in the midst of the ear'. The penny contained 24 Troy grains, thus giving the 3 to 4 ratio for wheat to barley.

of the monads of these systems being what they said they were, as against the purely hypothetical theories that the monad of the Babylonian mina was the weight of a certain cubic quantity of water.

I conclude, therefore, that

(i) the Babylonian mina (B.M.) was $60 \times 60 \times 3 = 10800$ wheat grains (w) and the stater ($\frac{1}{60}$ B.M.) was 180 w.

(ii) the Egyptian kat was $6 \times 6 \times 6$ w, so that 100 kats = 2 B.M.

(iii) the Lydian mina (L.M.) was $60 \times 60 \times 2 = 7200$ barley grains (b) and the Lydian or Phoenician shekel ($\frac{1}{60}$ L.M.) was 120 b.

(iv) the Roman lb. was $1728 \times 3 = 6912$ w

so that 1 Roman lb. = 32 kats

$\qquad$ 1 B.M. $\qquad$ = 50 kats

$\qquad$ 1 Roman lb. = $\frac{16}{25}$ B.M.

II THE WHEAT–BARLEY, GOLD–SILVER AND SILVER–COPPER RATIOS

We have seen that the monad of the Babylonian mina is a wheat grain of 0·047 grm. less rather than more, say 0·0465 grm., and the monad of the Roman lb. is a wheat grain of 0·047 grm. more rather than less, say 0·0475 grm. This yields a primitive barley grain (for the Lydian mina) of 0·0604 grm. if we take 10 to 13 for the wheat–barley ratio and of 0·06175 grm. if we take 3 to 4 for the wheat–barley ratio; and it yields a Roman barley grain of 0·0633 grm. taking the 3 to 4 ratio. The monads of the Babylonian mina and of the Roman lb. were wheat grains by contemporary *definition* not by *a posteriori* hypothesis. Similarly the avoirdupois grain is by contemporary definition the medieval wheat grain and the troy grain is the medieval barley grain. It is, therefore, interesting to compare the results given by the medieval standards with those given, as above, by the ancient standards. The troy grain weighs 0·0648 grm. and the old avoirdupois grain was therefore 0·0486 grm. Thus it seems, if my argument is correct, that the conventional weights of the wheat and barley grains increased by about 2 per cent in the two thousand years from 2500 B.C. to 500 B.C. and by a further 2 per cent in the next two thousand years from 500 B.C. to A.D. 1500, the Roman monad being 2 per cent heavier than the Babylonian, and the medieval 2 per cent heavier than the Roman. Progress has been much more rapid lately!

Passing from the traditional ratio between the barley grain and the wheat grain to that between gold and the tenfold of silver, I may point out the interesting fact that they were the *same*, namely approximately 4 to 3. If we accept the traditional 3:4 (i.e. 0·75) for wheat into barley and the traditional 3:40 for silver into gold, it follows that 10 barley grains of silver were worth 1 wheat grain of gold. The same is true of the variant traditional ratios namely 10:13 (i.e. 0·77) for wheat into barley and 1:13 for silver into gold, which pair of ratios is used or implied concurrently by Herodotus. Thus Herodotus' statement that the Euboic talent was $\frac{6}{7}$ of the Babylonian requires precisely the same ratio between wheat and barley, in order to justify the view set forth above that the relationship between the monads of the two systems was that of 2 barley grains to 3 wheat grains, as is given by him in the same context as the ratio between gold and the tenfold of silver. Perhaps of the two approximations the 13:1 ratio is the most ancient and the most popular and the 40:3 ratio the later and the most convenient for precise reckoning in divisionary units. The primitive metrological fact may have been that 13 wheat grains were the same *weight* as 10 barley grains and the primitive monetary fact that 10 barley grains weight of silver were *worth* 1 wheat grain weight of gold. Later on there was a tendency to get rid of the awkward figure 13:1 in favour of the more convenient 40:3 and to reckon 4 wheat grains as being conventionally of the same weight as 3 barley grains without disturbing the equality of value between 10 barley grains weight of silver and one wheat grain weight of gold.

It may help the reader if I mention at this point a possible conclusion which my argument may suggest. I believe that apart from a possible movement of the conventional wheat–barley weight ratio from 0·77 (i.e. 13 : 10) to 0·75 (i.e. 4 : 3), and a slow, slight increase in the absolute weight of these grains, the fundamental weight standards of Western civilisation have *never* been altered from the earliest beginnings up to the introduction of the metric system, which was the first real revolution in these matters away from the Sumerian and Egyptian ideas. All weight standards of the ancient and also of the medieval world in Babylonia, the Mediterranean Basin and Europe have been based on either the wheat grain or the barley grain as their monad, the higher weights being derived from these monads by the convenient multipliers 2, 3 or 10. The conservatism which I attribute to the ancient world in this matter is no matter for surprise. Prior to the introduction of modern strains of corn, the weights of the wheat and barley grains were physical facts stable within a fairly narrow range. Nor was there any reasonable motive for altering the accustomed monads of weight or any obvious or advantageous alternative to them.

When, however, we come to currency questions it is a different matter. The copper–silver value ratio and the silver–gold value ratio were very far from stable physical facts but depended on the varying relative abundance or desirability of the three metals. The tendency of these ratios to change over a period of time may have been, therefore, at the root of the currency difficulties in the ancient days of trimetallism and a cause of the complications of currency standards which perplex numismatists. During historic times the second of these two ratios seems to have presented less difficulty than the first. The successful silver–gold bimetallism of the Persian Empire preserved the stability of the silver–gold ratio until Alexander the Great upset the Empire and the ratio at the same time. But there was no similar influence to steady the copper–silver ratio, and I think that the clue to the perplexities about the early currency standards may be found in the fact that during the seventh and sixth centuries B.C. the Greek world was passing over from copper monometallism first to a loose copper–silver bimetallism and then to silver monometallism, and that during this period of transition the value of silver in terms of copper was tending to fall. Throughout this period the currency reformers may have been trying to adapt their units to a long familiar convention that a drachma of silver was worth a mina of copper—a convention just as difficult to upset as the corresponding English convention that there are twenty shillings to the £ sterling, even when the shillings are silver and the £ sterling has become gold.

Let us take first the gold–silver ratio. Our most convenient starting point is to be found in the known ratio established by the stable bimetallic system of the Persian Empire. Darius coined gold darics and silver shekels, the weight of the shekel being $\frac{4}{3}$ that of the daric and ten shekels being equal in value to one daric, i.e. silver and gold circulated at the value ratio 40:3, assumed above. This ratio persisted without variation down to the destruction of the Persian Empire by Alexander the Great. It would be spoken of popularly, as by Herodotus, as being a 13:1 ratio. The 13:1 ratio may have been a popular approximation or it may have represented a more ancient convention. In either case it would be true, near enough, that ten barley grains of silver were worth one barley [wheat?] grain of gold.

How far back can we carry to the 40:3 or 13:1 ratio? It would be convenient to suppose with Lehmann-Haupt that this was an immemorial ratio, though not so easy to agree with him that it was chosen on astronomical grounds, since gold represented the sun and silver the moon, whilst the period of the former stands to that of the latter in the approximate ratio 40:3. Lehmann-Haupt alleges that the 40:3 ratio between the metals has its roots in the Babylonian system, but I do not know his evidence.* Unfortunately the documentary records do not support either this ratio or any constant ratio in the earliest times. Scheil (*Revue d'Assyriologie*, vol. XVII (1920), p. 208) quotes the following ratios recorded in documents of the early Babylonian period:—

1. Agade   8 to 1
2. 8th year of Bur Sin   10 to 1
3. 6th year of Gimil Sin   7 to 1
4. 35th year of Hammurabi   6 to 1

I am not sure that these interpretations of what is meant in the passages in question are all reliable.† But if they are, there does not seem to be any means of reducing them to a uniform convention. No doubt many other records will be deciphered in course of time which will settle the matter one way or the other. Meanwhile I know no record approximating to the figure of 40 to 3 or 13 to 1 earlier than the middle of the 6th century B.C., Scheil (*l.c.*) quoting a record of 12 to 1 in the new Babylonian Empire in the 11th year of Nabonidus. Then during the epoch of the Persian Empire comes the stable bimetallic ratio of 40 to 3. But the dissipation of the gold hoards of Persia by Alexander the Great seems to have reduced the figure for many years thereafter to the figure of 10 to 1.‡

In Egypt at any rate gold had great importance for royal and religious purposes and in Babylonia it was probably used side

---

* It is characteristic of the standards of evidence prevalent amongst writers on this subject —which have made it a dark pit of falsehood—that Lehmann-Haupt alleges an official ratio of 40 to 3 for the early Babylonian period merely (so far as I am aware) because this was the official ratio elsewhere two thousand years later; and when positive evidence turns up for the existence of other ratios, he gets round it by arguing that the market ratio was not necessarily the same as the official ratio.

† The record of 10 to 1 from the reign of Bur Sin looks, on the face of the document in question, to be a reliable one.

‡ As regards later times the figure of 18 to 1 is quoted for the reign of Theodosius II. In the later middle ages before the discovery of America 11 to 1 or 10 to 1 was current in England. In the sixteenth century the ratio was 12 to 1. In the early eighteenth century when Newton was reforming British currency the value of silver had fallen, after great fluctuations, to 16 to 1. The bimetallic systems of Europe during the first three quarters of the nineteenth century were based on 14½ to 1. Nowadays the breakdown of bimetallism and the widespread adoption of gold monometallism, silver, no longer a standard outside Asia, has fallen to somewhere about 100 to 3.

by side with silver as a standard of value.* But in classical times its currency uses were mainly confined to Persia, Greek countries being upon a basis of silver monometallism. Probably Persia held, during the period of its strength, so large a proportion of the available gold that they had not much difficulty in maintaining their fixed parity. Nevertheless it seems likely that it would not have been maintained unless the authorities had supported it by accepting the metals alternatively at the legal parity for taxes or temple dues.

I suspect, however, that the 40 to 3 ratio may have tended to overvalue gold,† and that this may have been the explanation of a preponderance of gold in Persia and a preponderance of silver elsewhere.‡

Since from early Babylonian times onwards until the secular days of Alexander and Caesar the bulk of the gold and silver reserves were held by the temples, the bimetallic ratio must have been largely governed, within limits, by the relative valuation placed upon the metals by the priests for religious purposes and dues. The view that this valuation was constant over epochs and had an astronomical origin, as well as the convenience that ten barley grains of the moon's metal were worth one wheat grain of the sun's, would therefore, be plausible, if only, which at present it is not, it were compatible with the evidence.

If any generalisation is permissible I should be inclined to say that the traditional ratio between silver and gold, both before and after the Persian Empire, was more often 10 to 1 than any other figure, and unless this is to be interpreted as 10 of barley

---

* On the whole, however, I think that silver predominated in Babylonia as the standard of value. Johns found that this was certainly the case in Assyrian documents of the 7th century B.C. and that prices were never expressed in terms of gold.

† I have seen a statement—I know not on what authority—that the ratio of 10 to 1 was current in Greece so early as the time of Plato. Scheil also quotes an authority for 10 to 1 as the ratio prevalent before the Achaemenid dynasty established the 40 to 3 standard for Persia.

‡ The fall in the silver value of gold after the dissipation of the Persian temple hoards indicates that these hoards must have contained relatively more gold than silver. Pythius, the Lydian millionaire of the time of Xerxes, of whom Herodotus tells, owned, according to the story, 2,000 talents of silver and nearly 4,000,000 gold darics (i.e. more than 1,000 talents of gold) so that his gold was worth nearly 8 times his silver.

to 1 of wheat, the Persian ratio of 40 to 3 tended to overvalue gold in the long-period judgement of the ancient world.

In the case of copper and silver the traditional ratio, generally accepted by the authorities, was 120 to 1. This figure fits in very well with the fact that for the Babylonian mina, the Lydian mina and the Egyptian kat there were in each case two standards one double the other. If we suppose that the heavy mina was used for weighing copper and the light mina for weighing silver, we have the convenient result that a heavy talent of copper was worth a light mina of silver, a heavy mina of copper was worth a light shekel of silver, and so on.* That this was the primitive ratio, I am ready to accept as plausible. But I am afraid that the positive evidence for it is not quite what it might be. Dr Johns held that in Assyria in the 7th century B.C. the ratio was anything between 100 to 1 and 180 to 1. I shall suggest in a later section that the growing relative abundance of silver was the occasion of the change-over to a monometallic silver standard.

The final set of drafts, which involved some re-working of earlier material, was accompanied by a table of contents.

Chapter   I   The Babylonian mina, the Egyptian kedet (?), and the Persian daric and shekel

II   The Lydian–Euboic mina

Appendix A Wheat–Barley Ratio

B Silver–Gold Ratio

C Bronze–Silver Ratio

III   The Origins of Money

Appendix D The Backwardation on Corn in Antiquity

IV   Primitive Greek Standards

V   The Pheidonian and Solonic Reforms

VI   Attic Standards

VII   Roman Standards

---

* In Assyrian documents of the 7th century B.C. the minas 'of the king' and 'of the country' seem to have been heavy, whilst the minas 'of Carchemish' and 'of the merchant' were light (Johns, *Assyrian Deeds and Documents*, vol. II, p. 269). But it seems probable that the mina of Carchemish was of a different standard from those 'of the king' or 'of the country', i.e. did not stand to the latter in the simple proportion of one half. In this case it may have been the light Lydian–Phoenician mina.

I THE BABYLONIAN STANDARD

In the latter part of the second millennium B.C. it was traditional in Nineveh that the weight standard, which was then in use had been instituted by Dungi, a King of the third dynasty of Ur *circa* 2456 B.C. Some of the weights which Layard discovered in the Palace of Nineveh bear his name, and Prof. Sayce recorded a Babylonian weight thus inscribed: 'One maneh standard weight, the property of Mersdach-sar-itani, a duplicate of the weight which Nebuchadnezzar, King of Babylon, the son of Nabopolassar, King of Babylon, made in exact accordance with the weight prescribed by the deified Dungi, a former King'.

This tradition has now been verified by the results of more recent excavations into Sumerian remains in the neighbourhood of Ur. Three objects, in particular, have been found, two from the reign of Dungi himself and one from the reign of his grandson Gimil-Sin (2384 B.C.), which are inscribed with the name of the ancient weight which they are supposed to represent. These weights agree reasonably well with the Nineveh weights of more than 1,000 years later.

The mna, or mina, which Dungi prescribed for Ur in the middle of the third millennium B.C., is, within the limits of our present positive knowledge, the earliest standard of weight. Recent discoveries have, however, thrown back the genesis of organised economic life to a date so much earlier than was previously supposed, that weights must have existed centuries and, perhaps, even millennia before Dungi, in whose reign money, prices, interest, contracts, and receipts are fully established, the archaic civilisation of the Sumerians being far more fully developed in these respects than those which succeeded it.

We know not only the approximate weight of Dungi's mna, but also the table of weights then current, which was as follows:—

1 talent   = 60 mna
1 mna   = 60 gin or shekels*
1 shekel   = 60 gin-tur or little shekels
1 little shekel = 3 she or grains

The best evidence for the weight of mna of Dungi is as follows :–

(1) A diorite weight (No. 3 in Weissbach's list) from the reign of Dungi which is inscribed $\frac{1}{2}$ mna, weighs 248 grammes, giving 1 mna = 496 grammes. This weight is slightly damaged and it is estimated that it would weigh 3 grammes heavier in perfect condition, yielded a mina of 502 grammes. There is also a weight of similar standard and epoch found in the temple of Naumar at Ur (No 2 in Weissbach's list) which is inscribed 2 mna on the standard of Dungi, dedicated to Naumer, weighing 999 grammes which, allowing for slight damage, would probably weigh 1004 grammes in perfect condition.

(2) A diorite weight (No. 4 in Weissbach's list) from the reign of Gimil-Sin (2384–2378 B.C.), which is inscribed 5 mnas, weighs 2510·975 grammes, giving 1 mna = 502·2 grammes.

(3) The Nineveh weights discovered by Layard in 1853, which are important, because (bronze and stone together) they are numerous (about 30), many of them have their weights inscribed, they are concordant, and the place of their discovery was such as to suggest that they were authoritative.

(4) The bronze lion, representing a royal talent (120 mna) discovered at Khorsabad and now in the Louvre, which gives a mna of 502·5 grammes and the bronze lion of Susa (240 mna) which yields a mna of 506·4 grammes. The last named is the largest weight extant and has probably suffered, therefore, the least proportionate wastage.

(5) Two stone weights of the reign of Darius Hystapes, of which one ($\frac{1}{2}$ mna) yields a mna of 500·172 grammes and the other (apparently 400 silver shekels) a mna of 500·24 grammes. Both are in good condition (see Weissbach's list) and cannot have lost more than a fraction of a gramme in weight.

* Shekel is the Semitic translation of the Sumerian word.

(6) These figures are further confirmed by the agreed weight of the daric* or gold stater, which was $\frac{1}{60}$th of the Babylonian mina, and is given by all authorities at 8·34 to 8·42 grammes (130 grains) which yields a mina of 500·4 to 505·2 grammes,† the former being the weight of the average of extant specimens and the latter of the heaviest.

No primitive weight standard, indeed, is so well authenticated or so undisputed as is the Babylonian mna at 500–505 grammes with 502 grammes as the full normal weight in Sumerian times and perhaps 505–506 in later periods.

In spite of a variety of conjectures,‡ I see little reason to doubt as to what the basis of this weight standard was. The mna was what it said it was, namely the weight of 60 × 60 × 3 she or grains of wheat, just as the qa, the measure of capacity, is the volume occupied by the number of she included in the qa. Thus the unit of weight is given by counting grains of wheat. It follows that the weight of the she must have been

$$= \frac{1}{10800} (502\text{--}506) \text{ grammes}$$

$$= 0\cdot046\text{--}0\cdot047 \text{ gramme}$$

This is, as we shall see below, exactly the same figure (or within 1 per cent) as that of the traditional weight of the grain of wheat as given by the Roman lb, the weight of which we know to a high degree of accuracy. It is also the exact figure for the wheat grain evaluated by Professor Ridgeway.§

* This name seems not, as might have been supposed, to be derived from Darius, but is older than he. The coin was never debased and continued to be coined to the end of the Persian Empire. It was the ancestor of Caesar's *areus* and hence of most gold coins down to the present day. As Greece possessed no gold currency of her own, the gold daric obtained a considerable currency in Greece also, and was the gold coin of classical Athens, where it did not much differ in weight (24:25) from the Attic silver didrachma.

† The question between 500 and 505 grammes as the full theoretical weight of the mina and between 8·34 and 8·42 grammes for the stater is discussed further below. The numismatic evidence as to the weight of the stater or daric is conveniently collected by Viedebantt in *Antike Gewichtsnormen* (1923), p. 27. Out of 182 darics which have been separately weighted 159 lie between 8·27 and 8·41 grammes. The average weight of 255 darics and double darics is 8·245 grammes.

‡ E.g. that it represents the weight of a certain cubic volume of water or of stones or has some astronomical significance.   § *Origins of Currency*, p. 182.

These figures seem to me to establish almost beyond controversy that the Babylonian weights were based on a sexagesimal system with the wheat grain of about 0·0465 grm. as its monad.*

There are two derivative standards of some importance:

(1) *The Heavy Mina*

In the neo-Babylonian and Assyrian periods there is evidence of a standard just double the Babylonian of 500–505 grms, heavy shekels and heavy minas (but not, so far discovered, heavy talents). Many authorities write as though the heavy standard had always existed alongside the normal standard. But Viedebantt points out,† with truth I think, that we have no evidence of the heavy standard before the 8th century B.C.

Since at that date the bronze–silver ratio was 120,‡ and since the heavy mina contained 120 light shekels, I conjecture that the heavy standard was for weighing bronze, so that a heavy mina of bronze was worth a light shekel of silver.

(2) *The Persian Silver Shekel*

This, so far as I know the evidence, was a still later derivation of the normal Babylonian standard, and was a product of the Persian Empire. Under that Empire there was established and maintained down to its disruption by Alexander a gold–silver bimetallic system in which the metals were noted at 3 to 40. For purposes of convenience silver shekels were then minted of such a size that they would run 10 to the gold daric. Consequently their weight was $\frac{40}{3} \div 10$, i.e. $\frac{4}{3}$ of the daric. Since the daric was

---

* Thurea-Dangin approaches this solution (*Journal Asiatique*, vol. XIII (1909), p. 79) and then sheers off in favour of the mna being the weight of a certain cubic capacity of water (a far more advanced idea than one based on counting grains) partly because he takes the mna, rather than the she as the ultimate unit and partly because he gets the relative weight of wheat and barley the wrong way round. See also *Revue d'Assyriologie*, vol. XVIII (1921), p. 123. Lehmann-Haupt seems to ignore almost entirely the monads of the ancient systems.

† *Op. cit.* p. 15.

‡ See Chapter 2 below for the evidence.

$\frac{1}{60}$ of the mina, it follows that the Persian shekel or siglos was $\frac{1}{45}$ of the mina. It is sometimes alleged that there was also a Persian silver mina fifty fold of the silver shekel, but I do not know of the evidence for this.

The reader will notice that both these derivations (like, as I shall argue, most of the complications of standards) were probably due to the prevailing ratios of value between the monetary metals, the heavy mina being a product of the silver–bronze ratio and the silver shekel of the gold–silver ratio.

So far all seems simple:—and so indeed all is. But certain German writers, of whom Lehmann-Haupt is the chief, have wasted much of their own and other people's time in devising complicated systems which are not plausible in themselves, and are not, in spite of their authors' learning, as one discovers if one has the patience to work through the details, supported by the evidence.* Lehmann-Haupt has enlarged the three related standards defined above, namely the standard, the silver and the heavy Babylonian minas (or, as they might well be called, the gold, the silver and the bronze Babylonian minas) into twenty-four by (i) adding to these three a gold mina of 100 (instead of 60) darics, (ii) assuming that the silver and his alleged gold minas, as well as the standard mina, existed both on the heavy and on the standard scale, and (iii) assuming that each of the six standards thus arrived at existed on four related scales, namely a 'common' scale and scales respectively $\frac{1}{20}$th, $\frac{1}{24}$th and $\frac{1}{36}$th heavier than the common. Most of this is a figment in my opinion, and the less said about it the better.†

The evidence for a mina slightly heavier than the mina of Dungi falls to the ground, because the weight, provenance and

---

* In particular the theories range over a period of about two thousand years with too little regard to the *chronology* of the evidence. For instance, Lehmann-Haupt holds that the heavy mina is as ancient or more ancient than the light mina, which is contrary to the positive evidence up to date, and that the 40 to 3 gold–silver ratio of the Achaemenid Empire holds right back to the third millennium, which is not the case. He seems to take little or no account whether his evidence is from the sixth century, the eighth century or the twenty-first century.

† Some effective criticism will be found in Viedebantt's *Antike Gewichtsnormen*, Chapters 1 and 2.

epoch indicate without much doubt that the specimens alleged in evidence represent didrachmas on the Attic or Euboic-Lydian standard and have nothing to do with the Babylonian.* There remains, however, one set of facts, not yet mentioned, which does require further explanation, namely the existence of a set of weights both in Sumerian and in later times which seem to conform to a standard (i.e. about 2 per cent) lighter than Dungi's, namely about 490 grms (say 489–491 grms). Some of the weights of this standard belong to neo-Babylonian times but one at least seems to date from the dynasty of Lagash (circa 2950–2500 B.C.).

Considering what ancient weights are and over what wide ranges most known series are scattered, I am not clear that a variation of so little as 2 per cent in weights from different epochs and localities is sufficient to justify the inference of an independent norm. Nevertheless Viedebantt (*op. cit.* pp. 18–20) does adduce some plausible evidence for associating these somewhat light weights with the temple of the god Marduk and with Babylon, and argues that the temple standard of Marduk in Babylon may have been over long epochs a trifle lighter than the temple standard of Naumar in Ur, which latter is what I have called the Dungi mina of 502–505 grms.

This must remain conjecture. It is consistent with the evidence to suppose that the mina was by definition 10800 sound grains of wheat and that this lead at different epochs and different places to a mina of round about 500 grms, ranging from 2 per cent less than this to 1 per cent more. For a period of 2,000 years even this range exhibits an almost incredible stability, the maximum range representing a difference which for the smaller units of weight would be indistinguishable.

For the purpose of comparing the Babylonian standard with other standards in historical times, we may take it, I think, most

---

* The stater or didrachma ($\frac{1}{50}$th mina) on the Euboic-Lydian standard being within 4 per cent of the stater or daric ($\frac{1}{60}$th mina) on the Babylonian standard, it is difficult, when it comes to epochs and places where the existence of either standard is plausible, to be quite sure to which of those two standards the extant coins conform.

conveniently for practical purposes at the figure of 501 grms. I think that the full theoretical standard was a little higher—perhaps 502·5 grms in the Sumerian period and 505–506 grms under the Achaemenids;—at any rate weights and darics exist which suggest this. But the ordinary run of reasonably good specimens of darics, for purposes of comparison with similar specimens of (for example) Attic drachmas or Roman denarii, conform rather, for practical purposes, to about 501 grms (i.e. 8·34 grms for the daric). The question of the probable distribution of extant specimens about the theoretical norm is discussed further in an appendix to this chapter.

Appendix to Chapter I: The relation of extant specimens to the theoretical standard

The numismatic world has not yet made up its mind about this. Three methods of deriving the full theoretical standard from the evidence of extant weights and coins have their adherents:–

(i) To prefer the heaviest known specimens;

(ii) To calculate the average of the whole number of reasonably well-preserved specimens;

(iii) To take (in the case of coins) the most frequent value of extant specimens and to add (say) 1 per cent to this for wastage, etc.

A good deal depends, when we are dealing with coins, on how far the ancient world accepted coins by tale and how far by weight. I know no direct evidence on this point. On general grounds it seems plausible to suppose that in large transactions and for foreign trade payments of gold and silver would always be made by weight; but for retail transactions at home and possibly payment of taxes and official or religious dues a coin which looked a fair specimen would be accepted by tale at its face value—a drachma would be a drachma, a shekel a shekel, and a daric a daric. The pocket scales would not be a universal possession or come out on every occasion. Moreover, when the state itself was paying not newly minted coins, it might be in a position to insist that they be taken at their face value.

In this case there would be some temptation to the minting authority to take a modest seignorage, if only to discharge the expenses of the mint, within the limits to which the public were accustomed or which public opinion would allow. It seems to me almost certain that there would be some bias against issuing over-weight or even full-weight coins, or, if there was not, that such coins would be separated out by money changers for sweating or clipping or melting down, so that even exceptionally good specimens in circulation or in hoards would run (say) 1 or 2 per cent below the full theoretical standard, a discrepancy indistinguishable by the ordinary person in the transactions of daily life.

In this case method (ii) above will clearly lead to too light a result, besides which it allows nothing for inevitable wastage. On the other hand method (i) is liable to depend on a very small number of specimens which may be merely aberrant, ancient methods being not sufficiently precise to avoid occasional over-weight results by accident; moreover, coins occasionally gain weight by oxidisation. Something on the lines of method (iii) seems to me to be right, the question being how much percentage allowance ought to be added to the most frequent value to allow for light-weight bias and for wastage to attain the full theoretical standard.

This third method has been well worked out by Mr G. F. Hill of the British Museum.* His conclusion is to take one per cent above the mode or most frequent value given by his Frequency Table to get the full weight. This may be quite an adequate allowance for wastage, etc., but I am not sure whether it is enough to cover light-weight bias as well. Something between 1 and 2 per cent might yield safer results.†

* 'The Frequency Table', *Num. Chron.* 5th series, vol. IV (1924), p. 76.
† Mr Hill has some useful observations on the exactitude of ancient weighing generally. He takes a hoard of gold staters of Lysimachus of the same date and showing no wear and finds a range of 2·3 per cent. 'These coins belong to a period (323–281 B.C.) when the weighing

This line of thought is confirmed by the evidence from extant weights as distinguished from coins. In the case of weights there is less reason to suspect a light-weight bias, and where they are of stone and of regular shape it is often possible to estimate closely the amount of loss by damage. The result is that the preponderant evidence from weights, whether Babylonian, Greek or Roman, leads to an appreciably higher value for the standard than the preponderant evidence from coins. Unfortunately weights, when they are made of lead, which is not uncommon especially in Greece, may err seriously in the other direction, since lead gains in weight by time and exposure.

In a sense the question is not of much consequence, since the absolute value does not really matter within one or two per cent, which is the margin of error in question. But it has this amount of importance—that where, as often in this book, we are investigating the theoretical relations between different standards we must apply the same method in both cases. In particular we must be careful in comparing evidence derived from weights with evidence derived from coins. For the most ancient periods, we depend entirely on weights; and for later periods mainly on coins. For this reason I shall, in what follows, take the Babylonian mina at 501 grms for comparative purposes, whilst believing that its full theoretical weight was slightly more.

III   THE ORIGINS OF MONEY

An article may be deemed to have some at least of the peculiar characteristics of money (1) if it is regularly used to express certain conventional estimates of value such as religious dues, penalties or prizes, or (2) if it is used as the term in which loans and contracts are expressed, or (3) if it is used as the term in

of coins may be supposed to have been as highly organised as at any period of antiquity.' 'We are not justified', he concludes, 'in assuming that the Greeks cared about weights less than 0·05 grms'—which is somewhat more than 1 per cent of a drachma and less than 1 per cent of a daric.

which prices are expressed, or (4) if it is used as an habitual medium of exchange. In the first three cases the article in question is the term in a *money-of-account*, in the fourth case it is used as actual money. Now for most important social and economic purposes what matters is the *money of account*; for it is the money of account which is the subject of contract and of customary obligation. The currency reforms which matter are those which change the money of account.

When we turn to the actual records of antiquity, we find in the earliest Greek history a community very primitive in its use of money, but in the earliest Babylonian history a community very advanced indeed in all these matters even in the remotest records of the third millennium B.C. Individualistic capitalism and the economic practices pertaining to that system were undoubtedly invented in Babylonia and carried to a high degree of development in epochs more distant than the archaeologists have yet explored. The immigrating Greek tribes were Northerners having a social system (of clans or feudalism) very remote from individualistic capitalism (just as the theocratic slave state socialism of Egypt was remote from it in the opposite direction). The old Babylonian power had been swept away long before the Greeks appeared on the scene; but its economic system had continued without much modification through the Assyrian and neo-Babylonian periods and had probably penetrated to a considerable degree the whole of Asia Minor during the Persian Empire.

Perhaps the clue to the economic history of Greece from the Homeric period to the fifth century B.C. may be partly found in the gradual adaptation of the primitive economy of the tribes to the individualistic capitalism which they found in Asia Minor in a decadent and confused form but reaching back in its origins and in the experience behind it to a highly developed and complex system of great antiquity. Exactly as was the case in the Renaissance of our own era, the discovery of traditions and fragments of ancient learning, which became the instruments of revolutionary innovations of thought in the hands of the discoverers, coincided with economic contacts strongly tending away from feudalism towards individualistic capitalism. Solon was a Renaissance character.

Some historians underestimate, I think, the contrast between the economic development in the Greek lands in the seventh or eighth centuries B.C. and that in the areas which had long been under Babylonian influences. Because a particular kind of sealed or coined money was first minted in Asia Minor in the sixth or seventh century B.C., it has been supposed that the characteristics of a monetary economy were not much more ancient there than they were in Greece. In fact, however, the device of sealed money was an invention of very trifling significance. The first important innovation on Babylonian practices is essentially a modern one, namely the invention of representative money. The stamping of pieces of metal with a local trademark was just a piece of bold vanity, patriotism or advertisement with no far-reaching importance. It is a practice which has never caught on in some important commercial areas. Egypt never coined money before the Ptolemies and China (broadly speaking) has never coined silver, which is its standard of value, down to this day. The Carthaginians were reluctant coiners and perhaps never coined except for foreign activities. It is absurd to suppose that the coins of the city states of Greece and Asia Minor, of widely varying weight and very susceptible to clipping, ever passed in any sense as legal tender outside their own narrow territories (even if they did within them) and must have been reckoned by weight in all important transactions. The dealer or moneylender would not move without his *scales*.* It is more

* And apart from this the tradition, recounted by Herodotus, as to the Lydian coinages between the first in history, is in itself uncertain. Dr Johns makes out a *prima facie* case for not rejecting the idea that plaques of metal which perhaps bore of the head of Istar where coined in Nineveh before the 7th century B.C. He conjectures, not without evidence, that these coins were called Istars and that the Greek στατήρ may be derivative from the Istar or Astarte of Assyria (*Assyrian Deeds and Documents*, vol. II, pp. 278–291). More probably, however, στατήρ is a Greek word which came to be used as specially applicable to the Asiatic coins owing to the suggestive similarity of sound.

likely that the stamping of coins was intended as a certificate of the fineness of the metal than as one of weight. A particular coin might obtain a reputation and a trade value as being of a standard fineness, but scarcely as being of a standard weight. So far from the act of coinage constituting the veritable introduction of money, it could be argued that the races, which founded the monetary economy and have shown special aptitudes for its development, have been especially suspicious of the inexactitudes and pitfalls of coinage, have coined reluctantly if at all, and have preferred the straightforwardness and simplicity of bullion. The presumption of many writers that where there were no coins there was barter is far from accordance with the truth.

On the other hand the full-blown use of the precious metals as money for each of the four essential purposes outlined at the beginning of this section had already prevailed universally within the sphere of Babylonian influence for more than two thousand years at the least. The introduction of a money, in terms of which loans and contracts with a time element can be expressed, is what really changes the economic status of a primitive society; and money in this sense already existed in Babylonia in a highly developed form as many years before the time of Solon as separate Solon from Mr Pierpont Morgan and had had a continuous tradition during the whole interval in the districts of its origin.

What is the evidence concerning the introduction of the Babylonian economy into Greece? It is clear that in the Homeric age there was not much occasion for money in the settlement of strict business transactions between individuals. Mentions of price have a certain vagueness quite appropriate to the contexts in which they occur but not compatible with business transactions on the Babylonian or Wall Street model. The famous cow standard of Homer will be misunderstood if it is applied or even thought to be capable of application beyond the first of the uses of money distinguished at the commencement of this chapter, namely to express certain conventional estimates of value such as religious dues, penalties or prizes. I conceive the primitive state and its evolution towards a true monetary economy to have been as follows.

In an agricultural community of the bronze and iron age, the principal objects of transferable wealth, other than land and slaves, i.e. the principal raw materials of exchange were the ox or cow, the sheep, the measure of corn, iron and bronze, with the horse, gold and silver, wool, the measure of oil and the measure of wine as foreign, scarcer or secondary commodities. The more important of these, taken in their usual units, would have a conventional *order* of value and even a conventional *relation* of value for customary purposes. For example a cow would be a handsomer prize, a severer penalty, a richer sacrifice than a sheep, a copper pot or a measure of barley; and so on. It might also be felt that, if a cow was not forthcoming on an occasion where a cow had been customary, that ten sheep or a given quantity of bronze or iron was a reasonably suitable equivalent. It is not necessary for such conceptions that cows or sheep should be standard animals of unvarying value or that their market prices should be at all times in the strict relationship 10 to 1. Indeed it is obvious that neither of these conditions would be in fact even approximately true. Nevertheless these vague standards would be perfectly satisfactory for many semi-economic purposes. For example, one could speak of a rich man being worth so many cows or sheep, just as Dukes still record in *Who's Who* that they are worth so many acres; one could fix a scale of penalties or fines for certain offences in terms of those objects; one could denominate the customary prizes for Olympian victors in such terms; the suitable sacrifice at a particular shrine on a particular occasion could be so fixed. The element of vagueness in the standard would not seriously matter for these purposes. If the victor in an athletic contest got a scraggy animal, the local patron might get a bad name for meanness; the priest might refuse a blemished beast; but that would be the worst which could happen. In such conditions there can be no effective guarantee of the quality and precise value of this article delivered other than public opinion as to what is suitable in the circumstances. There are abundant examples of a similar vagueness as to precise exchange value in the practice of primitive races in recent times who have not come into close contact with the ways of an advanced profit-seeking economic society. Take, for example, the custom of trading by the exchange of 'gifts' which should be of approximately equivalent value before public opinion.

On the other hand for trading proper in the strict economic sense, where each party is keen for a profit and a trading 'turn', or for the purposes of everyday exchange in the market, it seems to me to be absolutely out of the question that the cow standard can ever at all have been employed. For it is entirely lacking in the essential qualifications for employment as money in any of the uses outlined above except the first. To begin with it is far too large a unit for ordinary use and has no obvious lesser derivative units,*—we are driven at once to sheep or measures of wheat or bars of iron and bronze which are really, if anything, alternative standards since they have no steady relationship of market value with the cow from which we started. Next there is the obvious objection that the cow is not a standard article, the value of which can be generalised and expressed without reference to the particular. Even if a trader were to take cows to market, he would be forced to trade individual cows against each particular purchase—which is barter. No-one would ever price goods or advance a loan in terms of cows in general without reference to the particular. Lastly there is a not less fatal objection, which has received less attention,—even a particular cow does not have a steady value throughout the year but fluctuates in accordance with the seasons or difficulty of finding fodder

---

* Lamm in his interesting and useful volume *Heiliges Geld* has suggested that a helping from a cooked cow at a feast was the original subsidiary unit, the ὀβελίσκος being not the spit itself but the quantity of meat which could be fished with one out of the common pot. But such an idea is surely but one more product of *mania nomismatika*.

and the expected date of its calving. I cannot believe that cows, sacred or otherwise, were ever money or standards of value in Greece or anywhere else in the full sense of the word, any more than turkeys and plum-pudding are in England.

These objections hold good against most commodities other than metals. Wheat is free, or almost free, from all but the last. But the seasonal fluctuations in the value of wheat according to the date in relation to the harvest introduce special difficulties— difficulties, as it happens, which were well-known to the ancient world*—in the case of any wheat contract into which a time-element enters.

These difficulties were not fatal, however, for all purposes. Specified measures of wheat remained useful standards for many purposes of an annual character, as for example the daily wage of a worker hired throughout the year or for agricultural rent payable at the harvest. There is plenty of evidence for corn-wages and corn-rents from the Babylonian age onwards to medieval times. For such purposes, though *not* for the purposes of trade which lacked this regular annual character, wheat or barley have been much more truly money than cows can ever have been.

Now by the eighth or seventh century B.C. the Greek world was not so primitive as to be able to do without money proper altogether. Already they were eminently traders and they were trading with peoples who had had the tradition of metallic standards of value for decades or centuries. Commercial practices of all kinds were rapidly undermining feudal and religious customs; and there is much evidence that loans, mortgages, debts and interest were becoming established features of life. The Babylonian economy had already made considerable conquests on the European littoral of the Mediterranean.

I am sure, therefore, that for trading purposes Greece of (say) the 8th century B.C. already had a metallic standard of value and exchange. And when we come to the question what metal was employed, the evidence is very strong that in Greece as in Italy

* See note on 'The Backwardation of Wheat in Antiquity'.

the primitive standard was either iron or bronze (or copper*)—
not silver or gold. There is even a tradition as to the table of
weights and the inter-relations of the units. The pre-Pheidonian
Greek bronze weights were probably somewhat as follows:—†

$$1 \ \tau\acute{a}\lambda\alpha\nu\tau o\nu \ = 10 \ (\text{or } 6) \ \pi\epsilon\lambda\acute{\epsilon}\kappa\epsilon\iota\varsigma$$
$$1 \ \pi\acute{\epsilon}\lambda\epsilon\kappa\upsilon\varsigma \ = 6 \ (\text{or } 10) \ \mu\nu\alpha\hat{\iota}$$
$$1 \ \mu\nu\hat{\alpha} \ = 6 \ \grave{o}\beta\epsilon\lambda\acute{\iota}\sigma\kappa o\iota$$
$$1 \ \grave{o}\beta\epsilon\lambda\acute{\iota}\sigma\kappa o\varsigma = 6 \ (\text{or } 12) \ \chi\alpha\lambda\kappa o\acute{\iota}$$
$$1 \ \chi\alpha\lambda\kappa\acute{o}\varsigma \ = 4 \ (\text{or } 2) \ \kappa\acute{o}\lambda\lambda\upsilon\beta o\iota$$

I think it probable (some confirmatory evidence will be given
later) that the basis of the standard was the same as that
prevalent in Etruria and Italy generally, from which the historic
Roman standard was derived. Thus the κόλλυβος was equal to
the Roman ounce and consequently the ὀβελίσκος to the libral
asses.

I conceive, therefore, that to begin with there existed in
Greece three types of monetary or quasi-monetary practice
persisting side by side:—

(1) A cow–sheep standard, traditional from more primitive
    times, for purposes of ostentation, religion, rewards and
    punishments;

(2) A corn standard for agricultural rents and wages, and
    possibly also for corn-loans repayable after harvest on the
    Babylonian model.‡

(3) An iron or bronze standard for the purposes of the market
    and of exchange and commercial purposes generally, and
    possibly for loans.

I conceive further that monetary evolution was proceeding
along two different lines simultaneously. There was, first of all,
the normal progress of adaeration, that is to say the gradual

---

* The date of the transition from copper to bronze (by admixture of tin) is somewhat obscure,
owing to the tendency to use the same word for both. In Assyria, however, bronze, rather
than copper, had become the standard article long before the earliest Greek age. I do not
know the evidence as regards Greece.

† The question of the number of μναῖ to the πέλεκυς and of χαλκοί to the ὀβελίσκος will
be discussed below.

‡ In Italy where the last two factors were not operative the transition came much later.

tendency for the metallic standards to oust the others; and secondly a tendency first for bronze to take the place of iron and then for silver to take the place of bronze from convenience of bulk, from commercial contact with the silver-using countries of Asia Minor, and as a result of the growing abundance in Greece of silver from Laurium (and elsewhere).* The problems of the early currency reformers (Pheidon if that dubious figure ever was such, and Solon certainly) arose out of these two tendencies. They may or may not have been tackling at the same time social difficulties arising out of the growth of indebtedness in a society comparatively unused to the Babylonian economy.

Chapter V

The Pheidonian and Solonic Reforms

Ever since the discovery of Aristotle's *Constitution of Athens* the interpretation of the passage relating to the Currency Reforms of Pheidon and Solon has been a favourite crux of metrology. The passage runs as follows:–

Before his legislation he (Solon) carried through his cancellation of the debts, and after it the augmentation of the measures and weights, and of the currency. For under him the measures were made larger than those of Pheidon, and the mina which previously was the weight of 70 drachmas was made to contain 100. (But the coin denomination in old times was the didrachma.) He also made as a standard of weights corresponding to this coinage a talent weighing 63 minas, and the extra minas were added proportionately to the stater† and the other weights.

Until recently there has been no secure evidence, based on actual coins, as to what the Pheidonian drachma or the pre-Solonic drachma of Athens did in fact weigh. Old-fashioned numismatists have identified the Pheidonian drachma with a variety of extant coins, doubtless Aeginetan, bearing the device of the

* Possibly as the result of an overvaluation of silver in terms of bronze—see a later section.
† I.e. the double mina, not, as Sandys supposes (*Constitution of Athens*, p. 42) the coin weight of $\frac{1}{50}$th the mina.

turtle. But whilst the Aeginetan drachma of classical times which was widely current throughout the Peloponnese and elsewhere in Greece has been established by numismatists at a normal weight of 6·2 grms (96 grains),* coins bearing the turtle do not conform to a single standard, but fluctuate from (say) 5·96 grms (92 grains) to 6·87 grms. Thus archaeologists have had a wide range of choice and have been inclined to fix the value to suit their own convenience. For example, Professor Ridgeway states on p. 217 of his *Origins of Currency* that the Aeginetan drachma weighed 98 grains, the heaviest coins exceeding 100 grains, on p. 306 that it weighed 92 grains, on p. 307 that it weighed 97·5 grains, and p. 311 that it weighed 90 grains, in accordance with the varying exigencies of his arguments.

More recently, however, the numismatic labours of Mr Seltman have put the matter on a sounder basis† As a result of his census of the earliest Athenian coins he finds that the series which immediately precedes the Solonic Reform conforms to a standard of 6·2 grms (which is, in fact, Hultsch's figure for the normal Aeginetan drachma), whilst the series which immediately follows it conforms to a standard of 4·34 grms (which is, in fact, the recognised standard of the historic drachma of Athens).‡ This gives us the necessary firm ground of fact on which to base our theory.

It also, as it happens, confirms the first part of Aristotle's statement. For 4·34 is exactly seven-tenths of 6·2. Moreover 4·34 grms is exactly one hundredth part of the now familiar Lydian–Euboic mina and 6·2 is exactly one seventieth part of the same mina. I do not see how we can doubt any longer but that the Pheidonian drachma was obtained by dividing the

* E.g. Hultsch, *Metrologie*, p. 188.
† Seltman, *Athens, Its History and Coinage*.
‡ Mr Seltman seems to me to be disposed not to allow quite enough for wastage. It is obviously the best preserved and heaviest coin specimens which are the clue to the standard and not the average. The above figures, however, conform in each case to the normal value of well preserved specimens in his census. For the purposes of this chapter I take the values of the Aeginetan and Attic drachmas at 6·2 and 4·34 grms respectively, so as to not confuse the argument. These are undoubtedly the norms of well preserved coins. But I shall argue elsewhere that the full theoretical standard was perhaps 1 per cent higher than this.

Lydian–Euboic mina into seventy parts and the Solonic drachma by dividing it into a hundred parts.

Two difficulties, however, remain. In the first place Pheidon certainly did not invent the Lydian–Euboic mina. What then were the famous Pheidonian standards? Herodotus narrates that Pheidon 'made their measures for the Peloponnesians'. Strabo quotes Ephorus to the effect that 'in Aegina silver was first struck by Pheidon', and that 'he invented the measures which are called Pheidonian and weights and stamped currency, both the other kind and that of silver'. According to the Parian Marble, 'Pheidon the Argive confiscated the measures...and remade them and made silver coin in Aegina'; and according to the *Etymologicum Magnum*, 'First of all men Pheidon of Argos struck money in Aegina; and having provided coin and abolished the spits, he dedicated them to Hera in Argos.' This is corroborated by a fragment of Aristotle, according to which the spits dedicated by Pheidon were still in his day to be seen in the temple of the Argive Hera.

In the second place, the last part of Aristotle's statement to the effect that Solon 'made as a standard of weight corresponding to the coinage a talent weighing 63 minas' remains unintelligible. No one yet, in my opinion, has been able to make consistent sense of this statement.* I believe, nevertheless, that the clue will be found by reading Aristotle literally. Does he mean that 63 new minas weighed one old talent or that one new talent weighed 63 old minas? Since he says in the same breath that Solon's measures were made *larger* than those of Pheidon, only the second of these two interpretations is consistent, namely that one Solonic talent weighed 63 Pheidonian minas, unless we take the quite different line of translation adopted by Mr G. F. Hill which is considered below. Let us start with this equation:–

$$1 \text{ Solonic talent} = 63 \text{ Pheidonian minas}$$

It follows that 1 Pheidonian talent

---

* I deal in an appendix to this chapter with alternative interpretations of Aristotle's statement propounded by Professor Percy Gardner and Mr G. F. Hill respectively.

$$= 60 \text{ Pheidonian minas}$$

$$= \frac{60}{63} \text{ Solonic talent}$$

$$= \frac{60}{63} \times 60 \times 100 \text{ Solonic drachmas}$$

$$= \frac{60}{63} \times 60 \times 70 \text{ Pheidonian drachmas}$$

$$= 4000 \text{ Pheidonian drachmas}$$

Thus Aristotle's two statements, taken together, namely that the Solonic drachma was seven-tenths of the Pheidonian drachma and that the Solonic talent was 63 Pheidonian minas, imply, by mere process of arithmetic, that the Pheidonian talent was equal to 4000 Pheidonian drachmas.

Now for the first of these statements, namely that the Solonic drachma was seven-tenths of the Pheidonian dracham, we have found exact archaeological corroboration in the coin census of Mr Seltman. Is there any archaeological corroboration for assuming a talent of 4000 Pheidonian drachmas?

Here again Mr Seltman's careful work has given us sound evidence for answering Yes. He finds (*op. cit.* p. 118) that the celebrated iron bar and spits dedicated by Pheidon in the Argive Heraeum and actually recovered by the excavations of Sir Charles Walston are based upon a 'drax' of 6 oboeloi weighing 400 Pheidonian drachmas and upon a talent of 10 drax (i.e. of 60 oboeloi) weighing 4000 Pheidonian drachmas.* This corroborative evidence has the added advantage (for when one enters the wicked world of metrology one must suspect everybody and everything) that Mr Seltman arrived at the factor of 4000 without being aware of its arithmetical conformity with Aristotle's statement. Moreover he has accepted the usual view that

---

* The iron bars and spits being considerably wasted by rust, Mr Seltman compares their weights with those of correspondingly worn Pheidonian drachmas. If we take the drachma at its full weight of 6·2 grms the large iron bar of 3 talents weight should scale 74,400 grms. Its actual weight is 73,000 grms after more than 2,500 years of wastage by rust. The spits, allowing for slightly more wastage, are in close conformity.

the spits dedicated by Pheidon represented the standard which he was introducing; so that he was cut off from connecting his archaeological results with the literary testimony of Aristotle.

I conclude that the chances of archaeological discovery enable us to reconstruct with considerable confidence the whole procedure of the Pheidonian and Solonic Reforms. I had better at this point abandon the method of exposition from the bottom upwards in favour of description from the top downwards.

For reasons already given I believe that the very ancient Lydian–Euboic mina of 434 grms (which possibly ante-dates the Babylonian mina of 505 grms) was the primitive standard of the Aegean and Mycenaean civilisation and (as I shall show in a later chapter) of the Italian and Etruscan also. The Mycenaean gold-rings, based upon an 8·68 grm standard, are exactly one-fiftieth part of this mina. I agree with Professor Ridgeway that this standard represents the primitive gold stater of the Greek world. The Greek world had very little silver at this date and was for monetary purposes on a gold–bronze standard.

Then come the Dorians bringing iron and establishing a gold–iron standard in place of the gold–bronze standard in those districts which they dominated.* Their conventional table of equivalence is between one gold stater and one talent of iron, which gives an iron–gold ratio of 3000 to 1. It is for this reason that Homer calls a gold stater a *talent* of gold,—it is an amount of gold worth a talent of iron.

The Dorian table of conventional equivalents of value in the Homeric age is, therefore,

1 talent of iron = 1 cow = 1 gold stater
1 talent of iron = 10 drax of obeloi
1 drax of iron = 1 sheep = 1 medimnus of corn
                        = 1 stater (or double-mina) of bronze
1 drax of iron = 6 obeloi of iron
1 obelos of iron = 1 hektus of corn = the daily wage

* The evidence for this is collected in chapter IV.

1 obelos *weighs* 1 mina of bronze
           50 staters of gold
           60 shekels of silver

All these talents, minas, staters and shekels are still on the Lydian standard, which the Dorians find and adopt, whilst introducing the iron units of talent, drax, and obelos into the table of conventional equivalents.

This was the standard upon which in the seventh century B.C. Pheidon sought to improve. I think that his main object was to introduce silver in place of gold and possibly bronze in place of iron as the predominant standards of value, though I think it is a mistake to suppose that he sought to abolish iron altogether. On the contrary, the evidence favours the opinion that in the districts under Pheidonian influence the use of iron-spits as currency continued for two or three hundred years after Pheidon's day. Their use in Sparta is familiar and Mr Seltman adds (*op. cit.* p. 120):– 'Their employment is recorded in other states, but only in such states as coined their silver on the Pheidonian standard.' In bringing in a silver currency Pheidon was introducing a monetary standard already prevalent in Asia Minor* and one better suited to the facts of the day and the economic relationships of Greece.

But apart from this it is probable that the old conventional equivalents between the metals were out of date and were no longer in sufficient accord with market values. In particular they may have under-valued silver which could not, therefore, circulate in Greece unless it was rated up. The Pheidonian standards, therefore, consisted in dividing the Lydian-Euboic mina into 70 parts instead of 60 for the purpose of the silver unit, and of making a new talent for iron 4000 times the new silver unit in place of 3600 times the old one. It is probable that the old-established Lydian mina continued to be used for

---

* The silver *standard* had always prevailed in countries under Babylonian influence. As to whether silver *coins* were minted in Asia Minor before the seventh century, I express no opinion.

weighing silver and bronze and the new Pheidonian talent with its divisionary units was limited to iron and served as a link with the existing iron standard.

In this case one of the objects of Pheidon's new silver coin standard and his new iron drax-obelos standard was to secure that his new silver drachma should be a conventional equivalent of his new iron drax, and also, perhaps, of a heavy mina of bronze on the Lydian standard, just as the old silver shekel may have been a conventional equivalent (no longer corresponding to market value) of the old iron drax and of the heavy mina of bronze. This means that he altered the conventional ratios of equivalence as follows:–

	Old ratio	New ratio
iron–silver	360	400
bronze–silver	120	140
iron–bronze	3	2·86

Lydian standards
   talent = 60 × 434 = 26,040 grms
   mina = 434 grms = 60 shekels = 50 staters
   shekel = 7·23 grms
   stater = 8·68 grms
Pheidonian standards
   talent = 5000 × 6·2 = 24,800 grms
   iron drax = 2480 grms
   iron obelos = 413 grms
   silver drachma = 6·2 grms

Thus the old iron talent weighed 3000 times the old gold stater and 3600 times the old silver shekel; the new iron talent weighed 4000 times the new silver drachma. At the same time the Pheidonian iron drax, whilst weighing 400, was worth 1 Pheidonian drachma.*

If this is correct, the spits and bars which Pheidon dedicated

---

* Mr Seltman agrees (*op. cit.* p. 119) that Pheidon rated iron and silver at 400 to 1.

in the Argive Heraeum were not, as has been supposed, on the authority of the *Etymologicum Magnum*, the old discarded standards, deposited there as a curious act of antiquarianism, but were his *new* standards, the depositing of which in a temple for record and safe custody was in accordance with immemorial Eastern custom, the great iron weight or kanon being the standard 3-talent weight. This interpretation is not only much more natural but makes better sense of the tradition. Pheidon, we are told, made their measures for the Peloponnesians, who, as we know, continued to use iron obeloi for two or three hundred years after his date. He invented the weights and stamped currency called Pheidonian, '*both the other kind and that of silver*'. 'The other kind', previously unexplained, is the iron talent of 4000 drachmas. He confiscated the measures '*and remade them*'. His reform consisted in remaking the talent, drax and obelos of a different weight from formerly.

Solon's reform, on the other hand, primarily consisted in going back to the international Lydian–Euboic standard, which was probably never abandoned for the purposes of weighing copper and silver. He was presumably influenced by the advantages of returning to the same standard as the outside world and of having one standard instead of two side by side. Moreover the use of iron spits was now out of fashion in non-Dorian centres, so that the relationship established by Pheidon between the silver units and the iron units had no longer any practical importance. It may also have been the case that the output of the mines of Laurium was making Pheidon's rating of silver out of date. If, as the wording of Aristotle suggests, he equated his new didrachma to the Pheidonian drachma and reckoned it as the conventional equivalent of the heavy mina of bronze he was changing the bronze–silver ratio from Pheidon's 140 to the figure of 100 more appropriate to the relatively greater abundance of silver in the Greek world in the sixth century.

Thus Solon got rid of the Pheidonian talent and its subsidiary units and returned to the Lydian talent, but divided the mina into 100 parts (or rather into 50 for the didrachma) for his silver currency instead of either 70 parts like Pheidon or 60 parts like the Asiatic shekel. The division into 50 parts, however, also had the advantage of making his silver didrachma of just the same weight as the ancient and traditional gold stater unit.

Our story is now in complete conformity with Aristotle's Solon 'augmented the weights', since the Lydian talent, which he restored, weighed 26,040 grms, as compared with the Pheidonian talent of 24,800 grms. He augmented the currency, if as we have supposed above, he equated his didrachma to the heavy mina of bronze which had previously been equated to the Pheidonian drachma, because the former weighed 8·68 grms and the latter 6·2 grms. He divided the Lydian mina into 100 parts instead of into Pheidon's 70. And, last but not least in corroborative value, 1 Solonic talent weighed 63 Pheidonian minas.

I see no evidence that Solon's currency measures were connected with his measures for the relief of debtors, which, according to Aristotle's statement, came first. Solon was concerned with restoring the international standard of the Aegean, with getting rid of what was no better than a Dorian provincialism brought into existence by their fancy for iron, and with correcting the fluctuation of the bronze–silver ratio.

Appendix to Chapter V

I. Professor Percy Gardner holds that Aristotle's passage as a whole is to be interpreted to mean that the drachma of Solon was $\frac{63}{60} \cdot \frac{70}{100}$ of the drachma of Pheidon, i.e. that the mina was raised 5 per cent and then divided into 100 drachmas instead of 70. As this fraction $= 0·735$, it is held to reconcile the Aristotelian account with the account given by Androtion, as transmitted by Plutarch in his *Life of Solon*, namely that Solon established a new drachma such that 73 of the old drachmas were equivalent to 100 of the new. It also accords with the theory that the Aeginetan drachma was about 5·96 grms (92 grains); for the weight of the Attic drachma is not very far from 73 per cent of 5·96 grms. If 5·96 grms were in fact the volume of the Aeginetan drachma, this interpretation might be worth considering in spite of the fact that it does not make matters much better since it is not really consistent with the first part of Aristotle's statement. But the conclusive objection is that 5·96 grms was not in fact the weight of the primitive or Pheidonian Aeginetan drachma.

II. Mr G. F. Hill's theory ('Solon's Reform of the Attic Standard', *Numisamtic Chronicle*, 3rd Series, vol. XVII (1897), p. 284) requires more detailed examination.* He translates both parts of Aristotle's statement differently from the translation which I have adopted:–

(1) ἡ μνᾶ πρότερον ἔχουσα σταθμὸν ἑβδομήκοντα δραχμὰς ἀνεπληρώθη ταῖς ἑκατόν.

he translates:

'the mina, which previously weighed 70 (new) drachmas, he increased so as to weigh 100 (new) drachmas'. That is to say he rejects the idea of there having been a Pheidonian division into seventieths, assumes that the Pheidonian mina was 100 Pheidonian drachmas just as the Solonian mina was 100 Solonian drachmas, and argues that Aristotle is telling us the weights of the old mina and of the new mina each of them in terms of new drachmas. Thus, according to Mr Hill, Aristotle is not in this statement comparing new drachmas with old drachmas in terms of the old mina, but *is* comparing new minas with old minas in terms of new drachmas. His main ground for this is that 'if we understand that the weight of the mina was retained and the weight of the drachma lowered, we must understand ἡ μνᾶ to refer to some other mina than the

---

* Not only on account of the high authority of Mr Hill, but because this theory has been adopted by Sandys in his edition of Aristotle's *Constitution of Athens* (p. 41), by Mathieu and Haussoullier in their translation of Aristotle, and by Professor Adcock in his *Cambridge Ancient History*.

Pheidonian'. As to this I agree but embrace the other horn of the dilemma and conclude that the mina here mentioned was the Lydian–Euboic mina which had never ceased to be used for weighing silver and bronze. I find the details as to excess of the Solonian mina over the Pheidonian not here but in the second part of Aristotle's statement.

I think that Mr Hill's translation assumes a very forced and awkward idiom. But apart from this it drives him to invent two standards for the first of which, namely a Pheidonian mina of 100 Aeginetan drachmas, he offers no evidence at all, and for the second of which, namely a Solonian mina of 200 Attic drachmas (for on his theory the Solonian mina is only heavier than the Pheidonian mina on the assumption that the Solonian mina contained 100 didrachmas) the evidence is very bad. For whilst double minas of this weight are found, such units are not called minas but staters, and are regularly inscribed as such (see Pernice, *Griechische Gewichte*, pp. 83, 84). I think that there is no evidence except the very ancient 10 stater weight in the Acropolis museum (Pernice, p. 82) which seems to weigh double the normal stater standard,* but this is poor evidence for the Solonic mina being double what an abundance of other evidence makes it.

In the face of the not easily disputed facts that

(1) the Lydian–Euboic mina was a pre-existing and widely prevalent standard

(2) the Aeginetan drachma weighed $\frac{1}{70}$ of this mina

(3) the Attic drachma weighed $\frac{1}{100}$ of this mina,

I do not think that we have a right to depart from a translation of Aristotle which is straightforward in itself and exactly consistent with these facts.

(2) ἐποίησε δὲ καὶ σταθμὰ πρὸς τὸ νόμισμα τρεῖς καὶ ἐξήκοντα μνᾶς τὸ τάλαντον ἀγούσας

he translates:

---

* The ἥμιον ἱερόν weight proves nothing (Pernice, p. 81), because it may have been a half stater.

'he also made trade weights, on the basis on the coinage, on a scale in which the talent was equal in weight to three-and-sixty of the (coinage) minae'. According to Mr Hill, that is to say, Solon introduced not one standard but two. He introduced a new currency mina $\frac{10}{7}$ of the old mina, and also a new trade mina 5 per cent heavier than the new currency mina. In doing so he attributes to Solon a very senseless proceeding. Apart from the inconvenience of having two standards current at the same time, one so nearly equal to the other as to invite confusion, and the folly of deliberately inventing such a system for no apparent purpose, Solon would be doing an absurdity for a trading state in introducing a trade mina just 5 per cent heavier than the widely current and old-established international Lydian–Euboic standard. There is, however, one point which Mr Hill has *not* noticed, counting partly for him and partly against him, namely that, if Solon did what he thinks he did, Solon's new trade mina was just half as heavy again as Mr Hill's supposed Pheidonian mina (for the new trade mina = $\frac{63}{60}$ new currency mina = $\frac{63}{60} \cdot \frac{10}{7}$ (i.e. $\frac{3}{2}$) old currency mina), i.e. it weighed 150 Pheidonian drachmas* and, incidentally, 210 Attic drachmas. It counts partly for him—because it makes rather better sense of Solon's procedure; but also against him because it provides an alternative explanation of the weights, the existence of which (if indeed they do exist which I dispute) he claims as evidence for his trade mina, namely that they are merely 150 Aeginetan drachmas.

I suppose that both translations are tenable. It all depends whether πρὸς τὸ νόμισμα is to be taken with σταθμά or with τρεῖς καὶ ἐξήκοντα μνᾶς. In the first case it means that Solon made a standard for weights, corresponding to (i.e. the same as) that for coins and then compares this standard with the pre-existing standard for weights as distinct from the standard for coins. In the second case it means that he made a standard for weights as distinct from coins, and that a talent weighed 63

---

* Whereas the Gardner theory makes the Solonian currency standard $\frac{63}{60} \cdot \frac{70}{100}$ of the Pheidonian, the Hill theory makes the Solonian trade standard $\frac{63}{60} \cdot \frac{100}{70}$ i.e. $\frac{3}{2}$ of the Pheidonian.

minas according to the currency (i.e. 63 currency minas). I should have thought that πρὸς τὸ νόμισμα τρεῖς καὶ ἑξήκοντα μνᾶς was not a natural way to express '63 currency minas'. But the graver objection is to be found perhaps in the entire lack of any trace in later times or any tradition whatever as to the existence of an Attic trade mina of 210 Attic drachmas.*

I prefer, therefore, the theory that Solon's weight standard was 5 per cent heavier than the Pheidonian standard and the same as his coin standard i.e. a return to the Euboic–Lydian standard, rather than that it was 5 per cent heavier than his own coin standard and a multiple (150) of the Aeginetan drachma.

My view is that before Solon the ancient Lydian–Euboic standard was still in use for the money-metals, gold, silver and probably bronze, whilst the Pheidonian standard was the standard for iron and for trade weights. Aristotle therefore, in describing the Solonic reform relates Solon's drachma to the Lydian–Euboic standard in the sentence where he deals with currency and to the Pheidonian standard in the sentence where he deals with trade weights; adding that Solon's standard for trade-weights corresponds to (i.e. was the same as) his standard for currency, since he restored the Lydian–Euboic standard for both purposes.

In conclusion I must say a word about Mr Hill's claim to support the existence of an Attic trade mina 5 per cent heavier than the currency mina by an appeal to the extant weights in Pernice's list. This is not supported by Pernice's own opinion. His weights form a continuous series ranging from 507 grms to 414 grms i.e. from 16 per cent above the Attic currency standard to 10 per cent below. The heaviest of these conform (apparently) to the Babylonian standard. It is not surprising that within this range Mr Hill can find some weights 5 per cent above the

---

* See the account of the next chapter of the traditions relating to Attic standards other than the currency standard. Mr Hill's assumption throughout of an Attic double–mina (as distinct from the stater which, of course, weighed two minas) partly depends, I think, on his acceptance of the theory that Hippias halved all the Solonic standards, a theory which is now generally discarded.

currency standard. But this is not the end of the argument. If we ignore the weights which have obviously suffered injury and loss, it is true that they average appreciably heavier than the Attic currency standard. Pernice faces this and explains it. Nearly all the Attic weights in the list are made of lead, and lead gains weight in course of time if it is exposed. Pernice illustrates this by leaden weights found at Pompeii which are obviously intended to be on the Roman lb standard but are decidedly too heavy (the majority 5 to 10 per cent too heavy) and range round the lb standard very much as the Attic leaden weights range round the currency standard. Further it is possible to check this conclusion, so far as concerns the Attic weights, (though Pernice himself does not do this) by an appeal to the small minority of *stone* weights to which the above argument does not apply. None of these support the theory of a standard 5 per cent heavier than the currency standard. The three best preserved and heaviest specimens (nos 275, 276, 278 in Pernice's list which are also outstandingly good indicators because they are 8 mina, 5 mina and 3 mina pieces respectively) yield figures of 446·6 grms, 442·82 grms and 440·47 grms. The average of these is 443 grms or 2 per cent above 434 grms. Whilst these figures do not help Mr Hill, they support my general view that the full theoretical weight standards were 1 or even 2 per cent heavier than the standards arrived at by numismatists on the basis of extant coins. Extant *weights* generally tend—which after all is not surprising—to yield a standard a little heavier than extant *coins*.

Some of these chapters were subjects of correspondence with C. T. Seltman and F. E. Adcock.

From C. T. SELTMAN, *27 January 1926*

Dear Keynes,

   This is really most attractive and, to my mind, thoroughly convincing. I am all agog to know when it is coming out and full of curiosity about the preceding and subsequent chapters.

Going through it for the fifth time with unabated interest the following points occur to me:–

p.1, last line; there is no doubt that these coins with the Chelonian reptile *are* Aeginetan since later (5th–4th Cent.) specimens bear at times the letters *AIΓ*.

p.2, line one. May I suggest 'device' or 'badge' rather than 'sign'? Also it is *not*, in Pheidonian times (not indeed before 404 B.C.) a tortoise, but a *turtle*.

p. 6. This is really *splendid*.

p. 8, line 4. Did the Dorians adopt the iron–gold ratio of 3000 to 1 because that had been the bronze–gold ratio in Mycenaean times as I have attempted to show (*Athens* p. 114)?

p. 8. '1 obelos *weighs* 1 mina of bronze.' This is an admirable point, I feel convinced.

p. 8, 6 lines from bottom; may I suggest putting 'Lydian–Euboic Standard' here which would save the first impression which one gets that the Dorians had to go to Asia Minor to find this standard which was, of course, in Greece before ever they came.

p. 9, line 11. 'A standard already prevalent in Asia Minor.' This is not quite clear to me. There is no evidence for any *Coined Silver* of earlier date than Pheidon (if Ure's dating and mine—floruit *c*. 668 B.C.—be accepted, and I notice Wade–Gery accepts it in *Camb. Anc. Hist.* III) anywhere. It is hardly possible to date the first coined electrum before 700 B.C. and that, with its fractions running as low as $\frac{1}{96}$th, seems, on the evidence of actual specimens, to have been the sole metal employed by Lydians for some 140 years, by Ionians until Chios began to coin silver about 620 (at a guess, but later anyhow than Pheidon).

Pheidon then would be the very first of anyone to coin silver. I am aware that the Pheidonian standard does occur on the Asiatic side of the Aegean, but it is later. I have got a paper out in *Num. Chron.* showing the chain of islands by which this standard wandered from Aegina across the Aegean, how it for a time 'stood up against' the 'Lydo–Milesian' and how the 'Lydo–Milesian' squeezed it out again. But of course uncoined bar or blob silver as a favourite *type* of currency did prevail in lands under Babylonian influence.

p. 11. This is splendid. I am quite converted and agree that the spits seem to be specimens of his *new* standard. And does this not gain additional support from the fact that the great iron weight or kanon was dedicated with them? It was then, on your showing, a standard 3-talent weight.

Last page, line 8. What about a footnote to say that, though the *Etymologicum Magnum s.v. Αἰγιναῖα* says 'the Aeginetan talent is heavier than the Attic', this late source is of no weight as set against the evidence extracted from Aristotle.

Very many thanks for letting me see this most interesting and instructive chapter. I hope the book will appear soon.

Yours,

C. T. SELTMAN

To C. T. SELTMAN, *31 January 1926*

Dear Seltman,

Ever so many thanks for your letter. I should like to talk to you some time about the whole thing. But there are just one or two points I might comment on now.

(1) I have given reasons in an earlier chapter, which I hope to send you soon, why I do not accept your argument (*Athens*, p. 114) that the bronze–gold ratio was ever 3000 to 1. So my apparent divergence from this was correct. I shall be interested to see what you think of the argument. My chief point is that you are supposing a value for bronze which is quite out of accord with all other evidence, except, perhaps, some of the theories currently held about the libral as of Rome. And as regards this last piece of evidence, I suspect, though not as yet confidently, that the original libral as of 12 ounces was an iron unit, very much like the obelos, and that the as of bronze or copper never at any time weighed so much as 12 ounces.

(2) In speaking of silver as a standard already prevalent in Asia Minor, I did not mean to suggest that there was coin silver there at an earlier date. I was referring only to the use of the metal as a standard of value. I am, however, in fact rather impressed by John's argument in favour of keeping an open mind as to whether there was not an Assyrian coinage of earlier date.

(3) I have an explanation of the statement of the *Etymologicum*

Magnum about the Aeginetan standard being heavier than the Attic in a later chapter.

(4) As regards the full theoretical standard weights of the Drachma and other units, I have taken in the chapter I sent you the usual figures as based on the best preserved coins. But having regard to the evidence as a whole, I am inclined to believe that the full theoretical rates all round were probably about 1 per cent heavier. This does not really make much difference to the argument, since it would not affect the relationships between the standards; but there are certain reasons, as I hope to show, why it would fit in better to make an allowance of 1 per cent against coins, even when new, being a shade less, rather than more than their theoretical weight, plus the inevitable abrasion of 2500 years. For example, I should like to put an Attic–Euboic–Lydian mina at 438 grms rather than 434. Does this seem to you to be inadmissible?

You say something at the beginning of your letter about my publishing these chapters. I have not any clear intentions about this. The thing has been done for my own amusement, and I feel rather nervous about printing on a matter where my knowledge is so insecure. There will also be the difficulty that my whole essay when it is finished will be too long for an article and too short for a book.

Yours sincerely,
[copy initialled] J. M. K.

From C. T. SELTMAN, *4 February 1926*

Dear Keynes,

Many thanks for your most interesting letter which raises my curiosity not a little. I must say, though so laborious at times, and wearisome to those who have not come under its spell, Metrology is a terribly fascinating subject.

I should much like to have a talk about it, and as I am to have the pleasure of dining at King's as McCombie's guest on the 16th I may see you there and have time to arrange a possible date for a talk.

As to certain points in your letter, there seems to be evidence for a North Italian *iron* unit. I am fortunate enough to possess a piece of early iron bar currency from Etruria. Where did Johns publish his theory about an Early Assyrian Coinage? And if there *was* any where is it now?

I should be inclined to doubt that full theoretical weights were 1 per cent heavier than the best preserved coins. Extant coin weight like the 'Lion of Abydos' and the 'Dekastateron' in Pernice's *Griechische Gewichte* don't support that. And I'm not convinced that *heaviest* specimens in any series give the true weight. Of course average weights won't do at all, but the table of frequency method, so well set out by Hill in *Num. Chron.* (1924), p. 76 ff., does appear to me to be sound. I am always open to conviction, though.

Whatever happens you must publish, though. It will be something entirely new in metrology and something approached from a new angle.

Yours sincerely,

C. T. SELTMAN

From F. E. ADCOCK, *29 January 1926*

My dear Maynard,

Thank you for the chapter. I am afraid I do not agree with the reading and translation of the passage from the *Constitution of Athens*. I think the right reading is as in the two editions which I send and that the right translation and explanation is in Sandys. In that case the 63 refers only to trade weights, not coin weights—at least Aristotle seems to say so. I have not studied the rest of your chapter yet. It may convince me that Aristotle ought to have said what your translation makes him say. Of course, some scholars read and translate as you do, because there are two little holes in the papyrus, but I feel sure that their view is not right. I will take the chapter away for the week-end and shall study it then.

As regards the price of iron: my Oxford authority knows no evidence earlier than Alexander but has given me a reference which I had overlooked, which I send along (see p. 317). I have not checked this man's figures but he is an accurate performer as regards his facts though no one ever agrees with him as to his interpretation of them.

Yours ever,

F. E. A.

To F. E. ADCOCK, *31 January 1926*

Dear Adcock,

I agree that Sandys's translation is much preferable. The passage which deals with mina weights, obviously relates to weights and not to coins, since there can be no coins of such a size. But unless I misunderstand your criticism, the point does not affect my argument. I understand the statement that he made weights 'corresponding to the coinage' to mean that he made them on the same standard. My argument is only affected if you mean to deny this, and to maintain, as the French translator seems to, that Solon made two totally different standards—one for his currency, and the other for weighing commodities. This theory, which I have not previously met with, seems to me to be objectionable for the following reasons:–

(1) The words 'corresponding to the coinage' either have no meaning, or contradict this theory.

(2) It is not likely that Solon would have done such a useless and inconvenient thing as to make a separate standard for goods 5% different to his currency standard. Why should he have done such a thing?

(3) There is no corroborative evidence as to the existence of any such standard. On the contrary, the evidence shows that the market mina, which was used for commodity purposes, was 50% heavier than the currency mina. (The reasons for which I go into in a later chapter.)

Many thanks for the 'iron' reference, which is very useful. It gives the figure of 250 to 1 for the iron–silver ratio, which is very near what my argument required.

I suppose that you are not the fellow who has had from the University Library the first Volume of Beck's *History of Iron*, which I tried to consult the other day?

Yours ever,

[copy initialled] J.M.K.

From F. E. ADCOCK, *23 August* [*1926*]

Dear Maynard,

Your note reached me here on Saturday. I haven't with me any books on numismatics so I must trust my memory, on which, it is true, the passages from Plutarch (Androtion) and Aristotle are indelibly branded from much puzzling. I quite agree that Gardner's explanation won't do. If he quotes the story about Hippias' recoining in (Aristotle) *Economics*, that is, to my mind, worthless as evidence. And I know of no other literary evidence for a change in the time of Peisistratus or his sons. The fact that the earliest Attic owl-drachmae may be dated on archaeol. grounds about 550 B.C. may be explained by assuming that, as the Solonian Attic dr. were slightly heavier than the Euboic which must have been still used in Attica to some extent, the Solonian drachmae were at first melted down. And there is no doubt that the weights and measures were Solonian and that the weights can't be separated from the currency reform. So rejecting that, and accepting the fact of an Aeginetan mina of 70 drachmae, there is no reason to suppose that Androtion and Aristotle are not trying say the same thing though it's a pity they didn't manage to be a trifle more lucid. The Aeginetan mina of 70 dr. is a newish discovery from inscriptions and until that was established it wasn't possible to make the two authorities agree. But with the 70-dr. mina to work with, I think your explanation is invincible and I send all my compliments. You will find it also put forward in De Sanctis 'Aτθίς *Storia della Repubblica Ateniese* 2nd edit. and accepted by Beloch 2nd edit. and by Linforth the latest American on Solon. All these I have read recently.

The portmanteau-ness of Androtion may be due to Plutarch telescoping him. The Aeginetan mina of 70 drachmae was of course made so as to be equivalent with the Euboic mina of 100 drachmae, and so the Euboic drachma works out at about 65–6 grains (i.e. Ae. dr. = 93 grains). The Attic drachma after Solon is *c.* 68–9 grains that is *c.* $\frac{63}{60}$ of the Euboic and that is what Aristotle is getting at with his statement about the distribution of the 3 minae (i.e. an extra $\frac{1}{20}$th) over the stater and the other weights. Whether the Attic talent was $\frac{63}{60}$ of the Euboic or whether the Euboic and Aeginetan table was 63 mina to the talent so that all three talents were the same weight I can't say without books to look up evidence. It rather looks as if Aristotle supposes an increase of the talent above the Euboic due to the fact that the new Attic drachmae are slightly heavier than the Euboic. The fact that the Aeginetan table had a mina of 70 drachmae certainly suggests that it was aiming at passing over into the Euboic standard for higher values and that there was no Aeginetan *talent*—for coin—different from the Euboic. And certainly one would expect the Euboic table to have been 100 dr. = 1 mina, 60 minae = 1 talent—but anyhow the important point is the drachma: how many Euboic minae went to a talent hardly touches the question. If then Aristotle and Androtion take the same view of the facts of the currency-reform of Solon it becomes more significant that Aristotle does not accept Androtion's view that this currency change was Solon's way of relieving debtors. He definitely separates the two things in time. That Solon did something more than play with the currency in the way of relieving debt is clear from the poems which are after all far the best evidence. It must be remembered that though drachmae of the Aeginetan standard were current in Attica Euboic drachmae circulated there too. That is proved by finds in Attica which can be dated about this time.

I may be pig-headed about it but I really can't believe that the new currency introduced by Solon did automatically relieve debtors without hurting creditors as Androtion says. It is hard to believe that the creditor who had lent 70 Aeginetan drachmae in 596 B.C. could be made to accept 70 Attic drachmae in 594 B.C. as payment of his debt, while his neighbour who had lent 70 Euboic drachmae at the same time was repaid just as much. And if the man who lent 70 Aeginetan drachmae had called it 1 mina in his bond—as he naturally would—I take it he had a claim to 1 mina in repayment and that is not 70 but 100 Attic drachmae. I can't imagine a primitive unbureaucratic state would have either the power or the machinery to deal with such complications. Nor does it seem possible that an Attic farmer could be either persuaded or compelled to give as large a lump of figs for an Attic drachma as for a 'fat' Aeginetan, as all his life he had given different amounts for Aeginetan and Euboic drachmae. Is the term 'debasement of the currency' rightly used except in the case of a country where an already existing currency is debased and then lives on its old prestige backed by the authority of the state, and where no currency is used except the national currency? But Solon's drachmae must have appeared to the Athenians to represent the Euboic rather than the Aeginetan and undoubtedly the Athenians for years continued to use other coins than those minted at Athens. In the time of Androtion when the Attic drachmae had a monopoly at Athens and had driven out most other silver currency in the Aegean world and the stater was far more powerful some such device might appear possible but hardly in the time of Solon. In Androtion's time when you said drachma you meant Attic drachma, but in the time of Solon 'drachma' at Athens must have had the same sound as 'pound' at Smyrna.

I would prefer to believe that Solon reduced all debts in terms of Aeginetan drachmae and declared by a special decree that the creditor was only entitled to one Attic drachma for each Aeginetan drachma he had lent. That would be a way of relieving the debtor of between 20 and 30 per cent of his liability, but when Androtion says the creditors were not injured or did not know they were injured I think he is talking through his headdress. And even such a reduction of the amount of the debt would be rather complicated to work, and the tradition isn't good enough to stand rationalising in this way. For I don't think Androtion can have had better evidence to appeal to than the tradition that it was Solon who introduced the Attic drachmae of the regular type and that before that Aeginetan coins or coins of that standard were the most current in Attica. If there was good evidence that

Solon used this currency change to relieve debt I don't see why Aristotle does not accept it. It does seem more probable that it was just a cleverish notion of Androtion to save the democratic Solon from being called a bolshevik.

I hope you haven't been bored by this long screed. I struggled with this coinage reform in my dissertation before the 70-drachma mina had been established and could find no satisfactory solution. And·I don't expect I should have discovered your solution even now. At least I read the like explanation in De Sanctis with much admiration and pass on the same admiration to you.

What I think Solon did was to meet two definite grievances for both of which there was good evidence. The first was that people were being sold into slavery for debt. This he met by declaring such debt-slaves free and cancelling debts secured only on the person of the debtor. The second was that owing to the operation of mortgage peasants had been reduced to being serfs on what was their own land paying over a large part of the produce to their creditors. This he met by restoring to these peasants the full possession of their land and declaring these mortgages null and void. He definitely forbade the pledging of the debtor's person and may have forbidden mortgage, though if so that law gradually ceased to be effective. There isn't any really good evidence for anything beyond this and I prefer to take Aristotle's view that the currency reform was a separate thing not intended to relieve debt.

Cookie[3] writes to say he'll be meeting you soon. Give him my love.

Ever yours
F. E. ADCOCK

To judge by its context, the last piece Keynes wrote was his chapter on Primitive Greek Standards. This chapter, a reworking of earlier drafts, remained unfinished.

III PRIMITIVE GREEK STANDARDS

In Babylonia silver was the standard with copper and then bronze as its subsidiary. In Assyria lead took the place of bronze as the subsidiary. In Egypt, and perhaps in Crete and the early Aegean civilisation generally, gold was relatively more important,

[3] S. Russell Cooke who had been at King's from 1911 to 1914.

281

compared with silver, than it was in Babylonia. In the Achaemenid Empire a strict gold–silver bimetallism was established, with perhaps a predominance of gold. Classical Greece had come over to pure silver mono-metallism with copper no better than a token. In the 4th century B.C. Rome seems to have been mainly on a bronze basis with silver gaining ground.

What was the primitive metallic standard of Greece and Italy in (say) the 8th century B.C.? It is agreed that it was iron or copper or both—not gold or silver. As regards the Dorian civilisation, and perhaps as regards Greece and Italy generally at that date, the evidence is predominant that the earlier standard was iron. I suspect that the history of Greece was as follows. The primitive metallic standards of the Achaeans and the Ionians were gold and bronze. The Dorians introduced the iron standard wherever they established themselves. The Pheidonian reform consisted in replacing the iron standard by a silver–bronze bimetallism; and the Solonic reform consisted in establishing a silver monometallism—a transition that was rendered feasible by the mines of Laurium. Iron being found in the Peloponnese and copper in Euboea, Seltman* plausibly suggests that iron was essentially a Dorian standard and copper an Ionic standard. The fact that iron was also found in Euboea weakens this particular argument. But all the evidence and all the traditions certainly agree that the iron standard was specifically Dorian.

At any rate the traditions as to primitive forms of money in Greece mostly relate to iron. No-one disputes, I think, that the ὀβελίσκος or spit was iron, that the ὀβελίσκοι dedicated by Pheidon in the Argive Heraeum were iron, that the drax or δραχμά or handful of 6 ὀβελίσκοι was iron, that the ancient standard of Sparta was iron, that the πελέκεις and ἡμιπέλεκκα which Achilles offered as prizes for the archers (*Iliad* xxiii, 650)[4]

* *Athens*, p. 122.
4 Actually 851 (Ed.).

were iron. The iron ὀβελίσκοι from the Argive Heraeum and iron ὀβελοί from Sparta have been actually found by excavations and are extant in museums. Iron ὀβελίσκοι were still in use in Bœotia in the fourth century, as shown by Plutarch's example of the poverty of Epaminondas. Aristotle in his *Constitution of the Sicyonians* spoke of iron obeloi.*

I know of no comparable evidence as to the existence of a copper standard in primitive Greece and I think that we are justified in assuming a Dorian iron standard somewhat as follows:

$$1 \ \tau άλαντον = 10 \ \pi ελέκεις \ \text{or} \ \delta ραχμαί$$

$$1 \ \delta ραχμά = 6 \ \dot{ο} βελίσκοι†$$

Nevertheless most scholars, in spite of the evidence in favour of iron which has accumulated recently, still follow the old tradition that bronze was the predominating standard in Greece and also in Italy. The decision as to this and other interesting cognate problems must depend, I think, on the view we take as to the relative values of iron, bronze and silver.

The traditional crux of this problem is to establish the relationship of weight and value between the Homeric τάλαντον of gold which was conventionally equivalent to a cow or ox and the talent equal to 60 minas in the familiar scale of weights; though, as I hope to show, the problem of the libral as of Rome may depend on the same considerations. The Homeric gold τάλαντον being clearly not a talent's *weight* of gold, the most obvious solution is to assume that it was a talent's *worth* of gold, i.e. a quantity of gold worth a bronze talent. Will this solution give a reasonable ratio between gold and bronze, account being taken of the evidence as to the value of the gold τάλαντον?

I see no reason to question the usual conclusion that the gold τάλαντον represented a quantity of gold approximately equivalent to a gold stater and also that it was a conventional

---

* For many references on this matter see Seltman, *Athens*, chap. xv.

† Perhaps we might add 1 δραχμά = 2 ἄγκυραι, 1 ἄγκυρα = 3 ὀβελίσκοι (see Dechelette, *Rev. Num.* 1911, 'Les origines de la drachme et de l'obole').

equivalent for the value of a cow.* It is, I think, generally agreed that Ridgeway (*Origins of Currency*) has made out a strong case for these conclusions, however much other parts of his thesis may be doubted.

If a cow was worth a gold stater on the Euboic–Lydian standard, it would be worth 10 silver shekels on the same standard taking 10 to 1 for the silver–gold ratio, and 10 silver shekels on the Babylonian standard taking 13 to 1 for the silver–gold ratio. That a cow or an ox was worth about 10 silver shekels in the 7th or 8th centuries B.C. is fully confirmed by the available Assyrio–Babylonian records.†

If, however, we take gold τάλαντον = gold stater = 10 silver shekels = cow as a fairly firm starting point for our table of equivalents, and if we suppose, further, that the gold τάλαντον was worth a light talent of bronze, then it follows that the bronze–silver ratio was 360 to 1 (and 720 to 1 if we equate the gold τάλαντον to a heavy talent of bronze). But this is very far from the theoretical ratio of 120 to 1, and we have seen in Chapter II that the extreme range for the bronze–silver ratio on the basis of Babylonian and Assyrian evidence is between 180 to 1 and 100 to 1. Unless, therefore, we can find corroboration‡ for so low a value of bronze in relation to silver, some other explanation must be found. My own supposition is that the gold τάλαντον was a quantity of gold worth a talent, not of bronze but of *iron*; and that the iron–bronze ratio was

---

* It is not necessary that I should quote the familiar evidence for this.

† Scheil, *Rev. d'Ass.*, vol. XI (1914), p. 186 quotes the following prices from documents relating (to) the sixth century B.C.:–

> 24th year of Nabuchadnezzar at Sippara
>   a choice ox   13 shekels
> 12th year of Nabonidus at Sippara
>   a cow   10 shekels
> ditto at Babylon
>   an ox   9½ shekels
> 4th year of Cambyses at Sippara
>   an ox   10 shekels

‡ The tablet discovered by Sir A. Evans at Knossos can only be regarded as 'literary evidence' (Seltman, *loc. cit.* p. 113) except as the result of a rather wild conjecture. There is in truth *no* direct evidence for equating the value of the gold τάλαντον to that of the bronze talent.

3 to 1, which would be consistent with 120 to 1 for the bronze–silver ratio.* To suppose that the original talent-value unit was based on iron rather than bronze seems to me to be consonant with the general evidence as to iron rather than bronze being the primitive standard of Greece,† and also, as we shall see later, with the substitution of the silver drachmas and obols for the iron drachmas and obols. Indeed, I hope to show that it will make better all-round sense. But first we must turn to the libral as of Rome and the Italian evidence.

Those who wish to assume a high bronze–silver ratio ignore the evidence from Assyrian and Babylonian sources and turn to Italian evidence. The divergence between the two sets of evidence is as old as Mommsen, who deduced that there was a bronze–silver ratio of 288 to 1 in 451 B.C. This deduction is based on the Tarpeian law which commuted 100 asses for 1 cow or 10 sheep. If we assume a conventional silver–gold value of cows and sheep the same as for primitive Greece, and the asses are full libral asses of bronze, the above ratio follows.

The primitive as of Rome was, it is agreed, a bar of metal very similar to the Greek ὀβελίσκος; there is plenty of evidence of iron–spit currency in Etruria as well as Greece; Plutarch translates the libral asses of early Rome by the Greek obelos.‡ I suggest that the old libral as was a pound of iron, not bronze; that the as as distinct from the pound was essentially the worth of a pound's weight of iron (just as I have supposed, above, that

---

* If the gold τάλαντον was worth a talent of iron there is a parallel to this in Mungo Park's account (*Travels* p. 39) of the currency practices of the natives of Gambia:

> In their early intercourse with Europeans the article that attracted the most notice was iron. Its utility in forming the instruments of war and husbandry made it preferable to all others; and iron soon became the measure by which the value of all other commodities was ascertained. Thus a certain quantity of goods of whatever denomination appearing to be equal in value to a bar or iron, constituted in the trader's phraseology a bar of that particular merchandise.

Thus a bar of tobacco was twenty leaves, a bar of rum one gallon of spirits. The English for their own convenience in the course of time fixed a bar at two shillings sterling. (E. E. Muntz, 'The Early Development of Economic Concepts', *Economic Journal: Economic History Series*, No. 1 (January 1926), p. 9.)

† In this case the 10 iron πελέκεις offered by Achilles were precisely one Homeric τάλαντον.

‡ Quoted by Ridgeway, *op. cit.* p. 356.

the old Greek talent was the worth of a talent's weight of iron); and that the copper *as* was a quantity of bronze worth a pound's weight of iron. This view will harmonise a good deal of conflicting evidence, for example:–

(i) the *as* is closely correlated to the obeliskos;

(ii) the difficulty about the rating of the richest class in the reign of Servius, as recorded by Pliny, being so high as 120,000 asses, is somewhat eased;

(iii) the discrepancy of evidence as to the bronze–silver ratio is avoided;

(iv) the early currency history of Rome, as affecting the varying weight of the as of bronze, is rendered more intelligible;

(v) the arguments of Mommsen and Soutzo are reconciled.

But there remains another argument, which is, perhaps the most cogent, for the view here put forward. It is agreed that Pheidon substituted silver for iron and it is assumed that the new silver drachmas and obols were equated to the old iron drachmas and obols. But this requires, as Seltman* shows, an iron–silver ratio of not more than 400 to 1. Indeed the direct evidence for some such ratio as this, based on the weights of extant iron obeliskoi and silver drachmas of the Pheidonian epoch, seems much better founded than any of the inferences as to the alleged bronze–silver ratio of around 300 to 1. But what has not been pointed out is this,—if both these ratios are right, iron and bronze work out at almost equal value. We are left with an iron–bronze ratio of 4 to 3 at highest, and I fancy that, if we apply a consistent calculation throughout, an equal value results.†

Now is it plausible to suppose that, so far on in the iron age as the seventh century B.C., iron was still worth practically as much as bronze?

[the new draft ends here—following on from this is an earlier draft that was not revised.]

---

* *Op. cit.* p. 119.

† If the 100 libral asses of Rome which the Tarpeian law equate to a cow are taken to be bronze, if a cow is worth 10 shekels of silver, and if a libral as weighs $\frac{16}{25}$ of a mina, the bronze–silver ratio becomes 384.

Keynes's interests in the ancient world also led him to contribute four anonymous book reviews to the *Nation*. The first appeared in January 1926.

From The Nation and Athenaeum, *16 January 1926*

WALLIS BUDGE, SIR E. A. *The Rise and Progress of Assyriology* (Hopkinson), 1925.

This book is primarily a record and justification of the Assyriological work done by the staff of the British Museum during the past sixty years, and also a vindication of Sir Henry Rawlinson's claims to priority. Sir E. Wallis Budge succeeds not only in establishing his point that the solid work has been done mostly in England and the doubtful theorising in Germany, but also in writing a most entertaining and readable volume. It is a good thing we have recorded over again the unforgettable feats of Rawlinson in copying and translating the inscriptions of Darius the Great from the Rock of Bihistun, and to have alongside this all the other queer and diverting incidents which have marked the early history of this great subject. Certainly no one who is interested in the foundations of early history which have been laid by Assyriologists during the last two generations can do without this volume. It is enriched by portraits of leading Assyriologists of all countries and by an extensive bibliography.

A second followed four months later.

From The Nation and Athenaeum, *12 May 1926*

THE ORIGINS OF CULTURE

DAWSON, CHRISTOPHER. *The Age of the Gods* (Murray), 1926. The secondary title of this book, 'A Study in the Origins of Culture in prehistoric Europe and the Ancient East', is a better indication of its contents than its rather meaningless title. For the book is a remarkably able synopsis of the history of civilisation up to the beginning of the Iron Age, which can be strongly recommended to the general reader who is interested in the extraordinary progress of this fascinating subject during the last generation. It is, in our opinion, a long way the best of several attempts which have been made lately to summarise the broad results of recent discoveries and theories. Mr Dawson's scholarship is exact, cautious, and thoroughly up-to-date, but the extent of his knowledge has not prevented him from covering adequately a great deal of ground in a moderate space and painting in the broad outlines of the picture with just that amount of detail which is necessary to make it live. He possesses the combination of a desire to generalise with an appreciation of the rashness of generalising at all, which the present state of the subject demands. For example, the fairness of his attitude to the theories of Professor Elliott Smith and Mr Perry is characteristic of his method; for he recognises how much real stimulus and useful suggestiveness they must have for a sympathetic reader—provided only that he does not actually accept any part of their conclusions. Mr Dawson has carried a difficult task to a most successful conclusion.

The book, as we have said, covers an enormous field. It begins by tracing the relations of the neolithic culture to the archaic civilisations of Sumeria and Egypt. Next follows the obscure and tangled story of the megalithic culture and of the earliest migrations of the Aryan stock. Then we pass through the two dark ages, the first near the beginning and the second towards the end of the second millennium before Christ, in which the discovery of the horse for purposes of war played as great a part as gunpowder in later ages. And finally we reach the later European civilisation which arose from the union first, at a remote date, between the peasant neolithic culture and the Aryan invader, and secondly between the European stock resulting from this union and the traditions of the Archaic civilisation—as exhibited in the Mycenaean culture and the beginnings of the Iron Age in Europe.

The Archaic civilisation reached its full development in the third millennium B.C. At that date, Mr Dawson claims, the general level of material culture stood higher in many respects than at any subsequent period of the ancient world—'all the great achievements on which the life of civilisation rests had already been reached, and there was no important addition to its material equipment until the rise of the great scientific and industrial movement in Western Europe in modern times'. In short, 'the Aryans in India, the Semites in Babylonia, and the Greeks in the Aegean have long enjoyed an undeserved reputation for the creation of a civilisation which was to a great extent inherited from their predecessors'.

Mr Dawson's absorbing book serves to show not only what a magnificent and intelligible story so-called pre-history has now become, with its progressive additions to our knowledge so rapid and so overwhelming as to make it one of the greatest living subjects for students of the present generation, but also that there is no longer any excuse for leaving it out of our regular educational curriculum. This is the subject to which we ought now to direct the minds and imaginations of our budding scholars and historians, rather than to the well-worked and outworn studies where they can scarcely hope to discover anything both new and important. Mr Dawson has supplied an ideal introduction, which should be in the hands of the young scholars of the public school sixth forms and of undergraduates as a necessary part of humanistic education.

The other two appeared in 1928.

From The Nation and Athenaeum, *12 May 1928*

ASSYRIA

SMITH, SIDNEY. *Early History of Assyria to 1000 B.C.* (Chatto & Windus), 1928.

This is the first of two volumes on the History of Assyria with which Mr Sidney Smith proposes to fill the gap left in the late Professor C. W. King's *History of Babylonia and Assyria* by the latter's premature death. The present volume assembles all the weapons of modern scholarship to tackle one of the most difficult and unsatisfactory sections of ancient history. In the first half of it Mr Smith is concerned with collecting such hints and scraps of information as are available concerning the inhabitants, language, and rulers in the third millennium B.C. of that part of the valley of the Tigris which was afterwards the seat of the Assyrian Empire. In the second half he deals with the history of the same geographical area during the second millennium B.C., a period of which our knowledge is at present far scantier than of either earlier or later epochs; indeed, Mr Smith admits that we are practically without any data from internal sources for Assyrian history from the end of the nineteenth century to the middle of the fifteenth.

It is a consequence of this unavoidable paucity of data that most of the book is occupied by somewhat jejune and highly doubtful inferences as to the influence of surrounding and contemporary powers and civilisations and by catalogues of monarchs and intricate questions of chronology—that is to say, with laboriously preparing the materials for more fortunate future historians rather than with writing real history itself. In two matters, however, Mr Sidney Smith succeeds in escaping into the realm of real historical writing—in his very able and important discussion of the origins of the Assyrian people and in his final confutation of the old-fashioned view of the barbarian and destructive character of the Assyrian power. No longer does the Assyrian come down like a wolf on the fold. Mr Smith discloses them to us as a people differing indeed in important respects of race, language, custom, and tradition from the archaic civilisation further south, but having successfully absorbed a great part of the Babylonian and Sumerian culture for many centuries before they emerged as a great power, and also as a trading people, much more influenced throughout their history by the desire for the security of trade than by motives of loot and pillage. Mr Smith represents the Assyrians to us 'as a developed product of a great civilisation and not, as the classical writers would have us believe, a primitive institution natural to barbarians', and the lands subject to the military state of Assyria as 'rarely better governed throughout the whole course of history.' Throughout the late eleventh and early tenth centuries the Assyrians defended civilisation, and from the ninth century onwards reimposed it in Western Asia, being in fact a necessary instrument of the great renaissance from the dark age which emerged near the end of the second millenium B.C.

On economic matters, which Mr Smith touches somewhat lightly in this volume, but may be expected to explore more fully in his next instalment, he is not quite so secure. Following other authorities, he fails to notice that the so-called 'loans without interest' to which many documents refer were most improbably made without consideration in an age for which interest was an habitual and familiar conception, and that these documents may reasonably be regarded as analogous to a modern bill of exchange which, if an orientalist were ever to see one, would probably appear to him to represent a loan without interest since it would carry on its face no reference to the payment of interest, but only to a sum due; that is to say, the Cappadocian documents in question had been discounted, the borrower receiving a smaller sum than that written in the document as due for eventual repayment. Further the low price-level current in the reign of Shamsi-Adad does not necessarily imply corresponding prosperity, but may have been due to the supply of silver not keeping pace with the general growth of business in settled times, whilst the dispensing of royal largesse might be expected, if made in silver, to raise prices, not, as Mr Smith seems to think, to lower them. Nor is any conclusion to be drawn from the use of lead as currency in later days than that this was the metal most freely produced and available within the country.

From The Nation and Athenaeum, *6 October 1928.*

CRETE AND GREECE IN THE BRONZE AGE

EVANS, SIR ARTHUR. *The Palace of Minos at Knossos.* 2 vols. (Macmillan), 1928.

HALL, H. R. *The Civilization of Greece in the Bronze Age.* (Methuen), 1928.

These two magnificent volumes on the Palace of Minos are in continuation of the first volume published by Sir Arthur Evans seven years ago, and are mainly concerned with the results of the excavations subsequent to 1921. They do not carry much farther his previous synthesis of the main evidence or attempt that final summary of the conclusions to be drawn from Sir Arthur's life's work, which we should have liked to have from him. But they are a treasure-house of evidence for the specialist and of curious items for the eye of the amateur.

The history of civilisation owes so much to the extraordinary flair and enthusiasm and perseverance of Sir Arthur Evans that it seems ungenerous to venture a criticism. But even as a treasure-house of evidence for the expert, the book seems to run a risk of not being quite as useful as it might be, on account of Sir Arthur's fondness for sketches, reconstructions, and restorations in preference to straightforward photographs of the actual objects uncovered. These volumes have been produced (at a very high price) with a great abundance of illustrations, many of them coloured, but it is not always as easy as it ought to be in a book of this description to disentangle Sir Arthur's theories from the material on which he builds them.

For historical generalisations and for an attempt to assess the contribution of Cretan civilisation to the long-subsequent Greek culture, we have to turn to Dr Hall's admirable volume on Greece in the Bronze Age, based on a course of lectures delivered in 1923 before the University of Edinburgh. The Cretan evidence naturally fills the greater part of it, but Dr Hall does his best to relate this to the Mycenaean and Aegean cultures generally and the transition to the Age of Iron. The main period covered by the book, say, 2000 B.C. to 1300 B.C., is one for which the evidence is fragmentary, perplexing and almost entirely archaeological. Dr Hall has probably made as good a 'story' of it as is possible for a prudent man, and the splendid and very well chosen collection of illustrations make it an ideal handbook (at a very moderate price) for anyone who wishes to get a general view of the existing evidence.

What is the impression produced on the mind by a conspectus of what we now know about the period of a thousand years which intervened between the great ages and extraordinary technical innovations of Sumeria and Egypt and the rise of the great age of Greece from which, admittedly, subsequent civilisation draws its origin? Ought we to regard the Cretan culture as the parent of Greek culture and therefore in the direct line of our own ancestry? Or was it only a curious, *fin-de-siècle*, slightly decadent offshoot of Babylonia and Egypt of no lasting significance? Sir Arthur Evans and Dr Hall lean strongly to the former alternative. And they can, indeed, make out a fairly strong case on grounds of technical archaeology. Yet the great gaps in the evidence still entitle us to hold opinions based on a general, imaginative impression, and to doubt whether the remarkable character of the archaeological discoveries may not cause us to exaggerate the influence of the Minoans on their geographical successors. There is the immense lapse of time for one thing. A dark age of several hundred years intervened between the collapse of Cretan culture and of the early Mycenaean culture which it influenced and the rise of anything which we can call Greek. Nearly a thousand years passed by between the fall of Knossos and the archaic art of sixth-century Athens. A certain continuity in techniques will often be handed down from one civilisation to another remote in time and race. But it is dangerous to trace affinities of culture and artistic inspiration between different races speaking different languages with many centuries of invasion and destruction lying between. Were these tight-lacing, codpiece-wearing fellows of rather light metal—so one feels—and furbelowed ladies of more dominant type than their partners, who decorated their houses with elegant dados in the style of Messrs Maple, and were the first to appreciate the delights of sanitation, the first *Europeans*—the first civilised beings to escape from the grimness of the East and to hand on the results of the technique and the science of Babylonia and Egypt to beings who could breathe a freer air? Dr Hall would have us believe that they were. He would make them of the same blood as the Pelasgians, and he would give the Greeks a large admixture of Pelasgian blood with their Aryan strain. The great age of Greece is the firstfruit, he thinks, of the marriage of the Nordic strength with the ancient Mediterranean inheritance; and perhaps, he adds, the Mediterranean peoples have since reverted to type, so that we find the ancient Cretan in the modern Italian.

It may be so, or the Minoans may have been no more than a brilliant ephemeral offshoot of their greater neighbours. We may one day know the answer, if we learn to read their language—written in something very like Greek letters yet almost certainly not (like the last deciphered puzzle—Hittite) of the Aryan family, but a branch of the unknown tongue, to which Etruscan also may perhaps belong, which was spoken by Mediterranean Europe in the Chalcolithic Age.

Chapter 3

KEYNES AND THE ARTS

Keynes's support for the arts was extensive and took various forms. During the 1930s *The New Statesman* was his main vehicle for the promotion of plays, of the Camargo Ballet, and of productions at the Arts Theatre, Cambridge. In addition, he wrote anonymous 'puffs' and short comments for the columns of *The Nation and Athenaeum*, prefaces to exhibition catalogues, longer articles, and letters to the press.

These years also saw the growth of Keynes's private collection of paintings, started in 1918 when he went to the sale in Paris of Degas' private collection. On that occasion he also had a Treasury Grant of £20,000 for purchases for the National Gallery.

Over and above all this, of course, came his contributions of time, effort and money to the arts in Great Britain. He was a buyer for the Contemporary Arts Society; treasurer of the Camargo Ballet Society (1931–5); and a Trustee of the National Gallery from October 1941. From February 1942 he was Chairman of the Council for the Encouragement of Music and the Arts (C.E.M.A.), which in 1945 became the Arts Council; and, at the end of the war, Chairman of the Trustees of the Royal Opera House, Covent Garden. Finally, there was the founding, building and nourishing of the Arts Theatre, Cambridge, and its presentation in 1938 to the University and the people of Cambridge.

The London Group of artists had emerged as an amalgamation of several small groups of artists who had been unhappy with the state of painting in Britain at the end of the first decade of this century. It was formed at a meeting on 15 November 1913 and held its first meeting in March 1914. Originally Roger Fry, Duncan Grant and Vanessa Bell were excluded from the new group, but by 1920 all had become members.

For its October 1921 exhibition, at the request of the President of the Group, Keynes provided a foreword to the catalogue.

From the Catalogue for the London Group Exhibition, Mansard Gallery, October 1921

LONDON GROUP

Not many rich persons in England take much interest in the work of young painters, who are not yet, if they are ever to be, of established reputation in the fashionable world. But there are a good many people, not rich, who are accustomed to visit such exhibitions as those of the London Group and to take pleasure in what they see there. It scarcely occurs to such people to buy a picture—that is a rich man's fancy. The conventions of picture exhibitions are partly responsible. There is generally a slight mystery about the prices, which can only be ascertained by those bold, inquisitive or wealthy persons who make enquiry at the desk. The enquiry, if made, generally discloses a price beyond what the purchaser feels he can pay merely for the adornment of his house; yet it needs great confidence in his own judgment for him to pay an appreciable sum for the work of a young, and perhaps almost unknown, artist 'as an investment'.

Some, however, of the members of the London Group (I hope most of them) have made up their minds that it is better to sell pictures cheap than not to sell them at all. Whilst those who are ready to pay higher prices are also provided for, they are offering a good number of finished oil paintings at £5, £10 and £12.

Since it can only be as a writer on financial topics that the President of the London Group has invited me to write this preface, I ought not to stray out of my field. But I should like to add that the London Group includes the greater part of what is most honourable and most promising amongst the younger English painters of today. It would be rash to name any one of them as being secure of permanent fame. But it is not so rash to affirm that it is from amongst their number that posterity will choose those whom it will celebrate as the leaders of English painting in the generation after to War;—which affirmation leads me back to my proper topic and allows me to add that the element of 'investment' may not be entirely absent after all, that great masterpieces have often cost their first owner very little, and that the discerning purchaser has a real chance of finding at the London Group a picture which public collections will covet some day. Besides, civilised ages have always recognised that a patron of the arts performs for the society he lives in a distinguished and magnanimous function. Without patrons art cannot easily flourish.

I hope, therefore, that those who visit the London Group this autumn will go with the thought at the back of their heads that, if they see something they like and the price is low, they will make the plunge and buy it.

J. M. KEYNES

In the course of 1925, Keynes originated a more ambitious means of supporting the visual arts when he conceived the idea of the London Artists' Association. By 8 February he had attracted Samuel Courtauld's support. The scheme came into being in July 1925 and the first sales came in October.

Keynes described the next few years of the Association's existence in an article for *Studio*.

From Studio, *June 1930*

THE LONDON ARTISTS' ASSOCIATION:
ITS ORIGIN AND AIMS

The London Artists' Association came into being towards the end of the year 1925, as the result of a meeting with a group of artists, who had found themselves without an efficient organisation for dealing with their work and had consequently sold almost incredibly few pictures during the previous year or two. Yet some of them were well-known painters who had had some excellent sales from time to time in the past. Nor was it only the difficulty of selling pictures which was hampering their work. It was the precariousness and the irregularity of their incomes. Even those of them who might on the average of two or three years expect to sell enough to get a living, had no regular prospects on which they could rely. Some of them had other sources of income, and to them this consideration was not so important. But others of those who joined in the discussion had practically nothing to depend on apart from their sales of pictures, except a certain income from teaching.

The result of our conversation was to make us feel that a small organisation formed on co-operative principles might, even if it had no great financial backing, at least do something to reduce the anxieties of promising painters and perhaps help to get a better market in the long run for their works. The idea was that an organisation could be formed which, acting as agent to a group of artists, would allow them to work in greater freedom from continually pressing financial considerations by providing them with a small guaranteed income and taking upon itself the entire management of the business side of their affairs. Three friends who were interested in modern painting came forward and offered to join with me in guaranteeing a certain sum for this purpose—Mr Samuel Courtauld, who is well known not only for his own private collection, but also for the famous modern French pictures which he has presented to the Tate Gallery, Mr Hindley Smith and Mr L. H. Myers, both of whom have collections of Modern English pictures. All of us knew some at least of the artists personally and felt that the scheme was worth a trial. The ultimate business responsibility for the Association has remained with these guarantors, who mainly decide such questions as the appointment of staff, arrangements with dealers, and the contracts made with members of the Association. But the artist members, on their side, determine the admission of new members, the choice of whom rests primarily with them and not with the guarantors.

The financial side

It may be a matter of some general interest that I should state quite frankly the financial principles on which we have worked and the results up to date. It is impossible, in my experience, to go on continually getting financial support for something which is perpetually losing money and presents itself as a bottomless sink to the friends and supporters who come in enthusiastically at the start. The aim has been, therefore, that the Association should always be run on the basis of being as nearly self-supporting as possible. The object is to cover the actual running expenses (apart from losses on account of the sales of individual members falling below the incomes guaranteed to them) by deducting a commission from the gross sale price of the artists' works on the same lines as those which any ordinary dealer would follow. The amount of the commission has varied, and a number of special arrangements are entered into to meet special circumstances. But at present the normal arrangement is to deduct 30 per cent from the selling price of all pictures sold for members of the Association, the cost of the frame and analogous expenses being deducted from the price before commission is reckoned and any commissions payable to dealers being met by the Association. If the Association were larger it would probably be possible to reduce this rate of commission. But the overhead expenses of keeping a small gallery open are so great that I should not expect a reduction below 20 per cent to 25 per cent to be possible in any circumstances. Indeed there are very few articles in the world of any kind which are sold at a lower retailing cost than this. We had at the start a good many minor troubles and extra expenses, having changed our gallery three times in four years, and began by buying our experience to some extent. But the commissions charged on sales have very nearly covered all our business out-goings.

Whilst the business side of the Association's work, though

intended to be self-supporting, has been helped by the presence of the guarantors in the back-ground, the main purpose of the latter is to cover the guaranteed incomes of the members, any losses in respect of these guaranteed incomes being charged against the guarantors and not against the running expenses of the Association. For obviously it would be unfair to the successful members to pay incomes to the less successful out of the proceeds of the commissions on their sales. It has not been practicable to fix these guaranteed incomes of the members on an absolutely uniform basis. But the most usual arrangement is to guarantee a member an income of £150 a year, paying him in addition to this the total receipts from the sale of his pictures or other works of art in so far as they exceed £150 a year after deduction of the Association's commission. Some members have voluntarily agreed to forego their guarantee in order to make it possible to add to the list of members. In some cases a substantially larger income has been guaranteed, either because the artist in question is one of our best sellers whose sales are practically certain to exceed the minimum, or because of the artist's special needs or expenses, or other circumstances of which it is right to take account. In the case of probationary members a guaranteed income is not always given, and when given may sometimes be less than £150.

In fixing the amount of the guaranteed incomes and the number of the members we have naturally had to be much influenced by the need of precaution lest we take up liabilities out of proportion to our resources. Nevertheless, so far, the actual losses as the result of the sales of individual artists falling short of their guaranteed incomes have been quite trifling, and the amount which we have finally written off on this score out of the guarantors' contributions has amounted in the course of four years to less than 1 per cent of our total sales. Of the total guarantees, on the basis of which the Association was founded, about £1,000 has been called up altogether to meet the losses of running the Association and in respect of guaranteed incomes and to provide working capital, and after four and a half years we still have some surplus in hand.

These results are a good deal better than our original expectations. For nearly all the members have earned their guaranteed incomes over an average of time, although most of them have had to draw upon their guarantee at one period or another when there was a temporary falling off in their sales.

It will put the above figures into perspective if I mention the actual results during the $4\frac{1}{2}$ years of the Association's existence. We have sold altogether more than 700 works of art by the members for an aggregate sum of about £22,000, being an average of about £30 a piece.

Our relations with the picture trade

It has never been the policy of the Association to supplant or do without the services of the regular members of the picture-dealing trade. Indeed, our relations with several of the more eminent members of this profession have been unbroken and of the most friendly character. In fact, it would have been impossible to have secured sales on anything like the scale described above without their assistance. English artists are, in my opinion, well served on the whole by the West End picture dealers, who to-day at least, whatever may have been the case in former years, treat modern movements and modern men with the greatest possible enterprise. I should like to add, too, that the amateur experience of the Association has served to convince me at least that the ordinary charges made by dealers are not excessive for the work they do: I am certain that if other associations were to be formed on the same model as the London Artists' Association, they would be wise to do their best to cultivate intimate and friendly relations with the principal picture dealers. We ourselves have had some of our most important and successful exhibitions at the Leicester Galleries. We have also been much helped from time to time by Messrs

Lefèvre, Messrs Brandon-Davis, the Redfern Gallery, the Goupil Gallery, the St George's Gallery, and many others. For there is no reason in the world to suppose that amateurs, merely because they are disinterested and lovers of art, are in the least likely to be the equals of experienced and seasoned professionals in the selling of pictures.

Our original quarters were in a small gallery opposite St George's, Hanover Square. From there we moved to a small room at 163 Old Bond Street. But for the last two years we have settled down in the occupation of a part of the Cooling Galleries at 92 New Bond Street, and the Association owes more than I can say to the friendliness and generosity and constant consideration of Messrs Cooling. A larger new gallery is shortly to be built on these premises specially designed to suit our requirements, where we shall have ample accommodation and good light. The Association has given exhibitions of the work of its members more or less continuously, holding a new exhibition, as a general rule, every month, either one- or two-man shows or general exhibitions. Representative works of all the members are kept constantly in stock and on view. In December last we held a successful Christmas exhibition consisting of watercolours, drawings and lithographs, and of all sorts of decorative work such as pottery, painted furniture, tiles, needlework, etc., designed and made by members of the Association.

One of the most important branches of the Association's work is the sending out of the members' pictures to exhibitions abroad, in the provinces, and in other galleries in London. Their work has been included in many of the exhibitions arranged by Sir Joseph Duveen's various organisations, such as the recent exhibition at Stockholm and the travelling exhibitions sent out for periods of a year or more to various provincial towns. But I have to confess that the actual volume of our sales outside London has been disappointing. For arranging all this business, and for looking after our own gallery, the Association maintains a whole-time secretary. We had valuable service in our early days from Mr F. Hoyland Mayor, who had some previous experience with a gallery of his own and is now with Mr Brandon Davis, and we were very sorry to lose him. Our present secretary is Mr Angus Davidson.

The choice of artist members

The basis of common sympathy which ought to exist between the different members of an Association of this kind has not always been a perfectly easy matter. All the original members of the London Artists' Association were members of the London Group. No new members are introduced without the approval of the existing members. But it is exceedingly difficult to get together and to keep together a group which is at the same time large enough for business purposes and yet is able to maintain the intimacy and *esprit de corps* between the members which is desirable in any cooperative body of this kind. We have lost some members from time to time whom we have been sorry to lose, and we have sometimes failed to secure new members whose membership would have been a great advantage to us. On the whole, I think we have succeeded in solving moderately well the problem which I have mentioned. But I have always felt this as an essential difficulty. One would wish the Association to be a consistent and coherent one made up of artists who like and approve of one another's work. On the other hand, it would be a great pity if the Association were to get into the hands of a small clique or become too much of a mutual admiration society of a very few persons all painting in much the same way. I hope that anyone who visits our exhibitions will agree that we have managed to combine together, not unsympathetically, a considerable variety of temperaments and methods of painting.

For getting the right members in future we must depend almost entirely on our own artist-members having sharp and sympathetic eyes for the work of promising newcomers. For it is surely the artists themselves who ought to be looking out for promise amongst the younger men and deciding who is really worth encouraging. It must be the case that they are better judges both of promise and of performance, than dealers or such people as the guarantors of this Association. If the artists will do their part in this way, after that the guarantors and the dealers come in—the guarantors to take away a little of the precariousness of those whose work has not yet reached the commercial stage and to make disinterested business arrangements, and the dealers to help us with the tremendously difficult job of bringing the pictures and possible buyers of them together. It is the artists who must spot budding talent.

Any English painter is eligible to submit work for consideration by the Association. Meetings for the purpose of electing new members are held twice a year, when work sent in by candidates is judged by the artist-members and the guarantors. Painters may also be invited by the Association, or by any member of it who knows their work, to stand for election. The original members were Bernard Adeney, Keith Baynes, Vanessa Bell, Roger Fry, Duncan Grant, Frank Dobson, and Frederick Porter. Two of these are no longer members, and there have been added, either as full or as probationary members, Edward Wolf, William Roberts, R. V. Pitchforth, George Barne, Raymond Coxon, Douglas Davidson, Rory O'Mullen, Sydney Sheppard and Morland Lewis. It will be seen from this list of names that the Association is in no way bound to any particular style. Duncan Grant and William Roberts, for instance, who are two of the most important English painters of the present day, are as wide apart as possible in style and feeling.

As I have mentioned, candidates sometimes submit work at the invitation of an existing member, who has seen something he liked at a general exhibition or elsewhere; and I hope that this may become the prevailing method in future. Indeed, I ought, perhaps, to sound a warning note lest the wide publicity which this article will receive in these pages leads to our being deluged with applications. We reject ten or more applications for every one we accept. The Association is not a charity organisation: it cannot afford entirely to neglect the commercial aspect of pictures. It does not set out to support absolute beginners in art, however promising, and is not anxious to elect a painter unless his work shows some reasonable sign of selling sooner or later.

One other difficulty I ought to mention, likely to crop up in any experiment of this kind, which others may make—as I hope they will. The artists for whom an association of this kind is most useful are those who, because they are young or unknown, have scarcely reached the commercial stage and cannot therefore expect a great deal of attention from the commercial world. But such an association would never be able to support its expenses unless it also had amongst its members some artists of established reputation whose works can regularly be sold for a substantial price. It is only by the support and the loyalty of artists in this position, who personally have perhaps not much to gain financially from their membership of the association, that lasting success can be obtained.

Pictures and the public

The question of price policy is a very difficult one, which is still not solved to anyone's satisfaction. Two principles are obvious. We want to get for an artist's pictures as high a price as the public will pay. On the other hand, almost any price is better than nothing. At the same time, it is clear that some uniformity of standard must be maintained, as otherwise buyers will become perplexed and doubtful whether they are receiving fair and uniform treatment. Our own prices have ranged from £5 to £200, the majority being priced at less than 30 guineas. I believe we should do better with lower prices than we actually charge for those artists who sell much less than their output, if only the picture-buying public could be greatly increased in numbers. It is the same with pictures as with books. To reduce prices in a particular case helps very little, because the habit of picture-buying has not spread widely enough. But if a lower range of price were universal and, as a result of this, picture-buying habits had been developed amongst the public at large, then I think it very probable that a lower price range would be advantageous for the majority of artists.

All the same, we could never hope to earn for artists a proper living on Mr Bernard Shaw's principle of the £5 picture. Of course he is quite right that it is much better for any artist to receive £5 and get his picture out into the world than to take it back again into his studio; but to stop at that is to view the problem too simply. The true solution of providing a living for the great majority of artists who are not at present best-sellers would be the growth of a really large picture-buying public which was prepared to pay £5 quite often for comparatively minor works, and £10 or £20 or even £30 not too infrequently. There is room for the £10 to £15 picture, but not, except for beginners or for minor works or as a policy of despair, the £5 picture. At present, however, no such public exists. The number of individuals in England who spend any appreciable sum on pictures in a year is extremely small. I think it is growing a little. But we are far too dependent on a small circle of faithful friends. For it never crosses the mind of the ordinary person to think of buying an original oil-painting, even though he could well afford it now and again and the price would not be out of line with what he spends in other directions.

Like all creative work where the occupation and the achievement are ends in themselves, painting can never be properly pursued for the express purpose of making money. In a sense an artist is an extraordinarily lucky person if anyone will pay him at all for products which he has probably produced mainly to please himself and as a natural emanation of his personality. 'When I get a sum down for a picture,' Walter Sickert is wont to say, 'it is as though someone were to pay me for my nail parings.' At the same time most artists having produced something are, naturally, anxious to get for it as much as possible. Thus the mixture of motives is apt to make them at the same time the nicest and the most difficult people in the world to deal with in a business way. They do not think about money, and yet they do. And apart from money, they most of them need success and recognition enormously, if life is to be satisfactory.

Then there is the public—very ignorant and hesitating for the most part. Yet with an immense respect for the prestige of art and anxious at bottom to enjoy and to help—if only that could trust rather more their own—or anyone's—judgment. When one sees how much money is spent in a year on useless and hideous objects, it seems monstrous that it should be a serious struggle to provide some of the most promising artists in the country—accepted as such by the consensus of their contemporaries and of the leading critics—with £150 a year. Why does the general public find it so extraordinarily difficult to get over its reserves and hesitations towards contemporary art? Was it always so? I suppose there are many reasons and many explanations. But if only the public could learn to enjoy as they deserve to be enjoyed the many delightful and beautiful things which the artists of their own age, just as much as of any other, are offering them, it would be a great improvement!

Keynes also provided a foreword to one London Artists' Association catalogue, that for an exhibition of flower paintings by some of its members in March 1931.

From the Catalogue of the London Artists' Association, Cooling Galleries, 11 March to 2 April 1931

ECONOMIC FOREWORD

It will not have escaped the notice even of the artistic public that the prices of many useful and attractive objects have fallen heavily in the past year. It may be that pictures should not be immune from the same influences that affect wheat, tin, silk and linseed-oil. I have, therefore, persuaded the members of the London Artists' Association who are showing pictures in this Exhibition to abate their prices in nearly every case to about half what it has been usual to ask hitherto. It is very desirable that the prices of wheat, tin, silk and linseed-oil should recover to their former level. When this happens I shall advise the members of this Association to follow suit. Meanwhile I hope that the artistic public will meet us half way by more than doubling their purchases. Indeed, I venture to beg them to do so.

6 March 1931

The Association did not survive the slump. In July 1931 it received the resignations of Keith Baynes, Duncan Grant and Vanessa Bell—all of whom moved to Agnew's—a cause of some coolness in Bloomsbury.[1] Finally in October 1933 the guarantors wound the scheme up after a period when they were called on to meet a quarter of the gross income. However even at this stage the three remaining guarantors[2] provided some support for one or two of the Association's oldest members—an arrangement that lasted in the case of William Roberts until 1937.

Keynes's involvement with the visual arts also led to a few anonymous contributions to *The Nation*.

From The Nation and Athenaeum, *5 May 1923*

It is instructive to compare the prices at the London Group (Messrs Heal's Gallery, Tottenham Court Road) this week with some of those at Mr Augustus John's exhibition. It would be possible to buy all the 150 pictures offered for sale by the London Group for one-quarter of what Mr John was asking for his 'Symphonie Espagnole'. Is it not possible that, if a public

[1] Roger Fry and Frank Dobson had resigned earlier.
[2] Myers had ceased to act in 1931.

gallery wanted to instruct the young and enrich the future and render itself a repository of what is strongest and most promising in English art, it might do better to lay out its money in the Tottenham Court Road? Our City Editor recommends the former purchase as the better lock-up of the two.

From The Nation and Athenaeum, *30 June 1923*

Holman Hunt's 'Scapegoat' and Herkomer's 'Last Muster' have made their funeral procession through Christie's Rooms to a final resting-place at the Lady Lever Art Gallery, Port Sunlight. Pears' Soap and Monkey Brand, the famous Veterans and the famous Goat are happily joined in a common ownership. 'The Scapegoat' was painted nearly seventy years ago at a place politely spelt Oosdoom on the shores of the Dead Sea, and exhibited at the royal Academy in 1856. The history of its price—475 guineas in 1862, 480 guineas in 1878, a failure to reach its reserve of 2,800 guineas in 1909, and 4,600 guineas to-day—illustrates how the fall in the purchasing power of money over *recherché* objects outbalances waning prestige. 'The Last Muster' (1875) fetched 3,100 guineas, Ford Madox Brown's 'Jacopo Fosca' (1870) 520 guineas, Burne-Jones's 'Green Summer' (1868) 380 guineas, Millais' 'St. Agnes' Eve' (1863) 1,500 guineas.

The great British illustrators of the 'sixties and 'seventies still command their price. But taste has turned, and the rich collector, even in England, begins to browse in other pastures. At the same sale a small sketch in oils by Manet fetched 780 guineas. Messrs Lefèvre's successful exhibition of pictures of the highest class by the French masters of the nineteenth century (to which, by the way, a fine Manet and a second Daumier have been added since the show first opened) has been followed this week by a similar show at Messrs Knowdler's and the exhibition of Manet's 'Le Bon Bock' by Messrs Agnew. Unfortunately, the Chantrey Fund is not yet available to purchase for the National Collections the best work of living Englishmen, and the future is dependent on the generosity of subscribers to such bodies as the 'Contemporary Art Society'. How much can be done even with small funds to secure contemporary works, can be seen at the Exhibition of the Society's recent acquisitions which has just opened (for one week only) at Grosvenor House, 32 Upper Grosvenor Street. Let the well-disposed, well-to-do, send their guineas to Mr Edward Marsh, the 'Buyer' for this year.

From The Nation and Athenaeum, *18 August 1923*

Mr Samuel Courtauld's munificent gift of £50,000, for the purchase of the works 'of painters centring round the great Frenchmen of the latter half of the nineteenth century' to fill the Modern Foreign Gallery which is being erected as an annexe to the Tate Gallery at the expense of Sir Joseph Duveen, comes just in time to fill a great notorious gap in our national collections. Within the last ten years the authorities of the National Galleries have refused to purchase works by Cézanne, and more lately even to accept on loan important examples of the master. But time is a mighty one and conquers all things,— even the obstinacy, ignorance and bad taste of the official custodians. Mr Courtauld's assault has been on a big enough scale to overwhelm them, and he deserves the thanks of the nation. It is a little ironical that the Directors of the Galleries in Trafalgar Square and Millbank, who have honestly disliked these pictures for so many years, should be entrusted with the duty of selecting them; and it would be worse than ironical—since the pictures they dislike least are liable to be those least characteristic of the masters—if it were not that their taste is to be corrected and supervised by three genuine lovers of these pictures, Lord Henry Bentinck, Sir Michael Sadler, and Mr Courtauld himself, who are to be associated with them in the task of selection.

Of course, at this time of day, big prices must be paid for the best examples,—enormous compared with those ruling when Mr Roger Fry began to educate the British public into an understanding of the great French masters of the last fifty years, painters as great as any that have ever lived. Nevertheless, heavy absorption into the United States has only lately begun, and it is still just possible to buy at a price the finest specimens of masters, who were by no means prolific, such as Cézanne, Daumier, and Manet, and even, perhaps, of a very rare master such as Seurat,—a thing which may not be possible at all ten years hence. The only regret to be felt is that the works of contemporary Frenchmen are apparently excluded. Would it not be well to secure first-rate specimens of (for example) Derain, Picasso, and Matisse, whilst they can be purchased at a comparatively modest figure, and whilst the living artist is still there to benefit? For, however much individual opinions may differ as to the enjoyment to be got from their art, the position of these original geniuses in the development of European painting is already sufficiently secure to justify their representation in the National Museums. Even if it is inevitable that the official world should move with a slower velocity, and that the voice of Mr Fry, swiftly voyaging into undiscovered lands amidst new flowers and yet untasted fruits, should seem to come from the wilderness rather than from the Promised Land of the future, one cannot but sigh a little that this should be so.

To the Editor of The Nation and Athenaeum, *25 June 1927*

Sir,

Sargent defined Impressionism as 'The observation of the colour and value of the image on our retina of those objects or parts of objects of which we are prevented by an excess or deficiency of light from seeing the surface or local colour'. Mr Woolf comments in last week's *Nation* that these words are 'the unintelligible definition of a man who is not merely inarticulate, but also does not know what he means'.

This seems unjust to a singularly precise statement. Shall I paraphrase it? When an object is either in shadow or in bright light, its natural colour is replaced to the eye by something else. Impressionism, according to Sargent, consists in paying particular attention to this something else and in trying to represent it at its true value to the eye. What is wrong with this? So far from verging on aphasia, Sargent's language is only open, I should have thought, to the criticism that it is more verbally correct than vivid.

Yours, &c.,

SIELA

(Mr Leonard Woolf writes: 'Siela's paraphrase is perfectly clear and is, I agree, part of what Sargent had in his mind. But you have only to compare it with Sargent's own words to see the difference between clarity and obscurity. Further, it is fantastic to say that impressionism is defined either by what Sargent says or Siela says, and Monet himself was amazed that anyone should define impressionism as Sargent did. I still think that the explanation is that Sargent did not know what he meant by impressionism.')

Keynes's activities in connection with the performing arts, other than as a frequent member of the audience, really date from his relationship with Lydia Lopokova. From an early stage, Keynes acted for her and advised her in negotiations with agents and impresarios.

As well, with the advent of *The Nation and Athenaeum* Keynes began to write short, unsigned notices for productions.

From The Nation and Athenaeum, *5 May 1923*

A second visit to the Italian Puppets makes one a little more alive, perhaps, to the dangers of the extraordinary technical virtuosity of the operators. The superb caricature of a music-hall entertainment with which the programme begins loses nothing by repetition; dolls and humans each, in one's imagination, enhance the other. The fantasy of the opera which follows—the frogs, the spiders, the horse, the equestrian lady, the professional mourners—is rich. But one notices the tendency for realism to conquer imagination. When puppets become just like humans, they lose all their point. We do not want to see something which at a sufficient distance we might mistake for Italian operetta. When the puppets are too successful we cease to be interested. But, of course, everyone ought to see them, if possible from somewhere in the dress circle; neither the front of the stalls nor the back of the gallery commands the whole stage.

From The Nation and Athenaeum, *16 June 1923*

Duse's return in Ibsen's 'Lady from the Sea' was a beautiful breath of the past. She still has that wise truth in her gestures and words that only talent can give. The play itself seemed dim and a little empty. Duse's method of the quietness of life, imposed on her company as well as on herself, emphasised too much Ibsen's realism at the expense of his poetry. Her physical weakness and flagging vitality could not quite sustain the mad intensity of Ellida. But her movements brought back the forgotten graces of the 'eighties. One understood that the fashion of an age goes deeper than dress. Her rhythm may be different from ours,—perhaps in us it is of a more complicated order. But after all, we were in sympathy with her, and she did create an emotion in all those present.

From The Nation and Athenaeum, *23 June 1923*

Serge Diaghileff's Russian ballet, by which London has been unhappily abandoned since the half-success of 'The Sleeping Princess' at the Alhambra early last year, is performing again at Paris for a very brief season,—with a programme mainly of the Stravinsky ballets, 'Petrouchka', 'Sacre du Printemps', 'Noces', 'Pulcinella', and others of the modern choreography, 'Chout', and 'Parade'. The only new production amongst these is 'Noces', a composition prepared by Stravinsky some time ago for an orchestra which includes four pianos, percussion instruments, and no strings or wood. Four soloists and a chorus, placed in the orchestra, chant words which no one needs to understand, and as a distinct, parallel interpretation of the music the corps de ballet manoeuvres mainly in front of curtains. The dancers also are in black and white, each sex in a uniform garb, that of the men being based on their traditional practice costume of white shirt and black knee-breeches, after designs by Goncharova. The dance, composed by Nijinska, is built on groups of human waves performing identical movements, and becoming a rhythmical ocean as more and more join in. A primitive and decadent mixture; and, altogether, a well-balanced madness in black and white.

From The Nation and Athenaeum, *28 July 1923*

Lord Howard de Walden's letter in another column heralds a very important theatrical project, which has been discussed behind the scenes for some little time past. It could not start under a management which better combines artistic strivings with a record of practical accomplishment than that of Mr Komissarjevsky and Mr Allan Wade. This is not the first occasion on which Lord Howard de Walden's munificence has tried to help the theatre, and this time we may fairly hope that a lasting success will be achieved. We shall all look forward very excitedly to the opening season.[3]

Serge Diaghileff has been appointed Director of the Ballet and Opéra Comique at Monte Carlo for the coming season, and expects to produce four new ballets. His old admirers in England will hope that this will pave the way to his return to London in the not too distant future, bringing with him these new productions as well as some old favourites.

[3] The letters in question announced the formation of the Forum Theatre and asked for potential shareholders.

From The Nation and Athenaeum, *15 September 1923*

The 'Fairy Doll', with which Pavlova opened her brief season at Covent Garden, gives an extraordinary opportunity of estimating the magnitude of what Serge Diaghileff did for the Russian Ballet. So far from this being, as many of the critics seem to have supposed, a flat imitation of 'La Boutique Fantasque', it is the famous original from which the 'Boutique' was derived. It represents the full glory of the Imperial stage before Fokine and his successors wrought their revolution. Apart from herself, Pavlova's company is rather weak. But one can see what a charming and even splendid thing it must have been when, some eighteen years ago, this piece was chosen for special representation before the Imperial Family at the Hermitage with the full cast of the Imperial Ballet, as yet undiminished by the claims of Western Europe,—Kchesinska, at the height of her fame, as the Fairy Doll; Pavlova herself as the Spanish Doll; Karsavina, Kyasht, and Eugenia Lopokova as the Porcelain Dolls; and Lydia Lopokova, a tiny schoolgirl twelve years old, in the Corps de Ballet. An Austrian production originally, perhaps suggested by 'Coppelia', staged in Petrograd by Legatt, it gives great opportunities for individual virtuosity. Yet how it lacks the ensemble, the management of the space, the simplicity, the wit, and the beauty of Diaghileff's 'Boutique'! By assembling and organising the genius of Rossini, Derain, and Massine, Diaghileff gave Leicester Square a more delicate banquet than the massed ballerinas of Russia could furnish the Grand Dukes.

From The Nation and Athenaeum, *12 January 1924*

After difficult and doubtful times, M. Serge Diaghileff's Ballet is established again at Monte Carlo, where three series of presentations are being given, spread over six months. The first season, mainly composed of old favourites, finished at the New Year; and the second season, which is to include four entirely new ballets, has just begun. It is a great achievement to have kept this remarkable organisation together with a company which, whilst a little weak perhaps in stars of the first order, reaches a high standard of accomplishment. Mme Trefilova, who danced in the 'Lac des Cygnes', still represents in almost full glory the traditions of the classical ballet; and M. Leon Woijikowsky, who will soon deserve to be acclaimed as a great star, dances the modern modes with a captivating, intelligent vitality, and with as fine technical powers as any of his predecessors. Mmes Nijinska, Tchernicheva, Sokolova, Nemchinova, and Ninette de Valois, and MM. Wilzak, Slavinsky, and Idzikovsky, make up a company capable of dancing the whole repertory well enough to make one feel that it is still one of the best things in Europe.

Mme Nijinska is choreographer for the new productions, the first of which, 'La Tentation de la Bergère' was given last week. It is a charming, somewhat slight affair of the Court of Louis XIV, with music of the period by Montclair. For the decor of this ballet, and of Gunod's 'Colombe', also given last week, M. Diaghileff has discovered in the Spanish painter Juan Gris an artist of exceptional talent for the stage. The scenery of 'Colombe' is a fascinating adaptation of the free use of perspective; and that of 'La Bergère' a witty and complete union of modern decoration and the spirit of Versailles.

Keynes even managed a brief, unsigned, cinema notice.

From The Nation and Athenaeum, *11 October 1924*

The Tivoli has put on this week a Metro-Goldwyn super-production entitled 'Tess of the D'Urbervilles', 'adapted from the famous novel by Thomas Hardy'. We are told in the programme that the producers have 'outdone their fondest expectations' and 'a masterpiece of literature has become a masterpiece of the screen'. The setting is modernised; Angel

Clare and Alec D'Urberville, both of immense wealth, pursue one another in Rolls-Royces; the meeting between Angel and Tess, when Angel comes back from Brazil, takes place in a London night-club to the music of a Jazz band; even at her lowest moments of fortune Tess wears a smart little costume from the Galeries Lafayette; the American film stars who take the parts of Angel and Tess are an advertisement-for-shaving-soap Jew-boy and a Ziegfeld Folly. The possibilities of the film are entirely neglected. Not a single cow is seen in this film, not a glimpse of the open downs, though, of course, Stonehenge gets is chance. Let anyone who wants to vomit see Angel take from his pocket a picture-postcard of Tess. I suppose one ought to be brave and take it all as a joke. But it is not possible to do so. The horror of modern exploitations strikes in this film with overwhelming force. Profanation, vulgarity, and falsehood cannot go much further. The Tivoli aspires to be a leading picture-house. Its management should understand that by putting on this film they have given many people a good reason for staying away from them in future.

In the late 1920s, Keynes's involvement in the performing arts increased and he began to act as a financial supporter of various small productions such as the Cambridge Amateur Dramatic Club's production of 'The Tale of a Soldier' and 'A Lover's Complaint' (1928) and a 'Masque for Poetry and Music' (1930), both of which went from Cambridge to London for brief seasons. Both productions provided roles for Lydia. For the 1928 production, Keynes also provided an unsigned 'puff' in *The Nation*.

From The Nation and Athenaeum, *3 November 1928*

The Cambridge A.D.C. is doing a bold and novel thing in presenting next week (November 8th, 9th, 10th at 8.30, and a matinee on November 10th—tickets from Elijah Johnson, Trinity Street, Cambridge) Stravinsky's 'Tale of a Soldier', followed by Shakespeare's 'A Lover's Complaint'. This great work of Stravinsky's has never been performed before in England (apart from the semi-private performance of the Arts Theatre Club last year). It is also rather a triumph to present the first performance of a work by Shakespeare! Two brilliant young Cambridge musicians, Mr Ord of King's, and Mr Arundell of St John's, will respectively conduct the orchestra and direct the plays; Mme Lydia Lopokova will play the Princess in the Stravinsky and has her first speaking part on the English stage in 'A Lover's Complaint'; the decor of the Stravinsky will be by Mr Humphrey Jennings, undergraduate of Pembroke, whose work was so successful in the production of Purcell's 'King Arthur', and that of the Shakespeare by Mr Duncan Grant.

With the 1930s Keynes became more seriously involved in the performing arts, first with the Camargo Society and then with the Arts Theatre, Cambridge.

In the case of Camargo, in an attempt to continue regular productions of ballet in London after the deaths of Diaghilev and Pavlova, Lydia was initially, if very reluctantly, the more involved of the Keyneses—an involvement that continued. After an early financial crisis, however, Keynes became honorary treasurer of the Society and gave its affairs considerable time as he raised funds for guarantees and became involved in other aspects of productions.

From this involvement, several printed documents from Keynes's pen survive, the first from 1931.

THE CAMARGO SOCIETY

Application to members for the renewal of subscriptions
by the treasurer

The audited accounts of the first year's operations will be duly submitted to a General Meeting of the Society at a later date. But members may be glad to have a brief summary of the results at the same time as they are asked to renew their subscriptions for the coming season.

The total expenditure has amounted, in round figures, to about £2,500 of which £1,900 has been obtained from the subscriptions of 550 members and the sale of guest seats, £450 from donations and £50 from hire and performing rights. This leaves a deficit of about £100 which is partly offset by certain assets such as scenery, costumes, etc. In view of the fact that the Society started with no tangible assets and has produced eleven new ballets, this is, in the opinion of the Committee, an extraordinarily satisfactory result. But it has only been achieved by means of the most resolute economy. Almost the whole of the expenditure has been incurred in the hire of theatres, the engagement of orchestras and the execution of costumes and scenery; whilst artistic services—of dancers, composers, choreographers and artist-designers—have been given either gratuitously or for a nominal payment. Opportunities for such craftsmen to earn an adequate income are infrequent nowadays and it would be more satisfactory if selection by the Camargo Society carried with it a reasonable remuneration. It is also felt that the Society has sufficiently justified its existence to be entitled to see a modest guarantee fund for its future season's work which will enable it to frame a budget instead of living from hand to mouth as in the past year. Members of the Committee can vouch for the fact that small financial anxieties, which ought to be unnecessary in the future, have very greatly hampered the preparation of programmes.

I venture, therefore, to appeal to you to renew your subscription for the coming year (a form will be found overleaf), and to send the Secretary names of possible new subscribers, not included in the enclosed list of members.

I also ask that any members who are prepared, in addition to their subscriptions, to contribute sums of £10 upwards to a Guarantee Fund or towards a fund to be specially earmarked for the better remuneration of artistic services, will kindly communicate with me personally as Treasurer.

The second took the form of a letter to the editor of the *New Statesman*. It followed a review in the issue for 1 July 1933 of the Society's gala performance for delegates to the World Economic Conference. The works performed were 'Coppelia' and the 'Lac des Cygnes'. The reviewer wondered whether the Society had not betrayed its origins in presenting two classics at Covent Garden rather than new ballets for subscribers and why Marie Rambert's Ballet Club, 'the best of English ballet dancing' and 'the home of choreographic invention in London' had not performed. Keynes replied.

To the Editor of The New Statesman and Nation, *2 July 1933*

Sir,

The remarks of your critic on the recent performances of ballet at Covent Garden by the Camargo Society show so extensive an ignorance of the conditions in which ballet can be suitably produced in London that a few comments may be in place.

Broadly speaking, there are three types of ballet which one would wish to keep alive; ballet on the grand scale, in the classical mode as a rule, or in the mixed modes of Diaghileff's earlier period; modern experimental ballet, generally too subtle and sophisticated in what it is attempting to convey to be adapted to the scale and distances of the great opera houses and better suited, therefore to a modern theatre in which the whole audience is comparatively near to the stage; and what, by analogy, one might call Chamber Ballet, a direction in which it almost seemed that Diaghileff himself was moving in his latest phase. All are important and desirable, and none of them easily preserved or developed in the meanness and indignity of the modern age, when the idea of doing anything except on commercial criteria fills our civic moralists with horror. The line between the first type and the second, and the line between the second and the third are not so sharp that there are not some ballets capable of adaptation from the first to the second or from the second to the third; but it is usually clear in any particular case which style of presentation is the most appropriate. There is, or should be, no competition between any of them.

It has been the primary object of the Camargo Society to keep alive the two former types. Since the society was first founded for occasional performances, a permanent organisation has come into existence in the shape of the Vic-Wells Ballet—the only permanent organisation of the kind in Great Britain—with similar objects. Fortunately—though it seems unsuitable to your critic—these two organisations, having similar objects, have found it possible to work together in amity and co-operative endeavour. It has been the role of the Camargo Society to take advantage of occasional opportunities to appear in the West End with the somewhat ampler (though still insufficient) material means which are so necessary for ballet if it is to attain the highest standards.

Opportunities for ballet on the grand scale, such as occurred last week at Covent Garden, are exceedingly rare. Fortunately, when they occur, the public support is substantial, since, as is the case with opera, it is the limited class of established favourites, chosen from the very few ballets which have gained a permanent place in the repertories of the opera houses of the world, which attract a great audience. On the other hand, the experimental ballet, to which the Camargo Society is not less attached and to which throughout its existence it has devoted the whole of its financial resources, is frightfully expensive in relation to the public which it can attract. The numerous experimental ballets, which the society has presented in the past three years, have never covered above two-thirds of their cost, even after including in the receipts the whole of the subscriptions of the Camargo members. The idea, therefore, that the presentation by the society of two of the masterpieces of ballet—one of which, by the way, has not been seen at Covent Garden in its two-act form for more than a generation—represents a betrayal of the modern ballet, can only occur to a mind which sees everywhere some occasion for grievance or competition—emotions so out of place, though, unluckily, so usual in enterprises of art.

To the third type, that of Chamber Ballet, Mme Rambert and her Ballet Club have been making contributions which we all applaud and support. But your critic is an indiscreet friend carried away by amiable enthusiasm, who runs the risk of making Mme Rambert ridiculous, when he suggests that it is her miniature ballets conceived for a piano and a fifteen-foot stage which the Camargo Society should have transferred to the vast spaces of Covent Garden.

J. M. KEYNES

The third comes from the period when the activities of the Camargo Society on a large scale effectively ceased after six programmes for members, one season for the general public and the Covent Garden affair for delegates to the World Economic Conference.

THE CAMARGO BALLET SOCIETY

Arrangements for 1934

When the Society was founded four years ago, shortly after the deaths of Diagileff and Pavlova, there was no other organisation in London for the production of ballet. The object of the Society was to fill the gap so as to provide opportunities for dancers and choreographs living in London, and thus to keep alive traditions too easily lost.

Since that time the Vic–Wells Ballet has been established as a permanent organisation giving very similar opportunities for dancers and choreographs as those which the Camargo Ballet Society was aiming at. In addition the successful visit last summer of Monsieur de Basil's Ballet Russe with Massine in principal charge of the choreography has served to raise materially the standards of production of ballet expected by the

London public, and to provide further opportunities for London to see ballets, old and new, produced by an accomplished and well disciplined company.

In these circumstances, the Camargo Society feel that they would be attempting something which could not be successfully accomplished if they were to offer new productions of ballet for special Sunday performances. They could not emulate the standards recently set without undue expense; whilst, so far from offering dancers and choreographs opportunities not otherwise open to them, their activities would probably tend in practice to a dispersion of the available talent.

The Society has, therefore, decided to use its actual and future resources to produce from time to time at its own expense a ballet which would then be offered to the Vic–Wells Company for production at one of their theatres and to be added to their repertory. By this means the Society would be able to do what lies in its power towards raising the standard of ballet in London without any risk of dispersion of the available talent; and they would be doing something to help the Vic–Wells Ballet to raise its production to a high standard without being as seriously hampered as they are at present by merely financial considerations. The Society believes that they will best serve the cause of ballet by this concentration on raising the standards so as to make financially possible well mounted and well considered ballets, drawing upon the best choreographic, musical and artistic talents available and guest artists from outside the regular Vic–Wells Company.

If this object is to be successfully attained, it will be necessary for the Committee to raise each year a substantial, but by no means extravagant, sum. Pending further experience, they aim for the present year at obtaining from £500 to £1,000, which sum will be sufficient to give a fair trial to the new policy.

They appeal, therefore, to their subscribers and to all lovers of ballet in England to contribute what they can afford to the above purpose. The Society invites subscriptions of any sum from 2/6 to £100 to be expended as set forth above.

It is not proposed that subscribers should be entitled to obtain tickets at the performances of the Vic–Wells ballet which the Society is assisting, except on payment of the usual price. The object is not so much to offer facilities for obtaining cheap tickets as to provide an organisation which will enable ballet lovers to combine to assist the development of the art in London. All subscribers, however, of 2/6 or more will be elected Associate Members of the Camargo Ballet Society, if they so desire, for the current year of their subscription (which involves a further legal liability not exceeding 1/– in the event of the debts of the Society exceeding its assets on its liquidation); and it is expected that the Vic–Wells management will be able to grant special facilities to such members for advance booking, and also to invite them to attend without charge the final dress rehearsal of the production which their support will have made possible.

Until some estimate can be made of the response to this appeal, the Committee cannot make any definite announcement regarding the first production, which it is hoped to give in the Autumn. Negotiations are, however, proceeding with an eminent English composer to write a ballet for the occasion.

Well-wishers of this scheme are asked to send their subscriptions as soon as possible to the Secretary, Miss J. M. Harvey, 56 Manchester Street, W.1 (Welbeck 2171). Miss Harvey will also be glad to receive lists of names and addresses of those to whom it would be worth while to send this announcement.

Keynes's final piece on the ballet dates from 1938 and relates to Camargo's successor in England.

From the Programme of the Second Buxton Theatre Festival, August–September 1938

A TRIBUTE TO THE BALLET AT SADLER'S WELLS

I write this as the Vic–Wells Ballet Company is completing a fortnight at the Arts Theatre, Cambridge, playing to crowded and enthusiastic audiences throughout. There are very few companies in the world which can fill a theatre to capacity in a town of this size for a whole fortnight, and it is a well-deserved tribute to the remarkable qualities of the Ballet Company which Miss Ninette de Valois has organised—supported through thick and thin by Lillian Baylis in days less prosperous than those which have now arrived.

The fortnight at Cambridge has given me the opportunity under the tutorship and the critical observation of Lydia Lopokova to take stock of the Company's achievements. There is no company in the world, Madame Lopokova says, which can make so fair a comparison in the conditions of its work and in its accomplishments with the old Imperial Ballet of St Petersburg. Dancing through their long season at Sadler's Wells only two or three times a week, the qualities and physique of the leading dancers—particularly the young ones—can be preserved and developed in the way which was possible for the famous ballerinas in Russia and which is quite impossible for companies perpetually on the road and dancing every night for month after month. The settled home and comparative leisure make it possible to work out important and significant new ballets to be added to the repertory, of which Ninette de Valois's 'Checkmate', magnificently dressed by Kauffer, is the latest triumph.

With recruits coming from their own school, with the training of the stage in the corps de ballet from the first opportunity, we find the conditions of the Imperial Ballet once more reproduced; and finally Sadler's Wells have taken the very wise step of engaging as Maître de Ballet M. Sergueeff (who was in fact Maître de Ballet at St Petersburg for a quarter of a century and carries in his head, as no one else now alive does, the traditions of the old teaching and the old technique).

Lillian Baylis and Ninette de Valois have in a surprisingly short space of time created a national ballet in this country solely recruited from English boys and girls which bears comparison with the best in the world.

By the time of the demise of the Camargo Society, Keynes was involved in a still larger project, the Arts Theatre, Cambridge. Here, a number of circumstances coincided to make the project possible, the most important being King's need for more undergraduate accommodation and the possibility of providing this around the outside of a site behind King's Parade in Cambridge. At the same time, there was a shortage of accommodation for productions in Cambrdge, for by 1933 Cambridge was without a commercial theatre—the New Theatre had become a cinema and the Festival Theatre had run out of wealthy sponsors. As well, the Amateur Dramatic Club's (A.D.C.) stage had been destroyed by fire.[4]

Keynes initially attempted to interest the A.D.C. and the College in a possible theatre in the area inside the King's project. When this did not come off, he shifted his ground and asked the College to lease the site to an outside group of which he would be the chairman. Once the College had approved of the principles of the scheme, Keynes completed the formation of the Arts Theatre of Cambridge Limited in December 1934. Although financial support from well-wishers in Cambridge was less than expected, Keynes had anticipated that he would have to take a substantial financial role in the enterprise. Ultimately he took up £10,000 in shares in the Company and loaned it £19,450. Construction occupied 1935. The theatre opened in February 1936 with a gala performance by the Vic–Wells ballet, followed by an Ibsen season in which Lydia took a major role in 'A Doll's House' and 'The Master Builder' and Jean Forbes-Robertson did the same in 'Hedda Gabler' and 'Rosmersholm'. Characteristically, Keynes provided an unsigned introduction to the programme for the Ibsen season.

From the programme for the Ibsen season, Arts Theatre, Cambridge, February 1936

IBSEN'S MIDDLE PERIOD

In 1879 Ibsen was fifty years of age and had behind him his poetical dramas and his social plays. Between 1879 and 1899 there were produced the eleven prose dramas upon which rests his reputation as the greatest dramatist of the nineteenth century. Ibsen died in 1906. Four of these eleven dramas are presented, in the order in which they were written, in the cycle

---

[4] In 1925 Keynes had been approached about the possibility of a new theatre in Cambridge, but occupied as he was with the London Artists' Association and *The Nation* he did not feel he could become extensively involved. He avoided even his conditionally promised financial involvement when the scheme failed to find a large backer.

of plays to be produced within the fortnight February 17th to 29th.

As is usually the case with the greatest plays, they can be understood and enjoyed, and are indeed in a sense complete, from several distinct aspects and on planes of varying depth below the surface. To begin with, they can be taken as carefully constructed realistic dramas, almost melodramas, of contemporary Norwegian life with exciting plots—super-Pinero 'problem plays' so to speak. From this aspect they have not a dull or unconvincing moment. This is a genuine aspect of these plays and to emphasise it they will be played in the costumes of their periods with the ladies' dresses gradually moving, as our fortnight proceeds, from the 'eighties to the 'nineties.

Or these four plays in particular can be regarded as a commentary on the profoundest social phenomenon of the period, the emergence of the modern woman; Nora the first Victorian wife to demand a serious life of her own, Rebecca the first bold egotist emancipated from the ancient moral bonds, whose will is nevertheless broken (as Ibsen truly foresaw) against her slower-moving environment, Hedda the first modern society woman to discover in her freedom nothing but boredom and a jealousy of those still capable of simpler feelings, Hilda the first hiker and Wandervogel.

But they can also be seen *sub specie eternitatis*, remote from contemporary moods and problems, as tragedies of character, exploring the depths and often the crannies of human motive with the imagination of a poet and the insight of a novelist. If the plays have sometimes been felt to be painful, it is because Ibsen can penetrate too deeply into regions which we prefer to keep concealed even from ourselves.

Moreover, the plays are of great importance to the art of the drama as essays in a new technique. During this period when Ibsen was exclusively engaged on prose dramas he still regarded himself as a poet. These plays can be read as poems of the purest aesthetic content conforming to strict rules of composition.

Ibsen's use of *leit-motiv* and certain recurrent phrases and symbols, especially in 'Romersholm' and 'The Master Builder' becomes highly developed, though not to the same degree as in his latest period. Many of his symbols, by which he suggests the supernatural and the magic of the north, the Vikings and trolls and little 'helpers and servers' who run about amongst the roots of the trees, became a part of the imagination of all of us in our childhood through the folklore and fairy tales of Northern Europe. But they obey a strict and inviolable law. The sense of the unseen world must never conflict or interfere with the realism of real life and a perfectly naturalistic and common sense interpretation. It is an overtone felt and heard by the sensitive, which will be out of proportion and almost vulgar if it is sufficiently emphasised to be obvious and inescapable.

These plays have been given not infrequently one at a time and in isolation. But this is the first time for at least a quarter of a century that there has been an opportunity for the present generation of play-goers to consider Ibsen's dramatic art as a whole, or rather (for Ibsen's last three plays are not yet represented in our series) that of his middle period. The plays will be given in William Archer's translation, subject only to minor modifications. His text is open to the charge of being queer and uncolloquial in places; but a dog-translation (as this is) of Ibsen's Norwegian speech probably conveys more of his essence to English ears than a more idiomatic, more anglicised version which might lose more through paraphrase and inexactness than it could gain in elegance.

Thus by 1936 Keynes had over a period of years been rather heavily involved in the cultural life of Britain. This involvement now began to be reflected in his publications.

During May 1936, Keynes prepared a talk for the B.B.C.'s Books and Authors series. It went out on 1 June 1936. A somewhat edited version of what went out on the wireless appeared in *The Listener* for 10 June. Below we print the version actually broadcast, indicating with square brackets the material that did not appear in the one-page published version.

ON READING BOOKS

The first step towards reading—I think you will agree—is to be able to read. Now, according to the law, we are all of us taught to read. Police magistrates are much shocked if a witness cannot read. Yet, in truth, there are very many people, even amongst the highly educated and professional classes, who read with difficulty. I mean by this that they read slowly and with effort, that it tires them—that they do not read as easily as they breathe. On the other hand, I expect that there are many of you, who earn your daily bread in ways for which reading is not important and yet do possess one of the best of all gifts—the eye which can pick up the print effortlessly. At any rate to acquire this—and many of you could acquire it merely by practice—is the first step. I emphasise this, because many people think they can read, but they can't. They do not know how far they fall behind the practised reader. We are inclined to think that of six people living in one house all will be much alike in their ability to read. But it is not so. Compare yourself with your friends and neighbours, and find out, first of all, whether you really know how to read—whether, as I have said, you read as easily as you breathe. [Newspapers are good practice in learning how to skip; and, if he is not to lose his time, every serious reader must have this art.]

When you can both walk and skip through a book, what next? I am afraid that I can give you very little advice on contemporary novels. I do not much care for them when I am lazy and relaxed; nor yet when I am contemplative and serious. They do not instruct or comfort or uplift me. It is thought almost a virtue in a modern writer to empty on us the slops of his mind just as they come. And their works are not even trash. For trash can be delightful, and, indeed, a necessary part of one's daily diet.

I read the newspapers because they're mostly trash. But when I glance into this contemporary stuff, I find such heavy-going, [such undigested, unenhanced, unintrinsic, unintuitive, such misunderstood, mishandled, misshapen, such muddled handling of human hopes and life; and] without support from the convention and the tradition which in a great age of self-expression can make even the second-rate delightful. So if you want a serious novel, read the old ones—older, at any rate, than the last ten years. [This year's novels are not so good, nor such pleasant easy reading, as Jane Austen's *Emma* or Thomas Hardy's *Tess of the D'Urbervilles* or E. M. Forster's *A Room with a View*. It is only commonsense advice to try these and their fellows first.]

Nevertheless—to begin on the groundfloor—there is one class of author, unpretending, workmanlike, ingenious, abundant, delightful heaven-sent entertainers, in which our age has greatly excelled. There are several of them and we are each entitled to our favourites. I mean Edgar Wallace, Agatha Christie, P. G. Wodehouse,—to name mine. I need not mention particular examples, you all know them, and each of them has what is a merit in a favourite author, that their different books are all exactly the same. There is a great purity in these writers, a remarkable absence of falsity and fudge, so that they live and move, serene, Olympian and aloof, free from any pretended contact with the realities of life, each in his world of phantasy moving through the heavens according to its own laws. There is no more perfect relaxation than these.

It is the mark of a species of work in which a particular period excels that even the inferior examples of it have some merit. On this test memoirs and biographies are our best speciality to-day. [Perhaps we owe it partly to Lytton Strachey that certain repressions and reserves which had a stranglehold on the last generation have sufficiently relaxed to let a little truth and character and the colour of life peep through. Virginia Woolf, who reads *all* of them, tells me that at least nine out of ten can be enjoyed.] The memoir or skimming autobiography is something which our generation *en masse* has somehow learned to write. The very old-fashioned are still too anecdotal and regard their autobiographies as no more than a last opportunity to tell once again all the good stories they have told before. But to-day a great many of such writers achieve much more than this. I could mention a number. Laura Knight's *Grease Paint and Oil Paint* and Eleanor Farjeon's *A Nursery in the Nineties*, both out this spring, are excellent examples. Or to go back three or four years, Karsavina's *Theatre Street* is a sweet book. Many even of the lives of public characters, who were distinguished in the War,—books which were unreadable written in the earlier fashion—have much interest and charm. I particularly enjoyed one which did not attract much notice, the Life of Lord Wester Wemyss by his wife.[5] But, [as Virginia Woolf says,] this is a class in which it is safe to-day to choose almost at random; so much more agreeable and amusing, so much more touching, bringing so much more of the pattern of life, than the daydreams of a housemaid, or, alternatively, the daydreams of a nervous wreck, which is the average modern novel. And in this context it is not out of place to mention Winston Churchill's enthralling history, so largely a memoir, of the World War.[6] Even two out of the few recent novels I have read and enjoyed, J. R. Ackerley's *Hindoo Holiday* and David Garnett's *Beany Eye* are, in fact, fragments of memoirs. It is a mixed lot you see. But they have splinters of truth and life in them. Besides we are just ready to be taken back, as a fair sprinkling of these books do take us, to the high comedy, the charm and security, of the Edwardian age in which most of us grew up. The early Victorian humours have grown a little stale by now, a little artificial, stereotyped and overdone. But the Edwardian age is near enough for us quickly to recognise hints and to know truth from falsehood. We want only to be reminded what it was like, and the research of

[5] Lady Wemyss, *Life and Letters of the First Lord Wemyss.*
[6] *The World Crisis.*

times past in our own memories will do the rest. Our nostalgia is for the charmed years before the War. [We need only a few hints of how we lived then, a few old photographs to bring back the taste of the biscuits we ate and the inner feeling in the whole body of what it was like to be alive in the reign of King Edward and Queen Alexandra.]

[The explanation of the comparative excellence of this class of writing is to be found, perhaps, in the principle that, if we cannot have art which is rare and particularly rare to-day, the next best is truth and actual experience. There is not much art in any writing to-day. But in the memoirs and autobiographies we seem to have caught the knack of recording quite a fair modicum of truth. And when this can be achieved, the memoirs of any age are delightful. I picked up the other day in a catalogue of remainders (the book was published in 1931, but failed, I suppose, to catch the public) the first English translation of *The Book of My Life* by Jerome Cardan, the Italian physician, philosopher and mathematician who lived in the sixteenth century, one of the earliest known of frank confessions and revealing autobiography, and a remarkable example of it.]

There is not much contemporary poetry to recommend. But we have one poet, the Anglo-American, T. S. Eliot, whose name will be spread, I believe, ever more widely as our ears become attuned to him. Two books of his have lately come our way,—*Murder in the Cathedral*, not a thriller as the title teasingly suggests, but a religious drama in verse concerning the murder of Thomas à Becket, and his *Collected Poems 1909–1935*, [which between them, Mr Eliot tells us, contain all of his poetry which he wishes to preserve]. Here we have, I am sure, the outstanding poetry of our generation, poetry in the great tradition with music and meaning. Mr Eliot's underlying significance and allusion is often obscure; but he has the rarest of possessions, the ear of a poet, and the music of his speech is apparent as soon as the reader becomes a little familiar with it, and the craft with which he freshly echoes older poetry, and the associations of word and meaning.

What seas what shores what grey rocks and what islands
What water lapping the bow
And scent of pine and the woodthrush singing through the firs
What images return
O my daugher.

There are many branches of knowledge to-day which are in no condition to be successfully and decently popularised. Much of anthropology and the history of very early civilisation is, however, in the stage where strange facts are being collected; [and even when some of the facts are disputed by other experts, it is intelligible reading for any of us;—for example *Adam's Ancestors* by Leakey, The *Old Stone Age* by Miles Burkitt and Dr Woolley's account of Sumeria. I advise the common reader to sample the current output of these fascinating subjects to see if they suit his taste.] But philosophy and physics, for example, are certainly no food for him just now and most popular books about them are better avoided. They flatter to deceive. I am not quite sure in which class that exciting, dangerous subject, psychology, now falls. But, for the moment, I am afraid, my own subject of political economy is scarcely fit for the general public; though a popular exposition may again be possible when the experts have become clearer amongst themselves. One book there is, however, falling within this field which every serious citizen will do well to look into—the extensive description of *Soviet Communism* by Mr and Mrs Sidney Webb. It is on much too large a scale to be called a popular book, but the reader should have no difficulty in comprehending the picture it conveys. Until recently events in Russia were moving too fast and the gap between paper professions and actual achievements was too wide for a proper account to be possible . But the new system is now sufficiently crystallised to be reviewed. The result is impressive. The Russian innovators have passed, not only from the revolutionary stage, but also from the doctrinaire stage.

There is little or nothing left which bears any special relation to Marx and Marxism as distinguished from other systems of socialism. They are engaged in the vast administrative task of making a completely new set of social and economic institutions work smoothly and successfully over a territory so extensive that it covers one sixth of the land surface of the world. Methods are still changing rapidly in response to experience. The largest scale empiricism and experimentalism which has ever been attempted by disinterested administrators is in operation. Meanwhile the Webbs have enabled us to see the direction in which things appear to be moving and how far they have got. It is an enthralling work, because it contains a mass of extraordinarily important and interesting information concerning the evolution of the contemporary world. It leaves me with a strong desire and hope that we in this country may discover how to combine an unlimited readiness to experiment with changes in political and economic methods and institutions, whilst preserving traditionalism and a sort of careful conservatism, thrifty of everything which has human experience behind it, in every branch of feeling and of action.

[May I conclude with a little general advice from one who can claim to be an experienced reader to those who have learnt to read but have not yet gained experience? A reader should acquire a wide general acquaintance with books *as such*, so to speak. He should approach them with all his senses; he should know their touch and their smell. He should learn how to take them in his hands, rustle their pages and reach in a few seconds a first intuitive impression of what they contain. He should, in the course of time, have touched many thousands, at least ten times as many as he really reads. He should cast an eye over books as a shepherd over sheep, and judge them with the rapid, searching glance with which a cattle-dealer eyes cattle. He should live with more books than he reads, with a penumbra of unread pages, of which he knows the general character and content, fluttering round him. This is the purpose of libraries, one's own and other people's, private and public. It is also the purpose of good bookshops, both new and second hand, of which there are still some, and would that there were more. A bookshop is not like a railway booking-office which one approaches knowing that one wants. One should enter it vaguely, almost in a dream, and allow what is there freely to attract and influence the eye. To walk the rounds of the bookshops, dipping in as curiosity dictates, should be an afternoon's entertainment. Feel no shyness or compunction in taking it. Bookshops exist to provide it; and the booksellers welcome it, well knowing how it will end. It is a habit to acquire in boyhood.]

Late in May 1936, Keynes was approached by the B.B.C. in another connection.

From J. R. ACKERLEY, *27 May 1936*

Dear Keynes,

I am trying to organise a series of articles for *The Listener* for the summer months, under the title of 'Art and the State'. It will form a kind of inquiry into the condition of modern art at home and abroad in relation to the social crisis. By art, perhaps I had better explain to start with, I mean painting, sculpture, architecture, and such new forms of art as, for instance, the pageantry of ceremony and festivity. I am trying to get nationals from Italy, Germany and Russia to give an account of what art is doing under their various political regimes; what its object is under Fascism, Nazism and Communism, and what are its achievements—what, in short, is, or should be, in their view, the relationship between art and the state. I think, and hope you will agree, that this is a fascinating subject.

After some investigations I have asked Staatskommissar Hans Hinkel, who has been newly appointed by Goebbels to direct German cultural matters, to put the Nazi point of view (and I understand that he has consented to do so); and for the Fascist and Communist theories, I have written respectively to Ugo Ojetti and Victor Lazareff. Georges Duthuit will probably write for France; and Kenneth Clark has consented to sum up the whole series. What I want now, however is somebody to write an introductory article, and I am wondering whether I could persuade you to do this? We

335

feel that this article should, so to speak, put the problems in connection with art and the state as they would present themselves to the ordinary intelligent man's mind, and that it would be better, therefore, to get a layman, like yourself, with an interest in the subject, to do this. I do hope you will feel inclined to accept this suggestion; and should be exceedingly grateful, also, for any advice you could give me.

Yours sincerely,
J. R. ACKERLEY

To J. R. ACKERLEY, *28 May 1936*

My dear Ackerley,

I always regret it afterwards when I get lured into taking on another job. However, the article you suggest does interest me and I am not disinclined to try my hand at it.

May I assume that you do not mean to exlude opera, ballet and drama?

The failure of the nineteenth-century democracies to maintain the grandeur and dignity of the state is, in my judgement, one at least of the seeds of their decay; and what I should offer would be a development of that theme. Is that the sort of thing you have in mind?

Yours sincerely,
[copy initialled] J. M. K.

From J. R. ACKERLEY, *12 June 1936*

Dear Keynes,

I am returning now to the subject of 'Art and the State' which, after receiving your exceedingly welcome and gratifying consent to open the series with an introduction, I put aside to await replies to my invitations abroad. These are now coming in.

Goebbels' new Director of Culture, Staatskommissar Hans Hinkel, is furnishing me with an explanation of the art principles of German National Socialism which, with its pictorial illustrations, is, I gather, to receive the authorisation of 'the leading personality in German Art matters' himself; L. Cherniavsky, Acting President of the U.S.S.R. Society for Cultural Relations, has actually written to say he has the matter in hand, and Georges Suthuit has promised to turn France inside out.

Only Italy so far refuses to answer my letters of entreaty—but if Severini, my present candidate, refuses, I believe that I can always fall back on Marinetti, unless the political situation is still too strained for even an art article to pass from Italy to us. I have asked all these people to tell me what in theory and in practice the relationship is, under their particular regimes, between art and the state: what its objects are, and how it works, and what are the fruits of that relationship.

I have defined art as painting, sculpture and architecture, with any new forms such as pageantry; but I am quite ready to include opera, ballet, drama and even the films too, if you think that they, besides yourself in your introduction, should treat of them. My only reason for not including them was that I was afraid of overloading comparatively short MSS. But I agree perfectly that you should not exclude them in your introductory article, and, no doubt, you will be mentioning, too, the commercial art of the poster, etc. This side of it naturally interests Tallents, and I thought it might interest you to see his pamphlet on the subject, which I enclose.

The point of view from which you wish to discuss the whole subject in your introduction to it is a very interesting one, I think, and I look forward with much eagerness to reading it. I am hoping to start the series off in the issue of July 29th, and, since we like to have scripts in our hands a fortnight in advance, that takes us back to July 15th; but if it would be possible for you to send me in your article even a week earlier than that—by July 8th—it would be convenient, as I am anxious to assemble the whole series as soon as I can, so that they can all be forwarded to Kenneth Clark for his summing-up. Another point is—will you be illustrating your article? My Editor always likes illustrations whenever possible, so if this is practicable and agreeable to you will you let me know what you would like, and I would set about procuring them.

Finally, we have not yet discussed a fee for your article. Would ten guineas be a satisfactory one?

Yours sincerely,
J. R. ACKERLEY

To J. R. ACKERLEY, *14 June 1936*

Dear Ackerley,

I will let you have the article in good time. Would you tell me the approximate number of words required? As regards illustrations, I am not very good at finding them, but possibly your pictorial department could supply some when they see the article. Will the question of illustrations affect the number of words you will want?

The question of fee raises rather a delicate question and also a matter of principle. My practice has been to make a distinction between papers which are not run for profit, where I accept whatever I am offered down to nothing, and papers which are run for profit. In the case of the latter, my practice for many years past has been to vary the rate, according to circumstances, from a minimum of 6d a word up to 1/– a word, and occasionally higher. As it happens, by the same post that I am writing this, I am refusing a request to write a series of articles for £100 a week which works out at 8d a word, and I have little doubt that, if I were to bargain, I could obtain a higher figure.

Now, I imagine that *The Listener* is run for profit. If not, it would make a great difference. Assuming it is run for profit. I think your rate should approach my normal minimum figure, that is to say, it should approximate to 6d a word, though I should raise no objection if you were to round the resulting figure off a bit in your own favour.

Yours sincerely,
[copy initialled] J. M. K.

From J. R. ACKERLEY, *16 June 1936*

Dear Keynes,

Thank you so much for your letter. I perfectly understand your principle and practice in the matter of fees, but the position with regard to *The Listener* is that, contrary to your impression, it is not a profit-making journal. In January, 1929, when it first appeared, the B.B.C. entered into a contract with the Publishers' Committee respecting the publishing and press interests of the whole country—the principal item of the contract being that *The Listener* was never to make a profit, and that if at any time its revenue exceeded its expenditure, it was to carry less advertisements, etc. You will see, therefore that *The Listener* does not contribute to the Corporation's revenue from publications, and is not to be numbered among profit-making journals. In the light of this, therefore, will you consider it possible to accept a lower fee for the article than the one mentioned in your letter?

The number of words required for this article should not exceed 2000, which is assuming that we should be able to give it about 3 inset illustrations. If it were not to be illustrated, the article could, of course, be a little longer.

Yours sincerely,
J. R. ACKERLEY

To J. R. ACKERLEY, *18 June 1936*

My dear Ackerley,

I am greatly interested in what you tell me in your letter of June 16th. But the peculiar result is that I shall apparently benefit no-one whomsoever by accepting less than my usual fee. I shall not benefit *The Listener* or the B.B.C. or the public, but merely defeat some would-be advertiser of his desire to advertise. I am afraid this can hardly be considered on all fours with assisting a publication which has no great financial resources. I am extremely amused that this should be the result of a contract with the Publishers Committee. For, obviously, it enormously increases your power to compete, since you are free to devote to the improvement and attractiveness of the paper sums which would almost certainly be diverted into the coffers of the B.B.C., if the contract had not been made. What the Publishers Committee ought to have stipulated for, if they wished to avoid competition, is that *The Listener* should never make a profit of less than x per cent of its published price!

Having said the above, and having pointed out that lower fee will benefit neither you, nor me, nor Sir John, nor the listener-in, nor the tax-payer, nor anyone else, I will leave myself in your hands with the suggestion that a fee of 25 guineas might be a proper compromise. I can honestly say that I am not in the least concerned from the financial point of view, and have given up writing as a means of income. But as a member, so to speak, of the Trade Union of writers, and by general habit of mind, I cannot bring myself altogether to neglect the point of principle.

Yours sincerely,
[copy initialled] J. M. K.

From J. R. ACKERLEY, *19 June 1936*

Dear Keynes,

I am so highly diverted by your letter and this correspondence that I cannot forgo the pleasure of continuing it to enquire whether I am to understand that because the B.B.C. is under an obligation not to make a profit out of *The Listener* it ought therefore to be content to make a loss? The object of the B.B.C. in conducting *The Listener* is to run it as a non-profit-making service, neither involving a financial liability in the shape of a loss, which presumably must come out of the licence-holder's pocket, nor a profit. This being so, it follows that by accepting less than your usual fee you would, in fact, be benefitting the listening public, because you would bring the accounts of *The Listener* nearer to that state of exact balance between profit and loss which will free *The Listener* from dependence upon the licence holder. On the other hand, if your argument were sound that you would apparently benefit no-one whomsoever by accepting less than your usual fee, this principle would be satisfactory if applied generally to all non-profitmaking undertakings. It would then follow that if you were writing for a charity or a public service of any kind, there would be no point in charging less than the standard fee. In fact, however, doctors and other professional people do make a considerable difference between the fees which they charge when they are working for a non-profit-making concern, and those which they charge when they are working for an ordinary profit-making commercial undertaking. Nor would your action defeat some would-be advertiser of his desire to advertise, since it is reasonable to suppose that he would spend the same money in advertising in some other organ, which would actually be a benefit to our competitors. So may I reduce your suggestion to 20 guineas?

Yours sincerely,

J. R. ACKERLEY

To J. R. ACKERLEY, *23 June 1936*

Dear Ackerley,

My letter was based on the assumption that you are already restricting your advertising revenue below its maximum. I was also assuming that the amount spent by advertisers on weekly papers is not a fixed amount, but depends on their view as to the value they are getting.

My argument only applies, of course, to a non-profit-making undertaking which is deliberately raking in smaller receipts than it could get. I know no other examples of such a state of affairs except your peculiar organ.

Yours sincerely,
[copy initialled] J.M.K.

To J. R. ACKERLEY, *3 July 1936*

My dear Ackerley,

I have now completed the first draft of the article which you asked me to write and I enclose it herewith. Let me know if any modification is required in its length.

As regards illustrations, it should not be difficult to find something suitable. But I am not very good at the job myself. Could your department of illustrations make suggestions? One suggestion of my own is the following:– Within the last four or five weeks there has been a photograph in *The Times* of a reach of the Thames with the announcement that it is going to be spoilt by a speculative builder or some such. This photograph with the words printed under it, as it actually appeared in *The Times*, would make a good illustration to one of my points. But I should like to hear what ideas for pictures the article puts into the minds of your experts.

Having composed the article I cannot help wishing, perhaps foolishly, that I was going to broadcast it. So I am venturing to send a copy on the chance to George Barnes, though, as I understood your proposal, this series of articles is entirely divorced from the actual Talks.[7]

Yours sincerely,
[copy initialled] J.M.K.

From The Listener, *26 August 1936*

ART AND THE STATE

The ancient world knew that the public needed circuses as well as bread. And, policy apart, its rulers for their own glory and

---

[7] The piece was not broadcast.

satisfaction expended an important proportion of the national wealth on ceremony, works of art and magnificent buildings. These policies, habits and traditions were not confined to the Greek and Roman world. They began as early as man working with his bare hands has left records behind him, and they continued in changing forms and with various purposes, from Stonehenge to Salisbury Cathedral, down at least to the age of Sir Christopher Wren, Louis XIV and Peter the Great. In the eighteenth and nineteenth centuries the rich nobility continued in a private, self-regarding and attenuated manner what had been the office of the monarch and the state, with the Church somewhat in eclipse. But there commenced in the eighteenth century and reached a climax in the nineteenth a new view of the functions of the state and of society, which still governs us today.

This view was the utilitarian and economic—one might almost say financial—ideal, as the sole, respectable purpose of the community as a whole; the most dreadful heresy, perhaps, which has ever gained the ear of a civilised people. Bread and nothing but bread, and not even bread, and bread accumulating at compound interest until it has turned into a stone. Poets and artists have lifted occasional weak voices against the heresy. I fancy that the Prince Consort was the last protester to be found in high places. But the Treasury view has prevailed. Not only in practice. The theory is equally powerful. We have persuaded ourselves that it is positively wicked for the state to spend a halfpenny on non-economic purposes. Even education and public health only creep in under an economic alias on the ground that they 'pay'. We still apply some frantic perversion of business arithmetic in order to settle the problem whether it pays better to pour milk down the drains or to feed it to school children. One form alone of uncalculated expenditure survives from the heroic age—war. And even that must sometimes pretend to be economic. If there arises some occasion of non-economic expenditure which it would be a manifest public scandal to forgo, it is thought suitable to hand round the hat to solicit the charity of private persons.

This expedient is sometimes applied in cases which would be incredible if we were not so well accustomed to them. An outstanding example is to be found where the preservation of the countryside from exploitation is required for reasons of health, recreation, amenity or natural beauty. This is a particularly good example of the way in which we are hag-ridden by a perverted theory of the state, not only because no expenditure of the national resources is involved but, at the most, only a transfer from one pocket into another, but because there is perhaps no current matter about the importance and urgency of which there is such national unanimity in every quarter. When a stretch of cliff, a reach of the Thames, a slope of down is scheduled for destruction, it does not occur to the Prime Minister that the obvious remedy is for the state to prohibit the outrage and pay just compensation, if any; that would be uneconomic. There is probably no man who minds the outrage more than he. But he is the thrall of the sub-human denizens of the Treasury. There is nothing for it but a letter to *The Times* and to hand around the hat. He even helps to administer a private charity fund, nobly provided by a foreigner, to make such donations as may be required from time to time to prevent such things as Shakespeare's cliff from being converted into cement. So low have we fallen today in our conception of the duty and purpose, the honour and glory of the state.

We regard the preservation of the national monuments bequeathed to us from earlier times as properly dependent on precarious and insufficient donations from individuals more public spirited than the community itself. Since Lincoln Cathedral, crowning the height which has been for two thousand years one of the capital centres of England, can collapse to the ground before the Treasury will regard so uneconomic a purpose as deserving of public money, it is no matter for wonder that the high authorities build no more hanging gardens of

Babylon, no more pyramids, parthenons, coliseums, cathedrals, palaces, not even opera houses, theatres, colonnades, boulevards and public places. Our grandest exercises today in the arts of public construction are the arterial roads, which, however, creep into existence under a cloak of economic necessity and by the accident that a special tax ear-marked for them brings in returns of unexpected size, not all of which can be decently diverted to other purposes.

Even more important than the permanent monuments of dignity and beauty in which each generation should express its spirit to stand for it in the procession of time are the ephemeral ceremonies, shows and entertainments in which the common man can take his delight and recreation after his work is done, and which can make him feel, as nothing else can, that he is one with, and part of, a community, finer, more gifted, more splendid, more care-free than he can be by himself. Our experience has demonstrated plainly that these things cannot be successfully carried on if they depend on the motive of profit and financial success. The exploitation and incidental destruction of the divine gift of the public entertainer by prostituting it to the purposes of financial gain is one of the worser crimes of present-day capitalism. How the state could best play its proper part it is hard to say. We must learn by trial and error. But anything would be better than the present system. The position today of artists of all sorts is disastrous. The attitude of an artist to his work renders him exceptionally unsuited for financial contacts. His state of mind is just the opposite of that of a man the main purpose of whose work is his livelihood. The artist alternates between economic imprudence, when any association between his work and money is repugnant, and an excessive greediness, when no reward seems adequate to what is without price. He needs economic security and enough income, and then to be left to himself, at the same time the servant of the public and his own master. He is not easy to help. For he needs a responsive spirit of the age, which we cannot deliberately invoke.

We can help him best, perhaps, by promoting an atmosphere of openhandedness, of liberality, of candour, of toleration, of experiment, of optimism, which expects to find some things good. It is our sitting tight-buttoned in the present, with no hope or belief in the future, which weighs him down.

But before we need consider what active part the state should play, we can at least abolish the positive impediments which, as some odd relic of Puritanism, we still impose on the business of public entertainment. Of the institutions which have grown up since the War, we should most of us agree, I think—in spite of all our bickering—that the B.B.C. is our greatest and most successful. But even the B.B.C. must be furtive in its progress. And, incredible to relate, instead of its receiving large subsidies from the state as one would expect, an important proportion of the ten shillingses which the public contribute is withheld from it as a contribution to general taxes. This was a new and difficult business requiring large-scale, costly experiments, capable of revolutionising the relation of the state to the arts of public entertainment, contributing more both to the recreation and to the education of the general public than all other mediums put together. Yet, even in its earliest and most precarious days, we considered it a proper object of taxation. On such dry husks are Chancellors of the Exchequer nourished; though probably these burdens were imposed in the spirit of fairness that requires equal injury all round. For the taxation of the B.B.C. is only the extreme example of the general principle that we penalise music, opera, all the arts of the theatre with a heavy, indeed a crushing, tax.

Architecture is the most public of the arts, the least private in its manifestations and the best suited to give form and body to civic pride and the sense of social unity. Music comes next; then the various arts of the theatre; then the plastic and pictorial crafts—except in some aspects of sculpture and decoration where they should be the adjutants of architecture; with poetry and literature, by their nature more private and personal. While

345

it is difficult for the state expressly to encourage the private and personal arts, fortunately they need it less, since they do not require the framework, the scale or the expense which only the organised community is able to furnish. But there remains an activity which is necessarily public and for that reason has fallen, in accordance with the aforesaid doctrine, into an almost complete desuetude—namely, public shows and ceremonies. There are a few which we have inherited and maintain, often in an antiquarian spirit, as quaint curiosities. There are none which we have invented as expressive of ourselves. Not only are these things regarded as the occasion of avoidable and, therefore, unjustifiable expense, but the satisfaction people find in them is considered barbaric or, at the best, childish, and unworthy of serious citizens.

This view of public shows and ceremonies is particularly characteristic of the western democracies, the United States, France, ourselves and our Dominions, I suggest that it is proving a weakness not to be ignored. Are there any of us who are free from strong emotion when an occasion arises for all the people dwelling in one place to join together in a celebration, an expression of common feeling, even the mere sharing in common of a simple pleasure? Are we convinced that this emotion is barbaric, childish, or bad? I see no reason to suppose so. At any rate the provision of proper opportunities for the satisfaction of this almost universal human need should rank high in the arts of government; and a system of society which unduly neglects them may prove to have done so to its peril. The late King's Jubilee, originally planned by the authorities on a very modest scale, provided an extraordinary example of the craving of a public, long deprived of shows and ceremonies, especially outside London, for an opportunity to collect in great concourses and to feel together. These mass emotions can be exceedingly dangerous, none more so; but this is a reason why they should be rightly guided and satisfied, not for ignoring them. This side of public life is one which we have so long neglected that we should scarcely know how to set about reviving it in a contemporary spirit, significant and satisfactory to this generation. For this reason we shall read with particular interest the succeeding articles in which those who are concerned with these manifestations in certain European countries will tell us something of their methods, both in this respect and in the general relations of the state to art, entertainment and ceremony.

The revival of attention to these things is, I believe, a source of strength to the authoritarian states of Russia, Germany and Italy, and a genuine gain to them, just as the lack of it is a source of weakness to the democratic societies of France, the United States, and Great Britain. In so far as it is an aspect—and it partly is—of an aggressive racial or national spirit, it is dangerous. Yet it may prove in some measure an alternative means of satisfying the human craving for solidarity. Much of the public ceremony and celebration now in fashion abroad strikes us, when we read about it, as forced and artificial, an occasion for bombastic oratory, and sometimes extremely silly. But we should like to know more. Here is an immemorial function of the state, an art of government regarded at most times as essential, which we have largely discarded as fit only for children and savages. Are we right to do this? This question, together with the wider problem of the relationship of the state to the arts, is the subject of these articles.

Our present policies are a just reflection of a certain political philosophy. I suggest that this philosophy is profoundly mistaken and that it may even, in the long run, undermine the solidity of our institutions. We shall only change our policies if we change the philosophy underlying them. I have indicated an alternative point of view. Let me conclude with two illustrations, as example of what might follow from a change of mind—one for the preservation of what we have inherited, the other for the enlargement of what we shall transmit.

(1) There should be established a Commission of Public Places with power to issue an injunction against any act of

exploitation or development of land or any change or demolition of an existing building, where it considered such act to be contrary to the general interest, with power to grant compensation to the extent that was fair in the circumstances, but not as of right. Similarly where the repair or maintenance or acquisition of a place or building was in the general interest, the Commission should have power to meet any part of the expense.

(2) Initial preparation should be made, so that some plans will be ready and available to ward off the next slump for the embellishment and comprehensive rebuilding at the public cost of the unplanned, insalutary and disfiguring quarters of our principal cities. Taking London as our example, we should demolish the majority of the existing buildings on the south bank of the river from the County Hall to Greenwich, and lay out these districts as the most magnificent, the most commodious and healthy working-class quarter in the world. The space is at present so ill used that an equal or larger population could be housed in modern comfort on half the area or less, leaving the rest of it to be devoted to parks, squares and playgrounds, with lakes, pleasure gardens and boulevards, and every delight which skill and fancy can devise. Why should not all London be the equal of St James's Park and its surroundings? The river front might become one of the sights of the world with a range of terraces and buildings rising from the river. The schools of South London should have the dignity of universities with courts, colonnades, and fountains, libraries, galleries, dining-halls, cinemas, and theatres for their own use. Into this scheme there should be introduced the utmost variety. All our architects and engineers and artists should have the opportunity to embody the various imagination, not of peevish, stunted, and disillusioned beings, but of peaceful and satisfied spirits who belong to a renaissance.

I affirm that there can be no 'financial' obstacle to such achievements, provided that the labour and the material resources are available. It is the relative abundance of the latter which should determine the pace at which we decide to work. It is not in itself advisable to aim at speed. The best buildings are planned and erected slowly, subject to patient criticism and evolving under the architect's eye. We should move, in London and in our other cities, at the rate made possible by the state of employment in other directions. If this condition is observed, the scheme must necessarily enrich the country and translate into actual form our potentialities of social wealth.

With his illness in 1937, except in connection with the Arts Theatre, these activities declined somewhat, but even a period in bed had interesting results.

To SIR STEPHEN TALLENTS, *12 July 1937*

Dear Tallents,

By ill fortune I am having to spend a considerable number of weeks in bed with a wireless set at my side. This means that I listen in at all hours of the day to all kinds of programmes. It occurs to me that you might, therefore, like to have a few of my reflections on the fare you are providing. At any rate, here are a few of them after the last weeks' experience.

1. First of all as regards the spoken word. The educational and high-brow talks which used to be such a feature have, of course, almost disappeared. In a way I regret them, but I rather think that, if they had been going on, I should not have listened in at many. I fancy they have to be of a high grade and particularly well done to be worthwhile. But of those that remain I find the talks for farmers only quite extraordinarily interesting and well done, and so far as I can judge, practically useful. I thought John Hilton's final broadcast[8] the most brilliant effort, as interesting and effective as such a thing could possibly be.

But at this point I should like to interpolate some general observations about voices. When I run through what I enjoyed,

---

[8] 'This and That', 1 July 1937.

I find that very few of such things were spoken in the thin, wretched cultured accents which you and I and the announcers employ. Provincial accents are an extraordinarily helpful qualification. What an enormous amount Hilton's broadcast would have lost if it had been in an announcer's voice. In the Carlyle play,[9] Carlyle himself was successful through his excellent Scotch accent, whilst John Stuart Mill was miserable beyond words. When Yeats introduced his poems the other evening,[10] he was magnificent in sharp distinction from those who recited his poems a few minutes later. Mr Penny[11] has been much overpraised, but was undoubtedly extremely amusing and successful, and this has to be put down to a very great extent to the peculiar and characteristic voice of Goolden. I found even the ghastly cockney accent of Reginald Foort at his organ[12] a relief after the announcer's. Somehow even that had character and personality which was effective. When on Sunday evenings I sample the services, I always find that I have to end up at some little Welsh Bethel in order to hear the Acts of the Apostles read properly.

Indeed, apart from special circumstances, I feel strongly that the cultured voice of the Universities is very unsuccessful, particularly when the announcers put on a tone which is reverend as well as cultured.

But, if the voices could be chosen right, I think there is an immense future for reading out loud. Last Sunday Beresford read one of his own short stories in an extremely amusing and agreeable way.[13] Obviously there are many readings which could not be properly given in provincial voices (though, on the other hand, there are many where such voices would be completely in place), but for those things where a cultured voice is essential I believe it would be much better to get older

[9] 'The Carlyles at Cheyne Row', 27 June 1937.
[10] 'My Own Poetry', 3 July 1937.
[11] 'The Strange Adventure of Mr Penny' was then in its second series with Richard Goolden as Mr Penny.
[12] The B.B.C.'s theatre organist who played regularly on the National Service.
[13] 'Professional Pride' read by J. D. Beresford, 11 July 1937.

persons. It is the immature cultured voice just down from the University which is at its worst, with the charm and unconsciousness of youth vanished, but the control and experience of the older, mature voice still unattained. I believe that many older people, particularly writers, can achieve what I want. Character in the voice is so essential and that is usually obtainable only in a more mature voice. This seems to me very important, because I feel that there is an immense field for really good reading out loud. This is something on which so many of us were brought up and is one of the best things to be communicated to the greater public.

As regards plays, I practically always find it impossible to attend. They still seem to me a complete failure. The only exception, so far as they are concerned, is where I know the play thoroughly already. For example, I enjoyed 'As You Like it' done by the Stratford-on-Avon players.[14] But that was because I already know the play by heart. If I had had to pick it up afresh, I could never have had the concentration and patience to do so.

One more passionate protest before I leave the spoken word. For what seemed a space of weeks, every programme in the middle day was liable to be broken into by comments from Wimbledon. Anything more boring and tiresome than descriptions of tennis you cannot see cannot be imagined. And surely a very small proportion of the B.B.C. public have the knowledge and experience of first-class tennis which is necessary to make such descriptions exciting. The uncertainty of when the wretched comments will come in makes it worse. One afternoon they broke off a Schubert symphony in the middle to give ten minutes description from Wimbledon, and then resumed the symphony where they had broken if off. The thing is an outrage and a disgrace and must surely present a hopeless misinterpretation of what the public want. This does not, of course, apply to all the comments on athletic contests, and I am sure some of them are very popular, and some of them can be

[14] On 4 July 1937.

enjoyed by anyone. But tennis, on every possible score, is hopelessly inappropriate.

2. Music. I am no musician, but I listen in to an enormous amount and, therefore, venture to give my views.

The last thing I should wish to do would be to discourage another engagement of Toscanini,[15] but I do think his concerts were an illustration of the fact that very complicated music performed by a huge orchestra comes through comparatively unsatisfactorily. One got Toscanini's dryness without any of his detail, most of which was inaudible. The result was to make one feel that it was in the bits of the cheaper Wagner that he was really supreme, the explanation being, I expect, that this was sufficiently simple for one to hear what he was actually performing. On the other hand, the Glyndebourne Opera comes through with absolute perfection. It seems to be ideally suited to broadcasting, and it would be well worth while to have five times as much. I should have thought that there ought to have been one act of opera at least three times a week. In general it is chamber music which is successful. One can really hear that exactly as it is played, whereas complicated symphonies performed by an orchestra of a hundred or more register only a fraction of what is going on.

The difficulty of there not being enough music to perform is obvious. But I should have thought there was an unnecessary amount of absolutely tenth-rate music. I am capable of thoroughly enjoying cheap music, and would be ready for more of it. But there are hours and hours of stuff which is neither cheap nor good, just hopelessly tenth-rate. I also think that very bad music by contemporary composers is given too good a show. Obviously it is your duty to support contemporaries. But quite a number of pieces are given which are clearly beneath any possible standard of merit. Speaking of cheap popular music, is there any special reason why Gilbert and Sullivan is never given? Nothing would be more popular, yet nothing is more

[15] As a guest conductor of the B.B.C. Symphony Orchestra.

rare. I think a great deal more could be done with good gramophone concerts. The existing stock of records gives you an enormous range. I would suggest that they should not be so scrappy as is usual at present, but definite concerts with long pieces in them. For example, in the long period of the year when there is no opera, why not give the whole sequence of the Glyndebourne records? I feel that the enormous range thus thrown open would make it possible to do without some proportion of the tenth-rate stuff; and on the gramophone one can have concerts of every sort of calibre and for every taste.

Two other points which are in a sense minor but quite important to one's enjoyment. Is it really necessary that the movements of symphonies and sonatas should be announced at length? They are recorded in the *Radio Times* for anyone who wants to know, and are a most dreary interruption of concerts; not made the less so by the announcers, to whom they mean nothing whatever, trying to introduce some sort of false meaning or emotion into the stage directions.

My second point is whether it is necessary to spend half of a gramophone concert announcing the numbers of gramophone records. Is there any known case of a listener taking out his pencil and hastily scribbling them down? The practice is particularly absurd, because the numbers (unlike the movements mentioned above) are not recorded in the *Radio Times*. From the point of view of gramophone companies, it would be infinitely more useful for them to be recorded in the *Radio Times* where, if one had enjoyed something particularly, one could look them up, rather than rely on the ravished listener hastily whipping out his pencil. The voices of the announcers giving the movements of the music and the numbers of the gramophone pieces are a really devastating interference to my enjoyment.

I am afraid this letter has got much longer than I intended, but here is for what it is worth.

Yours sincerely,
[copy not signed or initialled]

353

For the remainder of the 1930s, despite his illness, Keynes continued with his involvement in the Arts Theatre. On occasion he privately financed productions or took some, such as the Ibsen season, to the London West End. As well, in 1938, once the project was on its feet, Keynes transferred the theatre to a charitable trust. His exchange of letters with the Mayor of Cambridge then set out the position.

To the Mayor of Cambridge, 23 April 1938

Dear Mr Mayor,

When in 1934 I initiated proposals for the incorporation of a company to build and manage the Arts Theatre of Cambridge, my purpose was the promotion of the arts of drama, cinema, opera, ballet and music at Cambridge in a suitable home and under management which could maintain standards of educational purposes worthy of the town and the University.

The theatre has now been open for a little more than two years, and may be said, I think, to have found its feet and to have established a certain policy. We have given performances under the auspices of the Greek Play Committee, the University Musical Society, the A.D.C. and Marlowe Societies, the Rodney Dramatic Club, the Municipal Orchestra, the University In-formal Music Club, the Scientific Workers Association, the Cambridgeshire Rural Community Council, and the British Drama League Community Theatre (Eastern Area). We have ourselves produced plays by Shakespeare, Molière, Goldoni and Ibsen, and operas by Mozart, Arne, Handel and Vaughan Williams. We have given seasons of performances by the Vic–Wells Ballet Company, the Vic–Wells Opera, the Abbey Theatre of Dublin, the Westminster Theatre, the Mercury Theatre, Miss Ruth Draper, the Oxford Repertory Company, and many others.

Thus we have been able to show that the theatre is capable of serving a useful civic and University purpose. And I am now encouraged, therefore, to take a further step, which has always been in my mind, so as to make it clear that the theatre exists for public and not for private purposes. A charitable trust has been set up to which, as sole owner of the ordinary shares in the Theatre Company constituting more than five-sixths of its total capital, I have handed over all my shares as a gift; and I have also entered into a covenant to pay over to the trustees annual sums in cash over a period of years amounting to £5,000 in all.

In setting up the trust, the question has arisen as to the most suitable persons to be appointed trustees, and it is primarily in this connection that I am addressing this letter to you. It is proposed that the trustees should consist of five *ex officio* members, comprising two representatives of the town, namely, the Mayor and the Deputy-Mayor; two representatives of the University, namely, the Professors of English and of Music; the Provost of my own college, which is the ground landlord of the theatre; together with Mr Rylands, University Lecturer in English, and myself as representing the active management of the theatre. Presumably no official action is required by the Town Council or the University, since it must rest with the holders of these offices from time to time to decide personally whether they are prepared to act. I append a copy of the trust deed.

I was born in Cambridge and have lived there all my life, with the briefest intervals, closely associated both with the University and with the town. My father was secretary of the Council of the Senate for some 33 years and Registrary of the University. My mother has been Chairman of the Board of Guardians, Justice of the Peace, and Alderman and Mayor of the Borough. Through them I can claim a continuous contact of interest and devotion with the two institutions of University and town; and I like to think of the establishment of this trust, with its potentiality of equal service to both bodies, as being in some sense a memorial to their, as I well know, devoted services to Cambridge over half a century.

I am addressing a letter to the Vice-Chancellor in similar

terms, and am sending a copy of this to the Professors of English and Music, and to the Provost of King's.

Yours very faithfully,

J. M. KEYNES

From the Mayor of Cambridge, 29 May 1938

Dear Mr Keynes,

I thank you for your very interesting letter of April 23rd, referring to the formation of a trust in connection with the Arts Theatre of Cambridge.

I have shown your letter and the draft trust deed to the Deputy-Mayor, and we both feel that it is a project to which we personally would wish to give our wholehearted support.

As regards the proposal that the Mayor and Depty-Mayor for the time being should be *ex officio* members of the trustees, I observe that you appreciate that as the trust in contemplation will be in no sense connected with the Corporation, the decision of the Mayor and Deputy-Mayor to accept this position will only bind themselves, and not their successors, for whom they cannot vouch, though I should imagine that their successors in office will be willing to act as *ex officio* members for the period during which they hold their offices.

The Deputy-Mayor and I wish to express our appreciation of your great generosity in financing the trust, and have pleasure in acceding to your request to act as *ex officio* trustees.

Yours sincerely,

E. SAVILLE PECK

On 6 August 1938, W. J. Turner devoted the Miscellany column of *The New Statesman* to the proposal to build a National Theatre on a site in the Cromwell Road, raising questions as to the size and suitability of the site.

To the Editor of The New Statesman and Nation, *9 August 1938*

Sir,

May I write to support Mr W. J. Turner's article, as one who accepts, like him, the general desirability of a National Theatre, yet has, like him, hung back a little from the details of the present project?

Mr Turner is surely right in his insistence on a big site. He points out the importance of having both a large and a small theatre with a restaurant attached. I would add to this rehearsal rooms, workshops for scenery and costumes, ample storage and an indoor and outdoor café. For the National Theatre should be an institution, not just an auditorium. Clearly no such area is available in Central London except in Regent's or Hyde Park. But there the Crown could grant a site, capable of housing a great national monument, without cost to the taxpayer.

We are apt pupils of the Dictators in the arts of war. Let us, for once, imitate them on a modest scale in the arts of peace.

J. M. KEYNES

On 20 August, *The New Statesman* printed a letter from Dame Edith Lyttelton, Vice-Chairman of the National Theatre Appeal Committee and a member of the council of the Vic–Wells. She suggested that Keynes might help the existing appeal and pointed out that there was no Crown Land available for a larger scheme and that there was no public support for a scheme that took space from London's parks. Keynes replied:

To the Editor of The New Statesman and Nation, *22 August 1938*

Sir,

Dame Edith Lyttelton is quite right that in this country national institutions have often to come into being through private effort. In the realm of the theatre the Vic–Wells organisation is an example of this. Now I can conceive of a National Theatre on lines which could attempt projects which are beyond the scope of the Vic–Wells. I should welcome and support this. But on the scale contemplated by the sponsors what can the new National Theatre do that the Vic–Wells is not doing already? A third theatre in Kensington, allied to those in Islington and the Waterloo Road, would be a valuable addition and well placed. Of the objects and advantages of a competitive institution on the same or a smaller scale I have not yet heard, though ready to hear, a convincing account.

357

The force of Dame Edith's plea to the authorities for a gift of Crown Land in Regent's or Hyde Park which has been diligently explored and definitely proved impossible may have been weakened by the fact that she herself was evidently not in favour of it.

There are already a number of enclaves within those areas which do not spoil them and, indeed, add to their variety. Londoners will be hard to please if they are jealous of an encroachment of a People's Palace for the refreshment of mind and body, able to accommodate plays, opera, ballet and the choric drama of the future, both on a large scale and on a small, in a noble building, accessible, perhaps, from the new tunnel through the Park proposed in the Bressey Report.[16] Alternatively, it might occupy what is now largely a waste area, rising, let us suppose, above a café a hundred yards long on a terraced front by the south side of the river somewhere between Westminster and Waterloo Bridge. Are we, alone of ages, countries and civilisations, to leave no national monument behind us, except perhaps a bomb-proof shelter—and even about that our careful Government seems to hesitate?

J. M. KEYNES

With the war, Keynes continued his active interest in the Arts Theatre. However, he soon became involved in the Arts on a national scale. In October 1941 he became a Trustee of the National Gallery. Four months later he accepted an invitation to become chairman of the Council for the Encouragement of Music and the Arts (C.E.M.A.); a body set up by the Pilgrim Trust soon after the outbreak of war and later funded on an equal basis by the Trust and the Treasury. By the time Keynes took over, the Pilgrim Trust had bowed out and C.E.M.A. became completely Treasury financed.

Inevitably Keynes took an active part in C.E.M.A.'s activities and pushed it in new directions, most notably in leasing the Theatre Royal, Bristol to save it from destruction and reopening it in 1943. At the time Keynes provided an article for *The Times*.

---

[16] Ministry of Transport, *Highway Development Survey 1937 (Greater London)*, His Majesty's Stationery Office, 1938, paras. 79–80. Sir Charles Bressey was the engineer involved in the survey.

From The Times, *11 May 1943*

THE ARTS IN WAR-TIME

To-night, at the Theatre Royal, Bristol, Dame Sybil Thorndike, in the character of Mrs Hardcastle, speaks a new prologue before 'She Stoops to Conquer', with the company of the Old Vic, is played once again on the boards where Garrick's prologue was spoken in 1766. In 1766 the Theatre Royal was a new and, as it proved, an enduring experiment in the planning and aesthetics of the theatre. For it was the first to be built in this country with the seats rising from the pit tier above tier in a semi-circle. In these latter days, with its beauties undimmed, the oldest theatre we have was, like St Paul's, preserved by extraordinary chance from bombs and fire amidst surrounding desolation.

But in this peculiar country so much luck was not enough by itself to save a national monument—even when it was of rare beauty, when it echoed the voices of Siddons, Kemble, Kean, Macready, Irving, and Ellen Terry, and when it was still competent and useful to provide fresh delight to new multitudes. A year ago, saved from the enemy without, it was to be pulled down to make room for a warehouse. By timely action the citizens of Bristol opened an appeal fund and appointed trustees. That also was not enough to furnish and restore the place as the home of the living stage. So the Council for the Encouragement of Music and the Arts (C.E.M.A.), a body now wholly supported out of state funds, took over from the trustees the costs of equipment and the daily tasks of management, hoping in due season to hand the enterprise back to Bristol, unencumbered with debt, for local administration.

This is a new departure for C.E.M.A., and creates a precedent in the relation of the state to the theatre which deserves to be recorded. C.E.M.A. (as bad and forbidding a name as Bancor itself!) draws its funds from the Treasury and recognises the benevolent authority of the President of the Board of Education, But it has, I am thankful to say, an undefined independence, an anomalous constitution and no fixed rules, and is, therefore, able to do by inadvertence or indiscretion what obviously no one in his official senses would do on purpose.

> So, when Sir Kingsley told us that for staving
> Defeat, there was no saving grace like saving,
> We took him at his word, and, strictly loyal,
> For England's honour, sav'd—the Theatre Royal.

Thus in an undisciplined moment we accidentally slipped into getting mixed up with a theatre building. Making the best of a bad job, we shall come clean to-night, without shirking publicity, in hope of public absolution. And, the precedent having been once created, it will, I hope, be officially improper not to repeat it.

The functions of C.E.M.A. are evolving rapidly, and an account is soon out of date. In war-time an important part of them is to provide hundreds of factory concerts, to carry the drama to mining villages and war hostels where many of the audience see the living stage for the first time, to assist holidays at home and the provision of entertainment in parks and public places. With the aid of Mr W. E. Williams, who has been a great pioneer, we circulate through the British Institute of Adult Education large number of exhibitions of pictures and screen displays on such motives as 'The Rebuilding of Britain', having an educational aim and providing a worthy distraction for the mind. Last week a ballet company working in association with us (I pay a tribute to Mme Rambert) played to the wild delight of 3,000 workers within the walls of a Midland factory.

All our companies must perform their quota of such national service for the enlargement of public content in time of war. But we also seek, and increasingly, to aid all those who pursue the highest standards of original composition and executive performance in all branches of the arts to carry their work throughout the country, and to accustom the great new audiences which are springing up to expect and to approve the best. The leading symphony orchestras and string orchestras, most of the painters, and a large majority (I think I can now say), of the opera, ballet, and drama companies in the country pursuing a serious artistic purpose are working in occasional or continuous association with us. Our policy is to be satisfied with their work and purpose in general terms, and to leave the artistic control with the companies and individuals concerned; and they, with the plays, pictures, and concerts they offer, may be as many and as various as there are individuals of genius and good will.

The life of this country in the realm of the arts flows more strongly than for many a year. Our most significant discovery is the volume of popular demand. Apart from what we deliberately provide gratis or at nominal cost for war-time reasons, the money required to support so much activity is negligible. It is impossible to-day to offer in any large town in England a masterpiece worthily presented and to lose much money, if there is any building capable of holding the audience which assails the box office. It was not always so. We are capitalising, I fancy, the success of the B.B.C. (which we grumble against as against one we love) in stimulating and raising the popular taste.

But the lack of buildings is disastrous. The theatres, concert halls, and galleries well suited to our purpose, taking the country as a whole, can be counted in a few minutes. That is where money will be wanted when in due time we turn to construct instead of to destroy. Nor will that expenditure be unproductive in financial terms. But we do have to equip, almost from the beginning, the material frame for the arts of civilisation and delight. If it is thought fit to preserve after the war any part of the organisation and experience that C.E.M.A., which is on a temporary basis, will have acquired, this, I believe, is the fruitful line of development. If with state aid the material frame can be constructed, the public and the artists will do the rest between them. The muses will emerge from their dusty haunts, and supply and demand shall be their servants. To begin the good work, let us build temples for them as our memorial to the gallant endurance of Plymouth and Coventry and the rest, and of old London herself. Or to use language clearer to the departments concerned—let us give this bottleneck a high priority. At any rate, do not let us lose what we already have. So hold us well justified at Bristol. I have already quoted from the brilliant prologue (far, far better than Garrick's) which Mr Herbert Farjeon has written for this occasion. In another passage he has a couplet which C.E.M.A., and indeed all of us, might take as a motto :–

> Making it our endeavour, first and last,
> To serve the present and deserve the past.

On one occasion Keynes also defended C.E.M.A. in public following a public attack on the pictures it circulated.

To the Editor of The Times, *12 March 1944*

Sir,

You published on Saturday a letter from a number of signatories complaining that C.E.M.A. was unduly restricting the collections of pictures which it circulates to what were described as 'modernistic' art.

The letter suggests that our policy was calculated to deprave the public taste. It is, I think, somewhat scandalous that so distinguished a body of signatories should write that sort of letter with so little preliminary inquiry into the facts. As, however, the activities of C.E.M.A. are a proper subject of public concern and interest, I venture to trespass on your space to describe them as briefly as I can.

In its early days C.E.M.A. did not itself organise exhibitions of pictures, though we acquired at that time a small collection of inexpensive pictures out of a grant from the Pilgrim Trust. We limited ourselves to subsidising for this purpose the admirable pioneer organisation of the British Institute of Adult

Education. In 1942, however, in addition to continuing a substantial grant to the British Institute, we began to take a more direct responsibility. So far, our three major efforts have been the circulation through the provinces of the Sickert Exhibition, the Wilson Steer Exhibition, and the Tate Gallery's war-time acquisitions, all of which had been previously shown with general applause at the National Gallery.

Your correspondents do not particularise which of these exhibitions was more especially responsible in their judgement for degrading the public taste. We should have liked to supplement these outstanding shows of recent art by important exhibitions of old masters. But, not unnaturally, it has proved impracticable to persuade owners to allow such pictures to circulate through the country in present conditions. The same causes prevented a tour of the French pictures shown at the National Gallery and also led to the breakdown of arrangements for a representative show of the best American work of recent times. Nevertheless we were able to get together a satisfactory collection of old English landscapes, and the Tate Gallery have lately assembled for us a representative collection of the narrative pictures of the Victorian period which were once so popular and may prove so again.

For the most part, however, we have had to fall back for purposes of education in the historical development of art, on exhibitions dependent on photographs and reproductions. I may mention in particular those entitled 'The Artist and the Church', 'English Art and the Mediterranean', 'Portrait and Character', and 'English Book Illustrations since 1800'. Among others may be mentioned two series of water-colours called 'Recording Britain', commissioned by the Pilgrim Trust, of buildings of merit and interest which might suffer war damage; 'Rebuilding Britain' (prepared by the R.I.B.A.), and 'Ballet Designs'.

Out of the 25 exhibitions which we have circulated up to date there have been six mixed shows of contemporary artists, two of which were selections from the summer exhibitions of the Royal Academy, chosen on the responsibility of the Council of the Academy (two of the signatories of the letter of complaint were represented in these), and one of 'Living Scottish Artists', chosen by a special Scottish Committee. It is probably one of these selections which has called down the wrath of your correspondents. They do not explain whether it is their wish that no contemporary pictures should be circulated or only those of a particular school. The latter suggestion would be unworthy of the freedom and comradeship of art, besides being, in the light of the past history of taste, vain and childish. Our own practice and deliberate policy is to allow every form of serious endeavour its opportunity, and the above catalogue will show that we could scarcely have carried catholicity farther than we have.

In the choice of exhibitions C.E.M.A. acts on the advice of an art panel, consisting of the Directors of the National Gallery, of the Tate Gallery, and of the Leeds Municipal Gallery; of Mr Samuel Courtauld, who has served office as chairman of the National Gallery trustees and whose gifts to the national collections are outstanding, and Mr W. E. Williams, who initiated the work of the British Institute of Adult Education and is now the Director of the Army Bureau of Current Affairs; and of three working artists, Tom Monnington, R.A., Duncan Grant, and Henry Moore, whose achievement, you will agree, is in the public estimation an honour and an adornment to contemporary art. Our Director was in peace-time the Keeper of the Library of the Victoria and Albert Museum. In fact, our panel is as mixed a bunch of fogeys of repute as you could reasonably hope to collect. We have undoubtedly reached, on the average, the age of discretion.

Yours, etc.,
KEYNES

The spring of 1945 brought a C.E.M.A. exhibition of the previous fifty years of French book illustration. Keynes provided a foreword to the catalogue.

From C.E.M.A., An Exhibition of French Book Illustration, 1895–1945

With the liberation of France there naturally arises a strong desire for the resumption of those cultural relations between our two countries which have too long been severed, ties which in the past have meant so much to us. We should have liked to begin with an exhibition of contemporary French painting, so that we could learn how the catastrophe which engulfed France had affected her painters and what new tendencies had arisen during the occupation. Unfortunately the problem of transport, which is seriously affecting economic conditions in France, has prevented for the time being the assembly of a representative collection of paintings for exhibition in this country. But we have thought that, meanwhile, a collection of French illustrated books of the past fifty years, including the most recent graphic work of her greatest contemporary artists, would make an appropriate beginning.

A visit to Paris by Mr Philip James, the Art Director of C.E.M.A., who has selected and arranged this exhibition, revealed an unexpected wealth of books produced during the occupation with all the old regard for quality and style. Here there are still superb paper, ample margins, noble founts of type and original wood-engravings, etchings, aquatints and lithographs in many colours. Some may feel envious of such magnificence (though this does not mean that the ordinary book trade in France is not even more straitened than our own), when the cry for austerity here is having the unfortunate result of making those wretches, who like it as such, appear virtuous. But the sight of these books will at least encourage us to insist that we should forget austerity and 'war emergency agreements' at the earliest possible moment, and that there are such things as false economies in knowledge and the civilising arts, which in fact use up an infinitesimal quantity of materials in relation to their importance in the national life and the comfort they can give to the individual spirit. We shall welcome, therefore, this opportunity to admire the graphic work of Toulouse-Lautrec, Bonnard, Matisse, Rouault, Picasso and many other masters, and through them to pay a tribute to France. This is not the less true because our own taste and tradition in book illustration is, for better or worse, different.

The thanks of C.E.M.A. are given to the French Ambassador, M. René Massigli, and to M. Paris of the French Embassy without whose interest and help the exhibition could not have been arranged. For the collection of recent publications of the *Service des Oeuvres* at once accepted responsibility and we are grateful to MM. Laugier and Joubert of that organisation as well as to all the French publishers and galleries who have lent their books. A notable contribution has been made by M. Martin Fabiani of the fine books issued by the late Ambroise Vollard, several of whose projects have been or are now being completed by M. Fabiani himself. M. Henri Petiet has contributed from his collection and from his great knowledge of the subject. M. Dunoyer de Segonzac, who has many old friends in this country, has kindly lent some proofs of the plates for his long-awaited edition of the *Georgics*.

The response here has been no less ready. Mr A. Zwemmer in particular has made many loans of importance; and the Director of the Victoria and Albert Museum has allowed us to borrow a number of books from the national art library at South Kensington. All the other lenders must allow us to thank them collectively. Finally the help of the staff of the Chancellery at the British Embassy in Paris who despatched the books and of Miss S. Nechamkin and Mr Henrion in setting out the exhibition are gratefully acknowledged. After the London showing at the National Gallery, the Trustees and Director of which we thank for the hospitality of their galleries, the exhibition will, like other C.E.M.A. exhibitions, be shown in the provinces.

KEYNES

As the war progressed, the post-war future of C.E.M.A. came under consideration. After several months of discussion, after the end of the war in Europe, the Chancellor of the Exchequer announced on 12 June 1945 that the Government had decided to continue C.E.M.A.'s activities on a more permanent basis through the Arts Council of Great Britain. A few weeks later, Keynes gave a broadcast talk on the new organisation.

From The Listener, *12 July 1945*

THE ARTS COUNCIL: ITS POLICY AND HOPES

In the early days of the war, when all sources of comfort to our spirits were at a low ebb, there came into existence, with the aid of the Pilgrim Trust, a body officially styled the 'Council for the Encouragement of Music and the Arts', but commonly known from its initial letters as C.E.M.A. It was the task of C.E.M.A. to carry music, drama and pictures to places which otherwise would be cut off from all contact with the masterpieces of happier days and times: to air-raid shelters, to war-time hostels, to factories, to mining villages. E.N.S.A. was charged with the entertainment of the Services; the British Council kept contact with other countries overseas; the duty of C.E.M.A. was to maintain the opportunities of artistic performance for the hard-pressed and often exiled civilians.

With experience our ambitions and our scope increased. I should explain that whilst C.E.M.A. was started by private aid, the time soon came when it was sponsored by the Board of Education and entirely supported by a Treasury grant. We were never given much money, but by care and good housekeeping we made it go a long way. At the start our aim was to replace what war had taken away; but we soon found that we were providing what had never existed even in peace time. That is why one of the last acts of the Coalition Government was to decide that C.E.M.A. with a new name and wider opportunities should be continued into time of peace. Henceforward we are to be a permanent body, independent in constitution, free from red tape, but financed by the Treasury and ultimately responsible to Parliament, which will have to be satisfied with what we are doing when from time to time it votes us money. If we behave foolishly any Member of Parliament will be able to question the Chancellor of the Exchequer and ask why. Our name is to be the Arts Council of Great Britain. I hope you will call us the Arts Council for short, and not try to turn our initials into a false, invented word. We have carefully selected initials which we hope are unpronounceable.

I do not believe it is yet realised what an important thing has happened. Strange patronage of the arts has crept in. It has happened in a very English, informal, unostentatious way— half-baked if you like. A semi-independent body is provided with modest funds to stimulate, comfort and support any societies or bodies brought together on private or local initiative which are striving with serious purpose and a reasonable prospect of success to present for public enjoyment the arts of drama, music and painting.

At last the public exchequer has recognised the support and encouragement of the civilising arts of life as part of their duty. But we do not intend to socialise this side of social endeavour. Whatever views may be held by the lately warring parties, whom you have been hearing every evening at this hour, about socialising industry, everyone, I fancy, recognises that the work of the artist in all its aspects is, of its nature, individual and free, undisciplined, unregimented, uncontrolled. The artist walks where the breath of the spirit blows him. He cannot be told his direction; he does not know it himself. But he leads the rest of us into fresh pastures and teaches us to love and to enjoy what we often begin by rejecting, enlarging our sensibility and purifying our instincts. The task of an official body is not to teach or to censor, but to give courage, confidence and opportunity. Artists depend on the world they live in and the spirit of the age. There is no reason to suppose that less native genius is born into the world in the ages empty of achievement than in those brief periods when nearly all we most value has been brought to birth. New work will spring up more abundantly in unexpected quarters and in unforeseen shapes when there is a universal opportunity for contact with traditional and contemporary arts in their noblest forms.

But do not think of the Arts Council as a schoolmaster. Your enjoyment will be our first aim. We have but little money to spill, and it will be you yourselves who will by your patronage decide in the long run what you get. In so far as we instruct, it is a new game we are teaching you to play—and to watch. Our wartime experience has led us already to one clear discovery: the unsatisfied demand and the enormous public for serious and fine entertainment. This certainly did not exist a few years ago. I do not believe that it is merely a war-time phenomenon. I fancy that the B.B.C. has played a big part, the predominent part, in creating this public demand, by bringing to everybody in the country the possibility of learning these new games which only the few used to play, and by forming new tastes and habits and thus enlarging the desires of the listener and his capacity for enjoyment. I am told that today when a good symphony concert is broadcast as many as five million people may listen to it. Their ears become trained. With what anticipation many of them look forward if a chance comes their way to hear a living orchestra and to experience the enhanced excitement and concentration of attention and emotion, which flows from being one of a great audience all moved together by the surge and glory of an orchestra in being, beating in on the sensibilities of every organ of the body and of the apprehension. The result is that half the world is being taught to approach with a livelier appetite the living performer and the work of the artist as it comes from his own hand and body, with the added subtlety of actual flesh and blood.

I believe that the work of the B.B.C. and the Arts Council can react backwards and forwards on one another to the great advantage of both. It is the purpose of the Arts Council to feed these newly-aroused and widely-diffused desires. But for success we shall have to solve what will be our biggest problem, the shortage—in most parts of Britain the complete absence—of adequate and suitable buildings. There never were many theatres in this country or any concert-halls or galleries worth counting. Of the few we once had, first the cinema took a heavy toll and then the blitz; and anyway the really suitable building for a largish audience which the modern engineer can construct had never been there. The greater number even of large towns, let alone the smaller centres, are absolutely bare of the necessary bricks and mortar. And our national situation today is very unfavourable for a quick solution. Houses for householders have to come first.

And so they should. Yet I plead for a certain moderation from our controllers and a few crumbs of mortar. The re-building of the community and of our common life must proceed in due proportion between one thing and another. We must not limit our provision too exclusively to shelter and comfort to cover us when we are asleep and allow us no convenient place of congregation and enjoyment when we are awake. I hope that a reasonable allotment of resources will be set aside each year for the repair and erection of the buildings we shall need. I hear that in Russia theatres and concert-halls are given a very high priority for building.

And let such buildings be widely spread throughout the country. We of the Arts Council are greatly concerned to decentralise and disperse the dramatic and musical and artistic life of the country, to build up provincial centres and to promote corporate life in these matters in every town and country. It is not our intention to act on our own where we can avoid it. We want to collaborate with local authorities and to encourage local institutions and societies and local enterprise to take the lead. We already have regional offices in Birmingham, Cambridge, Manchester, Nottingham, Bristol, Leeds, Newcastle-on-Tyne, Cardiff and Edinburgh. For Scotland and for Wales special committees have been established. In Glasgow, in particular, the work of the Citizens Theatre is a perfect model of what we should like to see established everywhere, with their own playwrights, their own company and an ever-growing and more appreciative local public. We have great hopes of our new Welsh Committee and of the stimulus it will give to the special genius of the Welsh people. Certainly in every blitzed town in this country one hopes that the local authority will make provision for a central group of buildings for drama and music and art. There could be no better memorial of a war to save the freedom of the spirit of the individual. We look forward to the time when the theatre and the concert-hall and the gallery will be a living element in everyone's upbringing, and regular attendance at the theatre and at concerts a part of organised education. The return of the B.B.C. to regional programmes may play a great part in reawakening local life and interest in all these matters. How satisfactory it would be if different parts of this country would again walk their several ways as they once did and learn to develop something different from their neighbours and characteristic of themselves. Nothing can be more damaging than the excessive prestige of metropolitan standards and fashions. Let every part of Merry England be merry in its own way. Death to Hollywood.

But it is also our business to make London a great artistic metropolis, a place to vist and to wonder at. For this purpose London today is half in ruin. With the loss of the Queen's Hall there is no proper place for concerts. The Royal Opera House at Covent Garden has been diverted to other purposes throughout the war. The Crystal Palace has been burnt to the ground. We hope that Covent Garden will be re-opened early next year as the home of opera and ballet. The London County Council has already allotted a site for a National Theatre. The Arts Council has joined with the Trustees of the Crystal Palace in the preparation of plans to make that once again a great People's Palace.

No one can yet say where the tides of the times will carry

our new-found ship. The purpose of the the Arts Council of Great Britain is to create an environment to breed a spirit, to cultivate an opinion, to offer a stimulus to such purpose that the artist and the public can each sustain and live on the other in that union which has occasionally existed in the past at the great ages of a communal civilised life.

One sentence in Keynes's broadcast caused problems, when the publicity director of United Artists Corporation wondered in *The Times* of 11 July whether his words 'Death to Hollywood' represented a declaration of war on Hollywood by the Council and whether such a conflict was either necessary or desirable. Indeed the film industry might even support the Council's schemes. Keynes replied.

To the Editor of The Times, *11 July 1945*

Sir,

Mr Pole and the United Artists Corporation are so much in the majority that they must forgive me my eccentricity. But perhaps my wording was faulty. I was extolling (*a*) the presentation of art by the living artist 'with all the added subtlety of flesh and blood' and (*b*) a world in which 'different parts of this country would again walk their several ways as they once did and learn to develop something different from their neighbours and characteristic of themselves'. Thus what I ought to have said is—'Hollywood for Hollywood!'

In response to Mr Pole's friendly final sentence, I am open to any helpful proposal.

Your obedient servant,

KEYNES

Chapter 4

HUME

In 1933 Keynes, who had been collecting the works of David Hume for almost as long as he had collected books, received from his brother Geoffrey a copy of a pamphlet *An Abstract of a Book Lately Published entitled A Treatise of Human Nature, etc.*, originally published anonymously in London in 1740. According to tradition, the author of the *Abstract* was the young Adam Smith. On examining the work, Keynes began to doubt the accepted story, doubts that he confirmed in discussions with Piero Sraffa, another Cambridge economist–book collector. They were able to show that the pamphlet was not the product of Smith but rather of Hume himself. Keynes and Sraffa republished the pamphlet with Cambridge University Press in 1938, adding a joint introduction. This appears below.

From An Abstract of A Treatise on Human Nature 1740: *A Pamphlet hitherto Unknown by David Hume (1938)*

I

In the summer of 1734 Hume left Bristol for France. There he remained for three years, first of all at Rheims and then at La Flèche in Anjou. In this period the *Treatise of Human Nature* was mainly composed. In the autumn of 1737 he wrote to his friend, Henry Home:*

I am sorry I am not able to satisfy your curiosity, by giving you some general notion of the plan upon which I proceed. But my opinions are so new, and even some terms I am obliged to make use of, that I could not purpose, by any abridgement, to give my system an air of likelihood, or so much as make it intelligible. 'Tis a thing I have in vain attempted already, at a gentleman's request in this place, who thought it would help him to comprehend and judge of my notions, if he saw them all at once before him. I have had a greater desire of communicating to you the plan of the whole, that I believe it will not appear in public before the beginning of next winter. For, besides that it would be difficult to have it printed before the rising of the Parliament,

* *The Letters of David Hume*, ed. by J. Y. T. Greig, Oxford, 1932, Vol. 1, p. 23.

I must confess, I am not ill pleased with a little delay, that it may appear with as few imperfections as possible. I have been here near three months, always within a week of agreeing with my printers; and you may imagine I did not forget the work itself during that time, where I began to feel some passages weaker for the style and diction than I could have wisht. The nearness and greatness of the event roused up my attention, and made me more difficult to please, than when I was alone in perfect tranquility in France.

On 26 September 1738 Hume entered into an agreement* for the publication of the first two volumes with John Noon (or Noone) of Cheapside.† This agreement assigned to the publisher the first edition of the first two volumes of the book 'not exceeding one thousand copies thereof'‡ in return for £50 and twelve bound copies. Hume seems to have had difficulty§ in finding a publisher owing to his insistence on parting with the rights in the first edition only, and he had to agree to a clause 'that upon printing a second Edition I shall take all the copys remaining upon hand at the Bookseller's Price at the time'. In fact no second edition was published during Hume's lifetime;‖ and it is possible that the above clause may have played a part

---

* A copy exists amongst the manuscripts of the Royal Society of Edinburgh.

† John Noon appears to have been in business as a publisher between 1737 and 1760. 'He seems to have confined his publications to works of a religious character. The stock of John Noon deceased was sold by auction 10 Feb. 1763.' (*Notes and Queries*, 1931, Vol. CLXI, p. 351.)

‡ The book comes up for sale so seldom that one may doubt whether more than one or two hundred can be extant. 'The book', says Birkbeck Hill (*Letters of David Hume*, 1888, p. xx), 'had become so scarce by the time of Hume's death, that the reviewer of his *Life* in the *Annual Register* for 1776, ii, 28, thinks it needful, he says, to give some account of it.'

§ Cf. his letter to Hutcheson, 16 March 1740 (Greig, *Letters*, Vol. I, p. 38): 'I concluded somewhat of a hasty Bargain with my Bookseller from Indolence & an Aversion to Bargaining, as also because I was told that few or no Bookseller wou'd engage for one Edition with a new Author. I was also determin'd to keep my Name a Secret for some time tho I find I have fail'd in that Point.'

‖ The *Treatise* was not reprinted in English until 1817, and its next appearance was in the German translation *Ueber die Menuschlich Natur*, published in Halle in 1790, by Heinrich Jacob, who was, perhaps, the first to point out its superiority over the *Enquiry* and its much greater completeness (*vide* his excellent preface). In spite of T. H. Green's presumption to the contrary (Introduction to his edition of the *Treatise*, Vol. I, p. 3), modern Kantian scholars are convinced that before 1790 Kant had no direct acquaintance with the *Treatise* (knowing it, if at all, only through the passages quoted in Beattie's *Essay*, of which a German edition appeared in 1772) but used the *Enquiry*, which appeared in 1755 in a German translation, a copy of which is recorded as being in his library (*Immanuel Kants Bucher*, by A. Warda). No complete translation of the *Treatise* has ever appeared in French.

in his desiring (as we argue below) a Dublin edition which would enable him to make at once the corrections appropriate to a second edition.*

The book was issued anonymously at the end of January 1739 in two volumes octavo—*A Treatise of Human Nature: being an Attempt to introduce the experimental Method of Reasoning into Moral Subjects*, London, Printed for John Noon, at the White Hart, near Mercer's Chapel, in Cheapside MDCCXXXIX... *Vol I, Of the Understanding...Vol II, of the Passions.* On 13 February 1739 he wrote to Henry Home:†

Tis now a fortnight since my book was published; and besides many other considerations, I thought it would contribute very much to my tranquillity, and might spare me many mortifications to be in the country, while the success of the work was doubtful. I am afraid 'twill remain so very long. Those who are accustomed to reflect on such abstract subjects, are commonly full of prejudices; and those who are unprejudiced are unacquainted with metaphysical reasonings. My principles are also so remote from all the vulgar sentiments on the subject, that were they to take place, they would produce almost a total alteration in philosophy: and you know, revolutions of this kind are not easily brought about. I am young enough to see what will become of the matter; but am apprehensive lest the chief reward I shall have for some time will be the pleasure of studying on such important subjects, and the approbation of a few judges.

On 22 February 1739 he wrote to Michael Ramsey:‡

As to myself, no Alteration has happen'd in my Fortune, nor have I taken the least Step towards it. I hope things will be riper next Winter; & I wou'd

* Nine years later (in 1748) the necessity was superseded, in Hume's own view, by the publication of his *Philosophical Essays concerning Human Understanding*, which he later (1758) called *An Enquiry concerning Human Understanding*, though in the judgement of posterity a much inferior book. In 1751 Hume wrote to Gilbert Elliot: 'I believe the philosophical Essays contain every thing of Consequence relating to the Understanding which you would meet with in the Treatise: & I give you my Advice against reading the latter. By shortening & simplifying the Questions, I really render them much more complete. *Addo dum minuo.* The philosophical Principles are the same in both: But I was carry'd away by the Heat of Youth & Invention to publish too precipitately. So vast an Undertaking, plan'd before I was one and twenty, & compos'd before twenty five, must necessarily be very defective. I have repented my Haste a hundred, & a hundred times.' (Greig, *Letters*, Vol. 1, p. 158).) See also Hume's published disclaimer which was printed as the 'Advertisement' to the editions of the *Enquiry* from 1777 (cf. Birkbeck Hill, *Letters of David Hume*, pp. 289, 302).
† Greig, *Letters*, Vol. 1, p. 26.
‡ Greig, *Letters*, Vol. 1, p. 28.

not aim at any thing till I cou'd judge of my Success in my grand Undertaking, & see upon what footing I shall stand in the World. I am afraid, however, that I shall not have any great Success of a sudden. Such Performances make their way very heavily at first, when they are not recommended by any great Name or Authority.

On 1 June 1739 he wrote to Henry Home:*

I am not much in the humour of such compositions at the present, having received news from London of the success of my Philosophy, which is but indifferent, if I may judge by the sale of the book, and if I may believe my bookseller. I am now out of humour with myself; but doubt not, in a little time, to be only out of humour with the world, like other unsuccessful authors. After all, I am sensible of my folly, in entertaining any discontent, much more despair, upon this account; since I could not expect any better from such abstract reasoning; nor indeed did I promise myself much better. My fondness for what I imagined new discoveries, made me overlook all common rules of prudence; and having enjoyed the usual satisfaction of projectors, 'tis but just I should meet with their disappointments. However, as 'tis observed with such sort of people, one project generally succeeds another, I doubt not, but in a day or two I shall be as easy as ever, in hopes that truth will prevail at last over the indifference and opposition of the world.

By the summer of 1739 no review or notice of any kind had appeared. It is of his feelings at this time that Hume wrote in *My Own Life*: 'Never literary attempt was more unfortunate than my *Treatise of Human Nature*. It fell dead-born from the press† without reaching such distinction as even to excite a murmur among the zealots.' In the autumn of the year Hume seems to have reached the conclusion that something desperate must be done to provoke attention to the book. He proceeded himself to write—if the argument of the following page is to be accepted—a review, indeed a puff, of his own work, anonymously of course, which was in part an abstract or epitome of what he himself considered the most striking parts of the *Treatise*, such as Henry Home had asked him for in 1737 and he, at that time,

* Greig, *Letters*, Vol. I, p. 30.
† Echoing Pope, as Birkbeck Hill points out:

> 'All, all but truth, drops dead-born from the press,
> Like the last Gazette, or the last Address.'
>
> *Epil. Sat.* II, 226.

had 'in vain attempted',* and in part embodying some of those additions and improvements occurring to him whilst he was working at the completion of his book, which were to be published a little later as an appendix to the third volume. It seems that he had originally intended to offer this abstract as a review for publication in the periodical *The History of the Works of the Learned*; but before he had sent it up an extensive review of the book had already appeared in this publication in November and December.† Hume made arrangements, therefore, for its publication in London in 1740 as a separate pamphlet‡ under the title 'An Abstract of a Book lately Published; entitled A Treatise of Human Nature, &c. wherein the Chief Argument of that Book is farther illustrated and explained'. The publisher is given on the title page as 'C. Borbet, at *Addison's Head*, over-against *St. Dunstan's Church*, in *Fleet-street*'. But the name is evidently a misprint for C. Corbet, who is known to have been publishing at Addison's Head in Fleet Street at the date in question.§ The receipt of a copy of this publication was noted in the *Gentleman's Magazine* for March 1740, where the name of the publisher is correctly given as Corbet.‖ It is this pamphlet, hitherto unknown to Hume's biographers and of which until recently no

---

* *Vide supra*, p. 373.

† It was this review which Hume described in a letter to Hutcheson as 'somewhat abusive' (Greig, *Letters*, Vol. I, p. 38). Yet the reviewer had written of his book: 'It bears, indeed, incontestable marks of a great capacity, of a soaring genius, but young and not yet thoroughly practised. The subject is vast and noble as any that can exercise the understanding; but it requires a very mature judgment to handle it as becomes its dignity and importance: the utmost prudence, tenderness, and delicacy are requisite to this desirable issue. Time and use may ripen these qualities in our author; and we shall probably have reason to consider this, compared with his later productions, in the same light as we view the juvenile works of Milton, or the first manner of a Raphael or other celebrated painter.' A fair example of the fact that authors are hard to please.

‡ Letters to Hutcheson, 4 March 1740 (Greig, *Letters*, Vol. I, p. 37).

§ Cf. *Notes and Queries*, 1931, Vol. CLXI, pp. 80 and 171.

‖ 'Register of Books in March, 1740' contains, p. 152: 'An Abstract of the Treatise of Human Nature price 6d. Corbet'. This announcement in the *Gentleman's Magazine* has been overlooked hitherto; so that earlier commentators, besides not knowing the contents, were unaware that it has been in fact published. (See Bonar's *Catalogue of the Library of Adam Smith*, 2nd ed. 1932, p. 204: 'It is hardly probable that the Abstract of Hume's *Human Nature* made by "Mr Smith" for Hutcheson, and sent by Hume to a London journal 1740 (Hill Burton, I, 116), will yet be discovered.')

copy was known to exist, which is here reprinted. It has been the occasion, however, of a curious legend which we must now describe.

II

In the letter to Francis Hutcheson of 4 March 1740 already referred to, in which Hume mentions the *Abstract*, the following passage occurs:

My Bookseller has sent to Mr Smith a Copy of my Book, which I hope he has receiv'd, as well as your Letter. I have not yet heard what he has done with the Abstract. Perhaps you have. I have got it printed in London; but not in *the Works of the Learned*; there having been an article with regard to my Book, somewhat abusive, printed in that Work, before I sent up the Abstract.*

John Hill Burton in his standard *Life of Hume*, published in 1846, after quoting this passage adds the following (Vol. 1, pp. 116, 117):

The 'Smith' here mentioned as receiving a copy of the Treatise, we may fairly conclude, notwithstanding the universality of the name, to be Adam Smith, who was then a student in the university of Glasgow, and not quite seventeen years old. It may be inferred from Hume's letter, that Hutcheson had mentioned Smith as a person on whom it would serve some good purpose to bestow a copy of the Treatise: and we have here, evidently, the first introduction to each other's notice, of two friends, of whom it can be said, that there was no third person writing the English language during the same period, who has had so much influence upon the opinions of mankind as either of these two men.

Burton does not suggest any connection between Adam Smith and the authorship of the *Abstract*. But in John Rae's *Life of Adam Smith* (1895, pp. 15, 16) the story is carried a stage further:

Though Smith was a mere lad of sixteen at that time, his mind had already, under Hutcheson's stimulating instructions, begun to work effectively on the ideas lodged in it and to follow out their suggestions in his own thought. Hutcheson seems to have recognised his quality, and brought him, young

* Greig, *Letters*, Vol. 1, pp. 37, 38.

though he was, under the personal notice of David Hume. There is a letter written by Hume to Hutcheson on the 4th of March 1740 which is not indeed without its difficulties, but if, as Mr Burton thinks, the Mr Smith mentioned in it be the economist, it would appear as if Smith had, while attending Hutcheson's class,—whether as a class exercise or otherwise,—written an abstract of Hume's *Treatise of Human Nature*, then recently published, that Smith's abstract was to be sent to some periodical for publication, and that Hume was so pleased with it that he presented the young author with a copy of his own work. [Here Rae quotes the passage in quesion.] If the Mr Smith of this letter is Adam Smith, then he must have been away from Glasgow at that time, for Hutcheson was communicating with him by letter, but that may possibly be explained by the circumstance that he had been appointed to one of the Snell exhibitions at Balliol College, Oxford, and might have gone home to Kirkcaldy to make preparations for residence at the English University, though he did not actually set out for it till June.

Leslie Stephen, *s.v.* David Hume in the *Dictionary of National Biography*, follows Burton, but makes the mistake of relating the above to the third volume of the *Treatise* which was not then published: 'A copy (of the third volume) was sent to "Mr Smith", possibly Adam Smith, then a young student at Glasgow.' But *s.v.* Adam Smith (written at a later date) he follows Rae in tentatively attributing the *Abstract* to Adam Smith: 'A letter written by David Hume to Hutcheson (in March 1740) shows that a "Mr Smith" had made an abstract of the *Treatise of Human Nature*, by which Hume was so well pleased as to send a copy of his book through Hutcheson to the compiler. Whether "Mr Smith" was Adam Smith is, however, uncertain.'

In Professor W. R. Scott's *Francis Hutcheson* (1900, pp. 120, 121) the legend becomes a little more convincing by an explanation as to how Adam Smith might have come to write the *Abstract*:

Both Burton and Mr Rae, the biographer of Adam Smith, agree in thinking that this refers to the future economist, who had just been appointed to a Snell exhibition at Oxford, but was probably at this time at home in Kirkcaldy. From Carlyle's *Autobiography* we learn that it was customary for Hutcheson and Leechman to require promising members of their classes to prepare abstracts either of new or standard works, and that these summaries often attracted considerable notice in the University. In this case, Hutcheson evidently sent the abstract to Hume, who thought it worthy of being printed. It was an age of young philosophical authors, but, assuming that the 'Mr Smith' of the letter was Adam Smith, we have a reviewer of only seventeen years of age. This is not to be taken as tending to discredit the early connection of Adam Smith with Hume, rather, it is a remarkable instance of Hutcheson's success as a teacher, and the enthusiasm with which he inspired his pupils for Philosophy.*

To-day it is a commonplace amongst the biographers of Hume and Adam Smith that Adam Smith at seventeen wrote a review of Hume's *Treatise*. The following, for example, appears in Mr Greig's *David Hume* (p. 112) published in 1931:

> Hutcheson performed yet another service for his new acquaintance: he put him in touch with Adam Smith, then a youth of seventeen, but a Glasgow student of some three years' standing.

> It was Hutcheson's practice as a professor to lend newly published philosophical works to his brightest pupils, telling them to make a precis and submit it to him; and in 1739 Adam Smith wrote so good a precis of the *Treatise* (Books I and II) that Hutcheson, with pardonable pride, sent it to Hume. Hume in turn felt so highly pleased with it that he despatched a presentation copy of the book to Smith. He also sent the precis up to London, hoping that some learned journal there would print it; but apparently in vain.

III

Nevertheless, apart from the character of the contents of the *Abstract*, which was, of course, not known to these writers, Hume's letter to Hutcheson, which is the basis of the whole matter, does not easily bear the interpretation which has been put on it.

In the first place, as Burton and Rae noticed, the letter implies that 'Mr Smith' was not at Glasgow, since Hume refers to his hope that Hutcheson's *letter* to him has been received; whereas

---

* Convinced by the new evidence hereafter produced which the present writers had communicated to him, Prof. Scott has taken the opportunity of his recently published *Adam Smith as Student and Professor* (1937) to correct his previous error (pp. 34, 35).

it is probable that Adam Smith, who did not set out for Oxford until June 1740,* was still at Glasgow in March 1740. Moreover Hume explicitly states that he has already had the *Abstract* printed in London; which makes the sentence 'I have not yet heard what *he* has done with the Abstract' meaningless, if *he* is supposed to refer to Adam Smith. Thus the attribution to Adam Smith is, in any case, not plausible. It may be added that Prof. W. R. Scott finds no evidence of a meeting between Hume and Adam Smith until ten years later, sometime between 1749 and 1751, when Hume, having returned to Scotland about 1749, was living at Ninewells in Berwickshire. 'It must have been during one of his (Hume's) visits to Edinburgh,' Prof. Scott writes,† 'before Adam Smith moved to Glasgow in September or October 1751, that the two men met.'‡ This confirms the evidence mentioned by Dugald Stewart.§

In the second place, however, the context of Hume's letter‖ indicates a much more probable identification of 'Mr Smith'. Hume's letter is mainly concerned with asking Hutcheson's advice about the terms he should accept for the third volume of the *Treatise* and for an introduction to a London publisher which would render him less dependent on his previous publisher Noon. ¶ The letter begins: 'You will find that the Good-Nature & friendly Disposition, which I have experienc'd in you is like to occasion you more Trouble; & tis very happy, that the same Good Nature, which occasions the Trouble, will

---

* See Rae's *Life of Adam Smith*, p. 16.

† *Adam Smith as Student and Professor*, p. 64.

‡ 'It was then', Callander records, 'that he first became acquainted with Hume.' (Edin. Univ. Library MSS, La II, 451/2. We are indebted to Professor Scott for the quotation).

§ 'From some papers now in the possession of Mr Hume's nephew, their acquaintance seems to have grown into friendship before the year 1752.' (*Biographical Memoirs of Adam Smith*, etc., 1811, p. 11).

‖ This was not available to most of the previous commentators. Burton gives only the Smith paragraph and the letter was first published in full by Greig.

¶ In fact the third volume was not published by Noon but by Longmann, to whom Hume was introduced by Hutcheson whose London publisher he was. Though the publisher was different, nevertheless the printer was clearly the same, as is shown by the identity of the ornaments. It may be, therefore, that the third volume had been partly set up before Hume had insisted on parting from Noon.

incline you to excuse it'.* This suggests that Hume had already troubled him on a similar matter; in which case the final paragraph (quoted above p. 437) of Hume's letter concerning 'Mr Smith', which clearly refers to a previous conversation,† or possibly correspondence, with Hutcheson, relates to Hume's earlier request. Our hypothesis, elaborated below, as to the nature of 'the trouble' which Hume had then given him, is that he had invoked Hutcheson's aid with a view to arranging a *Dublin* edition of the *Treatise*.

Scotland had been brought under the English Copyright Act in 1710, but Ireland was not covered by it until 1801.‡ Thus throughout the eighteenth century English authors were liable to piratical editions in Dublin (though their importation into England was, of course, forbidden, together with all foreign reprints of books first published in England). In fact, many important English works were also published in a Dublin edition, with or without the approval and supervision of their authors. But apart from the additional publicity for the book and the avoidance of a possible piracy, the exemption of Dublin from English copyright offered a special advantage to Hume, since it would allow him to publish immediately a second and revised edition without infringing the conditions to which he had imprudently submitted (*vide* p. 374 above) in his contract with his London publisher, Noon. We know that he had just prepared additions to the first two volumes,§ which were eventually published as an Appendix to the third volume with directions as to the pages where they were to be inserted. We know that Hume was extremely anxious to issue a second edition; for he wrote to Hutcheson on 16 March 1740: 'I wait with some Impatience for a second Edition principally on Account of Alterations I intend to make in my Performance

---

* Greig, *Letters*, Vol. I, p. 36.
† Hume's letter to Hutcheson of 16 March 1740 shows that about this time they met and conversed (Greig, *Letters*, Vol. I, p. 39).
‡ See Birkbeck Hill's note on Irish editions, *Letters of David Hume*, p. 176.
§ The additions are thus described by Hume. But in fact the additions are only to the first volume.

...Our Conversation together has furnish'd me a hint, with which I shall augment the 2d. Edition';* and since what he had told Hutcheson a few days earlier,† namely, that 'the Sale of the first Volumes, tho' not very quick, yet it improves,' was not good enough to have given him any hope of a second edition in London, the edition which he was waiting for 'with some Impatience' must have been a Dublin edition. Finally, we know that precisely the same idea of defeating his London publisher by a revised Dublin edition occurred to Hume many years later, when he wrote to William Strahan (11 March 1771): 'It vexes me to the last Degree, that, by reason of this detested Edition of my History, I should have so distant or no prospect of ever giving a correct Edition of that Work. I assure you if Mr Millar were now alive, I should be tempted to go over to Dublin, and to publish there an Edition, which I hope wou'd entirely descredit the present one. But as you are entirely innocent in the conduct of this Affair, I scruple to take that Resolution.'‡

Now Hutcheson had a bookseller in Dublin, who had published his first two books, namely John Smith 'at the Philosopher's Head on the Blind Quay', with whom he was in particularly close touch inasmuch as Smith was in partnership with Hutcheson's cousin, William Bruce, their joint names appearing from 1728 onwards on the Irish editions of Hutcheson's works.§ In 1728, the same year as the English edition, Smith published in Dublin Hutcheson's *Essay on the Passions*, 'with the errors of the London edition emended'. ‖ Near the date in question (1740) there are several references in Hutcheson's letters to 'Jack Smith', as he called him, the Dublin publisher. ¶

Our conjecture is, then, that Hume had asked Hutcheson to recommend him to a Dublin publisher, with a view to an Irish

---

* Greig, *Letters*, Vol. I, pp. 38, 39.   † Greig, *Letters*, Vol. I, p. 37.
‡ Greig, *Letters*, Vol. II, p. 235.
§ W. R. Scott, *Hutcheson*, p. 26.
‖ Advertisement, quoted by Scott, *op. cit.* p. 53.
¶ 'Saunter in Jack's shop all day, among books' is Hutcheson's advice to a friend visiting Dublin. (Letter to Drennan, 8 July 1741, quoted by Scott, *Hutcheson*, p. 133; see also the references to 'Jack Smith' in 1737, p. 71, and in 1739, p. 138).

edition of his *Treatise of Human Nature*, and that naturally Hutcheson had suggested John Smith; that Hume had accordingly sent Smith a copy of the *Treatise*, while Hutcheson wrote recommending it for publication; and that, at the same time, Hume had sent Smith a copy of the *Abstract* (then still in manuscript), in the hope that he would arrange for its publication in some review in Dublin, just as Hume had originally intended in London, so as to awaken interest in the proposed edition of the *Treatise*. The Dublin edition would, no doubt, have contained the illustrations and explanations to the first two volumes, which, failing a new edition, Hume had to be content with appending to the third volume, published in London later in the same year.

Some hitch must have occurred, since no trace has been found of Dublin editions either of the *Treatise* or of the *Abstract*. But a gap of more than two years in Hume's correspondence, after the last letter quoted, prevents us from discovering its nature. If, however, our conjecture is correct, Hutcheson's introduction of Hume to John Smith was not without fruit, since John Smith did in fact publish a Dublin edition of the first instalment of Hume's *History of Great Britain* in 1755.*

In view of all the above hints there cannot, we suggest, be much doubt that the 'Mr Smith' of Hume's letter to Hutcheson refers to John Smith of Dublin 'at the Philosopher's Head on the Blind Quay.'

IV

So far we have assumed without discussion that Hume himself was the author of the *Abstract*. If a copy of the pamphlet had been available to earlier commentators, it is impossible that they could have doubted this conclusion. It is true that there is one (but only one) sentence in the Preface† intended to imply that it is not written by Hume; but this disclaimer, weak and

* Greig, *Letters*, Vol. I, p. 210.
† 'I hope the Author will excuse me...,' p. 4 below.

half-hearted as it is, is the least that could be expected in any case, for the publication would have defeated its own purpose if it had been confessedly by the author of the *Treatise*. Apart from considerations of style, the contents could not have been contributed by anyone but Hume himself, since they involved an anticipation of Hume's additions to the *Treatise* which were not published until *subsequently*. The internal evidence of Hume's authorship of the *Abstract* can, therefore, best be judged by comparing it with these additions, although they cover altogether only a few pages.

It should be remembered that Volumes I and II of the *Treatise* were published in January 1739, the Abstract was probably written in October–November 1739, and certainly printed not later than March 1740.

Volume III contains an Appendix 'Wherein some Passages of the foregoing Volumes are illustrated and explain'd'.* This Appendix, which takes up twenty-eight pages, is divided into two parts—an arrangement the reason for which is not obvious on logical or expository grounds, as the first refers to passages in Parts III and IV of Book I of the *Treatise*, and the second almost entirely to Parts I and II of the same Book. The first part is made up of an introductory discussion on the nature of belief, followed by a series of passages (five in number), on that and other questions, which are to be inserted in certain places in Volume I which are indicated. The second also opens with a discussion, in which Hume confesses the inconsistency of his Section on personal identity, and acknowledges two other errors of less importance; and is followed by four passages, on various subjects, to be inserted in their proper places. On comparison we find that the *Abstract* anticipates most of the points discussed in the first part of the Appendix, but none of those, and particularly not the corrections, in the second part.

Thus, in the first part, the two proofs of the falsity of the

---

* This is the description on the title-page. The similarity ('illustrated and explained') with the title of the *Abstract* should be remarked.

hypothesis that 'the belief is some new idea...which we join to the simple conception of the object'* are largely a paraphrase of the two proofs given on pp. 17–18 of the Abstract; and the conclusion, that what distinguishes belief is its being accompanied by 'a certain feeling, different from what attends the mere *reveries* of the imagination' follows almost verbatim the *Abstract* (p. 18, last sentence). Again, the passage† to be inserted on the difficulty of finding a word to describe this feeling, is anticipated in the *Abstract*, pp. 19–20; and the insertion,‡ which illustrates the same feeling by contrasting it with that arising from poetry, is an expansion of a brief allusion to this contrast in the *Abstract*, p. 20. Finally, the insertion,§ on the lack of connection between the will, considered as a cause, and its effects, which examines the statement 'that we feel an energy, or power, in our mind' is anticipated in the *Abstract*, p. 23. None of these points occurs in Volume I of the *Treatise*, and it is clear that Hume did not regard them as evidently implied in it, if he thought it necessary to add them later. Yet the author of the *Abstract* mentions them, not as his own criticisms or development, but in the casual way he would adopt were they contained in the work under review; it is, in effect, as if he were reviewing a new edition in which the additions had already been embodied —an edition which at the time only existed in Hume's desire.

Turning to the second part of the Appendix, however, we find that it has very little in common with the *Abstract*. Indeed, one of the corrections made in the Appendix (to the effect that two ideas of the same object can be different, not only by their 'degrees of force and vivacity' but also by their 'feeling')‖ is ignored in the *Abstract*, where (p. 9) the erroneous statement is repeated in the original form. It is true that another

---

* Vol. III, p. 284 (Selby-Bigge's ed., Oxford, 1888, p. 632).
† Vol. III, p. 293, for insertion in Vol. I, p. 174 (Selby-Bigge, pp. 628 and 97).
‡ Vol. III, p. 295, for insertion in Vol. I, p. 218 (Selby-Bigge, pp. 630 and 123).
§ Vol. III, p. 298, for insertion in Vol. I, p. 282 (Selby-Bigge, pp. 632 and 161).
‖ Vol. III, p. 306, referring to Vol. I, p. 171 (Selby-Bigge, pp. 636 and 96). The correction would have been better referred to p. 11 (Selby-Bigge, p. 1), where the original statement is made in a more definite form than on p. 171.

insertion,* concerning the opinion of the 'many philosophers' who refuse to define equality, which had not been considered in Vol. I, is anticipated in the *Abstract* (p. 27), to the extent of taking that opinion into consideration; but whilst here it is criticised and 'left to the learned world to judge', in the Appendix Hume declares his agreement with it. Of the other insertions and corrections in the second part of the Appendix there is nothing in the *Abstract*.

It would appear, therefore, that the two parts of the Appendix were written at different periods. The first part must have been prepared by Hume at about the time of his writing the *Abstract*, or at any rate when that state of the development of his ideas was complete in itself and the results were ready for insertion in the proposed Dublin edition; the second part was composed later, of which there is conclusive evidence in Hume's letter to Hutcheson of 17 March 1740, i.e. after the completion of the *Abstract*, where he writes: 'Our Conversation together has furnish'd me a hint, with which I shall augment the 2d. Edition. 'Tis this', and here follows the proof, from the case of simple ideas, that there may be similarity even though there be no possibility of separation, which we find in almost identical terms in one of the passages belonging to the second part of the Appendix.† The two parts were then printed, rather oddly, in the chronological order of their composition, and not in the order which would have been natural on other grounds.

There are, moreover, two passages in the *Abstract* which are not to be found in the *Treatise* or its Appendix, but of which Hume made use in the *Philosophical Essays concerning Human Understanding* (afterwards called the *Enquiry*) published in 1748. These are the criticism of Locke's theory of innate ideas (*Abstract*, pp. 9–10, *Philos. Essays*, pp. 28–29)‡ and the striking

---

* Vol. III, p. 307, for insertion in Vol. I, p. 88 (Selby-Bigge, pp. 637 and 47). The next following insertion, on the dilemma of the mathematicians, is to the same extent anticipated in p. 27 of the *Abstract*.
† Vol. III, p. 306, for insertion in Vol. I, p. 43 (Selby-Bigge, pp. 637 and 20).
‡ Selby-Bigge's ed., Oxford, 1894, p. 22.

example of the billiard balls (*Abstract*, pp. 11 ff., *Philos. Essays*, p. 52).*

It is, therefore, beyond doubt that we are here able to bring back to light a philosophical essay written by Hume, as Newton said of himself in 1666, 'in those days when he was in the prime of his age for invention and minded mathematics and philosophy more than at any time since'. It remains as good a brief introduction to the essence and original genius of the *Treatise* as can be found. Hume has pointed with infallible finger to those passages which, in the eyes of posterity as well as in those of the author, 'shake off the yoke of authority, accustom men to think for themselves, give new hints, which men of genius may carry further, and by the very opposition, illustrate points, wherein no one before suspected any difficulty.'†

He entirely neglects Book II of the *Treatise*, 'On the Passions,' apart from a single paragraph (p. 28), though he comments; ''Tis of more easy comprehension than the first; but contains opinions, that are altogether as new and extraordinary.' He barely touches in his first pages on the early apparatus of Book 1, 'Of Ideas'. 'I have chosen', he writes, 'one simple argument, which I have carefully traced from the beginning to the end. This is the only point I have taken care to finish. The rest is only hints of particular passages, which seem'd to me curious and remarkable.' The argument thus selected for emphasis and re-expression is the author's theory of causation, and is, in the main, a re-statement of the middle third of Part III of Book I of the *Treatise*. But there is no summing up in the *Treatise* so concise and effective as the statement in the *Abstract*, pp. 11–20; and of the various passages in the *Treatise* tracing the origin of belief from custom none is more Humian than the following from the *Abstract* (p. 16)

'Tis not, therefore, reason, which is the guide of life, but custom. That alone determines the mind, in all instances, to suppose the future conformable to

---

* Selby-Bigge, p. 28.
† Preface to *Abstract*, p. 4 below.

the past. However easy this step may seem, reason would never, to all eternity, be able to make it.

Finally, he 'concludes the logics of this author with an account of two opinions which seem to be peculiar to himself, as indeed are most of his opinions.' The first (*Abstract*, p. 24) relates to the soul or mind and leads up to a criticism of Descartes, and the second to the infinite divisibility of the extension and the exact standard of equality. He also adds a summary of his treatment of the freedom of the will which 'puts the whole controversy in a new light' (*Abstract*, pp. 29–31).

The concluding paragraph is a great contrast to the modesty and meiosis of the Preface to the *Treatise*. 'Thro' this whole book, there are great pretentions to new discoveries in philosophy...'Twill be easy to conceive of what vast consequence these principles must be in the science of human nature...' The eagerness of the author, after months of silence had greeted the appearance of his provocative masterpiece, could be restrained no longer. He must force the world to attend by strong and overt claims when too modest a demeanour has led to neglect. All is characteristic of Hume—the calculated demureness of his first appearance, the inability to resist the temptation to write and print an anonymous puff of his own work, and, when this too falls flat, a shamefaced suppression of the whole episode so completely successful that near two hundred years have passed before its rescue from oblivion.

The following is a line-for-line reprint of the *Abstract* in a fount almost identical, in design and size, with that of the original. The ornaments and the initial letters are reproduced in facsimile. The collation of the original is: A–D4.

The copy used for the reprint was purchased in 1933 from Messrs Pickering and Chatto, and is now in the possession of Mr J. M. Keynes. Two other copies have since been located, one in the Library of Trinity College, Dublin, whilst the other is now in the possession of Professor W. R. Scott. The copies belonging to Mr Keynes and Professor Scott contain no indication of *provenance*. The copy at Trinity College, Dublin, belonged to the library of François Fagel, Greffier to the States General of Holland, which was bought for the Library of Trinity College in 1802; it is entered in Christie's sale catalogue of the Fagel library as part of lot 1945 classed under 'Increduli celebriores eorumque Refellentes'.

Chapter 5

MISCELLANY

Keynes's journalism for *The Nation* sometimes took unexpected forms. On two occasions he commented briefly on books or reviewers.

To the Editor of The Nation and Athenaeum, *25 June 1927*

Sir,

Is it worth a column of *The Nation* (June 18th, p. 374) to tell us that Mr Richard Aldington does not like Wordsworth? Anyhow, it seems to make him an unsuitable reviewer for a minor work on Dorothy Wordsworth which could not be expected to have much appeal outside the (not very narrow) circle of Wordsworthians. So, after one depreciatory word for the authoress he passed on to what interests him—himself and the influence of modern French poetry on his taste. But one does not need to be a Wordsworthian to know that only an ass could write: 'If one sincerely likes modern French poetry, Wordsworth recedes.'

Yours, &c.,

J. M. K.

To the Editor of The Nation and Athenaeum, *24 February 1929*

Sir,

The appearance of two more volumes of the Centenary Edition of the works of Tolstoy moves me to make a protest about the type in which it has been printed.

Here is a set of volumes which should be the much-needed definitive Tolstoy for English readers for many years to come, satisfying a very great want. Each page consists of abnormally wide margins with some very small print in the middle of them, so small as to be uncomfortable for almost any reader. Indeed, the printed matter only occupies a little more than a third of the total area of the page. It is a typographical imbecility, of which the Oxford University Press—as a rule so exceptionally reliable on all matters of taste and common sense—ought to be ashamed. Is it too late to print the later volumes otherwise?

Yours, &c.,

J. M. KEYNES

On other occasions he was more constructive. Thus after *The Nation* had published, in the issue for 13 June 1925, a review by A. G. Tansley of Volume III of *The Collected Papers of Sigmund Freud*, and a correspondence had rumbled on for most of the summer either praising or denigrating Freud's contribution to psycho-analysis, Keynes ended the discussion with an anonymous letter.

To the Editor of The Nation and Athenaeum, *29 August 1925*

Sir,

I venture, as an outsider, to suggest that the truth about the importance to be attached to the ideas of Professor Freud lies somewhere between the views expressed by your learned correspondents.

Professor Freud seems to me to be endowed, to the degree of genius, with the scientific imagination which can body forth an abundance of innovating ideas, shattering possibilities, working hypotheses, which have sufficient foundation in intuition and common experience to deserve the most patient and unprejudiced examination, and which contain, in all probability, both theories which will have to be discarded or altered out of recognition and also theories of great and permanent significance.

But when it comes to the empirical or inductive proof of his theories, it is obvious that what we are offered in print is hopelessly inadequate to the case—that is to say, a very small number of instances carried out in conditions not subject to objective control. Freudian practitioners tell us that they are personally acquainted with a much greater number of instances than those which have been published. But they must not complain if others base their criticism merely on what is before them.

I venture to say that at the present stage the argument in favour of Freudian theories would be very little weakened if it were to be admitted that every case published hitherto had been wholly invented by Professor Freud in order to illustrate his ideas and to make them more vivid to the minds of his readers. That is to say, the case for considering them seriously mainly depends at present on the appeal which they make to our own intuitions as containing something new and true about the way in which human psychology works, and very little indeed upon the so-called inductive verifications, so far as the latter have been published up-to-date.

I suggest that Freud's partisans might do well to admit this, and, on the other hand, that his critics should, without abating their criticism, allow that he deserves exceptionally serious and entirely unpartisan consideration, if only because he does not seem to present himself to us, whether we like him or not, as one of the great disturbing, innovating geniuses of our age, that is to say as a sort of devil.

Yours, &c.,

SIELA

Similarly in 1927, he summed up a correspondence on vivisection.

To the Editor of The Nation and Athenaeum, *22 January 1927*

Sir,

Mr A. A. Milne, writing to you last week, purports to be very wise and judicious. But is he?

His first point, alleging that doctors sometimes deem an operation 'successful' even if the patient dies, which he intends as a criticism on the 'expert', is just feebly facetious—worse than Mr Shaw at his worst! His second point, arguing that the pain involved in vivisection would be intolerable if it were merely a sport, loses its effect when we remember that sport involving physical suffering to animals must in this country cause hundreds or thousands of times more pain in a year than is caused by vivisection. When, instead of being undertaken seriously on account of its utility to science and the cure of human suffering, vivisection *is* a sport, it is called hunting or shooting and no troubles are put in its way.

His third point stresses what most people accept, namely, that the question is one of the balance of advantage. But, judged by this standard, there cannot be the faintest vestige of a doubt, in the mind of any reasonable being who has considered the evidence, where the balance of advantage lies. Out of all the many classes of cases where we inflict pain that good may come, vivisection is surely amongst the least doubtful.

No! The real crux of the controversy is something different— something which was perhaps half present in Mr Milne's mind in the closing passage of his letter. The real point of difference is that the true anti-vivisectionist believes that it is *not* a question of the balance of advantage. He believes that it is absolutely wrong in itself to inflict pain on animals in the interests of physiological science, however great the advantage to the latter. He prefers quite deliberately that millions of children should die in pain than that a dozen dogs should suffer vivisection, or even than that one dog should be given indigestion, because he refuses to accept or allow that kind of calculation. He is liable, in controversy with people who do not accept this point of view, but do accept the balance of advantage position, to bolster up his argument by grossly exaggerating the pain and grossly belittling the advantages. But this is not his real case. His real case is based on a particular application of absolutist ethics about which it is very difficult to argue and where—I agree with Mr Milne—the opinion of the physiologist is worth no more than that of anyone else. The controversial anti-vivisectionist is exasperating because, knowing that his real reasons do not appeal, rightly or wrongly, to the majority, he tries to reinforce them with other arguments which are seldom fair or candid.

Yours, &c.,

SIELA

On another occasion, one of Keynes's unsigned contributions to *The Nation* had a sequel.

In one of his unsigned notes Keynes commented on the cost of betting.

From The Nation and Athenaeum, *11 July 1925*

WHAT IT COSTS TO BET

A little time ago, when a tax on betting was under discussion, a good many calculations were made as to the average losses of the betting man. What does the 'bookie' take out of him, on the average, to meet expenses and to pay profits? Various estimates were current at the time. A table lately compiled by *The Times* for this season seems to furnish some sort of answer to the question. It shows the position and percentages of the eleven leading jockeys, together with the result of investing £1 on each of their mounts:—

	Won	Lost	Total	£	s.	d.
				£1 stake system		
S. Donoghue	40	237	277	−35	12	0
G. Richards	36	242	278	−36	2	0
C. Elliott	32	168	200	−8	0	5
H. Wragg	30	214	244	−70	12	4
F. Bullock	29	115	144	−11	4	11
T. Weston	28	177	205	−40	11	4
C. Smirke	28	186	214	−21	1	10
R. Jones	27	204	231	−107	19	11
J. Taylor	26	108	134	−10	17	6

	Won	Lost.	Total	£1 stake system £ s. d.
R. Perryman	23	170	193	−33 15 10
V. Smyth	20	110	130	−20 16 10

If the results be aggregated and averaged the result shows a loss of 17·7 per cent of the stake. If this is, as it appears to be, a fair sample, it means that whenever a member of the public puts £1 on, 3s. 6d., on the average, goes to the bookmaker.

How does this strike the reader? Does it seem to him cheap or expensive? However it may strike him, a little mathematics is enough to show that anyone who operates with this percentage of charges against him is practically certain to lose, even in the comparatively short run, unless we suppose some special element of exceptional skill. Indeed, if people were sensible, surely it ought to be a prohibitive charge. Monte Carlo charges 3 per cent, yet succeeds in ruining its votaries without any undue delay. The bookmakers, it seems, charge a commission for their services six times as heavy as the Casino.

On 17 October he returned to the subject.

From The Nation and Athenaeum, *17 October 1925*

WHAT IT COSTS TO BET

In *The Nation* of July 11th we commented on a table published by *The Times* which showed the results of investing £1 on each of the mounts of the eleven leading jockeys. This table summarised the result of betting £1 on 2,250 occasions, and showed an average loss of 17·7 per cent of the stake, i.e. about 3s. 6d. in the £. The season is now farther advanced, and it is possible to give similar figures, as follows, summarising the result of betting £1 on twelve jockeys on 4,514 occasions, namely, a loss of £952:–

Jockey	Won	Lost	Total	£	s.	d.
				£1 stake system		
G. Richards	83	454	537	−67	18	11
C. Elliott	69	305	374	−8	10	3
H. Wragg	66	406	472	−135	13	11
S. Donoghue	59	350	409	−62	18	6
T. Weston	58	351	409	−91	6	3
C. Smirke	55	373	428	−121	4	3
F. Bullock	53	223	276	−36	3	6
R. Perryman	46	354	400	−64	19	4
R. Jones	45	367	412	−160	18	6
H. Jelliss	41	260	301	−68	6	8
J. Taylor	40	197	237	−51	12	6
J. Leach	39	220	259	−83	3	7
			4,514	952	16	2

This works out rather worse for the public than before, the loss averaging 21 per cent of the stake, so that out of every £1 which the public stakes, 4s. 3d. goes to the bookmaker.

P.S. In the week ending Oct. 3rd (next subsequent to the period covered by the above table), the loss would have been £69 on 168 stakes. Thus, as the season draws to an end, the bookmakers seem to become more rapacious—for the above represents an average loss of 8s. 9d. for every £1 staked.

Later, he had a chance to return to this and other issues, for on 10 October 1932 Edward Bridges, secretary to the Royal Commission on Lotteries and Betting, approached Keynes and asked if he would be prepared to give evidence as a person 'with experience of economic and financial questions'. His evidence could include the ground covered by the Commission's terms of reference—'to enquire into the existing law and the practice thereunder relating to lotteries, betting, gambling and cognate matters, and to report what changes, if any are desirable and practical'—'and, in particular, on such issues as the extent to which expenditure on lotteries and betting is detrimental to the economic welfare or financial position of the country'. Keynes, admitting that he had 'little positive to say on the matter' agreed to appear.

From the Royal Commission on Lotteries and Betting, Minutes of Evidence

ROYAL COMMISSION
ON
LOTTERIES AND BETTING

TWENTIETH DAY
Thursday, 15th December, 1932

Present: The Rt Hon. Sir Sydney Rowlatt, K.C.S.I. (*Chairman*)

The Lady Emmott
The Rt Hon. Sir F. S. Jackson,
   G.C.S.I., G.C.I.E.
Mr R. F. Graham-Campbell
Mr W. L. Hichens
Sir James Leishman

Mr A. Maitland, K.C.
Sir David Owen
Mr A. Shaw
Sir Sydney Skinner
Mrs J. L. Stocks
Mr E. E. Bridges, M.C.
   (*Secretary*)
Mr A. Johnston
   (*Assistant Secretary*)

Mr J. M. Keynes, C.B., called and examined

Statement of evidence submitted by Mr Keynes

1. I speak as an economist, not as a moralist, assuming that there exists a taste which people insist on gratifying, and that complete prohibition has been deemed either undesirable or impracticable.

2. On this premise, the object should be to furnish conditions for the gratification of this taste, which are of such a character that they are (1) fair and honest; (2) not subject to a ruinous percentage deduction for expenses or profits; (3) on a scale and with a frequency which minimise the temptation to people to ruin themselves.

3. As regards (1) above, putting on one side the question of fraud, it is in the public interest that opportunities for gambling should be (*a*) of a kind which does not mean a large waste of money in expenses and (*b*) where there is no pretence of skill.

4. Where there is a pretence of skill, it is likely that unfairness will creep in in some way or another, and also the attempt to acquire skill or to simulate the exercise of skill will cause gambling to occupy people's minds to an extent which is seriously detrimental to their other work. For this reason, lotteries or sweepstakes, for example, have much less bad indirect results than horse racing or Stock Exchange gambling.

5. The question of the percentage deduction is largely bound up with rapidity of turnover. For example Monte Carlo's 3 per cent may appear to compare favourably with the 20 per cent or whatever it is that the bookmakers take, whereas owing to the rapidity of turnover of the former, it is in fact far more certainly disastrous to the gambler. Thus nothing is more important than that facilities for gambling should be of an occasional rather than habitual character and should be in the nature of allowing people to have occasional flutters rather than to be perpetually occupied in this way. For example, a man who puts something on the Derby each year and limits himself entirely to that, is most unlikely to be ruined compared with a man who sits in a tote club all and every afternoon. From this point of view betting on the course, or periodic large-scale lotteries or sweepstakes are far preferable to credit betting off the course, tote clubs, or continuous greyhound racing.

6. In my judgment the ideal plan would be a weekly state lottery, less 10 per cent, or 15 per cent at the outside, for the benefit of taxation; all the expenses to be paid by the Sunday papers in return for getting for publication each Sunday a list of the winning tickets. Incidentally this might prove quite a powerful instrument of taxation. I should suppose that it might be worth as much as £10,000,000 a year to the Treasury. It would then be practicable to treat other gambling practices with greater strictness.

7. I consider that it is of considerable importance that gambling should be associated with amusement or with frivolous matters of no great significance. English racecourses for the British public are a vastly better amusement than Wall Street for Americans. The fact that grass won't grow in that country has led to the whole of its industry becoming a mere by-product of a casino. We have, in truth, much to bless our racecourses for.

8. To sum up, gambling should be cheap, fair, frivolous and on a small scale if its evil economic results are to be reduced to a minimum, and the fun and mild excitement to be maximised. I think it would add to the cheerfulness of life if practically everyone in the country was to wake up each Sunday morning stretching out for the Sunday paper with just a possibility that they had won a small fortune. It is agreeable to be habitually in the state of imagining all sorts of things are possible.

7820 (CHAIRMAN) *Mr Keynes, you have been good enough to give us a statement. I think what we really want to ascertain is whether, as an economist in the first place, you can help us as to the bearing of the habit of betting and gambling on national prosperity. Most of us think that betting and gambling certainly cannot increase national prosperity?* It depends upon whether enjoyment is part of national prosperity. Betting is certainly not a form of production.

7821 *Does it make any difference whether a man transfers his money to somebody else by losing a bet to him, or whether he transfers it to somebody else by rewarding him for some unproductive service?* The mere change of money from one hand to another is a matter of indifference, except in so far as it alters unfavourably, in all probability, the distribution of wealth; but the evils of betting, as I see them, are that it is a form of extravagance which may be carried to lengths far beyond what the individual can afford. On the other side, in practice it is not merely handing money from one person to another, because very great expense is involved. Regarded from that point of view, the only part which is a mere transfer is the profits of the bookmaking fraternity which is a comparatively small proportion of the total loss involved.

7822 *Can you help us as to how far betting is a habit of doing something foolish, if you like, but venial, and how far it is a social evil, causing public mischief. I do not know whether any statistics that you have had occasion to study give any help upon that?* I have never been able to find any reliable statistics bearing upon that matter. But it seems to me that it is, for most people who indulge in it, when it is done in moderation, a form of enjoyment, just as other people like a glass of wine or go to the opera. It is futile to condemn it by criteria which would apply equally to the opera or to any other form of enjoyment. The objection to it is that it is of the nature of a drug, and that it may easily, almost without the will of the man doing it, be carried beyond reasonable lengths, into an uncontrollable indulgence. It is particularly liable to do so, because it is very difficult for the man to calculate how much it is really costing him; it is all in and out. As to many of one's pleasures which one thinks worth while, at any rate one knows what they cost one, and that is a certain check. In the case of betting it is very much more difficult for a man to know that, and he always hopes he will win. Therefore, he does not look upon it as the extravagance that it is.

7823 *We recognise, of course, that betting, moderately indulged in, may give some pleasure, like going to the opera or anything else. But, over and above that, it brings serious evils. But it is difficult to find out the extent of the latter?* I should have thought the evil was undoubted; but it seems to me that the way to deal with it is not to attempt futile prohibition. After all, the laws of this country have discriminated against betting for a great many years with no signal success. It seems to me that the wise thing to do is to see that the facilities for it should be so fenced round that the enjoyment is at a maximum and the social evils are at a minimum.

7824 *I wish we could have your assistance in working out the details of that general principle?* I suggest that there are certain criteria. One is that it should be fair and honest. It is much more likely to be that, if there is no pretence to an element of skill, because the pretence of that would enable some people to be sharp at the expense of their neighbours.

7825 *Would you approve of newspaper competitions having no skill at all?* I think the law is precisely wrong at present. If there is no element of skill I see no harm in them, but if you waste people's time by fictitious pretence of skill, you are doing a much greater economic evil.

7826 *The* summum bonum *would be that you send in your coupons and try for the prize?* Yes, and most countries recognise that; in most countries there are state lotteries.

7827 *Do you approve of state lotteries?* It seems to me unquestionable that that is the best form. The expenses are at a minimum; the profits accrue to the state; there is no waste of time for anybody, and it lies within the power of the state to make the frequency of them not too great.

7828 *You suggest having them once a week?* Yes, I think that would be about right.

7829 *There would almost have to be a Ministry of Betting to run them?* It is a mere routine. In most Latin countries the greater part of the population participate in weekly lotteries, I think.

7830 *And rather live on the hope of it?* I think it is a cheering thing for the poorer members of the community to believe that there is at least a possibility of their getting a legacy, so to speak, I see no harm in that, but what I do see harm in is something which is not fair and honest, which is extravagant in its expenses, which enables a man to be at it every day of his life, wasting time, with a rapidity of turnover which ensures his ruin over almost any period. That seems to me to be the evil of it: in fact, I think that the existing state of affairs in this country is what we may call the *summum malum*.

7831 *You are entirely in favour of lotteries as against betting?* Yes; I think there would be great difficulties in prohibiting betting, but it seems to me that betting on the course is very much better than betting off the course.

7832 *In betting on the course you put your money on and see the horses run. There is something in that?* You have some fresh air and exercise, and you cannot be at it perpetually. It is the man who has something on practically every race that is run in the country from the beginning of the season to the end of the season who is suffering the maximum of injury and getting the minimum of enjoyment. I should like it to be an occasional flutter, such as most human beings indulge in from time to time. Sweepstakes which approximate to lotteries are of the kind that I should approve. If you were to allow sweepstakes in newspapers without any restriction you would have far too many of them. That is why I believe that a state monopoly is the only way of reducing it to right dimensions. The economic evils are at a minimum, if you put games of pure chance in the hands of the state and limit the opportunities somewhat strictly; and then, as regards betting, control betting on the course, but put great obstacles in the way of other forms of betting.

7833 (LADY EMMOTT) *Have you anything to say about greyhound racing as compared with horse racing with regard to its advantages or disadvantages?* The difference of animal does not seem to me to be important. I am not an expert on greyhound racing, but I gather that it is worked in this country to-day as a means of providing much more continuous opportunities for betting. I consider that evil, because I attach great importance to the evil of the rate of turnover. If you take Monte Carlo as a type of the most dangerous form of gambling, it is dangerous and disastrous to the individual because of the rapidity of the turnover. You can have a *coup* every two minutes as long as the rooms are open. At the opposite pole to that is the man who puts something on the Derby every year and otherwise has nothing to do with betting. Greyhound racing in its modern form is an attempt, as far as I can understand it, to approximate to the Monte Carlo rapidity of turnover, with the pretence of a race going on.

7835 *In a tote club, even more than on a greyhound racing track?* Yes; the tote clubs seem to me to be most evil institutions, because they infringe my criteria of the dangerous forms: a great deal goes in expenses; the rapidity of the turnover and the continuity of it are very dangerous; and I should have supposed that for any normal being the element of fun was almost at a minimum.

7835 (MR HICHENS) *Of course, state lotteries were legally practised in this country at one time?* A long time ago, I believe, yes.

7836 *Do you happen to know about the circumstances which led to their being abolished?* No, I do not.

7837 *That might throw some light upon the question?* Yes. For many years various forms of state lotteries were very much taken as a matter of course in the country. I am speaking without knowledge, but I should have expected that their suppression was an outcome of Puritanism. In this country the effort has always been to make gambling difficult or impossible. State lotteries is one of the easiest things for the law to prohibit.

7838 *The interest in the state lotteries did diminish; that is to say, the return from state lotteries became less?* I am not acquainted with the history of them.

7839 *We have had a great deal of evidence from social workers and social bodies of one kind and another, expressing to us very strongly the view that betting and gambling are the biggest social evils of the day. Their view is that it should not in any way be encouraged by the Government. It may be that it is the business of the Government to prevent certain of its evils and to minimise it; but they object very strongly to the Government taking a hand in the game, so to speak?* If that view is taken, it is perfectly open to the forces of the state to make all forms of betting illegal, but to think that you will somehow wash your hands of the matter and escape responsibility by not having a state lottery but, in fact, winking at a vast amount of betting and gambling, seems to me the worst hypocrisy.

7840 *If you take the analogy of drink, there are some people who say that the best way of controlling it would be to have state-owned publichouses?* I am strongly of the opinion, on the same kind of ground.

7841 (MR MAITLAND) *Mr Keynes, you think that newspaper competitions in which there is an element of skill are noxious?* There are competitions in which there is a genuine element of skill, such as 'Caliban's' problems in *The New Statesman and Nation*, in which the prizes are of negligible value, and which in fact are simply a game of skill. But I was referring to those competitions which have been widespread in the cheaper papers where the law is dodged by the pretence of skill, where in fact there is no skill but purely an element of chance. The game is either so easy that anybody can do it, and the first envelope that is opened gets the prize, or else there are a vast number of solutions, each of which is equally good, and it is a pure matter of chance whether the person purporting to exercise skill happens to fix on the same solution as the editor of the paper.

7842 *It has been suggested to us that those people who apply their leisure in solving these problems are better occupied than they might have been if they had not got them to apply their minds to. You do not seem to agree with that?* It is not a genuine exercise of skill.

7843 *You assume that if they had not got such newspaper competitions to solve they would be better occupied in something else?* I have no idea; I do not wish to make games of patience illegal.

7844 *If there were a genuine element of skill or interest of some kind, your objection would disappear?* I approve of the element of skill where the point is the enjoyment of exercising the skill; but where you get domestic servants puzzling over silly crossword puzzles, not because they enjoy doing it at all, but because they believe that by that means they will obtain a money prize, that I think is a bad way of spending time.

403

7845 (MRS STOCKS) *Mr Keynes, I gather from what you have said that you would be prepared to add to your first paragraph, in which you say 'there exists a taste for betting and gambling which people insist on gratifying and that complete prohibition has been deemed either undesirable or impracticable': you regard betting and gambling as a form of gratification, which has considerable social dangers and may give rise to abuses?* Yes, I should.

7846 *If you were to add to that and then go to paragraph 2, it seems to me there is somewhat of a non sequitur. If you think that an excess of gambling is likely to be dangerous, why are you so keen that there should not be a ruinous percentage or deduction for expenses or profit. Why not have a ruinous percentage?* The reason I consider that gambling is possibly socially injurious, is because of the large amount of money people will lose. If people could attend race meetings and have the enjoyment of them and, on the balance of things, it costs them very little, I should approve of it much more than if, whenever a man went to a race meeting, he was almost inevitably tempted into spending and losing far more money than he could afford.

7847 *Surely, the more you stand to gain, the more you are tempted to gamble?* I doubt whether experience bears that out. There is an enormous amount of gambling subject to a contrary condition. But it seems to me that the evil of it largely is the waste of money. Take the man who drinks: In the case of drink the great evil is not emptying the glass into your mouth, but the fact that it may injure your health and your purse. If it did neither, one would welcome the emptying of the glass into the mouth.

7848 *More expensive drinking is the result of some part of the profit being taken into taxation and it has led to less drinking. Why should not more expensive gambling lead to less gambling?* Because the taxation does not diminish the evil in any way; it may even accentuate it, because it makes it more damaging to the pocket.

7849 *There has been much less drinking because it is more expensive?* Your analogy would be that of putting poison into the drink; that beer should only be allowed to be brewed if it is bad beer?

7850 *That would be more like Prohibition, but it is an analogous position. It is an increased degree of the same medicine which you give the drinker when he takes the drink?* It all depends on whether you think the evil of gambling is the psychological one of hoping to obtain money that you have not properly earned, or whether the evil consists in the fact that the indulgence of this hope will cause you to lose a great deal of money. I consider it the second. If you consider it the first then, I think, your argument is valid.

7851 *What would you say if, instead of carrying on your paragraph 1, as you have carried it on, it were carried on in this way: 'Therefore, the gambling industry must be so organised that it is not to any individual's interest to stimulate a taste for gambling'?* Except the Chancellor of the Exchequer.

7852 *Except the Chancellor of the Exchequer or somebody representing the popular attitude?* Yes.

7853 *So that your gambling industry is in the position of the Russian vodka monopoly. The state says: 'We will give them the vodka; at the same time we will not give them pleasant places in which to drink it'?* I would agree to that in general, but I would not go as far as that. I think in all legislation against tastes, the liberty of the subject has a place. I think it would be oppressive to prohibit all forms of betting and all forms of wagering money upon a race, even if some sort of state lotteries were also supplied.

7854 *But is not there a considerable difference between the liberty of the subject to bet and the liberty of the subject to make money by encouraging other people to bet?* I think there is some difference there, yes.

7855 *So that the liberty of the subject would not necessarily be infringed in your sense if it were possible to cut out the private profit-making interest in the gambling industry?* I think that would be all to the good.

7856 *It has been put to us by one of our witnesses who has an interest in a tote club that there is in effect a sort of fixed gambling fund, and the implication of this gambling fund theory was that if you encourage people to gamble in one way they will gamble less in another way. That struck some of us as essentially false, and it seems to me there is something of the same sort of fallacy in your suggestion, that if you have a state lottery, it will be practicable to treat other gambling practices with greater strictness. It seems to me that if you have one sort of gambling, the tendency is to increase gambling all round by a kind of mass suggestion?* I should not have thought so, but I think I ought to say 'more reasonable' instead of 'practicable'. If you had state lotteries, it seems to me that newspaper competitions could be prohibited, and it would become much less oppressive to limit the opportunities for betting on sporting events to those who were actually present at those events.

7857 *Would it not work both ways. Would not the whole idea of betting attain such a sanction that people would come and point out to you the absurdity of saying they must bet in one way and must not bet in another?* Is not that the whole point: that one wants to provide comparatively harmless opportunities. I do not see why the existence of a state lottery should make me more inclined to bet on horses than before there was a state lottery. The notion that this is a new idea that you put into people's heads would be too innocent. The vast majority of the population indulge in greater or lesser degree in some form or another of gambling and betting.

7858 *Do we not know of hundreds of people who have had tickets in the Irish Sweepstake who were never conscious of the unsatisfied sort of urge to buy*

405

sweepstake tickets before? Yes, I think that is true. If you had a state lottery people would take tickets who do not take them at present, or for various reasons, go in for betting on horses, but I do not think that would be a great evil.

7859 *Except that it might really increase the betting habit?* Yes, but amongst those people who are not excessively indulging in it. The evil of betting, to my mind, is in those cases where it acts as a drug. For the healthy person who is not at all likely to overdo it, I do not think it is an evil.

7860 *In paragraph 7 you take another analogy, and you point out that 'English racecourses for the British public are a vastly better amusement than Wall Street for Americans.' But do the two types of betting compete at all? The vast mass of betting (at least, the great growth in betting and gambling) has been among the wage-earning classes. The Stock Exchange transactions have never touched them, have they?* Not in this country, but in America they have. I should say that in the boom in America Wall Street occupied much the same sort of position as betting on horses in this country.

7861 *Supposing betting was by some means effectively damped down, is there any machinery by which the ordinary wage-earner could get into industrial betting?* No; I do not think it would be likely in this country, because the organisation of our Stock Exchange makes that unlikely. I was really only quoting this as an example of worse forms of betting than horse racing, and I was also quoting it in illustration of my point that it is much better that gambling should be associated with frivolous matters of no great significance rather than be bound up with the industry and trade of the country.

7862 *Or with the health and possibly death of your relative?* Yes, gambling should be frivolous if it is to be healthy.

7863 *You say in your last sentence: 'It is agreeable to be habitually in the state of imagining all sorts of things as possible.' You have suggested that one economic objection to gambling is that it assists in the unequal distribution of wealth; a maldistribution of wealth, because lotteries collect small sums from many people and transfer them to one or two people. Is not there another possible economic evil, that it all tends to emphasise a general expectation of the fortuitous distribution of wealth?* I see no evil in that. It would be much fairer than the present system if fortunes were distributed by lot.

7864 *It might be fairer, but what reflex effect would it have upon productivity?* I should not have thought it would have any effect.

7865 *You mean that everybody would devote themselves to the common weal without any expectation of their income being related to their services?* It is depressing for an individual to look forward to a life of poverty without the slightest possibility of any amelioration in it. If everybody, for quite a small deduction from their wages, always had just the possibility of something turning up, I see no evil in it.

7866 *That has been put by other witnesses, who have put it more bluntly and said that betting preserves us from Bolshevism?* That would be something.

7867 *The danger is summed up, to my mind, in a poster which appeared in Manchester some time ago, and which said: 'Earn a year's wages tonight.' It would be very nice to earn a year's wages to-night; but a continual expectation that you might earn a year's wages to-night might have a certain damping effect upon the effort you made to earn the year's wages in the ordinary way, might it not?* It would be only a faint expectation.

7868 *When you meet people who hold sweepstake tickets, it is more than an expectation. It is a kind of excited certainty?* I think with a weekly lottery people would become milder in their expectations than that. They might indeed work harder in order to be able to afford more tickets.

7869 *On the other hand, there is the possibility that they will always hope that they are going to earn a year's wages next week?* I should have thought there would be the additional attractive object on which to spend one's wages, and that might be an additional stimulus to work.

7870 (SIR SYDNEY SKINNER) *I understand, Mr Keynes, that you consider it is almost impossible to eradicate betting?* I do not know that it would be absolutely impracticable from the legal point of view, but I think the difficulty is that total prohibition is felt to be oppressive, and partial prohibition is impracticable. That is the dilemma in which the law has always been placed in this country.

7871 *Would you be in favour of control?* I should want to hear details of the form of control proposed. As I have already said my quite uninstructed impulse is to favour control to the point of prohibition of off course betting, and to allow reasonable facilities for on the course betting.

7872 *Of course you are aware that there is a very large body of public opinion which does not want to recognise betting or to have anything to do with it; as a matter of fact certain people want to think that it does not exist?* I believe there are such people.

7873 *And you will have that view put forward, if there is any talk of control. It is a very large body of public opinion, is it not?* I do not know how large it is. It seems to me to be a survival of the old legalistic view of a man's conscience; that one's duty was to have a legal case for one's own self-justification. With that view I have no sympathy. The other view, with which I sympathise more, is that in one's behaviour one ought to consider the total effect of one's action on the situation taken as a whole. The kind of opinion you are mentioning is based upon the first criterion of one's duty, and I think that is a narrower view of one's duty than the other view.

407

7874 *You would consider that that is somewhat puritanical, would you?* It has been associated with puritan views, but I do not see any necessary connection between the two. It is a state of mind which arises out of a man considering his own duty very much in isolation from what happens to his fellows. He is thinking of himself, so to speak, as coming on trial as to whether he is free from personal responsibility. 'I did not do it.' That seems to me a poor defence. (MRS STOCKS) *Pontius Pilate, in fact.*

7875 (SIR SYDNEY SKINNER) *Many of us are very much exercised, I think, over this question of control. Could you, in your wisdom, tell us how to control street betting?* I much doubt if partial control of off the course betting is feasible. I should have thought that complete prohibition of that class of betting was easier; but I have no practical experience to help me in answering your question.

7876 *If it is ineradicable, what control are you going to put in place of it?* If it is ineradicable, you can do nothing.

7877 *But control it?* You are putting to me that you have had evidence that it is difficult or impossible to control it. I must take that from you. If so, there is nothing to be done. But I was under the impression that a good deal of the difficulty arose out of the vagueness of the point at which the law draws the line at present, and that if we were prepared to go so far as to prohibit off the course betting, it would be easier to handle it than it is at present with the rather vague line drawn between what is lawful and what is unlawful.

7878 (CHAIRMAN) *It is quite clear that it is unlawful to bet in the street?* But the difficulty always comes that the distinction between the street and some neighbouring places is so very arbitrary that it carries no force of conviction to the public. The idea that you must not bet on horse races unless you go to a race meeting is a perfectly clear idea.

7879 (SIR DAVID OWEN) *I do not quite know myself what an economist is. What is his function? Is it to add to the cheerfulness and frivolity of life?* My object, I think, in this was to promote clear thinking on these matters.

7880 *That is an economist's function, is it?* It is the function of the economist, among other things.

7881 *I thought an economist's function was to deal with concrete facts and statistics in order to prove things. I was interested in your statement that most human beings indulge in a flutter from time to time. Have you any statistics to prove that, or is it just a pure personal opinion?* I have not taken a census on the matter.

7882 *I should say you are a humorist. 'All the expenses to be paid by the Sunday paper.' 'Everyone in the country waking up on Sunday morning stretching out for the Sunday paper.' What economic factor underlies that suggestion?* You would have to have some means of publication, and this would be a means whereby the profits of the state would be intact, without the subtraction of the expenses.

7883 *But why Sunday papers?* I was taking that partly from Continental analogy. It is a thing that happens once a week there.

7884 *That is the weekly state lottery. You have already said that you do not know about the history of state lotteries?* I am not a student of the history of State lotteries in this country.

7885 *We have had evidence that there are very serious reasons for the discontinuance of state lotteries.*

7886 (SIR JAMES LEISHMAN) *Mr Keynes, I am not quite sure whether you would support or oppose the prohibition of betting off the course?* As I say, I have not the knowledge to say whether it is practicable or not. I have expressed the opinion, but I may have expressed it without sufficient warrant, that it would be easier to have a clear-cut prohibition of all off the course betting than to have the present rather complicated system.

7887 *We have been told that there is very much more betting off the course than on the course?* Yes. I have seen statistics which show that on the course betting is not more than 10 to 20 per cent of the total.

7888 *I wondered if you thought it would be practicable in any scheme dealing with this rather complicated and difficult question simply to prohibit all off the course betting?* As I say, that is not a matter upon which my knowledge entitles me to give a confident opinion.

7889 (MR SHAW) *Would you not think that that would be legislation of a most repressive character?* I said that that element came in and ought to be considered, but that if certain other facilities were being given I should consider it less oppressive than otherwise.

7890 (SIR JAMES LEISHMAN) *With regard to the weekly lottery, might I ask, with great respect, if that was a seriously thought out proposal, or was put up just as a cock-shy?* There are really two observations about that in my heads of evidence. I instance the lottery first of all as a good example of a form of gambling which reduces certain evils attendant upon gambling to a minimum. If you are going to have gambling, it seems to me that that is the least disadvantageous form of it. The further question is, whether one would positively favour such a thing. There I am just expressing a personal opinion, and it may be that I have gone beyond my province in expressing a personal opinion of that sort. I see no evil, and some benefits, in mild excitement of that kind, if suitably hedged round. But I would rather like to separate that from the way in which I introduced it, which was an example of a form of gambling which was relatively free of certain evils of extravagance, and so on, that I had been outlining.

7891 *Do you think that you would find £100,000,000 per annum for these weekly sweepstakes, out of which the state would take 10 per cent, or £10,000,000?* In advance of experience one is only guessing. I believe that the amounts which have been obtained in foreign countries are substantial, relatively to the national income. I was partly guided to this figure by the estimates which have been made of horse-race betting, which estimates are no doubt familiar to you. The order of magnitude of those suggest that £100,000,000 turnover for this was not putting it abnormally high.

7892 *Provided that the money at present going in horse-racing, either on or off the course, is diverted to the weekly sweepstake?* Yes.

7893 *That is a fairly large assumption, is it not?* No, because I was offering this as an alternative; not as an addition to the existing off the course betting. I agree with your suggestion that the figure would have to be smaller if the lottery was not in substitution for existing forms of betting.

7894 *I am a little puzzled about your remark that grass does not grow in America?* I believe it is the case that it is impossible, owing to the nature of the climate, to have a racecourse of the English type in America, with all the year round grass of that kind.

7895 *With regard to this dreamland of yours, do you think it is a good thing to lull people into these false hopes, having regard to the troublous times we are living in?* Why is it false? Some of them will win prizes.

7896 *I would have thought you would have been rather inclined to say: ' Your chances are five million to one against. Do not touch this thing.' You are only conjuring up disappointment and irritation in people's minds?* The richer classes have investments which they always hope will go up in value. It very seldom happens. But it seems to me that the feeling that there is this possibility of improvement is, on the whole, one which gives more pleasure than pain.

7897 (SIR F. S. JACKSON) *It has been estimated, I believe, that there is a turnover of £200,000,000 involved in betting and gambling in one way and another?* Yes. I have seen even higher figures.

7898 *As an economist, would you say that that is economically good or bad for the country?* A great deal depends upon the expense involved. I gathered, from certain statistics that I saw, that the gross proportion accruing to bookmakers might be nearly 20 per cent, perhaps not quite as much as that. On that basis, the gross losses of the public on a turnover of somewhat over £200,000,000 might be of the order of £40,000,000; it would certainly be more than £20,000,000. On the other hand, a bookmaker's profits are estimated at a very much lower figure than that. I think I saw a figure of £2,000,000 to £4,000,000 as the sort of amount they might be. Therefore, the actual expense might easily be of the order of £30,000,000 a year, and that is a pure economic waste.

7899 *Economically, in your view, it is bad for the country; I do not want to go into the morals of the thing?* Yes. Again, I must interpose that one has to set against that the amount of enjoyment, if you think there is enjoyment; or, if you think there is moral evil, add the moral evil to the expense. If you think there is moral evil, you have lost both ways. You have expended £30,000,000 of the nation's income on moral evil.

7900 (MR MAITLAND) *I do not quite follow why you say that £30,000,000 of expenditure is wasted. Is it not £30,000,000 handed from a certain section of the community to another; the money is still there in circulation?* Your argument would imply that no form of expenditure was wasteful.

7901 *I am asking you as an expert economist to explain why?* It is a very difficult question to answer briefly.

7902 (CHAIRMAN) *The effort represented by the money is wasted effort?* If you assume normal conditions in which there is normal employment, then I should say it is pure waste, because there is a reasonable expectation that the resources of the country, if not employed in this way, will be employed in some other way. If you are dealing with an abnormal condition where there is unemployment, the answer is much more uncertain.

7903 (SIR F. S. JACKSON) *If you wanted completely to demonstrate that gambling and betting was a terrible social evil, you could prove that it was a real economic disaster to a country to have gambling or betting to the extent to which it is supposed to be going on in this particular country?* You cannot really answer that question without deciding whether it is a moral evil or not, and how great a moral evil. There are all kinds of things which cost £30,000,000 a year for the nation as a whole, and the mere fact that they cost £30,000,000 proves nothing.

7904 (MR SHAW) *If we had a roulette table here, and £100 passed between the members of the Commission, would that be wasted?* The only sum that would be wasted would be the cost of the roulette board and the wages of the croupier. (MR MAITLAND) *But the man who sold the roulette board would have the £5, if it was sold for £5.* (MRS STOCKS) *And you would have to prove that each member of the Commission would handle the money as wisely as every other member when he got it.*

7905 (SIR DAVID OWEN) *We have been told that a large section of the so-called working class people in many districts, in London and other places, spend 5s. or 6s. a week out of a small wage on betting. They have 5s. or 6s. a week less to spend, and with people with that sort of income, as you know, there is no surplus; the money would be spent, in the ordinary course, on the necessities of life. Am I right in assuming that that is uneconomic in the country's interest, in your opinion?* Yes.

7906 *That money, although it is spent by somebody who has no surplus, is not an economic advantage to the country, is it?* No. I think it is a great evil.

7907 (MR HICHENS) *It has been put to us that every man is benefited by having a certain amount of amusement in this world, that it must not be purely a drab existence, and that if his amusement consists in putting so much on a horse or a dog, and the amusement of others consists in going to a cinema, you cannot say that the one is wasted any more than the other?* No; that is the point which I have been trying to bring out.

7908 (SIR SYDNEY SKINNER) *Would you also take into consideration not only the amusement side of it, but the appalling waste of time attached to it?* I should. Therefore, I attach importance in so far as it can be done, to providing that such gambling as takes place should waste as little time as possible, should be as inexpensive as possible, and should expose people to as little temptation as possible, not to spend more of their money than they can afford.

7909 *It is not only their own money sometimes?* No.

7910 (CHAIRMAN) *At the same time it will afford them a little amusement?* Yes. *On that happy note, I think we may say Good-bye. Thank you very much for coming, Mr Keynes.*

The witness withdrew.

Keynes's evidence was the subject of press comment. In two cases he answered the comment. The first came in reply to a letter from Professor John Murphy of Manchester University which appeared in *The Manchester Guardian* for 17 December. Professor Murphy suggested that Keynes had made a mistake in psychology in arguing that betting was one of the pleasures of the poor, for it was certainly the case that the costs of losing to the poor were so high that the slight chance of winning were overwhelmed. Keynes replied.

To the Editor of The Manchester Guardian, *17 December 1932*

Sir,

I wish that Professor Murphy had been able to see the whole of my evidence before the Royal Commission on Betting. I gave it subject to the hypothesis that there exists a taste which people insist on gratifying and that complete prohibition has been deemed either undesirable or impracticable. On this premise I endeavoured to make suggestions which would minimise the evils of gambling and the economic waste to the community as a whole, while at the same time maximising such legitimate enjoyment as it can provide.

I got into trouble with some members of the Commission partly because I recommended state lotteries and partly because I refused to deny that some permissible enjoyment could be derived from gambling under favourable conditions. But I am far from dissenting from what Professor Murphy says. Indeed, I shall be surprised if the Commission, in fact, recommend such drastic restrictions on the opportunities for gambling as I was prepared to support. For I proposed the total prohibition of off-course betting, of tote clubs, of continuous greyhound-racing, and of any form of lottery except under the auspices of the state.

I believe that the greatest obstacle in the way of a reasonable control of gambling facilities is the extremism of the reformers, doubtless based, excusably enough, on the strength of their feelings. But in denying any legitimate field whatever for the gambling propensities of man, for his enjoyment in taking a chance, and for the pleasurable anticipation of the possibility of a windfall, they run so counter to the instincts of the ordinary man as to ensure their own defeat.

Yours, &c.,

J. M. KEYNES

A week later, *The Economist* in one of its 'Notes of the Week' also discussed Keynes's evidence and took issue with Keynes's approach to the problem and his presumption that 'gambling makes for happiness'. Keynes replied.

To the Editor of The Economist, *27 December 1932*

Sir,

I'd be curious to know if the writer of the note on my recent evidence before the Betting Commission had read either the text of my evidence or my own summary of it in a letter to *The Manchester Guardian*. For he has been rash if he has relied for a balanced report of what I said on a Press *résumé* primarily prepared for papers belonging to groups which make their profits out of the provision of off-course betting news. At any rate, the reporters suppressed the passages in which I recommended, amongst other things, the total prohibition of off-course betting.

One may, it seems, make money out of facilitating off-course betting, which is socially the most disastrous form of gambling. That, as you express it, is being 'a servant of the public'. But one must not say that taking a chance is capable, in favourable circumstances, of adding to enjoyment, even if one couples this with drastic proposals for reducing the admitted evils to a minimum! To keep a public-house involves no loss of virtue. We save our hard words for the wretch who has the cynicism to declare that an occasional glass of beer may do a man good!

Yours, &c.,
J. M. KEYNES

[We confess that when we wrote our Note we had not seen the full text of Mr Keynes evidence, but we were not dealing in any general way with his views on the specific reform of the Betting Laws—merely with his reported *obiter dicta* on the psychological effect of financial risk-taking. If these were misleading, and if we misinterpreted the sense of his evidence as a whole, we owe him our apologies.—ED. *Econ.*]

Finally, we conclude on a domestic, Cambridge, note with two letters and a review.

The first letter followed a series of votes on the position of women in the University. On 6 December 1919, in response to a series of memorials, the University appointed a Syndicate to consider the relation of women students to the University. The Syndicate was unable to issue an agreed report and instead came up with two alternative schemes. The first scheme proposed to admit women to full membership of the University, subject to very few special restrictions. The second scheme suggested an alternative: that of a separate University for women with Newnham and Girton Colleges forming a nucleus. The reports of the Syndicate were discussed in the autumn of 1920 before voting took place. On 8 December a vote took place on the first scheme: it failed to pass with 712 in favour and 904 against. On 12 February 1921 a vote took place on the second scheme: it also failed with 50 in favour and 104 against. In its issue of 18 February, *The Cambridge Review* commented on the results, thus continuing the controversy.

To the Editor of The Cambridge Review, *21 February 1921*

Sir,

As you have given the prominence of your front page to a humbugging sort of a communication from an anonymous correspondent about the present position of the Women's question, there are two points which it is desirable to state plainly.

Your correspondent thinks that 'the only genuine grievance of the women' is the withholding of the titular degree. Quite apart from the right to vote in the Senate, it is, in the opinion of most male teachers in the University, a grievance that a woman, however well qualified, should be debarred on the sole ground of sex, from eligibility for University prizes and studentships and from University Lectureships, Readerships and Professorships, which are the reward and encouragement of sound learning. It is also a grievance, for the men teachers in the University as well as for the women, that we should be debarred from electing our women colleagues on Boards of Studies, however useful we may deem the assistance of particular individuals to be. The course of lectures on one of the compulsory subjects for Part II of the Economics Tripos, prescribed this term for members of the University, is being delivered by a Girton lecturer.[1] It is a small point in itself, capable of amendment, that this course should have been advertised to Students in the *Reporter* (p. 515), not in the main body of the lecture list, but in a footnote to a title apparently entered under the name of a male lecturer; but it is disgraceful to the University that this lecturer, however prominent a part

---

[1]   The lecturer in question was Mrs Barbara Wootton.

she may take in the teaching of the University, should be permanently debarred from the emoluments, now provided in part by the state, set aside for this purpose. No proposal can be accepted as a settlement, which does not remove these injustices.

Nor can your correspondent be permitted to suggest that Cambridge residents are weary of the persistence of the advocates of the Women's claims, or that action by the Commission would be improper interference from outside on a domestic matter, when your analysis of last term's vote shows that active University residents were, as a body, in favour of the full claims of Scheme A, that a substantial majority of Professors, Readers, and University Lecturers supported this scheme, and that the body, customarily the most tenacious of the claims of the traditional past, the Heads of Houses, were equally divided. If the Royal Commission consider that action on this question is within their reference, so far from interfering with the just claims of the University to settle its own business, they will be ridding us of the obstructions of the sentimental and ill-informed out-voter, some of whom vote on these questions frivolously, and will be only anticipating the much-needed reform by which a House of Residents will govern us.   Yours, etc.,

J. M. KEYNES

The review was a history of Clare College, Cambridge.

From The Nation and Athenaeum, *17 January 1931*

CLARE COLLEGE

FORBES, MANSFIELD D. (Ed.) *Clare College, 1326–1926.* 2 vols. (Printed for the College at the Cambridge University Press), 1930.

This monument, nearly as large as the court of Clare itself, celebrates, in 750 pages of text 9 by 13 inches and 238 pages of plates, at a rumoured cost of some £6,000, the sexcentenary of the College. It is a remarkable and singular work, as even a cursory glance will show, unexpected in style and content; yet a great success in my judgement, of which one can turn the pages with delight for many hours, deserving fame and circulation beyond that which the piety of Clare men have already accorded it. Certainly those, like myself, of the neighbouring foundation, who have spent much of their lives looking across their back lawn at the demure and exquisite habitation of our elder sister, will find here illumination and instruction to guide and warm the eye of sight and sentiment. They will, too, be glad to be reminded (passing by the attack on King's College made in 1454 with 'guns and all the habiliments of war') of the small exchanges of land and courtesies which have marked from time to time the five hundred years of their propinquity, beginning with the grant in exchange to Clare Hall by Henry VI of 13 King's Parade, which she still possesses, and particularly of Barnabas Oley, who, having secured from King's in 1638 the lease of the Clare river garden (the whole of the meadows across the river facing King's and Clare having belonged to the former College, as is still the case with the Clare 'Backs'), bequeathed a sum to that College as a compensation for any detriment thus caused them and 'as a means to perpetuate Love and amitie betwixt King's College and Clarehall', words which the Provost of King's still recites on Founder's Day. The chapter of this book on Barnabas Oley and his love of building—it was he who as Bursar planned the Court of Clare—and on the College living of Great Gransden which he held and adorned with several fine surviving houses, is an admirable sample of the range and charm of this History.

The seventeenth-century buildings of Clare naturally occupy pride of place. It is remarkable that the raising of so complete and perfect a piece should have been spread over nearly eighty years (1638–1715, the chapel being added so late as 1769), though it was mainly built by an uncle and nephew, Thomas and Robert Grumbold; but much more remarkable—at least to one who knows the building well but uninstructedly—that the characteristic and, one would have thought, inevitable balustrades which surround the court within and without, should be a late addition, having been substituted in 1762 for the battlements of the original design, thus demonstrating that perfection may be a growth of time and leisurely consideration—perhaps, where buildings are concerned, usually so. The photographs, here presented in dozens, of the details and the *ensemble* of Clare, are as fine and comprehensive as have ever been put together; and the series of Clare Bridge at various dates and at all seasons of the year may be particularly mentioned for their serene and cultivated beauty. 'I must be of opinion', as a freshman in the eighteenth century wrote home, 'that a college life, for one of a serious turn and contemplative disposition, is the most delightful situation imaginable. Since my being here I have taken a view of all the colleges, which has been, I think, the pleasantest time I ever spent in my life...I am, however, so singular as to prefer Clare Hall to any of the rest. It is neat beyond description.'

The worthies of Clare are, it must be confessed, for so maidenly a lodging, a motley crowd. They begin and end with two fine nonconformists, Hugh Latimer and Siegfried Sassoon, a poem by the latter opening each of the volumes. Between them there is a long procession. Two College scamps: Robert Greene, 'one of the small band of University men who made possible the development of the Elizabethan drama', who says in his 'Repentance', 'Being at the University of Cambridge I lit amongst wags as lewd as myself with whom I consumed the flower of my youth'; and Dr Dodd, tutor of Stanhope, first Earl of Chesterfield, whom Samuel Johnson's chivalrous humanity could not rescue from the gallows for forgery, but who still had the spirit (why does this book call it 'vulgar gaucherie'?) to seek publication of his comedy 'Sir Roger de Coverley' whilst awaiting execution in Newgate, and was the author of 'Dodd's Beauties of Shakespeare', which first introduced Goethe to

Shakespeare, and 'Dodd on Death' designed 'to be given away by well-disposed persons at funerals', both written at West Ham, thus apostrophised:—

> Dear were thy shades, O, Ham! and dear,
> O, Epping...

Lord Hervey, whose face was 'so finished that neither sickness nor passion could deprive it of colour', Pope's 'Lord Fanny' and 'Sporus',

> That thing of silk,
> That mere white curd of asses' milk...
> Yet let me flap this bug with gilded wings
> This painted child of dirt that stinks and stings,

the personal resemblance to whom of Horace Walpole has been the occasion of scandal. Horace Mann, into whose window Horace Walpole could already toss the first epistles 'of a series amounting to thousands' from across the way in King's. The three great Whig families of Pelham, Townshend, and Cornwallis, who dominated Clare in the eighteenth century; including Thomas Pelham, who beginning appropriately as Earl of Clare had himself created Duke of Newcastle-upon-Tyne, and then, to make sure of being Newcastle sole and *tout court*, Duke of Newcastle-under-Lyme as well; Charles Townshend, Chancellor of the Exchequer; and the Marquis Cornwallis, Commander-in-Chief in America and Governor-General of India. The Rev. Mr Thomas Seaton, by whose will the Vice-Chancellor, the Master of Clare, and the Greek Professor award a prize for a poem which shall enlarge on 'one or other of the Perfections or Attributes of the Supreme Being' annually for ever 'till the subject is exhausted'. William Cole the antiquary, who migrated to King's and wrote a History of that College in four volumes, but should, evidently, never have crossed the way, for to give King's the MSS. of his history would be, he wrote in 1778, 'to throw them into a horsepond', the members of that society being 'generally so conceited of their Latin and Greek that all other studies are barbarous'; and, when he had become tenant of the house at Milton which still belongs to the College and had spent £600 on it, 'Cooke, the snotty-nosed head of it, had the rascality with Paddon, a dirty wretch and bursar suitable to him, to alter my lease and put terms to it'. Doctor Butler, the famous physician and 'intolerable humorist'...But I must break off the endless list. It is certain that Clare men do not lack flavour.

Much more, too, belonging to the show and procession of these volumes we must pass by, the Lady of Clare herself, the College livings, what a difference it must make to a College to have had Mr Phipps as Butler for forty years (1879–1919), the College Plate, the College connections with American history, and, in particular, the fascinating chapter of more than 200 pages setting forth *in extenso* the singular career of Nicholas Ferrar and the story of Little Gidding. On the other hand, one regrets the paucity of detail concerning the College Estates, as illustrating the economic history of the realm. But the Estates were small and scattered, and the College Muniments were destroyed by fire, a third of the way through the life of the College, in 1521. One subtraction, moreover, from the glories of the College I must venture to make. It is certain that claret, much as the Clare High Table may wish the contrary, is *not* derived from the de Clares, but is *clairet*, light red wine, as distinct from tent or *tinto*, dark red wine.

Running through this book's enormous bulk, there is successfully achieved, as perhaps its highest quality, a certain magnificent *Silliness*—using this word, far from derogatorily, in its ancient sense—admirable and attractive to the reader. For it is this, I think, which carries off without pretence or pompousness what is, and must and should be, above all a work of sentiment. It does credit to the grave Fellows of a College that they should have lent themselves so willingly and with such harmonious collaboration of pen and sympathy to the waywardness and grace of one of their number, the Editor of the volumes, Mr Mansfield Forbes. Clothed in the finest dress of paper and black buckram, armed with intellect and learning, adorned with curiosity and fancy, there is here embodied the Sentiment of one of those of the ancient foundations of this country which have outlived the centuries with least loss of the past and least sacrifice of the present, a College. It is a gracious sight—worthy, but difficult, of imitation:–

> Clare Hall shall be your lasting Monument
> And, though in other tombs you'ld shrink away
> And melt into corruption, and decay,
> Your Fame this Charter to it selfe can give
> Within this monument you'l ever live.

The final letter reflected his continued interest in Malthus.[2]

To the Editor of The Cambridge Review, *25 February 1933*

Sir,

In your last issue you published a letter from Professor Trevelyan quoting a letter of the year 1710 to show that at that date £70 was considered a suitable income for an undergraduate of the University.

It is interesting to compare this with a figure given 75 years later. On May 15, 1785, Daniel Malthus, writing to his son Robert then at Jesus, said that he thought £100 a year a reasonable figure for the University expenses of ordinary folk. Daniel Malthus, it must be remembered, was a fairly well to do gentleman of independent means. He went on to say that, if it were to be more than £100, the Clergy would not be able to go on sending their sons to College. At Leipzig, he added, it could be done for £25. This letter is quoted in Dr Bonar's *Malthus and His Work*, p. 408.

Yours etc.,
[copy initialled] J.M.K.

2 See *JMK*, vol. x, pp. 71–108.

DRAMATIS PERSONAE

Agar, Herbert (1897–1980), author; special assistant to the American Ambassador in London, 1942–6.

Aitken, William Maxwell (1879–1964), 1st Baron Beaverbrook, 1917; financier, newspaper proprietor and politician; Chancellor of the Duchy of Lancaster, and Minister of Information, 1918; Minister for Aircraft Production, 1940–1; Minister of Supply, 1941–2; Lord Privy Seal, 1943–5.

Allen, Reginald Clifford (1899–1939), Baron, 1932; Labour propagandist and pacificist; Chairman, No Conscription Fellowship, 1914–18; Chairman and Treasurer, Independent Labour Party, 1922–6; supported 'National Labour', 1932–6.

Anderson, Sir John (1882–1958), 1st Viscount Waverley, 1952; M.P. (Ind. Nat.) Scottish Universities, 1938–50; Lord President of the Council, 1940–3; Chancellor of the Exchequer, 1943–5.

Angell, Sir Ralph Norman (1874–1967); author, lecturer, pacificist and socialist politician. Awarded Nobel Peace Prize for 1933.

Attlee, Clement (1883–1967), 1st Earl, 1955; M.P. (Lab.) Limehouse, 1922–50; Walthamstow West, 1950–5; leader of the Labour Party in the House of Commons, 1931–5; Leader, 1935–55; Lord Privy Seal, 1940–2; Secretary of State for Dominions, 1942–3; Lord President of the Council, 1943–5; Deputy Prime Minister, 1940–5; Prime Minister, 1945–51.

Auden, Wystan Hugh (1907–1973), poet.

Baldwin, Stanley (1867–1945), 1st Earl of Bewdley, 1937; Prime Minister, 1923–4, 1924–9, 1935–7; Lord President of the Council, 1931–5.

Barnes, George Reginald (1904–60); Asst. Secretary C.U.P., 1930–5; B.B.C. Talks Dept., 1935; Director of Talks, 1941; Head of Third Programme, 1946–8; Director The Spoken Word, B.B.C., 1942–50; Director of Television, B.B.C., 1950–6.

Barry, Gerald Reid (1898–1968), journalist; founder and editor of *Week-end Review*, 1930 (absorbed by *The New Statesman*, 1934); later a director of *The New Statesman*; editor *News Chronicle*, 1936–47; co-founder Political and Economic Planning.

Bartlett, Vernon (b. 1894), broadcaster and journalist; M.P. (Ind. Prog.) Bridgwater, 1938–50.

Beaverbrook, *see* Aitken.

Bell, Julian (1908–37), poet; elder son of Vanessa and Clive Bell; killed in Spain.

Bernhard, Prince (b. 1911), married Princess Juliana (b. 1909) in 1937. Juliana became Queen of the Netherlands in 1948 and abdicated in 1980.

Beveridge, Sir William (1879–1963), 1st Baron, 1946; Director, London School of Economics, 1919–37; Master, University College, Oxford, 1937–45.

Blackett, Patrick Maynard Stewart (1897–1974); scientist and government adviser; Fellow of King's College, Cambridge, 1923–33; Professor of Physics at Birkbeck College, London, 1933–7; at Manchester, 1937–53; at Imperial College London, 1953–65; Nobel Prize for Physics, 1948.

Blum, Léon (1872–1950); Prime Minister of France, 1936–7, 1938, 1946–7.

Bonham-Carter, Mark (b. 1922), son of Sir Maurice Bonham-Carter and Violet; Grenadier Guards, 1941–5; 8th Army (Africa) and 21st Army Group (N.W. Europe), captured 1943; escaped.

Bonham-Carter, Sir Maurice (Bongy) (1880–1960), businessman; husband of Lady Violet Bonham-Carter.

Bonham-Carter, Lady Violet (1887–1969), daughter of H. H. Asquith, 1st Earl of Oxford.

Boothby, Robert John Graham (b. 1900), Baron, 1958; M.P. (Con.) East Aberdeenshire, 1924–58; Parliamentary Private Secretary to the Chancellor of the Exchequer, 1926–9.

Bracken, Brendan Rendall (1901–58), newspaper proprietor; M.P. (Con.) Paddington North, 1924–45; Bournemouth, 1945–50; Bournemouth East, 1950–1; Minister of Information, 1941–5.

Brailsford, Henry Noel (1873–1958), journalist and historian.

Brand, Robert Henry (1878–1963), 1st Baron, 1946; Managing Director, Lazard Brothers, merchant bankers, 1919–60; member, Macmillan Committee on Finance and Industry, 1929–31; Head of British Food Mission, Washington, 1941–4; Treasury Representative, Washington, 1944–6.

Buck, Pearl (d. 1973), author; married to Richard J. Walsh; Nobel Prize for Literature, 1938.

Butler, Richard Austen (b. 1902), Baron, 1965; M.P. (Con.) Saffron Walden, 1929–1964; Under-Secretary of State, India Office, 1932–7; Parliamentary Secretary, Ministry of Labour, 1937–8; Under-Secretary of State for Foreign Affairs, 1938–41; President of Board (later Minister) of Education, 1941–5.

Cadbury, Laurence John (b. 1889); director, Bank of England, 1936–61; Nation Proprietory Co., 1958–67; Daily News Ltd., *News Chronicle*,

1930–60, *Star*, 1930–60; Cocoa Investments Ltd., 1937–64; Chairman, Cadbury Bros. Ltd., 1944–9.

Calder, Peter Ritchie (b. 1906), author and journalist; science editor *The New Statesman*, 1945.

Cassel, Sir Ernest Joseph (1852–1921), financier and philanthropist.

Cecil, Lord Robert (1864–1958), 1st Viscount Cecil of Chelwood, 1923; M.P. (Con.) Marylebone East, 1906–10; Hitchin, 1911–23; Parliamentary Under-Secretary for Foreign Affairs, 1916–19, Assistant Secretary of State for Foreign Affairs, 1918; Minister of Blockade, 1916–18; Lord Privy Seal, 1923–4; Chancellor of the Duchy of Lancaster, 1924–7; President, League of Nations Union, 1923–45; Nobel Peace Prize, 1937.

Chalmers, Sir Robert (1858–1938), 1st Baron, 1919; Permanent Secretary, Treasury, 1911–13; Governor of Ceylon, 1913–16; Joint Secretary, Treasury, 1916–19; Master of Peterhouse, Cambridge, 1924–31.

Chamberlain, Arthur Neville (1869–1940); M.P. (Con.) Birmingham Lady-wood, 1918–29; Birmingham Edgbaston, 1929–40; Minister of Health, 1923, 1924–9, 1931; Chancellor of the Exchequer, 1923–4, 1931–7; Prime Minister, 1937–40, Lord President of the Council, 1940.

Cherwell *see* Lindemann.

Churchill, Winston Leonard Spencer (1874–1965); M.P. (Con.) Oldham, 1900–4; (Lib.) 1904–6; (Lib.) Manchester N.W., 1906–8; Dundee, 1908–22; (Con.) Epping, 1924–45; Woodford, 1945–64. Prime Minister, 1940–5; 1951–5.

Clayton, William Lockhart (1880–1966); Assistant Secretary of State, U.S.A., 1944–5; Under-Secretary of State for Economic Affairs, 1945–6.

Coatman, John (1889–1963); Indian Public Service, 1910–26; member Indian Legislative Assembly, 1926–30; Professor of Imperial Economic Relations, University of London, 1930–34; chief news editor, B.B.C., 1934–7; North Regional Controller B.B.C., 1937–49; Director of Research in Social Sciences, University of St Andrews, 1949–54.

Cockburn, Claude (b. 1904), journalist; editor, *The Week*, 1933–46.

Cohen, Joseph L. (d. 1940), economist and Zionist propagandist.

Cole, George Douglas Howard (1889–1959), economist and socialist writer; Fellow of Magdalene College, Oxford, 1912–19; Fellow of University College, Oxford, and University Reader in Economics, 1921–44, Chichele Professor of Social and Political Theory, 1944–57.

Connolly, Cyril Vernon (1903–74), author and journalist; wrote for *The New Statesman* from 1927; founder and editor of *Horizon*, 1939–50; literary editor *The Observer*, 1942–3.

Cot, Pierre (b. 1895); French Minister for Air, 1933–4, 1936–8; Minister of Commerce, 1938.

Crossman, Richard Howard Stafford (1907–1974); assistant editor *The New Statesman*, 1938–55; editor, 1970–2; M.P. (Lab.), Coventry East, 1945–74.

Crozier, William Percival (1879–1944), journalist; editor *The Manchester Guardian*, 1932–44.

Cruikshank, Robert James (1898–1956); Director of American Division, Ministry of Information, 1941–5; Deputy Director-General, British Information Services in U.S.A., 1941–2.

Dacey, W. Manning (d. 1964), journalist with *The Financial News* and *The Financial Times*; editor of *The Banker*; economic adviser to Lloyds Bank, 1946–54.

Daladier, Edouard (1884–1970), French politician; President of the Council, 1938–40; Minister of Foreign Affairs, 1939–40; National Defence and War, 1938–40.

Davenport, Nicholas (d. 1979), stockbroker, journalist and author; financial correspondent for *The Nation and Athenaeum* (1923–30), *The New Statesman and Nation* from 1930; director, National Mutual Life Assurance Society, 1931–69, deputy chairman, 1960–9.

Davies, Emil; Fabian; financial editor *The New Statesman*, 1913–31.

Dawson, Geoffrey (1874–1944); editor of *The Times*, 1912–19, 1923–41.

De Gaulle, Charles (1890–1970); Chief of the Free French, 1940; President of the Provisional Government of France, 144–6; President of the French Government, 1958–9; President of France, 1959–69.

del Vayo, Don Julio Alvarez; Foreign Minister for Spain, 1935–7.

De Valera, Eamon (1882–1975); Head of Government in Ireland, 1937–48, 1957–59; President of Ireland, 1959–1975.

Dickinson, Goldsworthy Lowes (d. 1932); Fellow of King's College, Cambridge.

Duff Cooper, Alfred (1890–1954); Secretary of State for War, 1935–7, First Lord of the Admiralty, 1937–8; Minister of Information, 1940–1; Chancellor of the Duchy of Lancaster, 1941–3.

Durbin, Evan Frank Mottram (1906–48), economist and politician; lecturer, London School of Economics in the 1930s; Economic Section of the War Cabinet, 1940; Personal Assistant to the Deputy Prime Minister, 1942–5; M.P. (Lab.) Edmonton, 1945–8; Parliamentary Secretary, Ministry of Works, 1947–8.

Dyson, Sir George (1883–1964), director, Royal College of Music, 1937–52; a governor of Sadlers Wells.

Eden, Robert Anthony (1897–1977); M.P. (Con.) Warwick and Leamington, 1923–57; Secretary of State for Foreign Affairs, 1935–8, 1940–5, 1951–5.

Einzig, Paul (1897–1973), journalist and economist; *The Financial News*, 1921–45; *The Financial Times*, 1945–56.

Elmhirst, Leonard (d. 1974); founder and Chairman of Dartington Hall Trust, 1925; Chairman, Political and Economic Planning, 1939–53.

Evans, David Emrys (1891–1966); Principal, University College of North Wales, 1927–58; Vice-Chancellor, University of Wales, 1933–5, 1941–4, 1948–50, 1954–6.

Firth, Sir William John (1881–1957), businessman; Chairman and Managing Director, Richard Thomas & Co.

Fischer, Louis (1896–1970), journalist and author; American correspondent in Europe, especially Spain and Russia after 1921.

Franco, General don Francisco (1892–1975); Head of Spanish State, 1937–75.

Fyfe, Hamilton (1869–1951), author and journalist.

Gandhi, Mohandas Karamchand (1869–1948); Indian Congress leader and pioneer of civil disobedience.

Garnett, David (1892–1981), author.

Garvin, James Louis (1868–1947); editor *The Observer*, 1908–42.

Geddes, Sir Auckland Campbell (1879–1954); M.P. (Con.) Basingstoke, 1917–20; Minister of National Service, 1917–19; President, Local Government Board, 1918–19; Minister of Reconstruction, 1919; President, Board of Trade, 1919–20; Ambassador to U.S.A., 1920–4; chairman, Rio Tinto Zinc, 1925–47.

Geddes, Sir Eric Campbell (1875–1938), politician, administrator and businessman; M.P. (Unionist) Cambridge, 1917–22; Minister of Transport, 1919–21; Chairman, Committee on National Economy, 1921–2; Chairman, Dunlop Rubber Company and Imperial Airways.

George, Walter (1878–1957); U.S. Senator (Democrat), 1922–57; Chairman, Finance Committee, until 1953; Chairman, Foreign Relations Committee.

Goebbels, Josef (1897–1945); German Minister for Public Enlightenment and Propaganda, 1933–45.

Göring, Field Marshal Hermann (1893–1945); Commander in Chief of the German Airforce, 1933–45.

Graham-Little, Sir Ernest Gordon (1867–1950); M.P. (Ind.), University of London, 1924–50.

Gregory, Theodore E. (1890–1970), economist; Sir Ernest Cassel Professor of Economics, London School of Economics, 1927–37, Economic Adviser, Government of India, 1938–46, member, Macmillan Committee on Finance and Industry, 1929–31.

Grigg, Sir James (1890–1964); Principal Private Secretary to successive Chancellors of the Exchequer, 1921–30; Chairman, Board of Customs and Excise, 1930; Board of Inland Revenue, 1930–4; Finance Member, Council of the Viceroy of India, 1934–9; Permanent Under-Secretary of State, War Office, 1939–42; M.P. (Nat.) Cardiff East, 1942–5; Secretary of State for War, 1942–5.

Halifax, Lord, *see* Lindley-Wood.

Hammersley, Samuel Schofield (1892–1965); M.P. (Con.) Stockport, 1925–35; Willesden East, 1938–45.

Harmsworth, Alfred Charles (1865–1922), Baron, 1905, 1st Viscount Northcliffe, 1917; journalist and newspaper proprietor; founded *Daily Mail*, 1896; *Daily Mirror*, 1903; chief proprietor of *The Times*, 1905; undertook war mission to U.S.A., 1917; Director of Propaganda in enemy countries, 1918; brother of H. S. Harmsworth.

Harmsworth, Harold Sidney (1868–1940), Baron, 1914, 1st Viscount Rothermere, 1919; newspaper proprietor; founded *Daily Mail*, 1896; took over *Daily Mirror*, 1914; controlled Associated Newspapers, 1922–32; brother of A. C. Harmsworth.

Harris, Arthur Travers (b. 1892); Commander in Chief, Bomber Command, Royal Air Force, 1942–5.

Harrisson, Tom (1911–76), biologist, anthropologist and pioneer of social surveys; founder (with Charles Madge) of Mass Observation.

Hart, Sir Basil Liddell (1895–1970), military theorist and writer; military correspondent *Daily Telegraph*, 1925–35; *The Times*, 1935–9.

Hitler, Adolf (1869–1945); Chancellor of the German Reich, 1933–45; Head of the German State, 1934–45.

Hoare, Samuel John Gurney (1880–1959), 1st Viscount Templewood, 1944; M.P. (Con.) Chelsea, 1910–14; Secretary of State, Air, 1922–4, 1924–9, 1940; India, 1931–5; Foreign Affairs, 1935; Home Affairs, 1937–9; First Lord of the Admiralty, 1936–7; Lord Privy Seal, 1939–40.

Hobson, John Atkinson (1858–1940), heretical economist and publicist.

Howard, Brian (1905–58), aesthete, poet, author.

Howe, Quincy (1900–77), pioneer in radio and television news analysis; editor *Living Age*, 1929–35; editor-in-chief, Simon and Schuster, 1935–42.

Hull, Cordell (1871–1955); Secretary of State, U.S.A., 1933–44.

Hulton, Edward George Warris (b. 1906), newspaper proprietor.

Huxley, Aldous Leonard (1894–1953), novelist and critic.

Huxley, Gervas (1894–1971); Secretary, Publicity Committee Empire Marketing Board, 1926–32; Organising Director International Tea

Marketing Expansion Board, 1943; Adviser to Ministry of Information on Empire matters, 1939–45.

Huxley, Julian Sorell (1887–1974), biologist and writer.

Inskip, Sir Thomas Walter Hobart (1876–1947), 1st Viscount Caldecote 1939; M.P. (Con.) Bristol Central, 1918–29; Fareham, 1931–9; Minister for Co-ordination of Defence, 1936–9.

Ironside, Field Marshal Sir William Edmund (1880–1959), 1st Baron, 1941; Chief of Imperial General Staff, 1939–40; Commander in Chief, Home Forces, 1940.

Jay, Douglas Patrick Thomas (b. 1907), journalist and politician; on staff of *The Times*, 1929–33; *The Economist*, 1933–7; City editor *Daily Herald*, 1937–41; Ministry of Supply, 1941–3; Board of Trade, 1943–5; Personal Assistant to Prime Minister, 1945–6; M.P. (Lab.) Wandsworth/Battersea North since 1946.

Jebb, Herbert Miles Gladwyn (b. 1900), 1st Baron Gladwyn, 1960; entered Diplomatic Service, 1924; Private Secretary to the Parliamentary Under-Secretary of State for Foreign Affairs, 1929–31; to the Permanent Under-Secretary, 1937–40.

Joad, Cyril Edwin Mitchinson (1891–1953), philosopher and author; head, Department of Philosophy, Birkbeck College, London, 1930–53.

Joyce, William (Lord Haw Haw) (1906–46); entered Germany from Britain, August 1939; chief foreign commentator for German radio from July 1942; convicted of treason and executed January 1946.

Kerr, Philip Henry (1882–1940), 11th Marquis of Lothian; Chancellor of the Duchy of Lancaster, 1931; Parliamentary Under-Secretary of State for India, 1931–2; Ambassador to U.S.A., 1939–40.

Keyes, Admiral of the Fleet Sir Roger John Brownlow (1872–1945), 1st Baron, 1943; M.P. (Con.) Portsmouth North, 1934–43; Director of Combined Operations, 1941–2.

King, Wilfred T. C. (d. 1965), economic journalist; editor of *The Banker*, 1946–65.

King-Hall, William Stephen Richard (1893–1966); served in Royal Navy to 1929; subsequently publicist on defence policy and foreign affairs; M.P. (Ind.) Ormskirk, 1939–44.

Laski, Harold Joseph (1893–1950), political scientist, social theorist and politician; Professor of Political Science, London School of Economics, 1926–50; member of Labour Party Executive, 1936–49.

Layton, Walter Thomas (1884–1966), Kt, 1930, Baron, 1947; economist; editor *The Economist*, 1922–38.

Leith-Ross, Sir Frederick (1887–1968); Chief Economic Adviser to H.M. Government, 1932–46.

Lerner, Abba P. (b. 1903), economist.

Lindemann, Frederick Alexander (1886–1957), Baron Cherwell, 1941; Personal Assistant to the Prime Minister, 1940–2; Paymaster-General, 1942–5, 1951–3.

Lindley-Wood, Edward Frederick (1881–1959), 1st Earl of Halifax, 1944; 3rd Viscount Halifax, 1st Baron Irwin, 1925; Secretary of State for War, 1935; Lord Privy Seal, 1935–7; Lord President of the Council, 1937–8; Secretary of State for Foreign Affairs, 1938–40; Ambassador to the U.S.A., 1941–6.

Lloyd, C. Mostyn (d. 1945); member of staff of the London School of Economics, 1919–44; head of department of Social Science, 1922–44; editor from 1931.

Lloyd George, David (1863–1945), 1st Earl Lloyd George, 1945; M.P. (Lib.) Caernarvon, 1980–1945; President, Board of Trade, 1905–8, Chancellor of the Exchequer, 1908–15; Minister of Munitions, 1915–16; Secretary of State for War, 1916; Prime Minister, 1916–22.

Locker-Lampson, Oliver Stillingfleet (1880–1954), politician; M.P. (Con.) Huntingdonshire North, 1910–18, Huntingdonshire, 1918–22; Birmingham Handsworth, 1922–45.

Londonderry, 7th Marquis of (1878–1949); Secretary of State for Air,1931–5; Lord Privy Seal, 1935.

Lothian, Marquis of, *see* Kerr.

Low, David (1891–1963), cartoonist and caricaturist; director of *The New Statesman* from 1931.

Lucas, Frank Laurence (Peter) (1894–1967); Fellow of King's College, Cambridge, 1920–67, University Reader in English, 1947; served in Foreign Office, 1939–45.

Luce, Henry Robinson (1898–1967), publisher and editor; founder, editor and publisher of *Time*, 1923; founder and publisher of *Fortune*, 1930, *Life*, 1935.

McAdam, Ivison (1894–1974); Secretary and Director-General, Royal Institute of International Affairs, 1929–55; during World War II, Assistant Director General and Principal Secretary, Ministry of Information.

MacCarthy, Desmond (1877–1952), author and literary critic; literary editor *The New Statesman* until 1928.

MacDonald, J. Ramsay (1866–1937); M.P. (Lab.) Leicester, 1906–18; Aberavon, 1922–9; Seaham, 1929–31; (Nat. Lab.) Seaham, 1931–5; Scottish Universities, 1936–7; Prime Minister and Secretary of State for Foreign Affairs, 1924, Prime Minister, 1929–35; Lord President of the Council, 1935–7.

McKenna, Reginald (1863–1943), politician and banker; M.P. (Lib.) North Monmouthshire, 1895–1918; First Lord of Admiralty, 1908–11; Home Secretary, 1911–15; Chancellor of the Exchequer, 1915–16; Chairman of Midland Bank, 1919–43.

MacKenzie, Norman (b. 1921); assistant editor *The New Statesman*, 1943–59.

Macmillan, Maurice Harold (b. 1894); M.P. (Con.) Stockton-on-Tees, 1924–9, 1931–45; Bromley, 1945–64; Parliamentary Secretary, Ministry of Supply, 1940–2; Parliamentary Under-Secretary, Colonial Office, 1942–3; Minister Resident in North West Africa, 1942–5.

Maisky, Ivan Mikhailovich (b. 1884), Ambassador of U.S.S.R. in Great Britain, 1932–43; Assistant People's Commissar for Foreign Affairs, 1943–6.

Margesson, Henry David Reginald (1890–1965), 1st Viscount, 1942; M.P. (Con.) West Ham, Upton, 1922–3; Rugby, 1924–42; Government Chief Whip, 1931–40; Secretary of State for War, 1940–2.

Montgomery, Bernard Law (1887–1976), 1st Viscount 1946; Commander of Eighth Army, 1942–4 during campaigns in North Africa, Sicily and Italy; Commander in Chief British Group of Armies and Allied Armies in Northern France, 1944; Commander 21st Army Group, 1944–5, British Army of the Rhine, 1945–6.

Moore-Brabazon, John Theodore Cuthbert (1884–1964), 1st Baron, 1942; M.P. (Unionist) Chatham, 1918–29; Wallasey, 1931–42; Minister of Transport, 1940–1; Minister of Aircraft Production, 1941–2.

Morgenthau, Henry Jr. (1891–1967); Secretary of the Treasury, U.S.A., 1935–45.

Morrell, John Bowes, newspaper proprietor; Chairman of the Westminster Press Provincial Newspapers; Chairman, Rowntree & Co.

Morrison, Herbert Stanley (1888–1965), Baron, 1959; M.P. (Lab.) Hackney South, 1923–4, 1929–31, 1935–45; Lewisham East, 1945–50; Lewisham South, 1950–9; Minister of Supply, 1940; Home Secretary, 1940–5; Lord President, 1945–51; Foreign Secretary, 1951.

Mortimer, Raymond (1895–1980), author and critic; literary editor, *The New Statesman and Nation*, 1934–46.

Mosley, Sir Oswald Ernald (1895–1980); M.P. (Con.) Harrow, 1918–22; (Ind.) Harrow, 1922–4; (Lab.) Smethwick, 1926–31; Chancellor of the

Duchy of Lancaster, 1929–30; founder of New Party, 1931; British Union of Fascists, 1932.

Muir, John Ramsay Bryce (1872–1941), historian and politician; Professor of Modern History at Liverpool, 1906–13; at Manchester, 1914–21; Director, Liberal Summer School, 1921; M.P. (Lib.) Rochdale, 1923–4; Chairman, 1931–3, President, 1933–6, National Liberal Federation.

Mussolini, Benito (1883–1945); President of the Italian Council of Ministers, 1922–6; Prime Minister, 1925–43.

Nehru, Jawaharlal (1889–1964); Prime Minister of India, 1947–64.

Nicolson, Harold (1886–1968); Foreign Office and Diplomatic Service, 1909–29; M.P. (Nat. Lab.) 1935–45; Parliamentary Secretary, Ministry of Information, 1940–1.

Noel-Baker, Phillip John (b. 1889), Baron, 1977; M.P. (Lab.) Coventry, 1929–31; Derby, 1936–50; Derby South, 1950–70; Fellow of King's College, Cambridge, 1900; Sir Ernest Cassel Professor of International Relations, London, 1924–9.

Northcliffe, Lord, *see* A. C. Harmsworth.

Pétain, Philippe (1856–1951); Marshal of France, 1918; Prime Minister of France, 1940–2; Head of State, 1940–4.

Priestley, John Boynton (b. 1894), author and journalist.

Radek, Karl (b. 1885), Soviet politician; tried in January 1937 for plotting against the Soviet Union and sentenced to ten years' imprisonment; released after four years to serve as a propagandist.

Rathbone, Eleanor Florence (1872–1946); M.P. (Ind.) Combined Universities, 1929–46.

Ribbentrop, Joachim von (1893–1945); Minister for Foreign Affairs, Germany, 1938–45.

Roberts, John (d. 1967); assistant manager *The New Statesman*, 1914–1919; advertising manager, 1919–20; business manager, 1920–47; managing director, 1947–1957.

Robertson, Dennis Holme (1890–1963), economist; Fellow of Trinity College, Cambridge, 1914–38, 1944–63; Reader in Economics, Cambridge, 1930–8; Sir Ernest Cassel Professor of Economics, London School of Economics, 1938–44; adviser to H.M. Treasury, 1939–44; Professor of Political Economy, Cambridge, 1944–57.

Robertson, Miss; Kingsley Martin's secretary at *The New Statesman*.

Robbins, Lionel Charles (b. 1895), economist; Professor of Economics,

London School of Economics, 1929–61; member of Economic Section Offices of War Cabinet, 1939–41; Director, 1941–45.

Robinson, Edward Austin Gossage (b. 1897), economist; Fellow of Corpus Christi College, Cambridge, 1923–6; University Lecturer in Economics, Cambridge, 1929–49; Professor, 1950–65; Fellow of Sidney Sussex College since 1931.

Robinson, Joan Violet (b. 1903), economist; Assistant Lecturer in Economics, Cambridge, 1931; Lecturer, 1937; Reader, 1949; Professor, 1965–71.

Robson, William Alexander (1895–1980); Lecturer London School of Economics, 1926–33; Reader in Administrative Law, 1933–46; Professor of Public Administration, 1947–62; founder of *Political Quarterly*, 1930; joint editor, 1930–75.

Rodd, Francis James Rennell (1895–1978), 2nd Baron Rennell, 1941; banker, company director, author; Bank of England, 1929–32; Manager, Bank for International Settlements, 1930–1; served in the Army, 1939–44; Major-General, Civil Affairs Administration, Middle East, East Africa, Italy.

Röhm, Ernst (d. 1934); chief of staff of the storm troopers; shot 1 July 1934 for plotting against Hitler.

Roosevelt, Franklin Delano (1882–1945); President of the United States, 1933–45.

Rothermere, Lord, *see* H. S. Harmsworth.

Rowntree, Arnold Stephenson (1872–1951); Director, Westminster Press and Associated Papers; M.P. (Lib.) York, 1910–18.

Rowse, Alfred Leslie (b. 1903), author; Fellow, All Souls College, Oxford, 1925–74.

Russell, Bertrand Arthur William (1872–1970), 3rd Earl, philosopher and publicist.

Russell, Dora Winfred, second wife of Bertrand Russell; founded, with Russell, Telegraph House School, 1927.

Rylands, George Humphrey Wolferstan (Dadie) (b. 1902); Fellow of King's College, Cambridge since 1927.

Salter, Sir James Arthur (1882–1975); M.P. (Ind.) Oxford University, 1937–50; (Con.) Ormskirk, 1951–3; Gladstone Professor of Political Theory and Institutions, Oxford, 1934–44; member, Committee on Economic Information, Economic Advisory Council, 1931–7.

Schleicher, General Kurt von (d. 1934); Reichswehr Minister, 1932; Chancellor, 1932–3; shot in June 1934 for plotting against Hitler.

Schwartz, George Leopold (b. 1891), financial journalist; secretary, London and Cambridge Economic Service, 1923; Lecturer, London School of

Economics, 1929–44; deputy City editor *The Sunday Times*, 1944–71; editor *Bankers' Magazine*, 1945–54.

Sharp, Clifford Dyce (1883–1935), journalist; editor *The New Statesman*, 1913–29.

Shaw, George Bernard (1856–1950), playwright and publicist.

Sheppard, Hugh Richard Lawrie (1880–1937), churchman and pacifist; vicar St Martin-in-the-Fields, 1914–27; Dean of Canterbury, 1929–31; Canon of St Paul's, 1931–7; founder of Peace Pledge Union.

Shove, Gerald (1888–1947), economist; Lecturer in Economics, University of Cambridge, 1923–45; Reader, 1945–7; Fellow of King's College, Cambridge, 1926–47.

Sidebothom, Herbert (1872–1940), journalist; *Manchester Guardian*, 1895–1918; *Daily Chronicle*, 1922–3; 'Scrutator' of *The Sunday Times*, 'Candidus' of the *Daily Sketch*.

Simon, Ernest Darwin (1879–1960), 1st Baron Wythenshawe, 1947; M.P. (Lib.) Withington, 1923–4, 1929–31.

Simon, Sir John Allsebrook (1873–1954), 1st Viscount, 1940; M.P. (Lib.) Walthamstow, 1906–18; Spen Valley, 1922–31; (Lib. Nat.) Spen Valley, 1931–40; Secretary of State for Foreign Affairs, 1931–5; Home Affairs, 1935–7; Chancellor of the Exchequer, 1937–40; Lord Chancellor, 1940–5.

Sinclair, Sir Archibald Henry Macdonald (1890–1970); M.P. (Lib.) Caithness and Sutherland, 1922–45; Leader, Liberal Parliamentary Party, 1935–45; Secretary of State for Air, 1940–5.

Snowden, Philip (1864–1937), 1st Viscount of Ickornshaw, 1931; M.P. (Lab.) Blackburn, 1906–18; Colne Valley, 1922–31; Chancellor of the Exchequer, 1924, 1929–31.

Stalin, Joseph (1879–1953), Secretary, Central Committee of Communist Party of the Soviet Union, 1922–53.

Steer, George Lowther (1909–44), special war correspondent for *The Times* in Addis Ababa, 1935–6 and in Spain, 1936–7.

Stettinius, Edward R. (1900–49); U.S. Lend Lease Administrator, 1941–3; Under-Secretary of State, 1943–4; Secretary of State, 1944–5.

Stimson, Henry (1867–1950); Secretary of State, U.S.A., 1929–33; Secretary for War, 1939–45.

Strachey, Evelyn John St Loe (1901–63), author and politician; M.P.(Lab.) Birmingham Aston, 1929–31; Dundee, 1945–50; Dundee West, 1950–63; Minister of Food, 1946–50; Secretary of State for War, 1950–1.

Sweezy, Paul Marlon (b. 1910), economist and publicist.

Swithinbank, Bernard Winthrop (1884–1958); entered Indian Civil Service (Burma), 1909; Commissioner, 1933–42; Adviser to the Secretary of State for Burma, 1942.

Tallents, Sir Stephen (George) (1884–1958); Controller Public Relations B.B.C., 1935–40; Overseas Service, 1940–1.

Tawney, Richard Henry (1880–1962), historian and Christian Socialist; Professor of Economic History, London School of Economics, 1931–49.

Trenchard, Hugh Montagu (1873–1956), 1st Viscount 1936; Chief of Air Staff, 1918 and 1919–29.

Tukhachevsky, Marshal (d. 1937); former Assistant Commisar for Defence, U.S.S.R.; removed from office in May 1937, court-martialled and sentenced to death for treason, June 1937.

Turner, T. W. J., a music critic of *The New Statesman* and *The New Statesman and Nation* to 1940.

Tyerman, Donald (1908–81), journalist; assistant then deputy editor *The Economist*, 1937–44; deputy editor *The Observer*, 1944–5, assistant editor *The Times*, 1944–55; Editor, *The Economist*, 1956–65.

Utley, Freda (1898–1978), author and journalist; research fellow, London School of Economics, 1926–8; *Manchester Guardian* Japanese correspondent, 1928–9; senior researcher, Institute of World Economy and Politics, Moscow, 1930–6; China correspondent, *News Chonicle*, 1938; went to U.S.A., 1939.

Vallance, Aylmer (1892–1955), journalist; assistant editor *The Economist*, 1930–3; editor *News Chronicle*, 1933–6; financial editor *The New Statesman*, 1937–9; War Office, 1939–45, contributor to *The New Statesman* after 1945.

Vansittart, Sir Robert Gilbert (1881–1917); Permanent Under-Secretary, Foreign Office, 1930–8; Chief Diplomatic Adviser to Foreign Secretary, 1938–41.

Volpi, Giuseppe (Comte de Misurato); Italian Finance Minister, 1921–8.

Wallace, Henry Agard (1888–1965); Secretary of Agriculture, U.S.A., 1933–40; Vice-President, 1941–5; Secretary of Commerce, 1945–6.

Walsh, Richard John (d. 1960); president of John Day Publishers; publisher of *Asia Magazine*, 1941–6.

Webb, Beatrice (1858–1943), political scientist and socialist author.

Webb, Sidney James (1859–1947), 1st Baron Passfield, 1929; political scientist and socialist author; M.P. (Lab.) Seaham, 1922–9; President, Board of Trade, 1924; Secretary of State for Dominion Affairs, 1929–30; Colonies, 1929–31.

Wells, Herbert George (1866–1946), novelist and social critic.

Weygand, General Maxime (1867–1965); Commander in Chief, French Army, 1940; Minister of Defence, 1940; Governor-General of Algeria and Delegate-General of Vichy Government in French Africa, 1941; prisoner of Gestapo in Germany, 1942–5; prisoner in France, 1945–6.

Whitley, Edward (d. 1945); an original backer of *The New Statesman;* chairman of *The New Statesman.*

Wilhelmina (1880–1962), Queen of the Netherlands, 1890–1948.

Williams, Francis (1903–70), Baron, 1962; journalist; editor *Daily Herald,* 1936–40; Controller of News and Censorship, Ministry of Information, 1941–5; Adviser on Public Relations to the Prime Minister, 1945–7.

Willison, Ernst (1896–1954); advertising manager, *The New Statesman,* 1925–47; business manager, 1947; director, 1950.

Wilson, Sir Arnold (1884–1940); M.P. (Con.) Hitchin, 1933–40; Indian Political Department, 1909–20; Anglo-Persian Oil Company, 1921–32; Chairman, Board of Trade Advisory Committee on Cinema Films, 1931–8; Home Office Committee on Structural Precautions Against Air Attack, 1935–8.

Wilson, Sir Horace John (1882–1972); Chief Industrial Adviser to H.M. Government, 1930–9; seconded to Treasury for service with Prime Minister, 1935; Permanent Secretary of Treasury and Head of Home Civil Service, 1939–42.

Wilson, Woodrow (1856–1924); President of the United States, 1913–21.

Winant, John Henry (1889–1947); U.S. Ambassador to Great Britain, 1941–6.

Wintringham, Tom (1898–1949), socialist writer and publicist; served in British contingent, International Brigade; member of Common Wealth during World War II.

Woolf, Leonard Sidney (1880–1963), author and publisher; literary editor *The Nation and Athenaeum,* 1923–30; joint editor *Political Quarterly,* 1931–59; founded Hogarth Press, 1917.

Wright, Harold, editor of *The Nation and Athenaeum,* 1930–1.

DOCUMENTS REPRODUCED
IN THIS VOLUME

ARTICLES   *page*

Art and the State (*The Listener*, 26 August 1936)   341–9
Arts in War-Time, The (*The Times*, 11 May 1943)   359–62
British Foreign Policy (*The New Statesman and Nation*, 10 July
    1937)   61–5
Einstein (*The New Statesman and Nation*, 21 October 1933)   21–2
London Artists' Association: its origin and aims, The (*Studio*,
    June 1930)   297–307
Mr Chamberlain's Foreign Policy (*The New Statesman and
    Nation*, 8 October 1938)   125–7
Mr Keynes Replies to Shaw (*The New Statesman and Nation*, 10
    November 1934)   30–5
Plays and Pictures: The Camargo Society (*The New Statesman
    and Nation*, 11 April 1931)   9–10
Positive Peace Programme A (*The New Statesman and Nation*,
    25 March 1938)   99–104
What it Costs to Bet (*The Nation and Athenaeum*, 11 July 1925)   395–6
What it Costs to Bet (*The Nation and Athenaeum*, 17 October
    1925)   396–7

DRAFTS

Draft Contents (Ancient Currencies)   243
Babylonian Mina, the Egyptian Kat, the Lydian Mina and the
    Roman Pound, The   231–7
Chapter I, The Babylonian Standard   244–52
Chapter III, The Origins of Money   252–60
Chapter III, Primitive Greek Standards   281–6
Chapter V, The Pheidonian and Solonic Reforms   200–73
Fall in the Value of Money, The [pre 1923]   226–31
Further Thoughts on British Foreign Policy, 26 July 1937   73–8
Note on the Monetary Reform of Solon (1920)   223–6
Wheat–Barley, Gold–Silver and Silver–Copper Ratios, The   237–43

DOCUMENTS REPRODUCED IN THIS VOLUME

BOOK REVIEWS

Dawson, Christopher, *The Age of the Gods* (*The Nation and
Athenaeum*, 12 May 1926)   287–9

Evans, Sir Arthur, *The Palace of Minos at Knossos* (*The Nation
and Athenaeum*, 6 October 1928)   292–4

Forbes, Mansfield D. (Ed.), *Clare College* (*The Nation and
Athenaeum*, 17 January 1931)   416–421

Hall, H-R., *The Civilisation of Greece in the Bronze Age* (*The
Nation and Athenaeum*, 6 October 1928)   292–4

Low, David, *Low's Russian Sketch Book* (*The New Statesman and
Nation*, 10 December 1932)   14–16

Smith, Sidney, *Early History of Assyria to 1000 B.C.* (*The Nation
and Athenaeum*, 12 May 1928)   289–91

Wallis Budge, Sir E. A., *The Rise and Progress of Assyriology* (*The
Nation and Athenaeum*, 16 January 1926)   287

FOREWORDS, EXHIBITION CATALOGUES, PAMPHLETS

Camargo Ballet Society, The, 1934   322–4

Camargo Society, The, 1931   318–20

Economic Foreword (*Catalogue of the London Artists' Association
Exhibition*, March–April 1931)   307–8

Foreword (C.E.M.A., An Exhibition of French Book Illustration,
1895–1945), Spring 1945   365–6

Ibsen's Middle Period (programme for the Ibsen season, Arts
Theatre, Cambridge, February 1936)   326–8

Introduction to Hume's *Abstract* (with Piero Sraffa), 1938   373–90

London Group (Exhibition Catalogue, October 1921)   296–7

Programme of the Second Buxton Theatre Festival, August—
September 1938—excerpt   324–6

MEMORANDA, NOTES AND COMMENTS

Anonymous contribution (*The Nation and Athenaeum*, 5 May
1923)   308–9

Anonymous contribution (*The Nation and Athenaeum*, 30 June
1923)   309–10

Anonymous contribution (*The Nation and Athenaeum*, 18 August
1923)   310–11

Anonymous contribution (*The Nation and Athenaeum*, 25 June
1927)   311–12

DOCUMENTS REPRODUCED IN THIS VOLUME

Unsigned notice (*The Nation and Athenaeum*, 5 May 1923)   312–13
Unsigned notice (*The Nation and Athenaeum*, 16 June 1923)   313
Unsigned notice (*The Nation and Athenaeum*, 23 June 1923)   313–14
Unsigned notice (*The Nation and Athenaeum*, 28 July 1923)   314
Unsigned notice (*The Nation and Athenaeum*, 15 September
   1923)   315
Unsigned notice (*The Nation and Athenaeum*, 12 January 1924)   315–16
Unsigned notice (*The Nation and Athenaeum*, 11 October 1924)   316–17
Unsigned notice (*The Nation and Athenaeum*, 3 November 1928)   317–18
Why There is No Second Front, by Kingsley Martin, 21   176–81
   September 1942

MINUTES OF EVIDENCE

Royal Comission on Lotteries and Betting, Minutes of Evidence,
   15 December 1932   398–412

BROADCASTS

On Reading Books, 1 June 1936   329–35
Arts Council, The: its Policy and Hopes (*The Listener*, 12 July
   1945)   367–72

PUBLISHED LETTERS

To *The Cambridge Review*, 21 February 1921   415–16
To *The Cambridge Review*, 25 February 1933   421
To *The Economist*, 27 December 1932   413–14
To *The Manchester Guardian*, 17 December 1932   412–13
To *The Nation and Athenaeum*, 29 August 1925   392–3
To *The Nation and Athenaeum*, 22 January 1927   393–5
To *The Nation and Athenaeum*, 25 June 1927   391
To *The Nation and Athenaeum*, 24 February 1929   391
To *The New Statesman and Nation*, 2 July 1933   320–2
To *The New Statesman and Nation*, 15 July 1934   25–7
To *The New Statesman and Nation*, 11 August 1934   28–9
To *The New Statesman and Nation*, 24 November 1934   35–6
To *The New Statesman and Nation*, 21 January 1935   43
To *The New Statesman and Nation*, 13 July 1936   46–8
To *The New Statesman and Nation*, 8 August 1936   48–50

To *The New Statesman and Nation*, 15 August 1936   50–4
To *The New Statesman and Nation*, 29 August 1936   54–6
To *The New Statesman and Nation*, 12 September 1936   56–7
To *The New Statesman and Nation*, 3 April 1938   110–11
To *The New Statesman and Nation*, 9 August 1938   356–7
To *The New Statesman and Nation*, 22 August 1938   357–8
To *The New Statesman and Nation*, 22 August 1942   166
To *The Times*, 29 September 1937   82
To *The Times*, 12 March 1944   362–4
To *The Times*, 11 July 1945   372

UNPUBLISHED LETTERS

From Ackerley, J. R., 27 May 1936   335–6
To Ackerley, J. R., 28 May 1936   336
From Ackerley, J. R., 12 June 1936   336–7
To Ackerley, J. R., 14 June 1936   337–8
From Ackerley, J. R., 16 June 1936   338–9
To Ackerley, J. R., 18 June 1936   339
From Ackerley, J. R., 19 June 1936   340
To Ackerley, J. R., 23 June 1936   340–1
To Ackerley, J. R., 3 July 1936   341
From Adcock, F. E., 29 January 1926   277
To Adcock, F. E., 31 January 1926   277–8
From Adcock, F. E., 23 August [1926]   278–81
From Bonham-Carter, Violet, 15 May 1945   209
To Bonham Carter, Violet, 16 May 1945   210–11
From Boothby, Robert, 24 March 1938   104
From Cadbury, L. J., 14 May 1945   207–8
To Cadbury, L. J., 15 May 1945   208–9
To Crossman, Richard, 27 May 1940   142
From Jebb, Gladwyn, 9 July 1937   65
To Jebb, Gladwyn, 12 July 1937   65–6
To Jebb, Gladwyn, 29 September 1937   83
From Laski, Harold, 22 July 1934   27–8
From Layton, Walter, 25 March 1938   105
To Martin, Kingsley, 10 April 1923   1
To Martin, Kingsley, 2 August 1930   2
From Martin, Kingsley, 26 November 1930   3
To Martin, Kingsley, 8 January 1931   4–5
From Martin, Kingsley, 16 January 1931   5–6

DOCUMENTS REPRODUCED IN THIS VOLUME

To Martin, Kingsley, 1 March 1931	6–7
To Martin, Kingsley, 21 March 1931	8
To Martin, Kingsley, 19 April 1931	10–11
From Martin, Kingsley, 20 April 1931	11–12
To Martin, Kingsley, 21 April 1931	12–13
From Martin, Kingsley, 22 April 1933	16–17
To Martin, Kingsley, 23 April 1933	17–19
From Martin, Kingsley, 24 April 1933	19
To Martin, Kingsley, 9 May 1933	19–20
To Martin, Kingsley, 15 October 1933	20–1
From Martin, Kingsley, 27 August 1934	29
To Martin, Kingsley, 7 September 1934	30
To Martin, Kingsley, 2 December 1934	39
From Martin, Kingsley, 3 December 1934	39
From Martin, Kingsley, 22 January 1935	44
From Martin, Kingsley, 28 February 1935—excerpt	44
From Martin, Kingsley, 3 March 1935	44–5
To Martin, Kingsley, 13 July 1936	46
To Martin, Kingsley, 29 January 1937	57
To Martin, Kingsley, 1 July 1937	58
From Martin, Kingsley, 2 July 1937	58–9
To Martin, Kingsley, 4 July 1937	59
To Martin, Kingsley, 5 July 1937	60
From Martin, Kingsley, 6 July 1937	60
From Martin, Kingsley, 8 July 1937	66–7
To Martin, Kingsley, 11 July 1937	67–8
To Martin, Kingsley, 11 July 1937	68–70
From Martin, Kingsley, 12 July 1937	70–1
To Martin, Kingsley, 25 July 1937	71–3
To Martin, Kingsley, 26 July 1937; draft letter, not sent	73
To Martin, Kingsley, 27 July 1937	78
From Martin, Kingsley, 5 August 1937	79
To Martin, Kingsley, 9 August 1937	80–1
To Martin, Kingsley, 29 September 1937	86–7
From Martin, Kingsley, 11 October 1937	87–8
To Martin, Kingsley, 18 October 1937	88–9
From Martin, Kingsley, 26 October 1937	89
To Martin, Kingsley, 7 November 1937	90
From Martin, Kingsley, 9 November 1937	90–2
To Martin, Kingsley, 10 November 1937	92–4
From Martin, Kingsley, 12 November 1937	94

DOCUMENTS REPRODUCED IN THIS VOLUME

From Martin, Kingsley, 17 January 1938   94–5
To Martin, Kingsley, 19 January 1938   95
To Martin, Kingsley, 6 February 1938 (from Lydia Keynes)   96
To Martin, Kingsley, 23 February 1938   96–7
From Martin, Kingsley, 28 February 1938   97
To Martin, Kingsley, 21 March 1938   98
From Martin, Kingsley, 22 March 1938   98
To Martin, Kingsley, 25 March 1938   108–9
To Martin, Kingsley, 28 May 1938   111–12
From Martin, Kingsley, 22 July 1938   112
To Martin, Kingsley, 25 July 1938   113–15
From Martin, Kingsley, 25 August 1938   115–17
To Martin, Kingsley, 26 August 1938   117
To Martin, Kingsley, 27 August 1938   118
From Martin, Kingsley, 9 September 1938   118–19
To Martin, Kingsley, 11 September 1938   119–20
From Martin, Kingsley, 13 September 1938   120–1
To Martin, Kingsley, 1 October 1938   122–4
To Martin, Kingsley, 4 October 1938   124
To Martin, Kingsley, 23 November 1938   127–8
To Martin, Kingsley, 23 June 1939   130–1
To Martin, Kingsley, 14 August 1939   131–2
To Martin, Kingsley, 4 October 1939   133–4
From Martin, Kingsley, 10 October 1939   135
From Martin, Kingsley, 19 October 1939   135–6
From Martin, Kingsley, 27 January 1940   136
To Martin, Kingsley, 29 January 1940   137–8
From Martin, Kingsley, 25 May 1940   138–9
From Martin, Kingsley, 26 May 1940   139
To Martin, Kingsley, 27 May 1940   140–1
From Martin, Kingsley, 2 June 1940   142–5
To Martin, Kingsley, 20 June 1940   145–6
To Martin, Kingsley, 10 August 1940   146
From Martin, Kingsley, 13 August 1940   147
To Martin, Kingsley, 14 August 1940   147–8
From Martin, Kingsley, 16 August 1940   149
To Martin, Kingsley, 25 August 1940   149–50
To Martin, Kingsley, 10 December 1940   150
From Martin, Kingsley, 10 December 1940   151
To Martin, Kingsley, 17 December 1940   151
From Martin, Kingsley, 17 January 1941   152

From Martin, Kingsley, 2 February 1941   152–3
From Martin, Kingsley, 6 February 1941   154–5
To Martin, Kingsley, 7 February 1941   155–6
From Martin, Kingsley, 10 February 1941   156–7
To Martin, Kingsley, 12 February 1941   157
From Martin, Kingsley, 20 February 1941   158
To Martin, Kingsley, 26 February 1941   158–9
From Martin, Kingsley, 9 October 1941   160
To Martin, Kingsley, 14 October 1941   160–1
From Martin, Kingsley, 7 November 1941   161–2
To Martin, Kingsley, 12 November 1941   162–3
To Martin, Kingsley, 13 November 1941   163
From Martin, Kingsley, 14 November 1941   164–5
From Martin, Kingsley, 12 December 1941   165–6
To Martin, Kingsley, 5 January 1942   166
From Martin, Kingsley, 19 August 1942   167–8
From Martin, Kingsley, 24 August 1942   168–9
To Martin, Kingsley, 28 August 1942   169–71
From Martin, Kingsley, 28 August 1942   171
From Martin, Kingsley, 4 September 1942   172
From Martin, Kingsley, 9 September 1942   172–3
To Martin, Kingsley, 10 September 1942   174–5
From Martin, Kingsley, 12 September 1942   175
From Martin, Kingsley, 21 September 1942   175–6
From Martin, Kingsley, 8 January 1943   182
To Martin, Kingsley, 12 January 1943   183
To Martin, Kingsley, 24 January 1943   183
From Martin, Kingsley, 26 January 1943   184–5
To Martin, Kingsley, 28 January 1943   185–6
From Martin, Kingsley, 5 February 1943   186–7
To Martin, Kingsley, 9 February 1943   188
From Martin, Kingsley, 11 February 1943   189
To Martin, Kingsley, 15 March 1943   190
From Martin, Kingsley, 17 March 1943   190
From Martin, Kingsley, 18 March 1943   190–1
From Martin, Kingsley, 21 March 1943   191–3
To Martin, Kingsley, 1 April 1943   193–4
From Martin, Kingsley, 5 May 1943   195
To Martin, Kingsley, 6 May 1943   195–6
From Martin, Kingsley, 25 May 1943   196–8
From Martin, Kingsley, 27 May 1943   200

To Martin, Kingsley, 3 June 1943 200
From Martin, Kingsley, 3 June 1943 201
To Martin, Kingsley, 27 July 1943 201–2
From Martin, Kingsley, 29 July 1943 202–3
From Martin, Kingsley, 5 November 1943 203–4
To Martin, Kingsley, 9 November 1943 204
From Martin, Kingsley, 11 November 1943 205
From Martin, Kingsley, 14 September 1944 205–6
To Martin, Kingsley, 15 September 1944 206–7
To Martin, Kingsley, 29 June 1945 214–15
From Martin, Kingsley, 21 July 1945 215
To Martin, Kingsley, 25 July 1945 215–16
From Martin, Kingsley, 1 January 1946 216–17
To Martin, Kingsley, 3 January 1946 217–20
From Martin, Kingsley, 7 January 1946 221
To Martin, Kingsley, 9 January 1946 221–2
From Martin, Kingsley, 21 February 1946—excerpt 222
To Martin, Kingsley, 22 February 1946—excerpt 222
To Morrell, J. B., 6 January 1931 4
To Mortimer, Raymond, 20 February 1939 128–30
From Mortimer, Raymond, [May 1945] 212
To Mortimer, Raymond, 18 May 1945 212–13
To *The New Statesman and Nation*, 14 August 1937 82
From Nicolson, Harold, 24 March 1938 105
From Noel-Baker, Phillip, 29 March 1938 109–10
To Peck, E. Saville, 23 April 1938 354–6
From Peck, E. Saville, 29 May 1938 356
From Roberts, John, 15 May 1945—excerpt 211
To Roberts, John, 16 May 1945—excerpt 211
From Salter, Sir Arthur, 29 September 1937 84–5
To Salter, Sir Arthur, 30 September 1937 85–6
From Seltman, C. T., 27 January 1926 273–5
To Seltman, C. T., 31 January 1926 275–6
From Seltman, C. T., 4 February 1926 276–7
From Shaw, George Bernard, 30 November 1934 37
To Shaw, George Bernard, 2 December 1934 38
From Shaw, George Bernard, 11 December 1934 39–42
To Shaw, George Bernard, 1 January 1935 42
From Sinclair, Archibald, 26 March 1938 105–6
To Sinclair, Archibald, 4 April 1938 106–8
To Tallents, Sir Stephen, 12 July 1937 349–53

DOCUMENTS REPRODUCED IN THIS VOLUME

To Whitley, Edward, 15 February 1934   23–4
To Whitley, Edward, 13 March 1935—excerpt   45
To Whitley, Edward, from Kingsley, Martin, 8 July 1937   66–7
To Whitley, Edward, 3 October 1939   132–3
To Whitley, Edward, 10 October 1939—excerpt   134–5
From Williams, Francis, to Kingsley, Martin, 21 May 1943   198–9
To Woolf, Leonard, 15 May 1945   213
From Woolf, Leonard, 19 May 1945   213–14

ACKNOWLEDGEMENTS

We should like to thank the following for assistance: Professor W. H. Carr, Dr Dorothy Crawford, Dr Susan Howson, the late Kingsley Martin, C. H. Rolph, Professor Robert Skidelsky and Professor Anthony Snodgrass. For permission to reproduce documents we should like to thank the late Kingsley Martin, and the Society of Authors on behalf of the Bernard Shaw Estate.

The Social Sciences and Humanities Research Council of Canada and the Master and Fellows of Clare College, Cambridge provided financial support and accommodation.

INDEX

Aberystwyth, University College of North Wales, 30, 44–5

Abydos, bronze lion of, 234, 277

Abyssinia, 79; Italian invasion of, 50, 51, 55, 64, 65–6, 83, 90, 91

Academic freedom, and the London School of Economics, 24–9

Achaeans, 282

Achilles, 282–3

Ackerley, J. R., *Hindoo Holiday*, 331; correspondence on series of articles for the B.B.C., 335–41, 439

Adcock, F. E., correspondence on ancient currencies, 277–81, 439

Admiralty, 177

Advertisements, 66–7, 70, 109, 164, 195 n 89, 254; a 'personal' advertisement, 116, 117; of pro-Fascist publications, 136–7; in *The Listener*, 338–40

Aegean, 268, 281, 289, 293
    Aeginetan drachma, 269, 274, 280; mina, 279

Agar, Herbert, personal assistant to American Ambassador in London, 192, 422

Agnew's Gallery, 308, 309

Agriculture, 237; standard of value in primitive agricultural community, 256–60

Air Ministry, 152

Air Raid Precautions (ARP), 116, 176; shelters, 367

Air warfare, 126, 139, 145, 153; R.A.F., 139, 143, 193; bombing tactics, 167, 176, 178, 181, 192

Aitken, William Maxwell, *see* Beaverbrook, Lord

Albert, Prince Consort, 342

Aldington, Richard, novelist, 391

Alexander the Great, 277; seizure of Persian temple hoards, 228 n, 231, 239, 240, 241, 242

Allen, Lord (Reginald Clifford), 119, 120, 422

America, discovery of, 227 n, 228 n, 241 n

American
    edition of *New Statesman and Nation*, 182–4, 185, 193
    paintings, 363
    politics, 216, 219
    public opinion, 84

American League, 102

American Loan Agreement, 216–22

American Office of War Information, 184

Anderson, Sir John, Chancellor of the Exchequer (1943–5), 206, 405, 422

Androtion, ancient authority on Solon, 223, 224, 225, 227 n, 268, 278, 279, 280, 281

Angell, [Sir] Ralph Norman, 164, 422; 'The New John Bull', 57

Anglo-American relations, 162, 166, 171, 189, 208, 219; negotiations on post-war planning, 203; on the American Loan, 216–22

Anglo-Czech negotiations (1938), 115

'Anti-reds', 57

Archaic civilisation, 288–9, 293

Archer, William, translation of Ibsen, 328

Archimedes, 32

Aristophanes, 229 n

Armaments, 43, 46–8, 53; rearmament, 55, 75–6, 102; JMK's stand on, 47–8; 'A Contrast of Demeanours', cartoon, 103

Armstrong, John, theatre designer, 10

Army, 167, 177, 179; the unofficial soldier, 181

'Art and the State', B.B.C. series on, 335; correspondence on, 335–41; JMK's contribution (*The Listener*, 26 August 1936), 341–9

Article VII (Mutual Aid Agreement), 215, 219

Artists, 344–5

Arts Council, 295; 'The Arts Council: Its Policy and Hopes' (*The Listener*, 12 July 1945), 367–72

Arts Theatre, Cambridge: foundation (1934), 295, 326; opening productions, Ibsen season, 326–8, 354; Vic–Wells Ballet, 326; other productions, 128, 129, 324–5,

Arts Theatre (*cont.*)
    354; transferred to charitable trust, 354, correspondence on, 354–6
'Arts in War-Time, The', 359–62
Arundell, Dennis, of St John's College, Cambridge, 318
Aryans, 288–9, 294
Ashton, Frederick, choreographer, 10
Asia, 228 n, 229 n
Asia Minor, 235, 253, 254, 260, 265
Asquith, Herbert, Prime Minister (1906–16), 32
Assyria, 243, 253, 284–5; coinage, 259 n, 275–6; lead, 281
    History of Assyria, 289–91
Athens, 225, 227 n, 280; wages, 229–30; currency, 230–1, 261
Atlantic Charter, 162
Attic standards, 243, 270, 279, 280; Attic trade mina, 272
Attlee, Clement, M.P., Leader of Labour Party, 110, 150, 422
Auden, W. H., poet, 422; 'Spain', 61, 63, 65; with Isherwood, *On the Frontier*, 128
Aureus of Constantine, 229
Austen, Jane, *Emma*, 330
Austerity, 365
Austin, John, jurist, 31, 40
Australia, 198, 201
Austria, occupied by Hitler, 98, 144
Avoirdupois grain, 236, 237–8

Babylonia
    gold–silver ratio, 240, 241, 284–5; uses of gold, 241–2
    hanging gardens, 343–4
    Mina, 231–7, 243, 264
    monetary system, 253–60, 274
    standard, 235, 239, 244–50, 265 n, 272, 281
    History of Babylonia, 289, 290, 294
'Backwardation of Wheat in Antiquity', 243, 258 n
Bacon, 158
Balance of power, 37
Balance of trade, 227–8 n
Baldwin, Stanley, Prime Minister (1923–4, 1924–9, 1935–7), 48, 50, 53, 54–5, 57; his Government, 49, 51, 54, 55, 56, 71, 81; Cabinet, 47, 74; foreign policy, 73–5; on the 'hard-faced men' of 1918, 163
Balkans, 100, 126
Ballet: puff for, 9–10; M. de Basil's Ballet Russe in London, 322–3; at the Arts Theatre, Cambridge, 128–30, 324–6,

354; at the Cambridge Theatre, London, 9–10; Diaghileff Ballet, in Paris, 313–14; at Monte Carlo, 314, 315–16; in a Midland factory, 360; at the Vic-Wells, 322
    see also Camargo Society; Covent Garden; Diaghileff, Serge; Jooss, Kurt; Rambert, Marie; Sadlers Wells; Vic-Wells
Baltic States, 100
Bancor, 359
Bank of England: rescues Ebbw Vale steel company, 112–15
Banker, The, 206
Bankers, 13, 33
Bankers' Industrial Development Company, 113
Banks, 153
Banting, John, theatre designer, 10
Barcelona, 116
Barley: as measure of weight, 235–7, grain Troy, 236; ratio to wheat, 237–8, to price of wheat, 230 n
Barnes, George, Controller of the Spoken Word, B.B.C., 341, 422
Barry, Gerald Reid, journalist, 23, 145, 422
Bartlett, Vernon, journalist, 146, 422
Basque Provinces, 101
Baylis, Lillian, of the Old Vic, 325
Baynes, Keith, painter, 308
BBC
    'Books and Authors' series, 328; JMK's contribution, 329–35
    a public for the arts created by, 369, 371
    taxed, not subsidised by the State, 345
    see also Listener, The
Beaverbrook, Lord (William Maxwell Aitken), 117, 161, 167, 173, 422
Beck, *History of Iron*, 278
Belgium, 100, 141, 143, 144
Bell, Julian, death in Spain, 73, 77, 423
Bell, Vanessa, 295, 308
Bentham, Jeremy, 16, 40
Bentinck, Lord Henry, 310
Beresford, J. D., 'Professional Pride', 350
Berlin, 26, 65, 120
Bernhardt, Prince, 170, 423
Betting
    cost of, 395–8, 400
    Royal Commission on Lotteries and Betting, evidence from JMK, 398–412; views on betting off course, or through tote clubs, 399, 401, 407–8, 410, 413, 414
Beveridge, Sir William, Director, London School of Economics, 24–8, 423

Big Five banks, 113
Bihistun, Rock of, 287
Bilbao, 59
Bill of exchange, 291
Bimetallism: in antiquity, 239–42, 282; in 19th century Europe, 241 n
Birmingham, 34, 370
Blackett, P. M. S., scientist: wins King's Fellowship, 1 n 1, 423
Blake, William, *Job*, 10
Bliss, Sir Arthur, 'Checkmate', 325
Blockade, 74, 101, 148, 179, 192; of England, 121
Blocs, economic, 221
Blood sports, 394
Blood, toil and sweat, 221
Bloomsbury, 308
Blum, Léon, Prime Minister of France (1938), 108, 423
Boer War, 41
Bohemia, 101
Bolshevism, 35, 189, 407; anti-Bolshevists, 47
Bonham-Carter, Mark, son of Sir Maurice and Lady Violet Bonham-Carter, 209, 211, 423
Bonham-Carter, Sir Maurice (Bongy), 211, 423
Bonham-Carter, Lady Violet, 423; correspondence on article in *New Statesman and Nation*, 209–11, 213; a Governor of Sadlers Wells, 211
list of letters, 439
Bonnard, Pierre, 366
Bookmakers, 395–7, 399, 400, 410
Books
book-buying habits and prices, 305–6
bookshops, 335; book trade, 365
copyright, 382
French book illustration, 365–6
'on Reading Books' (*The Listener*, 10 June 1936), 329–35
Boothby, Robert, M.P., 104, 123, 172, 173, 207, 423
list of letters, 439
Boycott, 90, 92–3
Bracken, Brendan, Minister of Information, 164, 196, 198, 201, 423
Brailsford, Noel, journalist, 23, 68, 143, 154, 423; his leaders in *New Statesman and Nation*, 59, 60, 201–3, 207, 209; other contributions, 147–8, 196, 199; proposed pensioning off, 183; difference of opinion with Kingsley Martin over his defects, 184–8; a menace to the paper (JMK),

199–200, 212; retires, 215
health problems, 153, 197
Brand, R. H., 13, 423
Brandon – Davis, Messrs, picture dealers, 302
Bread and circuses, 341–2
Bressey, Sir Charles, Report on Highway Development, 358
Bretton Woods: JMK's performance at, 205–6; controversial article on Bretton Woods agreement, 205–7; Cole on Article VII and Bretton Woods, 215
Bretton Woods transitional period, 219–20
Bretton Woods Institution, at Savannah, JMK appointed a Governor (1946), 222
Bridges, Edward, secretary to Royal Commission on Lotteries and Betting, 397, 398
Brigand powers, 47, 48, 53, 55, 64
Bristol, Theatre Royal, 358; Old Vic production of *She Stoops to Conquer*, 359–62
Britannia Insurance Co., 69
British Association, 40
British Council, 367
British Dominions, 102
British Empire, 17, 33, 60, 82, 91, 100; imperial interests, 62, in the Mediterranean, 71; defence of, 110–11, 179; not challenged by Hitler, 126; Imperialist strategy on the Second Front, 167
British Expeditionary Force, 143
British-Franco-Russian understanding (1936), 46, 48, 55, 63–4
British Institute of Adult Education, 360, 362–3
British Museum, 37
British Union of Fascists, 136–7
Britten, Benjamin, music to *On the Frontier*, 128
Broadcasting: censorship in Europe, 168. *See also* BBC
Bronze: bronze–gold ratio, 274, 275, 283; bronze–silver ratio, 267–8, 284–5, 286; iron–bronze ratio, 286; bronze standard, 259–60, 265, 281, 283; as money-metal, 272
Bronze Age in Greece, 292–4
Brown, Ford Madox, 309
Browning, Elizabeth Barrett-, 40
Bruce, William, partner of John Smith, publisher, 383
Buchman, Frank, 46 n 26; Buchmanites, or Oxford Groupers, 46, 201–3
Buck, Pearl, *see* Walsh, Mrs Richard

Budge, Sir E. Wallis, *The Rise and Progress of Assyriology*, reviewed by JMK (*Nation and Athenaeum*, 16 January 1926), 287

Buell, Mr, 174

Building industry, 114; buildings for the arts, 370–1

Bullion, 227, 228 n, 255

Bur Sin, Babylonian Emperor, 241, 241 n

Burkitt, Miles, 333

Burma, 171, 172

Burne-Jones, Edward, 309

Burns, John, Labour Cabinet Minister, 41

Burton, John Hill, *Life of Hume*, 378, 379

Business arithmetic, 342

Butler, R. A., 104, 198, 423

Butter and cheese, 158

Byron, Lord George Gordon, *The Destruction of Sennacherib*, 290

Cabinet:
Baldwin's, 47
Neville Chamberlain's (1937–40), 74, 86, 107, 135
Winston Churchill's (1940–45), 167, 192; newspaper lords in, 159; Ministers, 168, 177; alleged wish to see Russia and Germany destroy each other, 178
Labour (1945), 220, 221

Cadbury, Laurence, company director, 152, 423; correspondence as shareholder in *New Statesman and Nation*, 207–9, 213; negotiates Agreement with Russia on raw materials, 208
list of letters, 439

Calder, Ritchie, journalist, 154–7, 424; taken from *New Statesman and Nation* for war service, 196, 199

Calvin, John, 37

Camargo Ballet Society: JMK Treasurer of, 295, 318
London season (1931), 7, 8, 9, 12; 'Plays and Pictures: The Camargo Society' (*New Statesman and Nation*, 11 April 1931), 9–10; application for renewal of subscriptions, 318–20
performance at Covent Garden for delegates to World Economic Conference (January 1933), 320–2
demise of Society, 326; 'The Camargo Ballet-Society, arrangements for 1934', 322–4

Cambridge, 19, 45, 87
Arts Council in, 370
dramatic and music societies, 354; New Theatre and Festival Theatre, 326. *See also* Arts Theatre, Cambridge
JMK's early connection with, 355
Mayor of, correspondence with, 354–6; Deputy-Mayor, 355, 356

Cambridge Review, The, letter to (21 February 1921), 415–16

Cambridge Theatre, London, Camargo Ballet Society production, 9–10

Cambridge, University of, 41
Amateur Dramatic Club (A.D.C.), 317–18, 326
Faculty of Economics and Politics, 2 n 4, 3
position of women (1919), 414–16
Professors of Music and English, 355, 356
undergraduates, 35
Vice-Chancellor, 355

Capital, 37, 102; for proposed *New Statesman and Nation*, 4–5
post-war capital levy, 137

Capitalism
in antiquity, 253–4; in ancient Greece, 227
and the arts, 344
capitalists, 36
Marxist view of, 32–3, 38, 40; Capitalism and Communism, 56–7

Cardan, Jerome, *The Book of My Life*, 332

Cardiff, 370

'Carlyles at Cheyne Row, The', 350

Carthaginians, 254

Cassel, Sir Ernest, 33, 424

Catalonia, 101

Cecil, Lord Robert, 104, 424

C.E.M.A. (Council for the Encouragement of Music and the Arts): JMK chairman of, 210–11, 295, 358; reopens Theatre Royal, Bristol, 359–62; exhibitions organised by, 362–6; reshaped for peace as Arts Council, 367–8

Censorship, 133, 134, 152, 168

Central Europe, 105

Cereals, 230 n. *See also* Barley; Wheat

Cézanne, Paul, 310, 311

Chalcolithic Age, 294

Chalmers, Sir Robert, Joint Permanent Secretary, Treasury, 163, 424

Chamberlain, Arthur Neville, Prime Minister (1937–40), 424; his Government policy on defence, 110; on Italy, 96–7, 105; search for peace 'in a secret cave', 99–100, 104, 107, 108, 111, 144; attitude to Hitler's aggression, 121, 'A Contrast of Demeanours', 103; speech in Parliament, 109; attempt to buy off Hitler, 119,

Chamberlain (*cont.*)
120, meetings at Munich (1938), 122–4, 127; recalls Parliament (September 1938), 122. 'Mr Chamberlain's Foreign Policy' (*New Statesman and Nation*, 8 October 1938), 125–7*

Chancellor of the Exchequer, 368. *See also* Anderson, Sir John; Simon, Sir John

Chantrey Fund, 309–10

Chaplin, Charlie, 22

Charity, 343

Chatham House, talk on Bretton Woods at, 206–7

Cherniavsky, L., 336

Cherwell, Lord (Frederick Alexander Lindemann), 179, 429

Children's allowances, 137

China, 16
Japanese aggression in, 82, 83, 84, 90, editorial on, in *New Statesman and Nation*, 90, 92–4; guerilla warfare, 181
money system, 254

Christian civilisation, 104

Christie, Agatha, 330

Christie's sale rooms, 309

Chronica, ballet by Kurt Jooss, 128–9

Churchill, Winston, 123, 127, 143, 424; understands the lion's roar, 104; as Prime Minister (1940–45), 150, 172; visit to Moscow, 178; policy on Second Front, 179, 192, 193; Indian policy, 189; defeat after the war, 218
The World Crisis, 331

Cinema, 370; Hollywood, 371, 372

City, the, 33, 89

Civil servants, 187; JMK as a member of, 203

Civilisation
and C.E.M.A., 361–2; and Arts Council, 372
Christian, 104
history of, 292; of Greek, 292–4
and liberty, 110–11

Clare College, Cambridge, 416–21

Clark, Kenneth, 335, 337

Class-war, 36, 37, 56

Clayton, William Lockhart, 216, 217, 219, 424

Clissold, William, 33

Coal, 115

Coalition Government, 367

Coatman, John, Professor of Imperial Economic Relations at London School of Economics, 17, 424

Cobden, William, 40

Cockburn, Claude, editor, *The Week*, 119, 424

Cohen, J. L., economist, 69, 70, 79, 80, 424

Coins, 226, 229, 240, 250–2, 254–5; Seltman's coin census, 263; coin standard of Solon, 272
see also Currency; Money

Cole, G. D. H., University Reader in Economics, Oxford, 7, 46, 115, 138, 424; regular connection with *New Statesman and Nation*, 146, 149, 196, 199, 215; ill-health, 199–200
'Industry – Where and Why', 90; obituary of Beatrice Webb, 195 n 90

Cole, William, antiquary, 419–20

Collective security, 71, 91, 101, 102–4, 106, 136, 144; 'The End of Collective Security', leading article in *New Statesman and Nation*, correspondence on, 45–57

Colonies, 126

Common sense, 76, 216, 328, 330

Communism
alleged Communist teaching at London School of Economics, 26
and Capitalism, 56–7
and Fascism, 81
fight against, and the Second Front, 168, 170, 173, 180
function of art under, 335, 336
as a religion, 34–5

Communist Party
in Soviet Russia, purges of, 72
communists on staff of *New Statesman and Nation*, 214

Compound interest, 342

Concentration camps in India, 135

Confidence, 368

Connolly, Cyril, journalist, 146, 424

Conscientious objectors, 52, 77

Conservatism, 16–17, 334

Conservative Party, 47, 75, 105, 107

Consols, 41

Contemporary Arts Society, 295, 310

Contractors, 33–4

Contracts, 252, 253, 255

Convertibility, 174

Cooke, S. Russell, of King's College, Cambridge, 281

Cooling Galleries, 302, 307

Copper, 235 n, 267; silver–copper ratio, 237, 239–40, 243; as measure of value, 259, 282, 283; in Babylon, 281

Corbet, C., publisher of Hume's *Abstract...*, 377

Corn-wages and corn-rents, 258, 259

Cot, Pierre, French Minister of Commerce, 121, 424

Courtauld, Samuel, industrialist and art patron, 297, 298, 364; gift for purchase of French Impressionist paintings, 310

Covent Garden, Royal Opera House, 371; JMK Chairman of Trustees, 210–11, 295; Pavlova season, 315; Camargo Ballet at, 320–2

Coventry blitz, 362

Cows: as standard of value, 255–9; equivalence with gold talent, 283–4, 285

Crete, 281; in the Bronze Age, 292–4

Crimea, 175

Critic, columnist on *The New Statesman and Nation*, 25, 28–9; 'London Diary', 59, 75, 76, 77, 140; 'Spanish Diary', 88

Croesus, 227, 228n

Cromer, 22

Crossman, Richard (Dick), Assistant Editor, *The New Statesman and Nation*, Labour M.P., 139, 141, 147, 167, 187, 196, 199, 425; articles and leaders, 140, 142, 150, 172

    leaves *New Statesman* for war service, 146, 149, 155–6, 157, 196, 206, 207, 215

    with Kingsley Martin, *A Thousand Million Allies If You Choose*, 169

    list of letters, 439

Crozier, William, journalist, 98, 425

Cruickshank, Robert James, Ministry of Information, 184, 193, 425

Crystal Palace, 371

Currency: problems in antiquity, 239–43; reforms, 253, 260; debased currency, 226–30, 280

Czecho-Slavakia, 75, 100; and Sudeten Germans, 101, 110n51, 115–22; Munich Agreement on frontier revision, 122; alliance with Russia, 126

Dacey, W. Marring, editor of *The Banker*, 146, 206, 425

Daily Express, The, 205, 222

Daily Herald, The, 98, 149, 154–5, 205; Laski's column, 24

Daily Telegraph, The, 24, 26; 'Pertinax' on Russia, 72, 81

Daladier, Edouard, President of the Council, France, 121, 425

Danzig, 131

Darius, Emperor of Persia, 240, 287

Dartington Hall, 129

Daumier, Honoré, 15, 309, 311

Davenport, Nicholas, financial correspondent, *New Statesman and Nation*, 12, 149, 152–3, 425

Davies, Emil, financial editor, *New Statesman*, 5–6, 425

Daville, French translator of *Das Capital*, 37

Dawson, Christopher, The Age of the Gods, reviewed by JMK (*Nation and Athenaeum*, 12 May 1926), 287–9

Dawson, Geoffrey, Editor of *The Times*, 119, 120, 425

Debasement of currency, 226–30, 280

de Basil, Colonel, Ballet Russe, 322–3

Debtors, 225–6; Solon's measures for the relief of, 226n, 260, 279–81

Defeatism, 18, 19

Deferred pay, 137–8

Dégas, Edgar, sale of his collection of paintings (1918), 295

De Gaulle, Charles, Chief of the Free French, 167, 168, 170, 425; De Gaullists, 176

Delibes, Léo, *Coppélia*, 320, 321–2

Del Vayo, Don Julio Alvarez, 87, 425

Demand, for music and the arts, 361–2, 369

Democracy, 14, 36, 144

    democracies and dictatorships, 49, 104, 106; attitudes to art and the State, 336, 346–7

    liberal democracies, 212

    Spanish democracy, 74, 76, 77, 97

Demosthenes, 229

Denmark, occupation by Germany, 144

Depreciation, distinguished from debasement, 226

De Quincey, Thomas, 31, 40

Derain, André, 311, 315

Derby horse-race, 399, 402

De Valera, Eamon, Head of Government in Ireland, 138, 139, 425

de Valois, Ninette, dancer and choreographer, 316; organises Vic-Wells Ballet Company, 325

    La Création du Monde, ballet, 10; *Checkmate*, 325

Devaluation, 12–13

de Walden, Lord Howard, formation of The Forum Theatre, 314

Diaghileff, Serge, 130, 314, 315; his death, 318, 322

    Diaghileff Ballet, 9; in Paris, 313–14; at Monte Carlo, 314–16; in London, 315

Dickens, Charles, *Hard Times*, 40

Dickinson, Goldsworthy Lowes, 6, 425

Dictatorships, 58, 63, 72; and democracies, 49, 104, 106
Dieppe raid, 177
Disarmament Conference, Geneva, Germany's withdrawal, 20–1
Dobson, Frank, sculptor, 308n1
Dodd, Dr William, of Clare College, Cambridge, 418–19
Dole, 41
Dollars, 158, 220; of Mexico and Maria Theresa, 229
Dorians, 268, 274; iron standard, 282, 283
Dover, 153
Drachma, 223–9
  Aeginetan, 223, 224, 225, 227n, 260–1, 269–72, 280
  Attic, 223, 224, 225, 227n, 229, 261n, 269, 270, 279, 280
  Euboic, 223, 225, 227n, 229n, 261–2, 280
  of Solon and Pheidon, 260–3, 268–72, 279
  in currency reforms, 260–8, 276
Dublin
  Hume's *Treatise of Human Nature* published in, 375, 382–3
  JMK gives lecture on National 'Self-Sufficiency', 19–20
  Kingsley Martin interviews De Valera, 138, 139
  Trinity College, 389–90
Duff Cooper, Alfred, 425: Secretary of State for War, 47, 48, 74, 89; First Lord of the Admiralty, 123
Dungi, deified King of Ur, 231–2, 235–6, 244
Dunkirk, 178, 179
Durbin, Evan, economist, 8, 425
Duse, Eleonora, 313
Duthuit, Georges, 335, 336
Duveen, Sir Joseph, art patron, 302, 310
Dyson, Sir George, director, Royal College of Music, 210, 425

Ebbw Vale, steel works, 112–15
Economic
  aspects of Assyrian history, 291
  interests, Marx on, 105
  sanctions, 82, 83, 86, 88, 99
  welfare, and betting, 398–412
Economic Consequences of the Peace, 109, 163
Economic Journal, obituaries of Beatrice Webb by Leonard Woolf and G. D. H. Cole, 195
Economics: 'standard system' of economists, 31–3, Shaw on, 40; communism and,

34–5; JMK's revolutionary new theory, 42
Economist, 156, 209; letter to (27 December 1932), 413–14
Economists
  at Bretton Woods, 207
  function of an economist, 408
  JMK speaks as, 32, 42, 398
Eden, Anthony, Secretary of State for Foreign Affairs, 48, 54, 68, 74, 91, 92, 425; Spanish policy, 64; resigns (February 1938), 96, 97; visit to U.S., 191
  passage on, in offending article on Poland, 208, 209
Edinburgh, 370, 381
  University of Edinburgh, 292
Education, 289, 342; schools of the future, 348
  Board of Education, 367; President of the Board, 360
Edwardian age, 331–2
Efficiency, 114
Egypt, 239, 288, 293, 294
  the Egyptian Kat, 231, 234–6, 237
  monetary system, 254
  use of gold, 241, 281
Einstein, Albert: sketch of, by David Low, with commentary (JMK, *New Statesman and Nation*, 21 October 1933), 20–2; also mentioned, 40
Einzig, Paul, journalist, 206, 426
Eliot, T. S., poet and critic, 332–3
Elliott, Gilbert, 375n
Elliott Smith, Professor, 288
Elmhirst, Leonard, of Dartington Hall, 147, 426
Emmott, Lady, member, Royal Commission on Lotteries and Betting, 398, 402
Engels, Friedrich, 42
England, 18, 37, 75
  academic freedom, 26–7
  English ballet dancers, choreographers and ballets, 9–10, 325
  English paintings, 296–8, 309
  Englishmen and Americans, 85
  founding of the Arts Council, 368
  the sovereign, 228n; shilling, 229
  see also Great Britain; United Kingdom
Enjoyment, 400–1, 411, 413, 414; benefits of amusement, 412
E.N.S.A., 367
Eton College, JMK at, 171n84
Etruria, 277, 285, 294
Etymologicum Magnum, 275–6

Euboea, 282
Euboic drachma, *see under* Drachma
Euboic mina, *see* Mina
Euclid, 21
Europe, 56, 107, 227
European Pact, proposal for, 100–4, 106–8
future of Europe, 197–8
gold stocks in 1450, 229n
origins of European civilisation, 288–9; the first Europeans, 294
Second Front, in Europe, 165–70, 172–3, 175–81
Evans, Sir Arthur, *The Palace of Minos at Knossos*, reviewed (JMK, *The Nation and Athenaeum*, 6 October 1928), 292–4
Evans, David Emrys, Principal, University College of North Wales, 44, 426
Evening Standard, The, 79; Low's cartoons, 15, 'A Contrast of Demeanours', 103
Evolution, 33
Excess Profits Tax, 162
Experiment, 334
Experts, 35
Exports, 8, 208, 218
exports and imports, 8

Fabian Essays, 40
Fabiani, Martin, 366
Fabius Maximus, the Cunctator, 63
Fagel, François, 390
Far East, 84. *See also* China, Japan
Farjeon, Eleanor, 331
Farjeon, Herbert, his prologue to *She Stoops to Conquer*, 360, 362
Farmers, 349
Fascists, 28, 52, 54, 80, 93, 96, 202, 203, 335; Baldwin's attitude to, 55; and Communism, 81; Joad, 'On Not Fighting Fascism', 108–9; in England, 124; alleged European revolution against, 166, 172–3, 180
Ferrar, Nicholas, 420
Feudalism, 253–4
Finance
and academic freedom, 26
'financial' obstacle to face-lifting London, 348–9
Financial News, The, 146
Financial Times, The, 113
Finland: Finnish War, 144
Firth, Sir William, 112, 426
Fischer, Louis, journalist, 108, 426
Fokine, Mikhail, 315

Food, supplies and storage, 148, 158–9, 162
Ministry of Food, 159
Foort, Reginald, theatre organist, 350
Forbes, Mansfield, *Clare College, 1326–1926*, review by JMK, 416–21
Forbes-Robertson, Jean, actress, 326
Foreign Minister, *see* Eden, Anthony; Halifax, Lord; Simon, Sir John
Foreign Office
incompetence of, 48, 71; on Abyssinia, 64, 65–6; on Japan, 83, 86; obsession with Secret Service, 168–9; anti-Stalin line, 178, 180
relations with *New Statesman and Nation*, 136; leading article on, 82; stops publication of letters in *The Times*, 88–9
Foreign policy
Baldwin's non-alignment policy, difference of opinion with Kingsley-Martin, 48–50, 55, 58, 71; failure of, during Abyssinian War, 51, 55, 64, 65–6, 91; non-intervention in Spain, 55, 62, 64–5
Chamberlain's policy of appeasement and inaction, 96–8, 99–100, 107–9; on China, 90–1, 92–3, 95; Czecho-Slovak crisis, 116–22; Munich Agreement, 122–4; war declared on Germany (3 September 1939), 132
first duty of foreign policy, to avoid war, 63, 92–4; problem of Fascist attitude to war, 55–6
'British Foreign Policy' (*New Statesman and Nation*, 10 July 1937), 61–5; 'Mr Chamberlain's Foreign Policy' (*New Statesman and Nation*, 8 October 1938), 125–7
Forster, E. M., *A Room with a View*, 330
Fortune, 171, 174–5
Foxwell, Herbert Somerton, economist, 40–1
France
alliance with Russia and England, 37, 46, 48, 55; in a reshaped League, 47, 100, 101; 'at a low ebb' (1937), 63; incompetence of Foreign Office, 48; Navy, 78; air force, 121, 122
concern in Spanish war, 62, 75; Mediterranean interests, 71; attitude to Czech frontier revision, 116, 121, 125; is refused guarantee by Chamberlain in case of German attack, 110n 51; signs Munich Agreement, 122, bought off by Hitler, 126
declares war on Germany (3 September 1939), 132; drive on Paris expected (June

France (*cont.*)

1940), 143; invasion of (February 1941), 153, 155, 168; fall of France, 172, 179, 180; opposition movement, 170, 173, 176, 181; ignored as base for Second Front, 169–70, 179–80; occupation, and liberation, 365; post-war loan from U.S., 219

David Hume in, 373

French paintings, 298, 309–11, 363, book illustrations, 15, 365–6; poetry, 391; 'Art and the State' in, 335, 336; absence of public entertainment and ceremony, 347

responsibility for Treaty of Versailles, 99

Franco, General don Francisco, Head of Spanish State, 426: U.K. attitudes to, 62, 73–4, 78, 168, 169, 170; in Low cartoon, 103

Free trade: 'Economic Notes on Free Trade', series for *New Statesman and Nation*, 8, 11–12; in a reconstituted European League, 102

Freedom, and Marxism, 27

French Revolution, 37

Freud, Sigmund, 21, 150, 151, 392–3

Fry, Roger, art critic, 295, 308n1, 311

Funeral Insurance, 68–9, 80

Fyfe, Hamilton, journalist, 164, 426

Gambling fund theory, 405; gambling for the rich and the poor, 410

Gandhi, Mahatma, 189, 426

Gardner, Professor Percy, 268–9, 278

Garnett, David, 44n24, 152, 426; 'Books in General' (*New Statesman and Nation* column), 160; *Beany Eye*, 331

Garrick, David, 359, 362

Garvin, James Louis, editor of *The Observer*, 90, 426

Gavarni, French lithographer, 15

Geddes, Sir Auckland, M.P., Minister of National Service (1917–19), 163, 426

Geddes, Sir Eric, M.P., author of the phrase 'the pips squeak', 163, 426

General Elections, 52; (1935), 51; after Munich (1938), 123, 124; Coupon Election (1918), 163; (1945), 208, 210

General Staff, 177; French, 121

Chiefs of Staff, 179

Geneva, 65, 102

Gentleman's Magazine, 377

George V, King of England, Jubilee celebrations, 346

George, Walter, U.S. Senator, 426; and the American loan, 216, 217

Germany

a Brigand power, 47, 48, 71; withdraws from Disarmament Conference, 20–1, 22; intervention in Spain, 75, 112; sanctions used against, 88

relations with Russia, 72, 135; Ukraine, Hitler's ultimate object, 126; Soviet-German Pact (August 1939), 132; attack on Russia, 166, 167, 176, 177, 181; mutual destruction, alleged aim of Allies, 178, 194

terms to Czecho-Slovakia, 101, 110n51; frontier manoeuvres, 115; threat of general war, 116–22; appeasement at Munich, 122; dominance in Eastern Europe, 105, 106; fate of Danzig, 131; invasion of Poland, 132; further ambitions, 144–5, 181

war declared against (September 1939), 132; brutality of German soldiers, 175, 179n; technical achievements, 176; victories, 179; fall of France, 172, 179, 180; Dunkirk, 170, 179; defeat of, expected (1943), 204; the war over (May 1945), 209

gold and silver mines, 228n; Art and the State, contribution to BBC series, 335, 336; public shows under the Nazis, 347

Reichswehr, 116, 135; Foreign Office, 119; air fleet, 121, 180; foregoes Navy, 126

also mentioned, 18, 24

Gilbert and Sullivan, 352–3

Gimil-Sin, King of Ur, 231, 232, 241, 244

Glasgow

barons of, 34

Citizens' Theatre, 370–1

University, Adam Smith at, 378, 379, 380–1

Glinka, Mikhail Ivanovich, *Valse Fantasie*, 10

Glyndebourne Opera, 352, 353

Gneisenau, German battleship, 177

Goebbels, Josef, Minister of Propaganda, 108, 335, 336, 426

Gold: gold monometallism, 228n1, 241n; in antiquity, 281–2; gold–bronze ratio, 274, 275, 283

Gold and silver

of ancient Persia, 228n; in Greece and Rome, 228n

bimetallism in, 282

as money-metals, 255, 272

ratio of gold to silver, 237, 238–43, 284

supplies, and prices, 227

Gold standard: and Bretton Woods Plan, 206, 207; English sovereign the first mono-metallic gold standard in Europe, 228 n

Goldsmith, Oliver, *The Deserted Village*, 41; *She Stoops to Conquer*, 359

Goncharova, ballet-costume designs, 314

Goolden, Richard, as Mr Penny, 350

Gordon Square, JMK's London home, 7, 21, 151

Göring, Field Marshall Hermann, 180, 426

Goschen, George Joachim, Viscount, Chancellor of the Exchequer (1887–95), 41

Goupil Gallery, 302

Government, 80, 106, 110; capitalist governments, 56; Catholic governments, 180. *See also under* Baldwin, Stanley; Chamberlain, Neville

Graham-Little, Sir Ernest, M.P. for University of London, 426; tries to suppress academic freedom of speech, 24–9

Grant, Duncan, artist, 295, 308, 318, 364

Great Britain
in proposed new League, 100, 101
'Recording Britain', and 'Rebuilding Britain', C.E.M.A. exhibitions, 363
see also England; Scotland; United Kingdom; Wales

Greece, 16; Anglo-Greek war successes, 150, 151
in antiquity, *see* Chapter 2, 'Keynes and Ancient Currencies', 223–94; in the Bronze Age, 292–4; introduction of Babylonian economy, 255–60; primitive Greek standards, 243, 281–6; monetary system, 253–5; silver monometallism, 242, 282

Greene, Robert, 418

Gregory, Theodore E., economist, 12, 426

Greig, J. Y. T., editor of David Hume's *Letters*, 373 n ff
David Hume, 380

Greyhound racing, 399, 402, 413

Grigg, Sir James, Secretary of State for War, 196–7, 198, 200, 201, 427

Gris, Juan, painter, 316

Grosvenor House, 310

Grumbold, Thomas and Robert, architects, 417

Guernica, 79

Gulliver's Travels, 34

Habits, 306–7

Halifax, Lord (Edward Frederick Lindley-Wood), 429; Foreign Secretary (1938–40), 120, 136, 167, 173, 178

Hall, H. R., The Civilization of Greece in the Bronze Age, reviewed (JMK, *The Nation and Athenaeum*, 6 October 1928), 292–4

Hammersley, Samuel Schofield, M.P., 427; article on Bretton Woods agreement, 205–7

Hammurabi, Babylonian Emperor, 241

Hard-faced men, 163

Hardy, Thomas, *Tess of the D'Urbervilles*, 330, adapted for cinema, 316–17

Harmsworth, A. C., *see* Northcliffe, Lord

Harris, Arthur Travers, Bomber Command, 167, 427

Harrisson, Tom, co-founder of Mass Observation, 146, 427

Hart, Sir Basil Liddell, military correspondent for *The Times*, 147, 427

Harvey, J. M., secretary, Camargo Society, 324

Haw-Haw, Lord (William Joyce), fifth columnist, 158, 428

Heal's Gallery, Messrs, 308

Health, Ministry of, 154
public health, 342

Henderson, Hubert, editor of *The Nation*, 1

Henlein negotiations, 116

Henrion, Mr, 366

Herbert, A. P., Marriage Bill, 78

Herbert, George, 'Peace', 99, 109, 110

Herkomer, Hubert, 'The Last Muster', 309

Herodotus, 228 n, 234, 235, 240, 242 n, 254 n, 262

Hervey, Lord, 419

Hewins, William Albert Samuel, 40

Hichens, W. L., member, Royal Commission on Lotteries and Betting, 398, 402–3, 412

Hill, G. F., theory of Solon's currency reforms, 269–73, 277

Hilton, John, economist, 'This and that', broadcast talk, 349, 350

Hinkel, Staatskommissar Hans, 335, 336

History, 289; fashion and history, 313

History of the Works of the Learned, The, 377, review of Hume's *Treatise*, 377, 378

Hitler, Adolf, Chancellor of the German Reich, 427; as leader of a Fascist power, 49, 54, 55, 59; intervention in Spain, 74, 78, 89; enters Vienna, 98; aggression against Czecho-Slovakia, 116, 117, 118, 120; meetings at Munich, agreement on frontiers, 122, 125; Allies declare war against, 132, 135; aims in Russia, 126, 136, 178, 191; plans on France, 145; proposed offer of terms to, 147
see also Germany

Hittite language, 294

Hoarding, 188, 227; gold hoards of Persia, 241, 242 n

Hoare, Samuel, Lord Privy Seal, 135, 136, 168, 170, 181, 427

Hobson, J. A., economist, 427; 'A World Economy', 10, 11

Holland, 100; and the Allied cause, 141, 144

Hollywood, 371, 372

Home, Henry, friend of David Hume, 373, 375, 376–7

Home Security, Ministry of, 154

Homer, 255, 283

Hood, Thomas, 40

Horses, 288
horse-racing, 399, 401–2, 404, 410

House of Commons, 78, 110

Houses, 370

Howard, Brian, author, 149–50, 427

Howe, Quincey, 427; *England expects every American to do his duty*, 84

Hull, Cordell, Secretary of State, U.S.A., 84, 85, 427

Hulton, Edward, newspaper proprietor, 162, 167, 168, 427

Human nature, 63, 81
Treatise of, see Hume, David

Humboldt, Alexander von, traveller, 41

Hume, David
An Abstract of a Book Lately Published entitled A Treatise of Human Nature, authorship of, established, 373–90; relation of, to *Treatise*, 385–90; assignment to Adam Smith exploded, 378–84
An Enquiry Concerning Human Understanding, 375, 387
History of Great Britain, 383, 384
My Own Life, 376
Treatise of Human Nature, 373–4; Vols I and II published by John Noon (1739), 375, 376, 385, reviewed, 377, 378; second edition, terms of contract, 374, 382–3; Irish edition, 382; 'puff' written by Hume, 376, 389, published by Corbet, 377. Vol. III, 379, 381; Dublin edition, 382, 383, 387; Appendix to Vols. I and II, 382–3, 384, 385; relation to *Abstract*, 385–90

Hunger riots, 41

Hunt, William Holman, 'The Scapegoat', 309

Hutcheson, Francis: relations with David Hume, 374 n, 377 nn, 378, 380, 381 n, 382; relations with Adam Smith, as tutor and pupil, 378–9, 379–80

Huxley, Aldous, 71, 427

Huxley, Gervas, Ministry of Information, 201, 427–8

Huxley, Julian, 147, 428; peace plan, 148

Ibsen, Henrik, *Lady from the Sea*, 313; Ibsen season at Cambridge, 326–8

Idzikovsky, M., dancer, 316

Imagination, 313, 327–8, 348; Freud's scientific imagination, 392; and gambling, 399, 406

Impressionism, definition of, 311–12

India, 16, 135, 181, 289
famine, 184, 188, 189
hoarding, 188
Indian White Paper, 'The Future Form of Government for India', 18
Indianisation of Civil Service, 188
as theatre of war, 135, 189
trade with Roman Empire, 228 n

India Office, 187

Industrial Democracy, 41

Industrial insurance, 66, 67, 80

Industry: captains of, 33; socialisation of, 368

Information, Ministry of, 153, 161, 169; appealed to, for release of *New Statesman and Nation* staff from war service, 199, 201

Inge, Dean, of St Paul's, 32

Inskip, Sir Thomas, Minister for Coordination of Defence, 50, 428

Instincts, 368

Insurance: Supplement to *New Statesman and Nation* on, 66–72, 79, 80

Interest
in antiquity, 258
on American loans to U.K. and to France, 216–17, 219

International Chamber of Commerce, 65

International conferences, 11

International Peace Front, 110

Intuition, 392, 393

Invention, 388

Investment, in paintings, 297

Ionians, 274; primitive metallic standards, 282

Ireland
copyright law, 382; publication of Hume's works, 282–4
Irish sweepstake, 405–6
the war in Ireland, 138, 139

Iron
Beck's *History of Iron*, 278
iron-bar currency, 276–7, 282–3, 285

Iron (*cont.*)
  iron–gold ratio, 274; iron–silver ratio, 278,
    286; iron–bronze ratio, 284–5, 286
  as measure of value for weight, 259–60,
    265–8, 272, 274–5, 276, 282, 285–6
  price in antiquity, 277
Iron Age, 286, 287; in Greece, 293
Ironside, Field-Marshall Sir William
    Edmund, 157, 428
Isherwood, Christopher, co-author with
    Auden of *On the Frontier*, 128
Isolationism 46
Italo-Abyssinian war, 50, 51, 55, 64, 65–6, 83,
    90, 91
Italy
  Abyssinian invasion, *see* Italo-Abyssinian
    war
  in antiquity, 276, 285, 294
  one of the brigand powers, 47, 48;
    intervention in Spain, 59, 75, 87, 97, 112;
    question of resistance to, 58, 71, sanctions
    against, 83, 86–7; Eden resigns over
    Government policy on, 96, 97; control of
    Mediterranean, 121; bought off by
    Germany, 126; in the World War, 151,
    176, 191, 192; plans for anti-Fascist
    changes, 180, 203
  entertainments in, 312–13, 347; invited to
    take part in BBC programme on Art and
    the State, 335, 337
Ivy Restaurant, 176

Jackson, Sir F. S., member, Royal Commis-
    sion on Lotteries and Betting, 398, 411
James, Philip, Art Director of C.E.M.A., 365
Japan: one of the brigand powers, 47, 64; aims
    in Manchuoko, 37; aggression in China,
    82, 83, 90, 99, 126, 179; sanctions proper
    for, 86, 87, 88; her economic position, 84
Jaurès, Jean, 121
Jay, Douglas, 153, 428
Jebb, Gladwyn, Private Secretary to Under-
    Secretary for Foreign Affairs, 65–6, 83,
    86, 428
  list of letters, 439
Jennings, Humphrey, 318
Jevons, William Stanley, economist, 42
Jews, 102, 136
Joad, C. E. M., 108, 211, 428
John, Augustus, 'Symphonie Espagnole', 308
Joint stock companies, 34
Jooss, Kurt, his Ballet company, 128, 129
Joubert, M., of *Service des Œuvres*, 366
Joyce, William (Lord Haw-Haw), 158, 428

Julius Caesar, 242
Justice, 16

Kant, Immanuel, 374n
Karinska, Madame, costume designer, 130
Karsavina, Tamara, ballet dancer, 9–10, 315
  Theatre Street, 331
Kat, of Egypt, 231, 234–7
Kauffer, E. McK., theatrical designer, 325
Kchesinska, dancer, 315
Kerr, Philip Henry, *see* Lothian, Lord
Keyes, Admiral Sir Roger, 177, 428
Keynes, Florence, mother of JMK, 163, 355
Keynes, John Maynard (JMK)
  and the arts: chairman of C.E.M.A., 210;
    of Covent Garden Committee, 210–11;
    founder of Arts Theatre, Cambridge,
    326, 354–6; collector of paintings, 295;
    buys French Impressionists for National
    Gallery, 295; book-collector, 373; visits
    to the Ballet, 128–30, 325, to the theatre,
    128, 313, to the Italian puppets, 312–13;
    'Art and the State', 341–9
  career: at Treasury in World War I, 143,
    148, 163, in World War II, 153;
    connection with *The Nation and Athen-
    aeum*, 1, with *The Political Quarterly*, 2;
    chairman, *New Statesman and Nation*, 6,
    45, as a Director writes to Secretary of
    State for War, 199–200, concern with
    affairs of paper, *see* Martin, Kingsley *and
    New Statesman and Nation*; director,
    insurance company, 68; evidence on
    Lotteries and Betting, 397–412
  domestic: family connections with Cam-
    bridge town and university, 355; a walk
    on the downs, 132; supper in the kit-
    chen, 213
  health: recovery from heart attack (1937),
    58, 59, 65, 71, 80, 84, 85, 87, 105, 106,
    110, 115, 128, 349, 354; leaves his 'Welsh
    prison', 86, 87, 88; still unwell, 94;
    allowed one visitor a day, 97; tonsils,
    149
  views: academic freedom, 24–9; as Liberal,
    29; pacifism, 53; peace and war, 62–3;
    long- and short-run, 62; Shaw on, 41–2;
    quoted in Simon's calendar, 154, 155
  visits: to U.S.A. (1931), 12, (1934), 83,
    (1941), 159, (1943), Bretton Woods, 203,
    his three-day exposition of Britain's
    post-war position, 216, (1946), Sav-
    annah, 222; at Tilton, 30, 87, 88, 112,
    124

Keynes (*cont.*)

writings: payment for articles, 79, 337–40; no longer 'writing for a living', 80, 339; free 'pulls', 7; foreign rights on articles, 7; views on journalists and journalism, 185–8; on words, 154; on function of a critic, 151

work on *General Theory*, 42; reviews, *see p.* 437; with P. Sraffa, introduction to *An Abstract of a Book Lately Published entitled a Treatise of Human Nature* (David Hume), 373–90

as Siela, 312, 395

Keynes, John Neville, father of JMK, 355

Keynes, Lydia, wife of JMK (Lydia Lopokova), 20, 28, 29, 42, 65, 87, 95, 97, 105, 106, 153, 206, 209, 223; her Russian newspaper, 72, 112; vets JMK's articles, 80; cares for his health, 94, 115, 119, 120; in America with JMK, 203

letter to Kingsley Martin, 96

see also Lopokova, Lydia

Kharkov, fall of, 191

Khorsabad, 232

King, C. W., 289–90

King, Wilfrid T. C., 146, 428

King-Hall, Stephen, 120, 428

King's College, Cambridge, 1, 6, 276; and the Arts Theatre foundation, 326, 355; links with Clare College, 417, 419

Provost of King's, 355, 356

Knight, Laura, 331

Knowdler's, Art dealers, 309

Koestler, Arthur, *Darkness at Noon*, 157

Komissarjevsky, 314

Koran, 38, 41

Kyasht, dancer, 315

Labour Government, and Bretton Woods, 220

Labour, Ministry of, 149

Labour Party, 36, 69, 107, 143; and collective security, 46, 55; anti-war policy, 73–4, 75; in House of Commons, 96, 110, Front Bench, 137

Executive, 187

Lady Lever Art Gallery, Port Sunlight, 309

Lambert, Constant, *Pomona*, 10

Landowners, 33

Laski, Harold, 138, 428; repercussions from his lecture tour in Soviet Union, 24–9

list of letters, 439

Lassalle, Ferdinand, 40

Latimer, Hugh, 418

Laugier, M. *Service des Œuvres*, 366

Laurium, silver mines, 282

Layard, Sir Henry, 231, 232, 244

Layton, Walter, 104, 164, 201, 429

Lazareff, Victor, 335

Lead: weights, 273; standard, 281; currency, 291

League of Nations, 56–7, 59, 106, 218; Germany withdraws from, 20 n 17; Covenant, and Italo-Abyssinian war, 50, 51, 53, 66; position in proposed new League, 100–4

League of Nations Union, 107

Leakey, Louis, *Adam's Ancestors*, 333

Leeds, 370

Municipal Gallery, 364

Lefèvre, Messrs, picture dealers, 301–2, 309

Left, 27, 36, 52; JMK sides with opinion left of Government, 96; leanings in *New Statesman and Nation*, 59, 143, 160; and Russia's entry into war, 180, 208; censored left-wing broadcasts, 168

Legal tender, 226, 254

Leicester Galleries, 301

Leishman, Sir James, member, Royal Commission on Lotteries and Betting, 398, 409–10

Leith-Ross, Sir Frederick, 65, 429

Lenin, 227

Lerner, Abba P., economist, 56, 429

Liberal–Labour: government in Spain, 89; anti-Chamberlain pact, 123

Liberal Party, 107–8, 210

Liberals, 19, 29, 40; Young Liberals, 16; liberal states, 73

economic reform through political liberalism, 29

Liberty, 73, 110–11

war of liberation, 180

Libya: Second Front in, 165; reverse for Allies, 179

Lincoln Cathedral, 343

Lindemann, Frederick Alexander, *see* Cherwell, Lord

Lindley-Wood, Edward Frederick *see* Halifax, Lord

Listener, The: a non-profit making paper, 338–41; (10 June 1936), 'On Reading Books', 329–55; (26 August 1936), 'Art and the State', 341–9

Liverpool: barons, 34; airport, 143

Lloyd, C. Mostyn, on staff of *New Statesman and Nation*, 3, 4, 23, 67, 90, 91, 92, 117, 133, 134–5, 153, 429

Lloyd George, David, Prime Minister (1916–22), 7, 429; 'conversation' in *New Statesman and Nation*, 127; in World War II, 143, 176, 192
'Lloyd George on the Warpath', review of *War Memoirs*, Vol. II, 22
Lloyd's Bank, 112
Loans, 220; in antiquity, 252, 255, 258–9, 291 *see also* American Loan
Local authorities, 370–1
Locke, John, 387–8
Locker-Lampson, Oliver S., M.P., 22, 429
London
  blitz on, 362, 371
  as centre for the arts, 371; ballet, 10–11, 322–3
  JMK in, 84, 87, 106, 124; in Gordon Square, 7, 21, 151
  plans for beautifying, 348, 358
  see also Covent Garden; Sadlers Wells; Vic-Wells
London Artists Association: article on, in *Studio*, 297–307, 326n4; 'Economic Foreword' to exhibition catalogue, 307–8
  JMK's idea for, 297; ceases to act for (1931), 308n2
London County Council, 41, 371
London Group of artists, 295, 303; foreword to exhibition catalogue (1921), 295, 296–7; prices of pictures on display at Heal's (1923), 308–9
London Mercury, 79
London School of Economics, 2; controversy over academic freedom, 24–9; terms of charter, 26
London University, 26, 42
  Principal of, 24–5; Vice-Chancellor, 25
Londonderry, Lord, Lord Privy Seal, 47, 429
Longmann, publisher, 381n
Long-run, and short-run, 62
Lopokova, Eugenia, ballerina, 315
Lopokova, Lydia (Mrs J. M. Keynes), ballerina, 315, 318, 325; dances in Camargo Society ballets, 9, 10; acts in *A Doll's House*, 326; praise for the Jooss Ballet, 128–9
  see also Keynes, Lydia
Lothian, Lord (Philip Henry Kerr), 84, 428
Low, David, 182, 429
  cartoons for *Shaw–Wells–Keynes...*, 36, 39
  'A Contrast of Demeanours', 103
  Low's Russian Sketchbook, reviewed by JMK in *New Statesman and Nation*, 13–19
  'This England' Christmas Card, 87–8

Lucas, Peter, 132, 429
Luce, Henry Robinson, 171, 174–5, 429
Ludmilla, Anna, American ballerina, 9
Luther, Martin, 37
Lydian Mina, 231–7, 261–2, 264–8, 270–2; coins, 254n, 274
Lynd, Robert (Y. Y.), columnist on *New Statesman and Nation*, 159. *See also* Y. Y.
Lyttelton, Dame Edith, letter to *New Statesman and Nation*, 357–8

McAdam, Ivison, Ministry of Information, 207, 429
Macaulay, Thomas Babington, 31, 40
McCarthy, Desmond, critic, 191, 429
McCombie, King's College, Cambridge, 276
Macdonald, Ramsay, Prime Minister (1924, 1929–35), 7, 41, 430
McKenna, Reginald, Chairman of Midland Bank, 156, 430
MacKenzie, Norman, assistant editor, *New Statesman and Nation*, 214, 430
Macmillan, Harold, M.P., 164, 430
Macmillan Committee, JMK's involvement in, 12
Madrid, 116
Mahomet, 41
Maisky, Ivan Mikhailovich, U.S.S.R. Ambassador, 430; obituary of Beatrice Webb, 195
Maitland, A., member, Royal Commission on Lotteries and Betting, 398, 403, 411
Malaya, 181
Manchester, 34, 228n, 370; Manchester school of economics, 40
Manchester Guardian, 2, 78; letter to (17 December 1932), 412–13
Manchuoko, 37
Manet, Edouard, 309, 311
Maple, Messrs, furnishers, 294
Margesson, Henry, M.P., 178, 430
Marinetti, Signor, 337
Market, 88, 115
Marsh, Edward, 310
Marshall, Alfred, economist, 40, 41
Martin, Kingsley
  career: fails King's Fellowship, 1, 60; teaches at London School of Economics, 2; leader writer, *Manchester Guardian*, 2; joint editor, *Political Quarterly*, 1–2; refuses Professorship at Aberystwyth, 30, 44–5
  editorship of joint *New Statesman* and *The Nation*, 2–6; as editor, 73–4, 90–1, 111,

Martin, Kingsley (*cont.*)

117, 119, 130–1, 138–9, 141, 187, 189; problem of staff in wartime, 196–201; advertising problems, 136–7; Vallence's offending article, 214–15; salary arrangements, 23, 45, 185

his leading articles, 8, 10–11, 44, 196; 'The End of Collective Security', 45–50; 'Will Stalin Explain?', 57; on foreign policy, 60, 82, 90; 'What We Ought to Do', 111; American Loan, 216–22

other leaders, 59, 140, 189, 201–2; policy on leading articles, 121

ill-health, 4, 23–4, 29, 128; boils, 79, 80; tonsils, 149, 153

pacifism, 16, 71, 80, 89

visits: to America (1923), 1, (1942), 172, 173, 175, 182, (1945), 207, 209, 210, 211, 214; to Russia, with Low, 13; *Low's Russian Sketchbook*, with text by Kingsley Martin, 14–16; to Spain, 87, 88; to Ireland, 138–9

writings: *Father Figures*, 13; *Propaganda's Harvest*, 163, 164; with Crossman, *A Thousand Million Allies If You Choose*, 169; obituary of Beatrice Webb, 195

list of letters, 439–43

Martin, Olga, wife of Kingsley Martin, 29

Marx, Karl, 21, 40, 41, 105; Marxism, 27, 28, 29; controversy with Shaw over, 30–42

Das Capital, 37, 38, 41

Mass Observation, 150

Massigli, René, French Ambassador, 366

Massine, Léonide, 129–30, 315, 322

Matisse, Henri, 311, 366

Meat, 158–9

Mediterranean

in antiquity, 239, 294

British interests in, 71, 75, 100; Italian, 121, 126

and Spain, 79

Meerut conspiracy case, 17, 18

Megalithic culture, 288

Merchant princes, 33

Mersdach-sar-itani, 244

Metric system, 239

Metrology, 276

M.I.5., 172–3

Midland Bank, 156

Milhaud, Darius, 10

Militarism, 99

Milk, 342

Mill, John Stuart, 16

Millais, John Everett, 309

Milne, A. A., 393–4

Mina, 224–5, 232–7, 270–3; in table of weights, 232, mina weights, 277; of Ur, 244; in Pheidonian and Solonic reforms, 260–8, 279; market and currency mina, 278

Ministers, 106

Minorities, 94

Minos, Palace of, 292–4

Missionaries, 84, 85

Monet, Claude, 312

Money

and academic freedom, 28

history of, begun by Solon, 226–7

money of account, 226, 253; representative, 254

moneylenders, 116,117

wasted in gambling, 404, 410–12

Monkey Brand, 309

Monnington, Tom, artist, 364

Monometallism, 240, 242–3

Monopoly, 402

Monte Carlo, 396, 399, 402

Montgomery, Bernard Law, commander of Eighth Army, 191, 430

Moore, Henry, sculptor, 364

Moore-Brabazon, J. T. C., Minister of Aircraft Production, 173, 178, 192, 430

Morals, 62, 104, 216; in advertisements, 116, 117; one's duty, 407; of gambling, 411

Morgan, J. Pierpont, financier, 40, 255

Morgenthau, Henry, Secretary of the Treasury, U.S., 83, 430

Morrell, J. B., newspaper proprietor, 4, 430

list of letters, 443

Morrison, Herbert, M.P., 127, 430

Mortgages, 258; Solon's reforms of, 281

Mortimer, Raymond, literary editor, *New Statesman and Nation*, 44 n 24, 133, 163, 165, 169, 202, 430; his salary, 185, 186–7; correspondence on an offending article, 212–13

Channel Packet, 186

list of letters, 443

Moscow, 26, 35, 165

Laski's lecture in, 27

retreat from, 126

as seat of government, 208

Mosley, Sir Oswald, 89, 430; 'The British Peace and How to Get It', 136–7

Motor industry, 114

Muir, Ramsay, Chairman, National Liberal Federation, 431; letter to *New Statesman and Nation*, 8

Munich: agreement on Czech frontier revision, 122, 144, 178

Murphy, John, 412–13

Music, 352–3, 361; demand for, 369
Professor of Music, Cambridge University
(Edward Dent), 355, 356

Mussolini, Benito, Duce of Italy, 31, 51, 143,
202, 431; British attitudes to, 54, 58, 74,
97, 126, 136; invasion of Abyssinia, 91;
intervention in Spain, 59, 78
in Low cartoon, 103

Mutual Aid Agreement, 219

Mycenae, 274, 288, 293

Myers, L. H., art patron, 298

Napoleon, 126, 176

Nathan, Montagu, secretary of the Camargo
Society, 10

Nation and Athenaeum, The: editor (H. Henderson), 1; JMK's involvement with
management, 1, 2, 326n 4; amalgamation with New Statesman, 2–6, 11, first
issue, 7; 'Nation' group on new Board of
Directors, 210
contributions from JMK: anonymous,
287–94, 295, 312–18, 395–97; by 'Siela',
308–12; signed reviews, 'Clare College'
(17 January 1931), 416–21; letters to,
391–5

National Gallery, 364, 366; JMK a Trustee
of, 295, 358; and French paintings, 310,
363

National Labour Party, 107

National monuments, 343–4

'National Self-Sufficiency', 19–20

National Socialist Party (Nazis), 118n57, 336

National Theatre, proposal for, 356–8, 371

Nationalisation, 68

Natural Law, 33

Navy, 52, 55, 56, 74, 75, 78; delay in
mobilisation, 125; Germany foregoes
fleet, 126

Nazis, 28, 105, 139, 147; and Einstein, 22;
pro-Nazis in England, 122; Nazi oppression in France, 176; point of view
on cultural matters, 335, 336

Nebuchadnezzar, King of Babylon, 231, 244,
284n

Nechamkin, S., 366

Nehru, Jawaharlal, Congress Party leader,
189, 431

Nemchinova, Mme, ballerina, 316

Neolithic culture, 288

Neutral countries, 138, 141, 144

New Deal, 83, 175, 187

New Republic, The, 182

New Statesman, The: founded by Beatrice
Webb and G. B. Shaw, 95; editorship
offered to Kingsley Martin, 2, 3;
amalgamation with Nation and Ath-
enaum, 2–6, 11

New Statesman and Nation
amalgamation of New Statesman and
Nation and Athenaeum, 2–6; first issue,
6–8; incorporates Week-End Review, 23
Board of Directors, 141, 145, 154, 162,
182–6, 203, 210, 211; JMK chairman of
Company, 6
Caliban's problems, 403
circulation, 112, 153, 162–3, 164–5, 200
City page, 149, 152–3, 155, 156, 157
editor, Kingsley Martin: appointment, 2–6;
difference of opinion with JMK on
editorial policy and leaders, 10–11,
16–19, 46–50, 59, 71, 90–4, 97, 134, 138,
140–1, 147–51, 166–70, 185–9, 190–4,
201–3; on 'Sanity in Poland', 207–15;
cases of approval, 25, 46, 57, 86, 88, 90,
108, 111, 113, 124, 140, 142, 149, 151,
195, 196, 214; wartime problems of
staffing, 154, 155–7, 196–201, of paper
shortage, 160, 161–3, 164–5
JMK, articles and letters: 'Plays and
Pictures' (11 April 1931), 9–10; 'Enjoying Russia' (10 December 1932),
14–16; 'Einstein' (21 October 1933),
21–2; 'Professor Laski and the Issue of
Freedom', (15 July 1934), 25–7; 'Mr
Keynes Replies to Shaw', (10 November
1934), 30–5; 'British Foreign Policy' (10
July 1937), 61–5; (15 March 1938), 'A
Positive Peace Programme, 99–104; (8
October 1938), 'Mr Chamberlain's Foreign Policy', 125–7; (28 January 1939),
'Democracy and Efficiency', published
conversation, 127
letters: 35–6, 43, 46–8, 48–50, 50–4, 54–6,
56–7, 110–11, 320–2, 356–7, 357–8
Libel case settled out of court, 203–5
London Diary, 24, 91, 128, 139, 158, 172,
216
Low sketches, 20; Einstein (JMK), 20–2
pamphlet: Shaw–Wells–Keynes on Stalin–
Wells Talk, 36–40
pictures, proposed and ruled out, 130–1
problems of advertising, 66–7, 116–17,
136–7
proposed American edition, 182–5, 193
reports: from America, 209, 210, 211,
216–17; from Spain, 88

New Statesman and Nation (*cont.*)
  salaries, 185
  Supplements, 12, 66–72
Newcastle-on-Tyne, 370
Newcastle Programme, 40
News Chronicle, The, 98, 146, 208
Newspapers, 15, 33, 217, 329, 330; Russian
  newspapers, 72, 112; newspaper lords in
  the Cabinet, 159; newspaper competi-
  tions, 401, 403, 405; Sunday papers, 399,
  408–9
  see also Press
Newton, Sir Isaac, 241 n, 388
Nicolson, Harold, M.P., 104, 105, 123, 431
  list of letters, 443
Nijinska, Mme, ballerina and choreographer,
  314, 316
1941 Committee, 162, 164
Nineveh, 231, 234, 244, 254n
Noel-Baker, Philip, M.P., 74, 104, 109–10,
  431
  list of letters, 443
Non-intervention, 74–5, 78, 97, 101
Noon, John, London publisher, 374, 381
Nordic peoples, 294
Norman, Montagu, Governor of the Bank of
  England, 112, 202
North Africa, as theatre of war, 176, 187, 192
Northcliffe, Lord (A. C. Harmsworth), news-
  paper proprietor, 164, 427
Norway: as a neutral country, 138, 141, 144;
  resistance party, 173
Nottingham, 370

Obols, 285, 286
Observer, The, 7, 185, 187
Occupied areas, 148, 167
Oil, oilseed, 16, 158, 308
Ojetti, Ugo, 335
Old Vic, The, 129
Oley, Barnabas, of Clare College, Cambridge,
  417
Opinion, 93, 96, 120, 372
  American, 218
  freedom of, 26, 27, 28
  influence on, of *New Statesman and Nation*,
  200
  see also Public opinion
Opposition, parliamentary, 50–1, 54, 106. *See
  also* Labour Party
Ord, Boris, of King's College, Cambridge, 318
Owen, Sir David, member, Royal Commission
  on Lotteries and Betting, 398, 408–9,
  411–12

Oxford, 379, 381
Oxford Group, 46 n 26, 201–3
Oxford University Press, 392

Pacifism
  extreme pacifists, 47; non-resistance, 53,
  94, 100, 105
  JMK's 'pacifist leanings', 53, 62
  Kingsley Martin's, 16, 71, 80, 89; in *New
  Statesman and Nation*, 53, 68, 143
  negative pacifism, 99–100
  pacific powers, 47, 48; pacific propaganda,
  56–7
Panikkar, Prime Minister of Bikaner, 189
Paper shortage, 160–3, 165–6, 365
Paris, 143, 295, 365
Paris, M., of the French Embassy, 366
Parliament, 367–8; Marriage Bill, 78
Patronage, of the arts, 297, 368, 369
Pavlova, Anna, 315, 318, 322
Peace, 49, 55, 73
  C.E.M.A. reshaped for, 367–8
  JMK's stance on, 62
  and Munich, 122–3
  Peace Ballot, 53
  proposed peace offer (1940), 147
  prospects in China, 93
Pearl Harbour, 178
Pearl Insurance Company, 69
Pears' Soap, 'Bubbles', 309
Peisistratus, 223, 227n, 279
Pelasgians, 294
Peleponnesians, 262, 267, 282
Pelham, Thomas, Duke of Newcastle, 419
People's Palace, 358, 371
Pericles, 228n, 229
Pernice, *Griechische Gewichte*, 270, 272–3, 277
Perry, Mr, 288
Persian Empire, 253; temple hoards, 227, 231;
  silver–gold bimetallism, 239–43; Persian
  daric and shekel, 243
Pertinax, *Daily Telegraph* columnist, 72
Pétain, Philippe, Marshall of France (1918),
  Prime Minister (1940–2), 153, 169, 431
Petiet, Henri, 366
Pheidon, 260, 274
  Pheidonian mina, 269, 270
  Pheidonian currency reforms, 260–73, 282,
  286
Phipps, Mr, College Butler, 420
Phoenician mina, 234, 235; shekel, 237
Picasso, Pablo, 311, 366
Picture dealers, 301–3
Picture Post, 310

Pilgrim Trust, 362, 363, 367
Pitcairn, Frank, 28–9
Plato, 32, 242n
Plebiscite, for Czechoslovakia, 119, 122
Pliny, 228n, 286
Plutarch, 229n, 268, 278, 279, 285
Plymouth blitz, 362
Poland, 17, 100, 123n; bought off by Germany, 126; invaded by Germany, 132, 144; guarantee of, 136, 143
‘Sanity in Poland’, leading article in *New Statesman and Nation*, controversy over, 207–15
Pole, J., of United Artists Corporation, 372
Political Economic Planning, 70, 72
Political economy, 333
Political Quarterly, The: JMK on editorial board, 2; ‘The New John Bull’ (Norman Angell, July–September 1936), 57
Political Warfare, 168, 169
Polycritic, *New Statesman and Nation*, 128
Pompeii, 273
Pope, Alexander, 376n
Pope, the, 31
Popular Front, 123
Population, 102
Post Office, 80
Poverty, 406–7
Practical men, 40–1
practical politics, 88, 106, 173
Preferences, under Mutual Aid Agreement, 219
Preservation of the countryside, 343–4, 347–9
Press, 14
censorship, 152, and betting news, 414
fascist, 121–2
German, 25
see also Newspapers
Prices: in antiquity, 226–31; in Assyria, 291
Priestley, J. B., 431; proposed for Board of Directors, *New Statesman and Nation*, 145–6, 162–3, 165; his 1941 Committee, 162, 164; lunch with JMK, 173, 175
Prime Minister, 348
see also Baldwin, Stanley; Chamberlain, Arthur Neville
Priority bag, 184, 193
Production, 177
productivity, and gambling, 406
Profit: in the gambling industry, 405, 410
Propaganda, 64, 85, 121, 164, 165, 190; *New Statesman and Nation* as a propaganda organ, 143, 173; Kingsley Martin's propaganda-conditioned mind, 193

Property, 37, 40
Pros and Cons, 43
Prosperity, 105
Prudential Insurance Company, 69
Psychology, 107, 176, 202, 216, 333; of gambling, 404, 412; Freud's theories of psycho-analysis, 150, 151, 392–3
Ptolemy Philadelphus, 228n, 231n
Public, the, and pictures, 305–7
public entertainment by the State, 344–7
Public opinion, 52, 53, 257
American, 84
on betting, 407
on the Labour Party, 76
Munich Agreement unsupported by, 122
and *The New Statesman and Nation*, 55, 56, 59
and sanctions, 82, 86, 92
see also Opinion
Puritanism, 345
Pythagoras, 32
Pythius, 242n

Quislings, 144
Quotas, 115

Radek, Karl, 431; trial in Moscow, 57–8
Radio Times, The, 353
Rae, John, *Life of Adam Smith*, 378–9, 381n
Rambert, Marie, Ballet Club, 320, 322, 360
Ramsey, Michael, correspondent of David Hume, 375–6
Rand, 228n
Rathbone, Eleanor, 67, 431
Raw materials, 208
Raw Materials Inquiry, 65
Rawlinson, Sir Henry, Assyriologist, 287
Reason and custom (Hume), 388–9
Reconstruction, 171, 198
Redfern Gallery, 302
Reds, 167; anti-Reds, 191
Rees, Miss, JMK's secretary, 11, 12
Reformation, 37
Refuge Insurance Company, 69
Refugees, 107
Renaissance, 253–4; in Assyria, 291
Resistance movements, 192, 193
Revelstoke, Lord, 33
Revenue tariff, proposals for, 6–7
Revolution, 34
French Revolution, 37
Russian Revolution, 37
Second Front as revolution against Fascism, 166–70, 172–3

INDEX

Ribbentrop, Joachim von, German Minister for Foreign Affairs, 118, 431

Ricardo, David, economist, 40, 41; Ricardian foundations of Marxism, 42

Right wing, 27, 173

'Rights of Man', (Kingsley Martin, *New Statesman and Nation*), 16

Risk, 414

Roads, 344

Robbins, Lionel, economist, 207, 431

Roberts, John, business manager of *New Statesman and Nation*, 4, 5, 45, 67, 68, 116, 152, 153, 154, 164, 182, 183, 184, 185, 186, 193, 431; correspondence on offending article, 211
list of letters, 443

Roberts, William, painter, 308

Robertson, Dennis, adviser to Treasury, 207, 431

Robertson, Miss, Kingsley Martin's secretary, 156, 198, 431

Robinson, Austin, economist, 3, 432

Robinson, Joan (Mrs Austin Robinson), economist, 146, 432

Robson, W. A., joint editor, *Political Quarterly*, 2, 67, 71, 432

Rockefeller, J. D., 40

Rodd, Francis, 432; 'libellous reference' to in *New Statesman and Nation*, 201–3, 432

Rodd, Lady, wife of Francis Rodd: an Oxford Grouper, 201–3

Röhm, Ernst, storm trooper, 25, 432

Roman Empire, 228n; bronze standard, 282
Roman pound, 231–7, 273; Libral As, 275, 283, 285, 286
Roman standards, 243, 259

Roosevelt, Franklin D., President of U.S.A., 107, 191, 432; meeting with JMK, 83, 85; and sanctions against Japan, 84, 86; his death, 217–18

Rossini, Gioacchino, *La Boutique fantasque*, 315

Rothermere, Lord (H. S. Harmsworth), newspaper proprietor, 52, 54, 57, 427

Rothschild, Lord, 33

Roualt, Georges, 366

Rousseau, Jean-Jaques, 16, 37

Rowlatt, Sir Sydney, chairman, Royal Commission on Lotteries and Betting, 398, 400–2, 408, 411, 412

Rowntree, Arnold, M.P., 5, 139, 432

Rowntree Trust, and amalgamation of *The Nation* with *The New Statesman*, 4, 5

Rowse, A. L., 10, 11, 432

Royal Academy, 364

Royat, JMK recuperates at, 131, 132

Ruhr, 79

Russell, Bertrand, 71, 432

Russell, Dora, 35, 432

Russia
alignment with 'peaceful nations', 37, 46, 47, 48, 55, 63, 100; potential militarism, 99; no guarantee by, for Czech frontiers, 121, 122–3, 125, or for Polish, 143; doubts on her cooperation, 117, 122–3, 160
German aims on, 123n, 126; Soviet–German non-aggression pact, 132, 136; German attack on, 162, 167, 173, 176, 177, 178, 190–1; British Government attitude to, 144, 173, 178, 179–80, 191, 192, 194, 208–9; and Western offensive, 165–6, 167, 173, 177–8, 189, 192–3; offending article on, in *New Statesman and Nation*, 206–9, 212, 215
art: Russian ballet, 9, 313–16, 322, 325; contribution to BBC series, 'Art and the State', 335, 336; authoritarian state shows, 347; theatres and concert-halls, 370
and India, 135, 189
Laski's lecture tour, 24–9
Low's Russian Sketchbook, 13–19
Russian Revolution, 37; controversy with Shaw over, 30, 34–9
Soviet Communism (Beatrice and Sidney Webb), 333–4

Ruthin Castle, Wales, JMK returns from, 97

Rylands, George (Dadie), 12, 355, 432

Sacco and Vanzetti, alleged miscarriage of justice, 17

Sadler, Sir Michael, 310

Sadlers Wells, 210, 325

St George's Gallery, 302

St Nazaire, 180

Salariat, 34

Salter, Sir Arthur, 83–6, 432
list of letters, 443

Sanctions: should be applied against Japan, 82, 83, 86, 90, 92–3; problem of Spain, 87, 88; used against Germany, 88; as part of new League of Europe, 99, 100, 101, 102

Sandys, translation of Aristotle, 277

San Francisco, 209, 210, 211

Sargent, John Singer, painter, 311–12

Sassoon, Siegfried, poet, 418

Savannah, JMK attends Bretton Woods Institution at, 222
Scandinavia, 91, 100
Scharnhorst, German battleship, 177
Schleicher, General Kurt von, 25, 432
School text-books, 43–4
Schubert, Franz, 351
Schwartz, George, 153, 154, 432–3
Scotland: 'Living Scottish Artists', C.E.M.A. exhibition, 364; Arts Council of Scotland, 370–1; copyright law, 382
Scott, W. W., 389; *Francis Hutcheson*, 379–80; *Adam Smith as Student and Professor*, 380n, 381
Seaton, Rev. Thomas, 419
Second Front, 165–73, 175–81, 191–4
Second generation, 33–4
Sedan, 122
Sedition, 51, 52; Sedition Bill, 27
Segonzac, Dunoyer de, 366
Seltman, Charles, archaeologist, 282; coin census, 263, 265; correspondence on metrology, 273–7
list of letters, 443
Semites, 289
Sergueeff, M., Ballet Master, 325
Seurat, Georges, 311
Severini, Signor, 337
Shakespeare, William, 22; *As You Like It*, 351; *A Lover's Complaint*, 317–18; *Macbeth*, 100; Shakespeare's Cliff, 343
Shamsi-Adad, King of Assyria, 291
Sharp, Clifford Dyce, journalist, 211, 433
Shaw, A., member, Royal Commission on Lotteries and Betting, 398, 409, 411
Shaw, Charlotte (Mrs G. B. Shaw), 42
Shaw, George Bernard, 306, 393, 433
'Mr Keynes Replies to Shaw', on Wells and Stalin, 30–5; objects to publication of *Shaw–Wells–Keynes on Stalin–Wells Talk*, 36–42
preference for tyrants, 36
share in foundation of New Statesman, 95
St Joan, 31
'Uncommon Sense about the War', 133, 134, 136
list of letters, 443
Shelley, P. B., 109
Sheppard, Dick, vicar of St Martin-in-the-Fields, 433: Peace campaign, 53–4, 90, 92
Shipping, 158, 178, 179; for the Dieppe raid, 177; shipowners, 33
Ministry of Shipping, 177

Shove, Gerald, 29, 433
Siberia, 126
Sicily, 191, 192
Sickert, Walter, 306, 363
Sidebotham, Herbert, journalist, 89, 433
Siela, pseudonym of JMK, 312, 395
Silesia, 126
Silk, 308
Silliness, 420
Silver
 in Assyria, 291
 in China, 254
 coins, in antiquity, 254, 262, 274
 silver monometallism, 240, 242, 243
 as standard of value, 260, 265, 275, 281, 286
 see also Gold and silver; Copper–silver
Simon, E. D., M.P., 8, 145, 433; his calendar, 154, 155
Simon, Sir John, 433; Foreign Secretary (1931–5), 83, 116; Chancellor of the Exchequer (1937–40), 137
Sinclair, Sir Archibald, Liberal Leader, 104, 433
Sinking fund, 230n
Sinn Fein, 121
Skinner, Sir Sydney, member, Royal Commission on Lotteries and Betting, 398, 407–8, 412
Slavinsky, M., dancer, 316
Slumps, 308, 348
Smith, Adam: not the author of *An Abstract of Hume's Treatise of Human Nature*, 373, 378–82
Smith, John, Dublin printer and bookseller: identified as 'Mr Smith' of Hume's *Abstract*, 378–84
Smith, Hindley, 298
Smith, Sidney, *Early History of Assyria to 1000 B.C.*, reviewed by JMK (*The Nation and Athenaeum*, 12 May 1928), 289–91
Snowden, Phillip, Chancellor of the Exchequer (1924, 1929–31), 7, 433
Social insurance, supplement to *New Statesman and Nation* on, 67, 68–70, 71–2
Social wealth, 349
Social workers, 403
Socialism, 7, 40, 89; involved in a Second Front, 180; in ancient Egypt, 253
'Socialist, A': replies to letters from, in *New Statesman and Nation*, 50–6, 110–11
Sokolova, Mme, 316
Solon
 'Note on the Monetary Reform of Solon',

466

Solon (*cont.*)
    223–31, further references, 243, 254, 255, 260, 261–4, 267–8, 279; Aristotle on, 268–73; silver monometallism, 282
    relief for debtors, 279–81
    Solonian mina, 269–71
Somme, 143
South Wales, and Ebbw Vale project, 115
Spain
    Civil War: difference with JMK on stance taken by *New Statesman and Nation*, 48–50, 55, 60–5, 68, 75–9, 80–1, 87–90, 97; could be saved by determined effort (Kingsley Martin), 87, 89, 105, 170; policy of non-intervention (JMK), 55, 68, 83, 88, 97, 101, proposal for negotiated peace, 101
    Italian intervention, 59, 87, 91, 97, 112; plans for anti-Fascist revolution, 172, 180
    gold and silver, 228n, 229n
    Government, 87, 89, 112, 126
    Posters, 150
    'Spain' (W. H. Auden), 61, 63, 65
    Spanish Provinces, 100
Sparta, 228n, 265, 282–3
Spectator, The, 17, 95, 161
Speculative building, 341
Spits, of iron, 262, 263–4, 265, 274–5, 282 285
'Spring Tale', ballet, 129
Sraffa, Piero, joint author with JMK of introduction to *Abstract of a Book Lately Published...* by David Hume, 373–90
Stalin, Joseph, 433
    interview with H. G. Wells, 30–3, 34; *Shaw–Wells–Keynes on Stalin–Wells Talk*, 36–9; 'a gramophone', 31, 41
    Moscow trials, 57, 59, purges, 72; 'Will Stalin Explain?' (Kingsley Martin), 57
    relations with Hitler, 135, 136, 178; his chestnuts, 177–8
    also mentioned, 157, 165, 192
Standard of living, 8
State lottery, 399, 401, 402–3, 405–6, 409–10, 413
Stater, 233, 237, 260, 264–6, 270, 283–4
Steel, 114
Steer, George Lowther, *Times* war correspondent, 79, 433
Steer, Wilson, artist, 363
Stephen, Leslie, on David Hume, 379
Sterling; penny of Henry III, 236n; £ sterling, 240

sterling area, transitional period for, under Bretton Woods Agreement, 219–20
Stettinius, Edward R., Lend Lease Administrator, 208, 209, 433
Stewart, Dugald, 381
Stimson, Henry, 84, 433
Stock Exchange, 399, 406
Stocks, Mrs J. L., member, Royal Commission on Lotteries and Betting, 398, 404–7, 408, 411
Stone weights, 273
Stonehenge, 342
Storage proposals, 115, 148
Strabo, 262
Strachey, John, M.P., 153, 171, 173, 174, 175, 433
Strachey, Lytton, 330
Strahan, William, 383
Stravinsky, Igor, composer, 313–14; *Tale of a Soldier*, 317–18
Strikes, 46
Studies (Dublin), 20
Studio: 'The London Artists' Association: Its Origins and Aims' (June 1930), 297–307
Submarine warfare, 177
Subsidies, 228n
Sudeten Germans, 101, 110n51, 120; under Munich Agreement, 122
Sugar, 158
Sumeria, 231, 232, 239, 244, 288, 290, 293
Sunday Times, The, 185
Supply, Ministry of, 149, 154, 161, 162
Surplus value, 37
Susa, bronze lion of, 232–3
Sussex Downs, 132
Sweden, 144
Sweezy, Paul, economist, 56, 433
Swift, of *The New Statesman and Nation*, 69, 70, 79
Swithinbank, Bernard, Adviser to the Secretary of State for Burma, 171, 172, 433
Switzerland, 100, 120

Talent, 224, 225, 279; bronze lions representing, 232, 234; in currency reforms, 260–8; Homeric, 283–6
Tallents, Sir Stephen, Controller of Public Relations, BBC, 337, 434; letter to, on listening to the radio, 349–53
Tansley, A. G., *The Collected Papers of Sigmund Freud*, 392
Tariffs, 12–13
    Tariff Reform League, 40
Tate Gallery, 298, 310, 363, 364

Tawney, R. H., 434; chairman, Committee on school text-books, 43
Taxation, and gambling, 399, 404
Tchaikovsky, Peter Ilyich, 'Lac des Cygnes', 320, 321–2
Tchernicheva, Mme, ballerina, 316
Technique, in drama, 327–8
Telephones, 17
The Times, 152, 343, 395, 396; on Czech frontier revision, 118–21; wartime size, 159
  'The Arts in War-Time' (11 May 1943), 359–62; letter to (11 July 1945), 372
Theodosius II, 241 n
'This England', 87–8, 89
Thomas, Richard and Company, Ebbw Vale steel works, 112–15
Thorndike, Dame Sybil, 359
Thousand Million Allies If You Choose, A, 169, 173
Thucidydes, 81, 89, 228 n
Tilton, JMK's country home, 30, 86, 87, 88, 112, 124
Time, 34, 310; in evolution of money system, 255
Time lags, 35, 40, 148
Time and Tide, 161
Tin, 308; tinplate, 114
Tolstoi, Leo, 391–2
Toscanini, Arturo, 352
Totalitarian states, 73, 99, 111, 126; success with public shows, 347, 357
Toulouse-Lautrec, Henri de, 366
Trade
  Assyria as a trading nation, 290–1
  standards of exchange value for, in antiquity, 257–60; trade mina, 271, 272; trade weights, 272, 277
Trade Unions, 41, 137, 339
  Trade Union Conference, 137, 138
Traditionalism, 334
Transitional period for sterling area, 219–20
Transport, 115, 365
Treasury, 187
  backs C.E.M.A. with money, 211, 358, 359, 367
  JMK at (1917–19), 142, 163, 295, (1940), 142, 153
  Treasury view, 342, 343
Treatise on Money, A, 223
Trefilova, Mme, ballerina, 316
Trenchard, Hugh Montagu, Chief of Air Staff, 434; bombing programme, 179
Trimetallism, 239

Troy weight (barley grains), 236, 237–8
Truth, 116
Tukhachevsky, Marshall, 59, 434
Tunis offensive, 190, 191
Turkey, 175
Turner, T. W. J., music critic of *The New Statesman and Nation*, 96, 434; plan for a national theatre, 356–7
Tyerman, Donald, Assistant Editor, *The Economist*, 156, 434

Ukraine, 126
Unemployment, 14, 41
United Artists Corporation, 372
United Kingdom
  arts: for ballet and paintings, *see under* England; theatres, *see* Arts Theatre, Cambridge; Theatre Royal, Bristol; bread without circuses, 341–9; beginnings of state aid for the arts, *see* Arts Council; C.E.M.A.
  foreign affairs: incompetence of Foreign Office, 48, 51, 55, 56, 64; position on Spanish Civil War, 48–50, 55, 73–8; responsibility for failure of League of Nations, 51, 106; 'negative pacifism', 99; paralysis of will, 102, 105; the isolationist alternative, 91
  Anglo-Czech negotiations, 115, 117–21; Munich Agreement with Hitler, 122–7; war declared on Germany 132; threat of invasion, 153; her year alone, 217; sea power, 55–6, 63–4, 126; secret service, 144, 145
  relations with U.S., 37, 47, 84–5, 92; with U.S.S.R., 208
  American loan, 216–22
  world position in 1945, 222
  see also England; Great Britain; Ireland; Scotland; Wales
United States of America
  Administration, 218; Congress, 218; Senate Committee, 217; State Department, 83, 191; and sanctions against Japan, 82–6, 92–3
  arts: purchase of French paintings, 311; absence of public entertainment, 347
  frame-ups, 17, 18
  JMK's visits to: (1931), 12; (1934), 83; (1941), 159; (1943), 203, 204, 216–22; (1946), 222
  Kingsley Martin's visits to: (1943), 169, 172, 173, 175, 182; (1945), 207, 209, 210, 211, 214, 216; Eden's visit, 191

United States of America (*cont.*)
  loan to U.K., 216–22
  the Midas touch, 228 n
  role in world politics, 82, 82–3, 118, 135; in World War II, 192
United University Club, 155
Universities, 350, 351; G. B. Shaw on, 40–1
Ur: excavations at, 231, 244; Ur mina, 232, 244
U.S.S.R., 135; relations with U.K., 191, 192, 218
  see also Russia
U.S.S.R. Society for Cultural Relations, 336
Utilitarians, 31, 342; utilitarianism as a political philosophy, 347
Utley, Freda, author, 87, 88, 434

V Campaign, 173
Vallance, Aylmer, journalist, Financial Editor, *The New Statesman and Nation*, 91, 92, 117, 434; goes to War Office, 196, attempt to get him released, 197–201; offending article on Poland, 209, 211, 212–14
Value, standard of, in antiquity, 252–3, 256–60
Vanderbilt, Cornelius, 40
Vansittart, Sir Robert Gilbert, 116, 434
Vaughan-Williams, Ralph, *Job*, a ballet, 10
Versailles, Treaty of, 99
Victoria, Queen, 33
  Victorian paintings, 363
Victoria and Albert Museum, 363, 366
Vic-Wells Ballet, 321, 322–4, 354, 357
Vienna, 98
Vivisection, 393–4
Voices, 349–51
Volga conversations, 14
Vollard, Amboise, 366
Volpi, Giuseppe, Italian Finance Minister, 201, 202, 434
Voltaire, 37

Wade, Allan, 314
Wages
  in ancient Greece and medieval England, 229–30
  reductions, 12–13
  wage-earners, 406, 411–12
Waiver clause, in Loan Agreement, 218, 219
Wales
  Arts Council of Wales, 370–1
  JMK's 'Welsh prison', 87
Wall Street, 399, 406
Wallace, Edgar, 330

Wallace, Henry Agard, Vice-President, U.S.A., 186, 187, 434
Walpole, Horace, 419
Walsh, Richard John, publisher, 182, 184, 193, 434; Walsh family, 182, 183, 184
Walsh, Mrs (Pearl Buck), 182, 183, 184, 423
Walton, William, *Façade*, 10
War
  attitudes of Fascist powers and of Britain to, 51, 53, 55–7; of Left-wing, 75–6; Treasury view, 342
  guerilla warfare, 180–1
  and peace, 94
  threat of world war (1938), 116, 117; not to be expected (August 1939), 131; declared (September 1939), 132. *See* World War II
  war debts, 218; war losses, 217
  war-mongering, 97
  Wars of Religion, 61
  see also Abyssinia, Japan, Spain
War Expenditure, Committee on, 197
War Office, 165–6, 168, 172, 196, 197, 199, 200
  Secretary of State for War (Sir James Grigg), 198; letter to, 199–200
Washington, 83, 189, 216; 'Big Army school', 191, 192, 194
Wealth, distribution of, 400, 406
Webb, Arthur, *Daily Herald* correspondent in Washington, 205
Webb, Beatrice, 434: her 80th birthday, 95; obituaries (1943), 195; an anecdote, 195 n 89
  with Sidney Webb: Supplement on Industrial Insurance, 66; *Soviet Communism*, 333–4
Webb, Sidney, 40, 434; Supplement on Industrial Insurance, 66, 71; an anecdote, 195 n 89
  with Beatrice Webb, *Soviet Communism*, 333–4
Week, The, 119
Wells, H. G., 157, 434
  on Beatrice Webb, 95
  censored by Foreign Office, 136
  his imagination, 32
  interview with Stalin, 30–2, 41; pamphlet on (*Shaw–Wells–Keynes on Stalin–Wells Talk*), 36–41
  'our stinks master', 35
Wemyss, Lady, *Life and Letters of the First Lord Wemyss*, 331
Western Europe, 126

Western Front, 177, 191, 194

Weygand, General Maxime, 143, 153, 435

Wheat, 158
  prices, in antiquity, 229n; in 1931, 308
  as standard of weight, avoirdupois, 233–7, 258
  wheat–barley ratios, 237–9

White, Freda, 196

White Paper, on relations with Germany, 125

Whitley, Edward, chairman of *New Statesman*, 154, 164, 182, 183–5, 205, 216, 435; letters to, 23–4, 45, 132–3, 134–5; from Kingsley Martin, 66–7
  list of letters, 443–4

Wilhelmina, Queen of the Netherlands, 170, 435

Williams, Francis, 435; journalist, 149, 153; at Ministry of Information, 196–201

Williams, W. E., of C.E.M.A., 360, 364

Willison, Ernst, advertising manager, *New Statesman and Nation*, 67, 154, 435

Wilson, Sir Arnold, M.P., 66, 435; *Industrial Assurance*, 70, 79, 80

Wilson, Sir Horace, Permanent Secretary of Treasury, 119, 435

Wilson, Woodrow, President of U.S.A., 218, 435

Wilzak, M., dancer, 316

Wimbledon, 351–2

Winant, John Henry, U.S. Ambassador to Great Britain, 192, 435

Winterton, Paul, *News Chronicle* reporter, 208

Wintringham, Tom, 168, 435

Wodehouse, P. G., 330

Woijikowsky, Leon, dancer, 316

Wolfe, Edward, theatrical designer, 10

Women
  Ibsen and the modern woman, 327
  position of, at University of Cambridge, 414–16

Wood, Sir Kingsley, Chancellor of the Exchequer (1940–3), 360

Woolf, Leonard, 23, 141, 145, 197, 435; acting editor of *New Statesman and Nation* in Martin's absence, 169, 172, 198, 208–9, 210, 211, 212; correspondence on offending article, 213–14
  obituary of Beatrice Webb, 195n90; on Impressionism, 311–12
  list of letters, 444

Woolf, Virginia, 330–1

Woolley, Leonard, 333

Wootton, Barbara, Economics lecturer at Girton College, Cambridge, 415–16

Wordsworth, Dorothy, 391

Wordsworth, William, 391

Working-class: French and Spanish, 169
  working-class saving, 80

Workmen's Compensation, 68

World Economic Conference (1933), 320, 322

World War I, 41, 228n; JMK at the Treasury, 142; involved with post-war food shortages, 148

World War II
  declaration of war (September 1939), 132; events in France, 138–9, 143, 145, 153, 167; fall of France, 172, 176, 179, 180, 181; surrender of neutrals, 141, 144; Anglo-Greek successes, 150–1; invasion of Britain threatened, 153
  German pressure on Russia, 166, 167, 173, 176, 177, 178, 181, 190, 191, 192; war on the Eastern Front, 175–6, 192; Dieppe raid, 177; Pearl Harbour, 178; Dunkirk, 178, 179; war in Libya, 179; Japan joins in, 179; Tunis offensive, 190, 191, 192
  policy of bombing from air, 139, 177, 179, 181; fire-watching at home, 176; Britain's year of going it alone, 217; blitz on London and elsewhere, 359, 370, 371
  defeat of Germany in sight, 204, 206; war in Europe over (May 1945), 209

Wren, Sir Christopher, 342

Wright, Charles, father of Harold Wright, 5

Wright, Harold, editor of *Nation and Athenaeum*, 2, 5, 435

Xerxes, 227, 228n

Yale Review, The, 20

Yeats, W. B., 'My Own Poetry', broadcast talk, 350

Yugoslavia, 181

Y.Y. (Robert Lynd), columnist in *The New Statesman and Nation*, 140, 149, 160–1

Zullig, Hans, dancer, 130

Zwemmer, A., book seller, 366